The N-Word in Music

The N-Word in Music

An American History

TODD M. MEALY

McFarland & Company, Inc., Publishers
Jefferson, North Carolina

Also of Interest

Equity in the Classroom: Essays on Curricular and Pedagogical Approaches to Empowering All Students, edited by Todd M. Mealy and Heather Bennett (McFarland, 2022)

Race Conscious Pedagogy: Disrupting Racism at Majority White Schools, by Todd M. Mealy (McFarland, 2020)

Glenn Killinger, All-American: Penn State's World War I Era Sports Hero, by Todd M. Mealy (McFarland, 2018)

ISBN (print) 978-1-4766-8706-3
ISBN (ebook) 978-1-4766-4649-7

LIBRARY OF CONGRESS AND BRITISH LIBRARY
CATALOGUING DATA ARE AVAILABLE

Library of Congress Control Number 2022016566

Front cover image by Alexander Budylin (Shutterstock)

Printed in the United States of America

McFarland & Company, Inc., Publishers
Box 611, Jefferson, North Carolina 28640
www.mcfarlandpub.com

For my good friend, Todd Allen

Table of Contents

Author's Note

It should be of no surprise to anyone that I was quite reluctant to write this book. The irony of writing a book about the N-word is that I must include those two ugly syllables in these pages. To be mindful of the broad spectrum of sensitivities that exists around this topic, I will use the euphemism "N-word" or other descriptors when writing in my voice. When the word falls within quotation marks because someone else is doing the talking, the reader will see the word's complete spelling. I am aware some will say that this approach might empower the slur, that my sidestepping the full word will only make it more dangerously taboo; however, it is safer and more considerate to the feelings of those who have been harmed by the history that lies behind it.

I reference several songs, concerts, comedy skits, and television shows throughout this book. I suggest readers take the time to find these texts on the internet. They will provide both context and proper tone, making the book more comprehensive and, I believe, more engaging.

Acknowledgments

Many people deserve my praise. First and foremost, thank you to my wife, Melissa, and our two children, Carter and Adeline. They are my everything. In particular, Melissa's honesty and insight guided me to the end of this project. Additionally, I must salute my parents, Maurene and Thomas J. Mealy. My brother, Tommy, and sister, Crissy, have always been supportive. I also need to thank my colleague, Streeter Stuart, a music enthusiast who helped me in the earliest stages of the project to frame the scope of the book. Speaking of getting the project off the ground, my former student Jordan Schucker helped synthesize ideas. I owe a tremendous debt to several mentors in the fields of race studies, philosophy, and performing arts. First, I relied heavily on the advice and wisdom of Dr. Todd Allen, Vice President for Diversity Affairs at Messiah University and founder of The Common Ground Project, a non-profit dedicated to teaching the history of the Civil Rights Movement. Dr. Allen provided valuable mentorship and encouragement to complete this book. Also, Lenwood "Leni" Sloan provided support when composing the first three chapters. I must also thank Dr. George Yancy for his support. It was a conversation in the spring of 2021 that convinced me to follow through on this project. Everyone mentioned herein played a crucial role in completing this book. I hope it gives you, your colleagues, and your students much to ponder.

the term, including removing it from historical literature, music, and film. And yet, throughout American history, the word has appeared in every music genre; it pervaded folk music throughout the nineteenth and early twentieth centuries before calls to remove the slur by progressive warriors failed to mitigate the word's incursion throughout popular culture in the 1920s. Bluegrass musicians used the word well into the 1980s. Rock 'n' roll artists peppered the genre with the appellation during the entire second half of the 1900s. Punk performers have used the word. Of course, hip-hop artists hardly make an album without a mention of the word.

Those two ugly syllables have come to embody so much more than just painful illiteracy and an obscene relic from the darker chapters of American history. Language, like statues and monuments, more so than any other cultural marker, symbolizes and reflects the era it defines. Like statues and monuments, language unveils truths about society by the inclusion, or revision, of words from one generation to the next. Yet, humanity has never quite figured out what to make of this spoken monument. Is the N-word something that should be bulldozed and melted? Should it be torn down and placed in a museum? Should it be kept in classroom textbooks? Should we preserve it in storage? Or, do we determine that it means different things to different people and, like some controversial monuments that remain standing depending on public opinion of the local population, the N-word, too, must live on in communities encompassing a consensus supporting its use and mention?

This debate is complicated because the word's usage, meaning, and spelling have changed over time. Linguists and historians agree that Europeans first used the word as a designation for racialized Africans. In the mid–Nineties, the eleven-month murder trial of O.J. Simpson planted seeds to make the word taboo in the twenty-first century. These concepts—descriptor and unspeakable slur—bookend the N-word's history. This book attempts to use music to understand the time between those conscious moments and recognize why we have constructed a zero-sum culture. A look back at the writing of the antebellum era's leading African American abolitionist shines a light on a time when the word was ordinary, unquestionably degrading, yet not forbidden. In a letter to Sydney Howard Gay, editor of the *National Anti-Slavery Standard*, on August 10, 1847, Frederick Douglass told the story of a violent mob in Harrisburg, Pennsylvania, threatening him while yelling, "Give it to him, give it to him! Let the d----d nigger have it!" as he ducked a cascade of stones, brickbats and raw eggs.[2] The fact that Douglass evaded a lynch mob is not the point of the story. Instead, readers should focus on Douglass's decision to redact "damned" while leaving the N-word in its fullest form. Indeed, profanity was unfit for print during the nineteenth-century's spiritual revival known as the Second Great Awakening. The N-word, nonetheless, had yet to fit the classification of profane. Obviously, attitudes about the impact of each word have flipped.

The N-word's evolution did not stop in the age of Frederick Douglass. During my grandparents' generation (Silent Generation), the N-word was relatively tolerable within white and Black societies. It was, in fact, still used as frankly in public spaces as non-slur profane terms "damn" and "hell" are used in the current era. Geographic landmarks, roads, house pets, consumer items, food, and even family board games acquired the N-word as if an honorific at the start of the twentieth century. In my parents' generation (Baby Boomers), it was acceptable (by other whites) for whites to use the word directly to Blacks, who had no choice but resignation due to lack of legal recourse. But for my generation (Generation X) and for those that follow, the N-word has become a hot potato. At times, the word is used to teach lessons on triumph over anti–Black racism. But often, it is taken only as a slur. Its taboo nature has made it *a word that must not be named* lest one would risk the derailment of career or acceptance into college. For good reason, linguist John McWhorter calls it "English's Voldemort term."[3] The N-word is still popular among many Blacks. Racist whites certainly still use the pejorative to harm, degrade, and dehumanize. Some whites—well, mainly Millennials and those from Generation Z— presume it is tolerable to call their Black friends the appellation and to sing the word aloud. For the rest of white people, this group, for the large part, is left wondering why white people (and other people of color) can't say the word although Black people can.

The N-Word in Music: An American History indeed responds to this compendium of questions and generational interpretations; however, providing answers to these questions is not its centerpiece. Neither is this book a history of music genres (i.e., ragtime or blues or jazz or hip-hop). Instead, I aim to chronicle the history of the word as it navigated through American music culture. As such, I present to the reader a biography of a word. In doing so, readers will come to respond to the questions mentioned above.

Music today, rap music, in particular, is quintessential in the argument for why the word is, in one instance, commonly used as a term of endearment, while also existing as a hair-pin trigger for termination of employment and cancellation from social media and the real world. But it was, among all music performers, John Lennon, musical genius, founding member of the Beatles, and peace warrior who drew me to this book. The question right now, I imagine, must be, where is the relevance? What does John Lennon, a Brit, have to do with the English language's nuclear bomb? Initially, I intended to write about one of Lennon's solo albums, *Some Time in New York City*. In 1972, Lennon and his wife Yoko Ono recorded the album to speak to the prevailing issues at that moment in time. One could say that *Some Time in New York City* was a musical version of *Nightly News*, aiming to inform the public about race relations, the criminal justice system, sexism and second-wave feminism, and the ongoing civil war in Ireland. Despite the couple's genuine belief that the album could reignite the counterculture revolution, it fell flat. It lacked the brilliance of the Lennon–McCartney numbers, such as "A Day in the Life," "Revolution 1," and "All You Need is Love," along with Lennon's signature solo songs "Imagine," "Happy XMass (War is Over)," and "Give Peace a Chance."[4] Moreover, *Some Time in New York City* offered listeners nothing in terms of kinesthetic. The album represents Lennon's struggle for an identity free of the Beatles and emancipation from Great Britain. It was a search for meaning behind his commitment to global peace. By producing an album full of songs that could become anthems for several different freedom movements, Lennon thought he could use his privilege as a white male celebrity to expose human experiences under captive conditions. That enterprise derailed from the start, when, in April 1972, Lennon and Ono released the album's first single, "Woman is the Nigger of the World." He sang the number at benefit concerts, on daytime television talk shows, and on the radio. The pushback was scathing. As Lennon nevertheless defended his use of the word, the hole he lay in grew bigger and bigger.

The project's scope changed after my editor read the first three chapters and suggested I reconstruct the manuscript to track the music industry's use of that word over the course of American history. Hence, here we are. The reader will still see John Lennon often in this book. However, this work has become a historical survey of a word as it has infiltrated each genre of music and permeated almost every aspect of American society. *The N-Word in Music* is a history of the word's use in lyrics. It also provides a history of the public debate over whose word it is to say and whether everyone has a right to use or mention it in any contextual setting.

Work on the book came intermittently; I often put down the project, knowing that laboring on such a topic would draw ire. The pushback against writing such a book never left my mind, especially as I kept abreast of virtue-signaling and performative behavior in the shape of cancel culture occurring in many professional fields during the summer and fall of 2020 and winter and spring of 2021. The attacks were coming from both sides. Conservatives condemned educators for pushing equity and social justice in schools. Progressives assailed professors, CEOs, and public personalities for mentioning the N-word as a teaching tool for lessons about anti–Black racism and racial justice. While I am a 20-year educator with a body of work on similar topics and founder of an institute that provides race-conscious and culturally responsive services to educational institutions and other organizations, it is impossible to avoid the recoil that is seemingly inevitable for writing a book about such an explosive topic. Who am I, a white man, to write about the N-word? Would readers misinterpret my framing? Other more established people have written on the topic, each in meaningful ways. In particular, Randall Kennedy's 2002 tome that places the word in the context of the legal system is the foundational study on the topic. Then there is Jabari Asim's 2004 historical analysis of the word's appearance in various aspects of American society since the abolition movement. Cultural critic Neal Lester's singular scholarship on the N-word made his Arizona State University course on the word nationally popular. For a decade, Lester and his students studied the word's omnipresence in various parts of American popular culture, including toys, television shows, and children's books. However, upon reading these works, I realized these scholars hadn't yet told the story I planned to tell. Lester's research was an essential roadmap for me, primarily because he focused on the word in both nineteenth-century minstrelsy and twentieth-century comedy. But the history I chose to write about is more concerned with the musicians—both Black and non–Black—who use the word, some of whom receive an in-depth analysis in these pages, especially John Lennon. *The N-Word in Music* is far more a story about who has included the word in music and why, as well as the social impact that is revealed by following the word's evolution throughout American music history.

But first, what this book is not. *It is not an argument to bowdlerize the word.* While I detest the word when said in any contextual, written, or enunciated form, I do not believe that the word must disappear. I also do not argue that the word should stay. This book is not a treatise about whether the word should or shouldn't be on death row. I am providing a qualitative analysis of the word's use in music since blackface minstrelsy preceding the American Civil War. A look at nineteenth-century music guides us into the word's appearance in other aspects of popular culture: at community carnivals, on antique ceramics, and in children's literature. From there, we find the word preserved in plain sight through Jazz Age productions, after which it would find another public spotlight for decades as racists used the word as a hegemonic device to maintain social order. Like the Confederate flag, the slur resurfaced as an expression of power. Upon the conclusion of the Civil Rights movement, white and Black cultural archetypes dueled over how the word should be said in public. Many white musicians wrote those two ugly syllables into antiracist songs. Black professional athletes and Black comedians, meanwhile, used the word—well, both variations of the word—in mixed company frequently enough that by the Eighties, public opinion columnists in the mainstream media were absent from a theoretical direction. When gangsta rap and conscious rap artists in the Eighties and Nineties imbued lyrics with the term, local and national governing bodies, *Merriam-Webster's Dictionary*, and the NAACP hit the roof. City councils passed non-binding resolutions denouncing the public use of the term. The dictionary modified the word's meaning. And, as previously mentioned, the NAACP symbolically buried the word in a public funeral. Naturally, the defense team in the O.J. Simpson trial did a remarkable job buttressing the taboo nature of the word during that period. People knew the N-word was forbidden fruit by the first decade of the twenty-first century, but few lost jobs for saying it. There was a degree of latitude given to those that distinguished between *use* and *mention*. But the rise of a new wave of antiracist activism lifted and animated by a dizzying number of Black Americans killed by law enforcement officers has settled society into a place of bewilderment. As of 2021, there is no way of avoiding questions about a racial double standard: Why can't whites say the word since Black rappers pepper lyrics with it? Are rappers responsible for the proliferation of the casual use of the word? Why can Trevor Noah use the word as an endearment on *The Daily Show,* but Bill Maher had to apologize for using the word as a joke on *Late Night*? Why did a tenured law professor receive a suspension from his university for including an abbreviated form of the N-word on a course exam (the N followed by five asterisks)? The threat of occupational termination for mentioning the word in a lesson plan about James Baldwin or during a diversity and inclusion board meeting is very real. This book cannot avoid dilemmas such as these. But the reason why music is essential in a story about those two ugly syllables is that, regardless of the era, music is the agent that has recurrently pushed the word back into public discourse.

Second, *I am not writing this book to tell Black people if they should or should not say the word; it is not my place.* It is not my aim to judge whether or not Black hip-hop artists should include the word in their music. While I provide the history of the debate over rappers' affinity for the word, I do not take a position on this. However, in the logical sense, it is irresponsible to tell my fellow white persons that a racial double standard exists while we still benefit from institutionalized privileges that the word helped build. I apologize if this logic sounds oversimplified. I find it unprincipled to claim that white teachers, musicians, and journalists can say or wield the word in any context without considering the personal or familial experiences of the Black person listening. Knowing what I know about the history of racism having spent two decades engrossed in research on race and society, I cannot in my righteous mind ignore the fact that American society has reached a point—whether rightfully so or not—that Black Americans and white allies will respond to the utterance of the word with guns drawn. Indeed, a peculiarly institutional form of racism privileges specific individuals to seize upon the imbalance of power afforded by social roles. One thing that white people can do is to choose not to say the word no matter the intent. A lesson plan will not lose its impact by censuring the word. The evening news reporter will not fail viewers. Lawmakers can still present an impactful case for antiracist legislation without using the word.

This book, then, is written with the goal of communicating with white people how horrible and violent the word is and how it has manifested in unspeakable forms of violence across time. In a manner of speaking, this is the N-word's genealogy. I trace its evolution and instantiation across musical genres and throughout American history. In what follows, however, I do more than examine the N-word's pervasion of American music culture. This book examines how music has helped keep the N-word alive in four ways: one, as a conduit for white racial control over the social order, first during the antebellum period, then in postbellum society, and finally after the demise of Jim Crow America; two, as a modified manifestation of affection (some will argue, and I am one of them, that the modified manifestation is a term entirely distinct from the racist cousin ending in a hard "r"); third, as a redemptive expression used to deride white supremacy in its historical, contemporary, and institutional forms; and finally, fourth, as a term used by people of all races and ethnicities to injure, slander, and dehumanize in-group members and people from an out-group. To make these points, I use narratives and counter-narratives that appear mostly in period music, but also in comedy, politics, and the athletic arena.

In the chapters ahead, I attempt to unpack why and how the slur has arrived at a stage that it elicits such strong emotions, intensifying the heart rate during the most innocent of utterances. In other words, using historical methods, I seek to understand the reasons why we have such a hard time mending racial misunderstandings accentuating these two ugly syllables. And within these arguments, how responsible are the various music genres for sustaining the word in its most vicious form while also contributing to its evolutionary change into, what many consider, a paradoxically endearing form. In this book, there are some instances where lyrics have been shortened beyond their original form; while record labels are known for being litigious against print, most of the modern lyrics are available online in their entirety and the reader is encouraged to find and reference them. Chapters One and Two of this book examines how minstrelsy, folk music, ragtime, and popular blues employed the

N-word to shape American popular culture in relation to how Black people were treated during the nineteenth and early twentieth centuries. White and Black artists in minstrelsy and ragtime, in particular, created the paradoxical tradition of using the word both casually and ruthlessly. In one sense, people said the word so much it became a regular term that it would appear in Disney cartoons. On the other hand, the N-word always possessed undertones of inferiority, shame, and alienation. Carnivals and carnival games capitalized on racist folk music as a means of entertainment. Like ice cream, Brazil nuts, and tobacco, many dark colored consumer items were named after the word, as were towns, locales, mountains, and creeks. These chapters examine how that term reinforced already-dismantled white supremacist institutions in children's literature and playground rhymes.

After understanding how the word saturated all aspects of American society by way of minstrelsy and folk music, Chapter Three looks at the trajectory of John Lennon-the-musician to John Lennon-the-advocate for world peace. It is in this arc that Lennon composed "Woman is the Nigger of the World." This is an exhaustive chapter on Lennon's actions between 1969 and 1972, with particular attention paid to the backlash and how he defended the song.

Given Lennon's relationship with the N-word, albeit fleeting, Chapter Four provides an analysis of varied and divergent opinions on N-word usage. This chapter explores what ten diverse intellects have said about who can say the word, when it can be said, and why particular groups can and cannot say it. Included herein are liberals and antiracist progressives, as are moderates and social conservatives. The ten voices represent men and women, as well as persons who are black, brown, and white. Most are academics in some fashion, while some are self-employed scholars on topics of critical whiteness. The voices highlighted in this chapter are Randall Kennedy, Jabari Asim, Cornel West, Michael Eric Dyson, Neal Lester, John McWhorter, Elizabeth Pryor, Imani Perry, Tim Wise, and Joe Feagin. Though not spotlighted in this chapter, the voices of renowned philosopher George Yancy and antiracist scholar Ibram X. Kendi appear regularly in these pages. The purpose of Chapter Four is to explore the tug of war between wielding and mentioning the N-word and acquiring a deeper understanding of the hair-trigger reaction to the word's utterance, which has more often resulted in the loss of employment or the suffering of social ostracism.

The fifth chapter offers a history of how the N-word has appeared in music written and performed by white artists. Titled "Philosorock: John Lennon, Bob Dylan, and Other White Musicians Who Sing the N-Word," I return first to John Lennon's "Woman is the Nigger of the World" to explore the enigma of white musicians doing the work of social justice. The chapter illuminates controversy around other artists too, such as Jane's Addiction's rendition of Sly and the Family Stone's "Don't Call Me Nigger, Whitey," Bob Dylan's "Hurricane," The Dead Kennedys' "Holiday in Cambodia," Guns N' Roses' "One in a Million," and Elvis Costello's "Oliver's Army." Moreover, I analyze music using the slur by the punk band X, the bluegrass group Virginia Mountain Boys, and rock-rap artists Frank Zappa and Europe's Clawfinger. Comparing Lennon's musical slip-up to those of Dylan, in particular, and the others reveals profound ways in which well-meaning white liberals find themselves caught in blind spots that offend others.

Given the analysis of white musicians who have used or mentioned the word in songs, Chapter Six redirects the word's focus in history by looking at Black comedians, namely Richard Pryor and Paul Mooney. This chapter looks at comedy to explain the word's entry into casual conversation; not just in the Black community, but on television and in the lyrics of Black hip-hop artists. The combination of comedy and hip-hop has helped soften the word's blow when spoken by someone who is Black, even on live television. This chapter considers how comedy, casual conversation, and hip-hop converged in the 1970s.

Chapter Seven explores the interplay between the N-word's ironic use, injurious use, and redemptive use through the personality of Muhammad Ali, a prolific boxing champion whom many historians consider to be one of the originators of contemporary rap. Ali relied on rhyming to market himself and the much-maligned sport of professional prizefighting. His blustering in the 1960s influenced rappers by the end of the decade, having inspired even the likes of Run DMC's Darryl McDaniels, who called some of Ali's trash-talking the "most famous rap lyrics ever." The chapter draws a line from the media's attacks on Ali for his use of the N-word to Jay-Z's defense of the word's use in rap while on *The Oprah Winfrey Show* in 2009. At the time, rap critics like Oprah Winfrey charged the music genre of being responsible for souring race relations and the Black psyche's degeneration over the regular use of the N-word.

"White noise," or a distraction from more serious issues, is what Jay-Z calls the debate over the N-word's use in hip-hop. Chapter Eight, titled "A Hip-Hop Icon," responds to Jay-Z's position by scrutinizing the difference between gangsta rap and conscious rap. The chapter also explores whether the N-word is used more as a cudgel against white supremacy than a term intending to insult rap competitors and fictional antagonists featured in the lyrics. In part, this chapter looks at how political bodies and civil rights organizations like the NAACP have responded to rappers' refusal to vacillate on the issue by attempting to legislate the N-word.

In the subsequent chapter, "A Sensible Rule: A Case Study," I examine those all too frequent times when whites vocalize the N-word while singing along to rap lyrics and whether rappers are responsible for the proliferation of casual use of the word by people of all races and nationalities. This chapter goes beneath the surface of Jay-Z and Oprah's 2009 spat by reconstructing the history of gangsta rap during the late Eighties and throughout the Nineties. The chapter also explores the N-word's various contextual usages in the lyrics of rap's most popular early artists. To be clear, this is not a history of rap music, vis-à-vis Jeff Chang's *Can't Stop Won't Stop* or Imani Perry's *Prophets of the Hood*; instead, the chapter provides a survey of the N-word's history in rap music, from the Eighties to the Trump Administration.

Chapter Ten is titled "Inviting Destruction Beyond the Music" for its deep-reading of the N-word in professions other than music. I discuss the climate of fear that haunts educators, corporate CEOs, journalists, and anyone of influence who might face professional and socially fatal consequences for saying the N-word, its congenial euphemism, and its cousin, which begins with an "N" and ends in an "o." I detail stories of administrators and boards of trustees giving in to performative demands by firing employees for uttering the word. The chapter looks at the very real quandary of how a Salem Witch Trial–like cancel culture has entered university and corporate management. I explore those moments when the intent is *not* to call someone a bad name and not to endorse the slur, but to actually dig deeper into a text or historical moment—when those moments result in hurt and occupational castigation. In addition to the debate over the fashion of zero tolerance of discussing something like Mark Twain, this chapter brings the book full circle by exploring music both before and during a time when the word was so explosive.

All of this begs the question, is it humane to either mention the word in an erudite context or to wield the slur with the intention of insulting another person so often that it no longer becomes offensive? Minstrelsy and ragtime music show us that nineteenth- and early twentieth-century white and Black artists started using the term so commonly that it launched the word into other aspects of popular culture, material culture, and language. Ragtime is perhaps the form of music that helps us make sense of our time's debate over whether rap artists are responsible for disseminating multiple variations of the word within many subcultures in the United States and abroad. Some have argued that if the public would just embrace the N-word today, that it would soon lose its bite. But yet, ragtime presents itself as a case study. It was a form of music that shows us that Black cultural archetypes, such as Ernest Hogan and Bob Cole, embracing Black stereotypes and the word through productions of ragtime's "coon songs" only helped to create an environment where the term became a mocking descriptor of anything with black or brown colors. Whether it be the Gilded Age or the new millennium, music shows us that it is not possible to use English's worst word often enough to blunt the emotional impact in the same way that the words "damn," "hell," and "ass" evolved over my lifetime.

To put it another way, can you strike someone repeatedly with a stick and have the impact become less hurtful? Is that rational thinking? Would that even be humane? The beating would become so prevalent that the victim would lose the desire to resist. The victim would likely reach the point of full submission. But the pain wouldn't dull. What about a battered wife? The physical and verbal abuse wouldn't get easier to absorb; it's just that the victim would grow so accustomed to the violence that she wouldn't fight back. Her submission doesn't make the domestic abuse hurt any less. It certainly never becomes less dangerous. In fact, it becomes more dangerous. To the point, there is no way to fight it. So she acquiesces to staying in the relationship for her own survival.

This quandary over the word is music's creation. The art form has made it much more than a racial slur. It is true that in different time periods, the word has had its supporters and detractors. The most interesting has occurred in the theater of those that argue the word's uncensored inclusion in music helps soften its bite.

Music history sings otherwise.

ONE

The N-Word's Musical Contours

The story of how America's ultimate slur rose from a racial descriptor into a vernacular superpower in the music industry is one that can't be told without a look at the effort to undo the earliest racial hierarchy. I choose the resistance to slavery when referring to the word's entrance into music because, at that moment, the illusory concept of the word's various contextual usages had just formed. It is true, slave-traders used the term as a designation for humans forced into servitude in the earliest days of settlement in this country. But it was the universally successful promotion of the minstrel show *Jump, Jim Crow* in the United States and Britain as "The Two Black Crows; Or, the White Negro. The Out and Out Nigger, Jim Crow" that transformed the slur into its most pernicious form of expression. The first great American theatrical practice, minstrelsy, was a caricature of Black life, with a particular stage tradition of using blackface paint or burnt cork to parody Black people for profit. In the process, *Jump, Jim Crow*, written by Thomas Dartmouth "T.D." Rice during the 1828–1829 theater season, introduced to the world a song and a dance that both became cultural fads. The outcome: a comedic art form that tormented Black Americans while emboldening white society into physical and mental acts of anti–Black violence. Writing in *The North Star* in 1848, Frederick Douglass called minstrel performers "the filthy scum of white society."[1]

The signature song in *Jump, Jim Crow* carried the same title. Rice, who went by the stage name "Daddy Rice" or "Jim Crow Rice," and has since been known as the "father of American minstrelsy," wrote the song "Jump, Jim Crow," sometimes called simply "Jim Crow," while working on an impersonation of an enslaved African named Jim (a character inspired by a real man named Cuffy) who belonged to a Mr. Crow, the owner of a stable yard near City Theater in Louisville, Kentucky. Like most folksongs, "Jump, Jim Crow" has numberless verses and the typical rhythm and nonsense of what early twentieth-century writer Frank F. Patterson called "the real Negro folksong."[2] The song's protagonist, a Black man who walked with a limp, was cheerful and hopped around as he sang at his work. At the end of each verse, the song repeated the chorus: "Wheel about, turn about, do jes so / An ebry time I wheels about / I jump Jim Crow." The song also features the stanza: "Now my Broder Niggars / I do not tink it right / Dat you should laugh at dem / Who happen to be White."[3] In that verse, Rice had included the N-word as a term of endearment, a descriptor for Jim's Black brethren. When the name Jim Crow grew to symbolize segregation, first in public transportation of the antebellum North and later throughout nearly every facility of the postbellum and Progressive-era South, the N-word evolved into a cudgel to distress Black Americans. This specific song, "Jump, Jim Crow," enabled the slur to move beyond the confines of plantation life and into the vestiges of urban America. The parody helped the word mature beyond the isolation of enslavement and into popular culture, material culture, food culture, and even when naming geographic landmarks.

It was during this era that the musical ditty "Jump, Jim Crow" opened the door for the N-word's entrance into the free parts of the country; as a manifestation not limited to slave labor, but to all people with Black skin, free or otherwise. "Jump, Jim Crow" redefined the meaning of the N-word as an assault on freedom, a statement that Black people could never be free.[4] The song helped the white population weaponize the word after the emancipation of four million enslaved Africans. In one sense, the word kept the newly freed Black populace in its place. Then again, it sustained racial resentment within the white community, even those who never encountered someone who was Black. It was a word conveying that Black people have no value in society and will be treated as such. In those instances when the word wasn't spoken aloud, a facetious performance of the dance steps to "Jump, Jim Crow" in front of Black individuals sent the same message.

Blackface minstrelsy is the first distinctively American contribution to theater, and by proxy, music. Music scholar Eileen Jackson Southern calls it a musical genre built on the "exploitation of the slave's style of music and dancing by white men, who blackened their faces with burnt cork and went on the stage to sing 'Negro songs,' to perform dances derived from those of the slaves, and to tell jokes based on slave life."[5] Judging by the genre's long popularity in the United States and abroad, and its sustained and wide influence among artists well beyond the antebellum period and into the Gilded Age and Progressive Era, the music came to fashion, directly and indirectly, the American public. Indeed, minstrelsy was, as one writer put it in 1928, something that "to the present America has produced little else that was original and at the same time worth while [sic] in the art of public entertainment."[6] Of course, these sentiments came at a time when ragtime and jazz challenged the notion that "Negro minstrelsy," as Patterson called it, was America's only original form of music. That is to say, minstrelsy prided itself on "maudlin ballads, coon songs, banjo solos and dancing," he wrote. In much the same way that blackface make-up flourished on the vaudeville stage throughout the 1900s, the art of imitating or spoofing Black Americans came to define minstrelsy's musical comedy. In song after song, from "Jump, Jim Crow" to "Old Dan Tucker," and from "Turkey in the Straw" to "Alabama Coon," and from "In Old Virginny" to "Stop Dat Knockin' at Mah Doah," the African in America was propagated as a humorous "Sambo" character: irresponsible, fun-loving, and content being the butt of the joke. Then when Jim Crow's figurative cousin, Zip Coon, worked his way into the public consciousness, Black Americans, urban Black men in particular, were characterized as conniving tricksters.

Returning focus to "Jump, Jim Crow," Rice would get into character by blackening his face and then donning the raggedy clothes of a Black man named Cuffy who hung around outside the Louisville theater where he performed. Rice would leave the unfortunate man "waiting in the alley almost nude in chilly weather." One critic wrote of Rice and "Jump, Jim Crow": "The song was a 'riot' and the encores were only stopped when the poor shivering coon crept in and, sticking his head from behind a backdrop, grumbled loudly, 'I wants mah cloes.'"

In 1843, the first minstrel troupe, the Virginia Minstrels, composed of a quartet also known as the "Big Four," including Daniel Decatur Emmett, author of "Dixie," Frank Brower, Dick Pelham, and Billy Whitlock, started performing "Jump, Jim Crow" to audiences across the United States and in England. Shortly after that, other minstrel troupes formed, including Christy's Callender's Troupe, Ethiopian Serenaders, Carncross's Troupe, Haverley's Troupe, Primrose and West, McIntire and Heath, Chauncey Olcott, and Lew Dockstader's Troupe. These musical ensembles proudly imitated Rice's Jim Crow caricature. Across the American North and abroad, the troupes used the Sambo stereotype as expressed in the Jim Crow character to entertain white communities that had never interacted with Black people.[7]

The minstrelsy genre quickly acquired the categorical name "Nigger Minstrel Show." It was sometimes referred to as the "Nigger phalanx" or the "Nigger stage" in the performing arts circuit. Troupes were often called "Two Good Niggers," "Nigger trio," or "Nigger quartet," depending on the number of singers, which, according to critics, "personated the most amiable of Niggers." Newspapers wrote of minstrel plots featuring a "sketch of Nigger eccentricities" and "Nigger with the inquiring mind."[8] White actors in blackface were called anything from "very respectable Niggers" to "excellent single-handed Nigger[s]."[9]

Blackface song-and-dance became the medium for performing

artists, vaudeville performers, and eventually many big screen actors and actresses began to hone the craft and obtain celebrity status. Although music historians credit minstrelsy for producing popular wartime tunes, such as the Civil War's "Dixie," the Spanish American War's "There'll Be a Hot Time in the Old Town Tonight," and the Great War's "Over There," much of the genre artists' success came at the expense of Black Americans.[10] Minstrelsy was a cultural appropriation atrocity, the act of exploiting Black spirituality cramped into a conventional form of white musical expression built on the theme of comedy. Black people were made the subject of laughter. Whites who knew nothing about Black Americans thought they were listening to authentic Black American music, all the while absorbing messages that represented Black people as irresponsible, apparently happy yet manipulative, and absent of common sense smarts. The stories went over big, winning audiences of millions throughout the world. Writing from his office at *The North Star*, Frederick Douglass criticized blackface performers for stealing "from us a complexion denied to them by nature, in which to make money, and pander to the corrupt taste of their white fellow-citizens."[11]

Douglass was far from being the only critic of minstrelsy. There was that time when one popular Black bass-baritone sang "Jump, Jim Crow" in mocking fashion. In 1942, Paul Robeson interrupted his concert in Kansas City to lecture his audience about the auditorium's Jim Crow seating arrangement. The former All-American football player and lawyer gave his speech without warning: "I have made a life-long habit to refuse to sing in Southern states or anywhere that audiences are segregated. I accepted this engagement under guarantee that there would be no segregation." Robeson hardly cared that several whites in the audience immediately left the venue. "Since many local leaders of my own race have urged me to fill this engagement, I shall finish the concert," he said, "but I am doing so under protest."[12] He later sang a rendition of "Jump, Jim Crow," slipping in ad-libbed verses of racial protest. More audience members left the auditorium throughout the remainder of the concert.

In very stark terms, the exploitation of African Americans turned profitable for a racial caste fixed on using language and imagery that devalued the very people who had become characters and caricatures of this early performance art form. As the song "Jump, Jim Crow" reveals, the N-word—and the racist stereotypes that accompanied it—was crafted tightly into the fabric of America's first musical genre.

✳ ✳ ✳

A year after T.D. Rice's "Jump, Jim Crow" took the public by storm, abolitionists started to push back against the rising tide of racist popular culture. Among the first to speak out publicly against anti–Black racism was Bostonian David Walker. In September 1829, Walker published *Appeal … to the Coloured Citizens of the World*, a treatise against slavery and segregation. It was a clarion call for enslaved persons to rise up against their enslavers. Walker dedicated parts of the *Appeal* to addressing the N-word. He said the word is rooted in Latin and was also used by the Romans to designate "inanimate beings [and] animals." White Americans, he said, "applied this term to Africans, by way of reproach for our colour, to aggravate and heighten our miseries, because they have their feet on our throats."[13] This account of the term is among the earliest descriptions on record detailing the Black perspective toward the slur; alleging white supremacists used the term with the intent to demean and harm Black persons.

A look into how whites hurled the N-word at the distinguished abolitionist and civil rights crusader Frederick Douglass after his escape from bondage reinforces Walker's point. If truth be told, a short survey into different moments of Douglass's life will offer a much-needed historical context for why there is a heightened sense of pain every time a white person speaks the N-word. Writing from the Victoria Hotel in Belfast, Northern Ireland, in 1846, Douglass explained how the N-word was so commonly tossed at him by whites while living free in the United States.

> … about two years [ago], there was in Boston, near the southwest corner of Boston Common, a menagerie. I had long desired to see such a collection as I understood were being exhibited there. Never having had an opportunity while a slave, I resolved to seize this, my first, since my escape. I went, and as I approached the entrance to gain admission, I was met and told by the door-keeper, in a harsh and contemptuous tone, "*We don't allow niggers in here*." I also remember attending a revival meeting in the Rev. Henry Jackson's meeting-house, at New-Bedford, and going up the broad aisle to find a seat, I was met by a good deacon, who told me, in a pious tone, "*We don't allow niggers in here*"! Soon after my arrival in New-Bedford from the South, I had a strong desire to attend the Lyceum; but was told, "*They don't allow niggers in here*"! While passing from New York to Boston on the steamer *Massachusetts*, on the night of 9th Dec. 1843, when chilled almost through with the cold, I went into the cabin to get a little warm. I was soon touched upon the shoulder, and told "*We don't allow niggers in here*"! On arriving in Boston from an anti-slavery tour, hungry and tired, I went into an eating-house near my friend Mr. Campbell's to get some refreshments. I was met by a lad in a white apron, "*We don't allow niggers in here*"! … On attempt to take a seat in the Omnibus.… I was told by the driver (and I never shall forget his fiendish hate,) "*I don't allow niggers in here*"![14]

While traveling as a lecturer throughout the United Kingdom and Ireland on behalf of the American Anti-Slavery Society, Douglass expressed nothing but approbation to his hosts abroad, who often delivered to him gifts while never turning him away with the American condemnation, "*We don't allow niggers here.*" Upon his return to the United States, he was nevertheless greeted with the racial slur once again. A year later, while still traveling as a speaker for the antislavery cause, a lynch mob met Douglass in Harrisburg, Pennsylvania. Douglass and William Lloyd Garrison spoke together at the Dauphin County Courthouse on the morning of August 9, 1847.[15] Garrison lectured first "with little or no interruption for the space of an hour," Douglass recollected in a letter to his wife. But when Garrison introduced Douglass to the audience, a mob gathering outside the courthouse turned hostile. "I spoke only for a few moments when through the window was poured a volley of unmerchantable eggs, scattering the contents on the desk in which I stood, and upon the wall behind me, filling the room with the most disgusting and stifling stench," Douglass recalled. He tried to carry on before the mob set off a barrage of firecrackers. It sounded like a "discharge of pistols," said Douglass. "I could occasionally hear amid the tumult, fierce and bloody cries 'Throw out the Nigger! Throw out the Nigger!'" Stones were launched at Douglass's head as friends ushered him to safety inside the home of a friendly Harrisburg resident.[16] A similar incident occurred in Chicago just a few months later, where men cursed him as "nigger" while hurling chairs in his direction.[17] A decade later, during peak moments of the Underground Railroad but also at a time when other countries were contemplating opening borders to Chinese immigrants, the Australians used Douglass as a testament to all people of color that were able to integrate into a foreign society after escaping a violent form of persecution. The publication called Douglass a "free nigger" who "obeyed the voice of nature and of God in running away from the horrors of slavery" only to prove himself an equal measure to white people in a foreign land.[18]

A popular blackface minstrelsy rhyme-turned-children's-ditty during Douglass's lifetime was "Ten Little Niggers." Performed regularly by G.W. Moore of Christy's Minstrels during the 1860s, the song taught children how to count by systematically killing off the title characters.

> Ten little nigger boys,
> Full of beer and wine!
> Rosenmiller soon collapsed,
> And then there were nine;
>
> Nine little nigger boys,
> Grieving o'er his fate!
> Lawyer Johnson squeaked awhile,
> And then there were eight!
>
> *Chorus*

One little, two little, three little, four little, five little nigger boys!
Six little, seven little, eight little, nine little, ten little nigger boys!

Eight little nigger boys,
To distraction driven,
Called on Fisher for a speech,
And then there were seven!

Seven little nigger boys,
Couldn't stand the mix;
Bill Buckius went to Franke's for a beer,
And then there were six!

Chorus—One little, two little, etc.

Six little nigger boys,
With loyalty alive!
Ell. Gable left (with Dixie dog)
And then there were five!

Five little nigger boys,
Not another more.
Ben Smith in search of Gable sloped,
And then there were four!

Chorus—One little, two little, etc.

Four little nigger boys,
Drinking whiskey free;
Chuck Boas got very drunk,
And then there were three!

Three little nigger boys
Saw it wouldn't do;
Jack Hiestand said, "Now let's adjourn,"
And then there were two!

Chorus—One little, two little, etc.

Two little nigger boys,
Deprived of all their fun;
Davy Nauman left the chair,
And then there was one!

One little nigger boy,
Standing all alone
Johnny Martin went to bed,
And then there was none!

Chorus

One little, two little, three little, four little, five little nigger boys!
Six little, seven little, eight little, nine little, ten little nigger boys![19]

In addition to counting, schoolteachers used the jingle to teach young children about personal safety.[20] Ten white students recited the song at a school holiday concert in 1887. Newspaper reports said the performance was "heartily encored."[21] Boston's Toyland sold a card game of "Ten Littler Niggers" for 10 cents in 1905.[22] Adaptations of the rhyme also emerged in the twentieth century. Here is one from Fall River, Massachusetts, in 1910.

Ten little nigger boys stealing grapes from a vine;
One got caught, then there were only nine.

Nine little nigger boys fixing a grate;
One got his finger jammed, then there were eight.

Eight little nigger boys in a balloon going to heaven;
One fell out and then there were only seven.

Seven little nigger boys piling up some large brick[s];
One let one fall on his toe, then there were six.

Six little nigger boys fooling with a hive;
One got stung and then there were five.

Five little nigger boys tried to fix a door;
One hurt his finger, then there were four.

Four little nigger boys tried to climb a tree;
One fell on his head, then there were only three.

Three little nigger boys trying to mend a shoe;
One put a nail in his finger, then there were two.

Two little nigger boys with a cat tried to have fun;
[One] got bit and then there was none.[23]

This 1912 version is from Wilkes-Barre, Pennsylvania:

Ten little nigger boys, going out to dine.
One got shot and then there were nine.

Nine little nigger boys slept very late.
One overslept himself and then there were eight.

Eight little nigger boys traveling in Devon.
One missed the train and then there were seven.

Seven little nigger boys chopping up sticks.
One chopped himself in half and then there were six.

Six little nigger boys playing with a hive.
A bumble bee stung one and then there were five.

Five little nigger boys got into law.
One got into the chancery and then there were four.

Three little nigger boys traveling through the zoo.
A big bear hugged one and then there were two.

Two little nigger boys sitting in the sun.
One got shriveled up and then there was one.

One little nigger boy living all alone.
He got married and then there was none.[24]

Here is a 1916 variation from Wilmington, North Carolina, that plays more on Black stereotypes:

> Ten little niggers, ragged and forlorn;
> In the Recorder's Court every Monday morn.
>
> Nine little niggers wonder what's their fate;
> One to the County Roads, then there were eight.
>
> Eight little niggers aged nine, ten, and eleven;
> Met a policeman, then there were seven.
>
> Seven little niggers up to all their tricks;
> One got arrested, then there were six.
>
> Six little niggers very much alive;
> Caught in their mischief, then there were five.
>
> Five little niggers were then very sore;
> Tried to get even, then there were four.
>
> Four little niggers, lively as can be;
> Auto killed one, then there were three.
>
> Three little niggers with no work to do;
> Were caught shooting craps, then there were two.
>
> Two little niggers shooting off a gun;
> Were a bit careless, then there was one.
>
> One little nigger grown to be a man;
> Steals a woman's purse, catch him if you can.[25]

Decades later, on November 6, 1939, the Collins Crime Club resurfaced the song when it published Agatha Christie's mystery novel about ten killings on a remote island inspired by her visit to an island off England's South Devon Coast. The book, initially titled *Ten Little Niggers* in the United Kingdom, released in the United States a year later as *And Then There Were None*, taken from the song's last five words. Later adapted as a stage-play, the story found audiences all over the world under varying titles. In London, the play ran under the name "Ten Little Niggers." The play was rewritten as "Ten Little Indians" in the United States. In Kenya, the play was called "Ten Little Redskins."[26]

In the wake of global decolonial efforts and the civil rights movement in the United States, activists mobilized to remove the children's ditty from circulation. In 1969, the American Jewish Congress's Commission on Law and Social Action launched a successful protest against the Xerox Corporation, which carried a reputation for unwittingly publishing reproductions of "Ten Little Niggers" complete with Black stereotypical illustrations in the classic *Mother Goose's Nursery Rhymes and Fairy Tales*.[27] The history of this song alone illuminates how popular music not only reflects but also helps shape public attitudes.

Just as significant in disseminating notions of Black inferiority with use of the N-word were Southern folk songs, such as "Jimmy Crack Corn" and "Shew! Fly, Don't Bother Me," along with "Polly Wolly Doodle," which evaded use of the N-word yet propped up the watermelon stereotype. Each tune sprang from blackface minstrelsy only to regain currency as children's songs in the twentieth century.[28] Minstrelsy songwriting is among various children's traditions culpable in perpetuating racist ideas. Among the greatest songwriters benefiting from minstrelsy music was Stephen C. Foster, whose compilation of music romanticizing antebellum and plantation life has left an indelible mark on the way Americans remember the mid-nineteenth century. Born in 1826 near the Pennsylvania steel city of Pittsburgh, some of Foster's songs—about 25 out of 400, according to Robert Perloff, distinguished University of Pittsburgh professor emeritus from the Katz Graduate School of Business—became the most popular numbers performed by blackface minstrel troupes.[29] Much like early white rock 'n' roll artists that were drawn to the unusual Black genre known as rhythm and blues in the 1950s, Foster biographers have noted that America's first professional songwriter was likewise drawn to African American music of his time.[30] Indeed, he appropriated and eventually profited from the melody and dialect of African Americans. His work helped future artists commercialize the key component of blackface minstrelsy—the music. "Foster as a youth ate up the minstrel songs," writes music critic Steve Terrell. Seizing upon elements of plantation life "is what made Foster's music unique and powerful."[31] The musical collection includes "Old Black Joe" and "Massa in De Cold, Cold Ground."

Foster's biggest hit was "Oh! Susanna," a song about a man traveling through the South looking for love. The song is representative of the period's allure of mobility, a novel time when people emancipated themselves from the land of their birth only to move greater distances from home and with greater frequency than ever before. In the song, the main character witnesses the death of hundreds of Black people and feels indifferent about it to the chagrin of many.

> I come from Alabama with my banjo on my knee,
> I'm goin' to Louisiana my true love for to see.
> It rained all night the day I left, the weather it was dry;
> The sun so hot I froze to death—Susanna, don't you cry.
>
> Oh! Susanna, do not cry for me;
> I come from Alabama, with my banjo on my knee.
>
> I jumped aboard the telegraph and traveled down the river,
> Electric fluid magnified, and killed five hundred *Nigger*.
> The bullgine bust, the horse ran off, I really thought I'd die;
> I shut my eyes to hold my breath—Susanna, don't you cry.

In the nineteenth century, "Oh! Susanna" was a hit. Music publishers fought one another to secure rights to sell it, which were eventually awarded to W.C. Peters in Pittsburgh.[32] Like "Ten Little Niggers," "Oh! Susanna" has undergone lyrical transformations during the twentieth century to remove the N-word and make it more accessible to the public. However, the act of changing the lyrics is a concession that there is something terribly problematic with the song. It also illuminates a level of indecency undertaken by Foster and Peters to profit from Black plantation life. Adding to the debate surrounding Foster's songwriting, in 1900, the City of Pittsburgh erected an 800-pound statue in his likeness at Highland Park (it would change locations after World War II). The statue shows Foster towering over a Black man, Uncle Ned, the celebrated character in the song "Old Uncle Ned" (1848). Sitting at Foster's feet, Ned happily strums a banjo. For 118 years, the statue stood unscathed as a city ornament, save an episode in 1937 when someone chiseled away Ned's banjo and took it as a souvenir.[33] Proponents of the statue asked viewers to see it for its context: that Uncle Ned was not some random fictional enslaved human sitting underneath Foster's gaze, but that he was the namesake of the character in one of Foster's most popular songs. Music historians recognize "Old Uncle Ned," a song about the death of a bald, blind, and toothless Black man, as the first antislavery number in the popular music market. Music historian and professor emeritus at the University of Pittsburgh Deane Root says a casual listener today would not see "Old Uncle Ned" as an antislavery ditty.[34] The language is vulgar: "Dere was an old nigga dey called him Uncle Ned / He's dead long ago long ago.... No more hard work for poor old Ned / He's gone where da good niggas go." But after the death of the song's protagonist, the lyrics illustrate the mourning of Ned's white slaveholder and mistress. "Massa take it mighty bad / De tears run down like de rain / Old Missus turn pale and she gets berry sad / Cause she nebber see Old Ned again." According to Root, this show of affection was considered a landmark breakthrough in the minstrelsy tradition that had customarily portrayed Black Americans as manipulative, brainless, and lawless. The argument that the Foster monument is representative of racial harmony between Blacks and whites would not stand the test of time. After a formidable effort to preserve the statue at its current location near the Carnegie Museum of Art in Schenley Park, widespread criticism over how the statue glorifies white appropriation of Black culture convinced city authorities to take Foster and Ned down in 2018.

Protest of Foster's legacy is not limited to a statue in Pittsburgh. Civil rights groups as early as 1914 orchestrated campaigns to remove his "plantation songs" from schools. Foster's "Oh, Susanna" was the driving force to remove music containing the words "darkey" and the N-word from music curriculum in Boston public schools. The Boston school board of directors voted on November 12, 1914, to withdraw from its curriculum a book titled *Forty Best Songs* after speeches by concerned citizens, including Francis J. Garrison, the only surviving son of the white abolitionist printer William Lloyd Garrison, disclosed information about how the songs emboldened racist bullying in their schools. In one case, a Black 10-year-old student returned home from Boston's Browning School distraught because white students called him a "nigger" and "darkey."[35] In addition to "Oh! Susanna," other Foster songs included in the ban were "Carry Me Back to Old Virginny," which contained several references to "darkey's heart"; "My Old Kentucky Home" for its minstrel melody; "Old Black Joe" for its appropriation of an African American spiritual; and "Massa's in de Cold, Cold Ground," which made references to "darkey's mournful song" and "darkey's" affection for his master. Years later, when the Republican Party voted to make "Oh! Susanna" the official song of Alf Landon's 1936 presidential campaign, the *Atlanta Constitution* decried the song as "an incoherent jabber which sounds like clever satire on the whole succession of hill-billy numbers and spirituals." The Republican Party, railed Westbrook Pegler, a conservative columnist well-known for his opposition to United States President Franklin Roosevelt's New Deal, was, by choosing "Oh! Susanna" to represent Landon's vision for the nation, "appealing to the worst and cheapest in the electorate in incompetent fashion."[36] But for a campaign strategy aimed at appealing to rural voters in the South, and during a time when most Black Southerners were disenfranchised, Pegler's disparagement of the Republican Party hardly mattered.

There were other musicians and other songs of this era that faced intense scrutiny in later generations for commercializing minstrelsy music to harden Black stereotypes and racist imagery. In March 1916, Columbia Records released the record "Nigger Loves a Watermelon Ha! Ha! Ha!" a parody of the 1820s fiddle-tune "Turkey in the Straw." One Northern newspaper called the song "a treat to tickle the musical palates of those who love to listen to the old-time, slave-day river songs." The song's first public performer, the popular early twentieth-century white baritone and banjo player, Harry C. Browne, was called a "genius" with a "real darkey fervor. And the laugh—well, it has all the joyous abandon of a watermelon banquet."[37] This song is known today as the beloved "Ice Cream Truck Song."[38]

As seen in the unpleasant history of blackface minstrelsy tunes becoming part of children's songs, schoolyard rhymes also added to racist innuendo's ubiquity in American society, making young people consciously and subconsciously racist and ready to use violent words against racialized counterparts. The origins of the counting-out game "Eenie, meanie, miney, mo" comes to mind. When one hears a group of adolescent children playing a game of elimination designed to choose who will be "It" in a game of tag or hide-and-go-seek, the leader of the group typically chants this rhyme:

> Eenie, meenie, miney, mo
> Catch a tiger by its toe.
> If he hollers let him go,
> Eenie meenie miney mo.

This alternative form of counting comes from the belief that there will be some misfortune at the end of the rhyme, that there is a luck of the draw impacting the fate of multiple players.[39] In the United States, this fate was tied to the plight of Black people. One of the earliest variations of the rhyme included the N-word:

> Ena, meena, mina, mo.
> Catch a *nigger* by the toe.
> If he squeals let him go,
> Ena, meena, mina, mo.

Other versions have been reported, depending on location and decade, such as the following:

> Eeny, Meeny, Miny, Mo,
> Catch a *nigger* by the toe.
> If he won't work then let him go;
> Skidum, skidee, skidoo.
> But when you get money, your little bride
> Will surely find out where you hide,
> So there's the door and when I count four,
> Then out goes you.[40]

In 1892, folklorist Joel Chandler Harris reintroduced to the public the old African American folk song "Run, Nigger Run" in his publication *Uncle Remus and His Friends*. The song narrates the experience of a freedom seeker trying to evade slave patrols.

> Do, please, marster, don't ketch me,
> Ketch dat nigger behine dat tree;
> He stole money en I stole none,
> Put him in de calaboose des for fun!
>
> Oh, run, nigger run! De paterroller ketch you,
> Oh, run, nigger, run! Hit's almos' day.

The song was sung on plantations throughout the South before the black-face minstrel troupe The White Serenaders procured it in 1851. After

Harris's unearthing of the ditty near the turn of the century, the song grew in popularity before it was finally reprised for commercial recording in the 1920s. A chilling rendition of the song appeared in the 2013 film *Twelve Years a Slave*, Hollywood's interpretation of the narrative account by the same title written by Solomon Northup, a free Black man drugged, kidnapped, and sold into slavery in 1841.

Disturbingly racist and causal references to the N-word in music increased in regularity as Black performing artists moved the field beyond minstrelsy during the Gilded Age. Ragtime, a new genre of music formed in the early 1890s known most for its pianist syncopation, wherein the notes fall on the off beats to produce an original sound and novel dance culture, got its start in the American Midwest. Subtle rhythmic modifications to folk music were already common in songs and dances of Ireland, Scotland, and Wales. Variants of the ragged music also derived from Germany, Austria-Hungary, and Russia as students of music during the era pointed to Beethoven's "Sonata Pathetique" and "Moonlight Sonata" as among the earliest renditions containing syncopated bars. Frantz Von Suppe's "Poet and Peasant Overture" and several numbers by the Russian composer Pyotr Ilyich Tchaikovsky are also referenced as forerunners to the ragtime form. Legend has it that an Irish comedy team performed a variant of the syncopated classics in St. Louis sometime in the early 1890s. Black St. Louisans fancied the new Irish sound and adapted it as their own.

The aspect that made ragtime distinct from classical music and minstrelsy is not the syncopated sound but the outlandish exaggeration of syncopated sound. "With the classics, syncopated time was merely a means for conveying musical ideas, often of fairy delicacy," wrote one music authority. With ragtime, "the displaced beat is the end, the all in all." With most ragtime performers on the piano, the style was to let the unimportant melody in the right hand "languish along as best it can, and, for the most part, permit itself to be drowned by the left hand's accompaniment of resounding octaves, as thunderous as blows upon a bass drum."[41]

It was in Sedalia, Missouri, where African American artists birthed this strange style of music-making that deviated from banjo tunes of minstrel performances. "It is well known that the negroes are peculiarly sensitive to rhythm," wrote James M. McLaughlin, chairman of the Boston Music Commission in 1901. "How very natural it is to put into melodic shape the syncopated rhythms of the juba!"[42] Another music critic, Herbert Johnson of the Ruggles Quartet, called ragtime "peculiar to negro melodies."[43] One reviewer called the fact that Black musicians outclassed white composers as manufacturers of ragtime both a "strength and weakness" for the genre. "The jungle African is excited to bodily ecstasy by the throbbing of drums and tom-toms, his musical development having never passed far beyond the stage of instruments of concussion." Blacks in the United States "have built ragtime by adding a frail structure of Caucasian harmony, restricted in nearly every case to three simple chord changes and the transition to the major third." In ragtime songs, the composer usually gave the verses a setting in a minor key and transposed to the major for the chorus. "But beneath the veneer of harmony throbs and pulses [there is] a vigorous savage rhythm, harking back to the jungle, and to frenzied ghost dances about enchanted fires," wrote a columnist for the *Herald and Review* in 1909.[44]

It hardly mattered if white or Black musicians wrote the songs; ragtime was so deeply entrenched in Black culture at the time that the genre regenerated an old minstrel slur referencing Black people: the "coon song." White ragtime artist May Irwin, once described as a performer who told it like it is and was "too honest, too sincere, too humorous," was among the most influential and opportunistic in writing and profiting from songs that exploited Black caricatures. Among her scores, Irwin published the 1897 hit "An Awful Wicked Nigger." The song contained many offensive lines, but perhaps none more insulting than, "I's an awful wicked nigger / Dat's w'at I am, Yes I am."[45] Irwin had been a leading figure on the theatrical bill since the 1870s and was known both for her vaudeville and stage performances.[46] But there were other white performers before Irwin, notably J.P. Skelly with "The Dandy Coon's Parade," and J.S. Putnam's "New Coon in Town" and "The Coons Are on Parade." Two of the most popular rag songs at the turn of the century were W.G. Wilmarth's "Hypnotized Coon" and "Dis Coon Has Got the Blues." Famous Black blackface singers included Sam Lucas, who became famous for "Coon Salvation Army," George W. Johnson, author of "The Whistling Coon," the first hit recorded song by a Black man, and Robert Allen Cole, who also made it big as a minstrel performer. Cole's first hit was "Parthenia took a Likin' to a Coon." In 1898, Cole wrote *A Trip to Coontown*, a musical comedy consisting of only Black actors but based on traditional minstrel stereotypes.[47] It was a production he grew to regret.

The ragtime song "Coon, Coon, Coon," with music and lyrics by two white musicians, Leo Friedman and Gene Jefferson, was considered song of the year in 1901. The song sheet cover features three caricatured Black men in red bow ties, red hats, and matching oversized red lips. Also on the illustration is a photograph of Lew Dockstader, a white minstrel performer in blackface who performed the song. The song describes a

> Coon, coon, coon,
> I wish my color would fade;
> Coon, coon, coon,
> Quite a lighter shade;
> Coon, coon, coon,
> Morning, night or noon,
> It's better to be a white man,
> Than a coon, coon, coon

Within a year of nation-wide syndication, carnivals and street fairs made the ditty a signature song, playing endlessly for days as the public—largely white—bustled among the games and concessions. "'Coon, Coon, Coon' seems to buz [sic] through the crowd at night, and even the orchestra and band took it up," wrote a review of the Mid–Winter Exposition in Topeka, Kansas.[48]

Author of *The Colored Four Hundred* J.W. Wheeler, said of the musical style:

> The effect of the "coon song" has, without question, been wonderfully good. When I say "coon song," I mean those remarkably catchy and melodious ones that send theatre audiences on their homeward way humming and whistling in the air, and the melody goes zipping over the country from New York city to the Klondike, back over Chilcoot [sic] Pass to Seattle, and from Seattle to Presque Isle, Maine…. Another good thing about the "coon song" is it sees all kinds of classes of people singing the same songs.

Not every ragtime performer bought into the "coon song" framework. As a matter of fact, Black pianist Scott Joplin wrote and performed ragtime's most profitable song "Maple Leaf Rag." The song was a classic named after a waltz unique to Sedalia choreographers. Published by W.P. Stark, "Maple Leaf Rag" sold half a million copies by 1910 and helped Joplin become the nation's first example of an artist who received royalty payments for a song. Before this moment, artists received a one-time payment from music publishers.[49]

An African American pianist earning a living as a music teacher in Sedalia, Joplin was part of an entertainment district possessing formal music halls, clubs, saloons and brothels. Since Joplin played the piano inside of brothels as frequently as he played in nightclubs, his songs, and, by association, all ragtime tunes, were called hustler music. Critics said ragtime's novel dance style of shuffling, clattering, and halting steps were deprived of morality.

Criticism unleashed upon ragtime was no different than what rock 'n' roll faced in the 1950s and 1960s and what hip-hop has received since its inception. Indeed, music critics and newspaper columnists spent 20 years wishing for ragtime's demise, but so did blue-blooded composers and conductors in a form of class politics playing out in the musical profession. In 1909, music conductor John Phillip Sousa prophesied that ragtime was doomed to extinction and eliminated any variant from his programs. One cutting review appearing in Decatur, Illinois' *Herald and Review* suggested, "[R]agtime pretends to make no address to the heart and mind. The message ... concerns the feet and the muscles only." The review went on to say, "the whole literature of ragtime may be searched without yielding one musical concept of the least value. The ragtime writers seemed to have concerned themselves little, if at all, with finding fresh and meaningful themes. Inspiration and originality are superfluous with them. The ambition is to achieve a barbaric violence of rhythm, crude and vigorous as the pounding of a tom-tom."[50] Charles Kunkel, a German immigrant, composer, and music teacher living in St. Louis at the birth of the musical form, said the problem with ragtime is that most of its Black writers were "musically illiterate." He called ragtime compositions "as painful as a sonnet, tolerable in meter and rhyme, but without a single idea and containing violations of every rule of grammar and orthography." Ragtime is doomed, he said in 1909, "because it contains no brains. There are no notes, no rhythms, in music which are intrinsically bad, just as no letters in the alphabet are bad in themselves."[51]

Ragtime's irregular piano melodies were the invention of Black pianist and vaudeville entertainer Ernest Hogan. Already known as a Black minstrel performer who regularly appeared in blackface, and later called the "Father of Rag Time Music" and "Moses of the colored theatric professional," Hogan, whose real name was Reuben Crowders, put ragtime in general, and Black entertainers more specifically, on the map with the 1895 publication of "La Pas Ma La."[52] "La Pas Ma La" is a choreographed dance number consisting of one step forward with three steps back. "Hand upon yo' head, let your mind roll back / Back, back, back, and look at the stars / Stand up rightly, dance it brightly / that's the Pas Ma La." The song, however, contains repeated uses of the N-word and the slur "coon." "Fus yo say 'my niggah' get yo gun / shoota dem ducks an' away yo run / Now my little coon come 'a down the shute / With the Sainta Louis pass and Chicago Salute" and "Fus yo say 'my niggah' Bumbisha / then turn 'round and go the other way / To the world's fair and do the Turkey Trot / Do not dat coon tink he look very, very hot."

A year later, Hogan published "All Coons Look Alike to Me." The song came to Hogan after being wrongly arrested by a police officer. While in police custody, Hogan pleaded to the officer, "I am not the guilty man." The officer replied, "Tell it to the judge, all coons look alike to me." Hogan used the experience to pen the hit. "All Coons Look Alike to Me" contains two verses. The first tells the story of a Black woman who leaves her partner for another Black suitor: "All coons look alike to me, I've got another beau, you see / And he's just as good to me as you Nig every tried to be." The passage mentions the N-word and another repetition of the theme, "All coons look alike to me." The second verse refers to the experience of a retail clothing merchant who had merchandise stolen by a Black thief. The verse's protagonist describes the crime to the police and gives the best description that he could of the offender and was sent for the next day to go down to the police headquarters to identify the thief. He could not distinguish one Black man in the line-up from the others. "All coons look alike to me," he said. The cover art for the record features six Zip Coon caricature images of Black men and one woman, each replete with oversized red lips. The song yielded Hogan more than $40,000 in royalties. Its title became, and still is, a catch phrase used to mock Black people throughout the United States.[53]

Hogan's success as a ragtime pianist helped catapult his theatrical career. By 1900, he moved east to boost his vaudeville vitae. He became a star among the theater-going public and assumed the stage name "Unbleached American." Choosing long before to use the Irish name Hogan and pasting burnt cork onto his face, plus his willingness to call himself and other Black people the N-word and coons, helped make white audiences think of him as among the greatest comedians of his time.[54] It also created an awkward predicament in 1908, a year before he died of tuberculosis in New York City.

That year, a group of Black entertainers led by Bert Williams, George Walker, and nine others created a fraternal organization for professional entertainers duly called "The Frogs," a name inspired by the Aristophanes' comedy *The Frogs*, which tells the story of Dionysus's travels to Hades to bring the playwright Euripides back from the dead. Through philanthropy, The Frogs aimed to "promot[e] social intercourse between the representative members of the Negro theatrical profession and those connected directly or indirectly with art, literature, music, scientific and liberal professions, and the patrons of art." The group despised blackface performances and loathed racist representations of Black people.

The founders of The Frogs admired the ailing Hogan, whose illness had been disclosed earlier that January when starring in *The Oyster Man*, and they had organized on his behalf a benefit to offset medical expenses. However, the founders never welcomed Hogan into their beneficial association for Black actors. And Hogan was not in attendance at The Frogs' inaugural event in August 1908, a masquerade ball called "The Frolic of the Frogs" held at the Manhattan Casino on 155th Street.[55] This episode is among the earliest documented debates playing out publicly in the Black community over Black music and Black comedy wherein the N-word is central.

The N-word's usage by Black musicians and comedians at the turn of the century only helped to numb the public—whites largely—to its biting impact. Of course, whites like May Irwin wielded the word in adverse ways in both casual conversations and music; however, the transitional period of the Gilded Age to the Progressive Era by way of Black entertainers like Ernest Hogan's compositions helped pass usages of the word off as a neutral descriptor, while, in a very nuanced manner, conveying contempt for African American people.

Two

Out of Music

The N-Word's Material, Environmental, and Social Contours

Minstrelsy, said James Weldon Johnson of Black entertainers engaged in the performance art, "provided an essential training and theoretical experience, which could not have been acquired from any other source." It is important to realize that this kind of defense was based squarely on the history of oppressing Black Americans that goes back to the postbellum era when trying to cross the color-line solicited violent consequences. Johnson understood that the best way for Blacks to gain "national notice" was in show business, which began in minstrelsy. Acting and singing in front of white audiences "has made possible the higher development of each period of the Negro in the theatre over the period preceding."[1] Sadly, he understood, the artists that came before him had to stoop to such debauchery.

Ironically, however, these performers helped etch racist misrepresentations into the nation's psyche. This explains why N-word usage peppered every aspect of society during the first half of the twentieth century, from school textbooks to house pets, and from local landscapes to recreational entertainment. One artist from popular blues, the newest form of music in the 1910s, utilized the N-word when releasing the genre's very first published song. In 1913, a white songwriter named Leroy Robert White, a blackface minstrel performer from Texas affectionately known as "Lasses," copyrighted and published "Nigger Blues." The song likely originated from Black artists in the South. White is believed to have collected the lyrics from African American folk artists in the streets of Dallas and then passed it off as his own. When submitting the song for publication in 1912, White's original title was "The Negro Blues." In unorthodox fashion, it contains no chorus and consists of 12-bar verses, and six verses altogether with two interludes.[2] The song isn't derogatory. In fact, the lyrics evade a single mention of the N-word. Instead, the song

32

speaks to a "good man feeling bad" who, when feeling the blues, ails from "the doggone heart disease." The song went on to reap commercial success, with on-stage performances and studio recordings throughout the 1910s. In 1916, Columbia Records signed George O'Connor to record the song and sell it commercially. O'Connor was an attorney who moonlighted as a singer who performed "negro dialect humor and song." Columbia Records advertised the song as "the catchiest tune of the season."[3] "Nigger Blues" was O'Connor's bestseller.[4]

Such actions, whether premeditated or not, helped the word pervade school fairs, Boy Scout banquets, and community festivals. One popular carnival game during the era was "African Dodger," also known as "Nigger Dodger," "Hit the Nigger Baby," and "Kill the Coon." The game originated during Reconstruction when carnival customers paid to throw soft balls at a minstrel artist outfitted in burnt cork and poking his head through a hole in a canvas background. In 1881, carnival promoters in Indiana replaced humans with a monkey chained to a pole. The monkey as a target was short-lived, however, as a result of a disinterested public plus a scathing review in the *Indiana Herald*, which said, "If a man is disposed to make a fool of himself and run the chances of being hit at all, well and good, but for any man to put an animal in this position, it is a shame and an outrage. It is nothing less than a severe case of cruelty to animals, and as such should be prohibited by the management of the grounds."[5] When proprietors of the African Dodger concessions reemployed human dodgers by 1886, replacements came in the form of Black men.

The contest operated as a very primitive version of the dunking booth. Instead of asking a willing victim to fall into a tank of water once a ball hits the right spot, the face of a Black individual was the unfortunate target. The game is played when the head of an individual is thrust through a hole in a canvas curtain. The dodger must remain alert at every instant as pitches from all angles include eggs, baseballs, and other projectiles. Contestants would pay a nickel for three balls. Hitting the dodger won a cigar. Despite the health risk, the dodger was expected to tease customers. Taunts and jests provoked carnival-goers into spending more money.[6] Apart from a New York bill sponsored by State Senator Charles F. Murphy of Brooklyn and signed by Governor Charles Seymour Whitman in May 1917 placing a ban on the carnival concession at Coney Island and other summer resorts across the state, African Dodger remained a popular amusement in the North and South before World War II.[7] Critics of the game, namely the prominent Black-owned newspaper *New York Age*, mocked the contest as "Kindergarten for Lynchers."

Newspaper reports show that carnival-contestants took as much joy in playing this game as any of the other contests, which included the fish bowl toss, dart games, house of horrors, and basketball throws.[8] The name of the game became a widely popular phrase used to describe people known for sidestepping personal harm. In the Twenties, sportswriters described Afro-Cuban boxer Eladio "Black Bill" Valdés as having footwork in the ring that was "more like those of the 'artful African dodgers of carnival fame.'" Wayward husband Dave Hutton, a famed baritone of the 1930s who was white, was called a "Nigger Dodger" for circumventing a $5,000 alimony payment to ex-wife Myrtle Jean St. Pierre.[9] Press secretaries in the 1950s were called "African Dodgers in a carnival" for evasive answers given to press corps reporters.

Racism was just as pervasive in material culture of the early twentieth century. Commercial advertisers well into the century saw no value in the African American market, which, according to historian Robert E. Weems, Jr., was presumed to be "a group with limited spending power." Some businesses accordingly marketed products to white Americans by insulting Black Americans. The American Tobacco Company sold a brand of tobacco called "Nigger Hair," which sold successfully throughout the North and South during the 1910s.[10] Invented in 1922 by the Baltimore-based company Hendler Creamery Co. and sold by confectioners across the United States, "Picaninny Freeze" was a watermelon-flavored ice cream dotted with chocolate seeds. Advertisements featuring a young girl with dark black skin, oversized red lips, and strings of thinning hair eating a slice of watermelon beneath a yellow moon marketed the ice cream flavor in both tin and cardboard signage, as well as in the nation's newspapers. Imprinted on every variation of advertising was the inscription "Eat seeds 'n' all!"[11] One modified version of the advertisement proclaimed in nineteenth-century folk dialect, "Picaninny [sic] Freeze is made of ice cream, with chocolate seeds and a reg'lar watermelon rind."[12]

Other mercantile aspects of consumer culture devalued Black life with use of the N-word. Brazil nuts were called "nigger toes."[13] The name of this peculiar snack originated in the American South and was called such because, according to one food expert, "they were humorously supposed to resemble the toes of negroes."[14] For decades during the late nineteenth and early twentieth centuries, fireworks were called "Nigger chasers," a nickname made famous by George W. Peck's 1909 "Peck's Bad Boy in an Airship" short stories.[15] "Nigger babies" became the name of licorice candy. "Nigger brown" was a fashionable color, used mostly to describe designer gloves and dresses.

During the Gilded Age, the N-word pervaded random terminology throughout various parts of American society. "Nigger flicker" was a long-blade knife or razor carried in the pocket as a weapon of self-defense or attack. "Nigger heaven" was the segregated balcony in a theater where Blacks had to sit. "Nigger luck" was a term created to ironically refer to putting the best face on a bad situation. "Nigger rig" has been used to describe any makeshift device or structure of poor quality. "Nigger mess" describes any messy personal or community affair involving African Americans.[16]

Several racehorses were named the N-word, including prize winner "Nigger Baby."[17] A popular 1900 storybook by Alma Porter with the title "Nigger Baby and Nine Beasts" was called "one of the best books of the kind."[18] In the book, the "Nigger Baby" was a black race horse "with a great soul." Sequoia National Park was home to a yearling black bear cub named "Nigger, the Bear cub."[19] Slingshots carried the nickname "Nigger shooters" before an 18-year-old youth from Jefferson, Iowa, started a movement in the 1960s to change the name.[20] "Nigger Mammie" was a popular costume at masquerade parties at the start of the twentieth century.

A common phrase used to describe something as suspicious, uncanny, or complex was "Nigger in the woodpile." Several abolitionists testified to using the phrase after many successful rescues of enslaved persons that hid among stacks of wood to evade slave catchers.[21] The phrase also turned up in the Congressional Record of February 6, 1900, with one representative saying, "Louisiana sugar planters have found a new 'nigger in the woodpile,' who was not as useful as the one they have now."[22] With roots in the Underground Railroad, the popular recognition of the dictum suggested that behavior shouldn't be taken at its face value. After Black men received the right to vote by way of the Fifteenth Amendment, the Democratic Party commonly used the phrase to allege foul play between Republican candidates and the recently enfranchised electorate. At the turn of the century, muckraking journalists penned the expression in their columns when unmasking suspicious behavior by lawmakers.[23] In 1907, the Lily White Brothers released the song "Nigger in the Wood Pile" to public acclaim in New York and San Francisco. The song's chorus recited: "There's a nigger in the woodpile / Who has got his lamps on you / There's a black man in the doorway / And a sure thing bugaboo / And he says he will not go / He is after one Chames Edward / So it's time for us to blow." The song's second chorus adds the lines: "There's a nigger in the woodpile / And a great big black one, too / Little Arthur's on the warpath / He's a-coming, Tom, skiddoo."[24] Popular culture references to the phrase still made appearances 30 years later. John McWhorter's book *Nine Nasty Words* reminds readers that even Looney Tunes got into the act. In one episode of *Porky Pig*, titled "Porky's Railroad," which aired in 1937, the title character, cast as a train engineer, races throughout the countryside against a nemesis. When one of the Pullmans zips past a pile of logs duly named "woodpile," a caricature of a befuddled Black man is revealed as the logs soar in different directions.[25]

As Black workers found employment in the Ford Motor Company after World War I, white workers coined the phrase "Niggermation" to describe the company's practice of increasing productivity by using Black labor, not automation, on the assembly line. Black workers were commonly forced to work overtime hours without overtime wages. Haste on the production line often led to severe injuries. For example, in April 1969, thousands of Black workers walked off the job at a Ford plant in Mahwah, New Jersey, for its reputation for harassing night shift workers. Workers on a 2,000-man night shift, which was half Black, charged the company of forcing Black laborers to work harder than whites. "It's called niggermation," said Monroe Head, a leader of the United Black Brothers of Mahwah Ford. "They make one black man do the same job three whites do."[26]

Owing much to the multitude of Black migrants relocating into urban settings in places like St. Louis, New York, Philadelphia, and Cleveland, the years between World War I and World War II were a time of magnified white resentment for Black people in northern parts of the country. For example, the release of "That's Why Darkies Were Born" by New York–based Columbia Records in 1931 divulges the essence of Great Depression-era antipathy among racial groups. Written by Ray Henderson and Lew Brown, but made popular by soprano Kate Smith, affectionately known as "The Songbird of the South" and "The First Lady of Radio," and later Paul Robeson, "That's Why Darkies Were Born" was a hit song for much of the Thirties and Forties, despite its first stanza being among the most offensive lyrics in music history up to that point: "Someone had to pick the cotton / … Someone had to slave and be able to sing / That's why darkies were born." White audiences at Smith's concerts regularly insisted on encores. Radio stations aired live performances of the song.[27] The live sketch-comedy Broadway revue, *George White's Scandals*, a multi-act theatrical performance that ran for 16 years between 1919 and 1939, and that combined music, dance, and comedy, boosted the song's popularity with successive shows in Atlantic City, Newark, Brooklyn, and New York City during the summer and fall of 1931. Opera singer and actor Everett Marshall commonly received glowing praise for his performance of the song for the revue. After hearing Marshall perform "That's Why Darkies Were Born" at Harlem's Apollo Theater on September 14, 1931, one reviewer said Marshall "reveals one of the most melodious and powerful baritone voices you are liable to hear this season."[28]

It is true, civil rights icon Robeson helped circulate and commercialize the song throughout the United States during this era. That fact hardly deterred most Black people from detesting the lyrics. In fact, Robeson performed it in redemptive fashion to avenge white supremacist culture. When he performed the song, he asked "Maybe," a derisive gesticulation against a backdrop of racial turbulence. He would sing, "*Maybe* That's Why Darkies Are Born." He sang it, critics believe, as a satirical critique of racist America.[29] The second verse gives credence to that intimation: "Someone had to laugh at trouble / Though he was tired and worn / … That's why darkies were born." It is in that final line where Robeson would add the query: "That would bring God's children to green pastures. *Maybe* [holding the note for effect in his baritone voice], that's why darkies were born [prolonged notes with 'born' too]."

Like the N-word in the current era, context in the 1930s made little difference when white people sang "darkies." Historians Thomas J. Davis and Brenda M. Brock document a racial fracas at the famed Apollo Theater on 125th Street in November 1938 after a white singer gave a rendition of "That's Why Darkies Were Born." The performance, broadcasted live over the radio, agitated Black Harlemites in and outside the theater into an uproar.[30]

Indeed, "darkies" and the N-word's formal usage among the white social archetypes played a role in the persistence of racist-naming during the Jim Crow era. An example is found in the outrageous frequency at which the title "Niggerhead" was applied to various aspects of American life and culture. A type of cactus, Echinocactus polycephalus, was called "niggerhead cactus."[31] Similarly, coal was sometimes called "nigger head."[32] Dark-colored fruits such as blackberries, gooseberries, black raspberries and strawberries were called "Nigger Head Brand." Food stores also sold "Niggerhead Oysters" and "Niggerhead Shrimp."[33] The Aughinbaugh Canning Co., a canning company with factories up and down the East Coast, from Baltimore, Maryland, to Biloxi, Mississippi, named its oyster line "Nigger Head Brand."[34] When forced to change its name in 1954, the new brand became "Negro Head Brand." A makeshift dart-game, where contestants dropped darts into the mouth of a Black figure, was called "Nigger-Head."[35] To play, participants stood overtop the image of a darkened face with oversized lips, teeth and tongue. From an elevated position, contenders would drop a dart onto the face; two points were awarded for landing the dart on the face's lips. The contestant received five points when the dart landed on the image's teeth; if the dart landed directly in the center of the tongue, the contestant received ten points. Hitting any other area of the tongue granted three points.

Throughout the United States, several locations that carried some type of association to a Black person or Black community received the

N-word in its name. Mountains in Florida, Arizona, South Dakota, North Carolina, Texas, and elsewhere were called "Nigger Mountain." Some of those same sites also named ponds and creeks "Nigger Pond" and "Nigger Creek." Orange County, California, possessed a canyon called "Nigger Canyon."[36] Also in the Golden State were the "Nigger Jack Slough Stream" and "Nigger Jack Slough Bridge" located near Yuba City in Yuba County. A road called "Nigger Nate Grade" on Smith Mountain was named after the formerly enslaved Nate Harrison, who was among the first African Americans to establish a homestead in the region.[37]

Hunting locations in several places throughout the country were called "Niggerhead."[38] One such site in West Texas became famous in 2011 when the public learned that Republican presidential candidate Rick Perry and his father, Ray, had leased a hunting camp near his boyhood home in Paint Creek that still bore that name. A boulder bearing the name "Niggerhead" greeted visitors at the hunting ground's entrance.[39]

Then there were cases of actual lynching of Black individuals. Lynching African Americans, it seemed, was the standard of justice in local communities where there was no power to enforce the law.[40] The northern press called lynching a "pastime below the Mason-Dixon line," and "altogether too popular an amusement among our noble brethren of the south."[41] In 1899, a Georgia newspaper ran a story about a lynching using the headline "Nigger on Toast." The editor's remarks were lighthearted: "The affair was enjoyed by all excepting the nigger who kicked because he was the star performer."[42] In 1901, a South Carolinian by the name of Pitchfork Tillman traveled through Wisconsin recruiting lynchers. Tillman spread the message, "lynching niggers is right [and] the people will again take the shot gun with them to the polls to kill niggers should any of them undertake to vote."[43] In 1913, the Arkansas legislature abolished its militia because, according to critics, it "interfered with lynching niggers."[44] In 1924, the Ku Klux Klan published the "Klan Song" that included the passage: "And when there's no game bigger, the Knights of the Ku Klux Klan Delight in lynching a Nigger / For when life gets dull and duller, we never give up hope, We search for a man of color, and dangle him from a rope."[45]

One of the most important studies explaining the psychological degeneration of self-perception in Black children caused by Jim Crow segregation, racial caricatures, and the N-word was the "Baby Dolls" study conducted by Kenneth and Mamie Phipps Clark in the 1940s.[46] In a series of studies, the Clarks used four dolls, identical except for skin color, to study the reaction of 253 Black children representing communities in the North and South with ages ranging from three to seven. Asked to evaluate how the children viewed their own race and status, the subjects had to answer eight questions about the dolls: point to the doll that you like to play with, point to the nice doll, point to the bad-looking doll, point to the doll that is a nice color, point to the doll that looks like a white child, point to the doll that looks black, point to the doll that looks like a Negro, and point to the doll that looks like you. The Clarks designed half of the questions to unmask preferences. The other half revealed knowledge of racial differences and to record how the children self-identified. One of the most heartbreaking moments of the study was when the Clarks showed a black doll to a boy in Arkansas, who responded, "That's a nigger. I'm a nigger."[47]

"The Dolls Test was an attempt," explained Kenneth Clark years later, "...to study the development of the sense of self-esteem in children." The Clarks' report was glaring. It showed 67 percent of the children preferred to play with the white doll; 59 percent considered the white doll "nice"; 59 percent thought the black doll looked "bad"; and 60 percent favored the white dolls over the black dolls. "The importance of these results for an understanding of the origin and development of racial concepts and attitudes in Negro children cannot be minimized," wrote the Clarks in the study's final report.[48] These self-defeating images were reinforced, unfortunately, in newly integrated schools following the landmark ruling in *Brown v. Topeka Board of Education*, an opinion citing the Clarks' study as evidence of psychological damage of Black children caused by living in segregated states. In the new integrated schools, Black students were isolated, without culturally responsive curriculum, and divorced from Black educators. Black voices were muted, and there was no talk of racial justice, lest they be removed from the classroom. And these were spaces where teachers would facilitate games of hangman to turn a spelling lesson into a fun review activity.

There is no secret that the brave students decorating the pages of American history textbooks endured regular blitzes of racial epithets. When confronted by a human fence of Arkansas national guardsmen ordered to block the entry of African American students into Central High School in Little Rock on September 4, 1957, 15-year-old Terrence Roberts encountered taunts to "Go [a]way, Nigger, we don't want you."[49] Roberts, one of nine Black students enrolling at the city's cornerstone school that day, dressed in an open sports shirt with a new yellow pencil over his left ear, was asked, "Are you scared?" He answered, "Yes, I am. I think the students would like me … once I got in and they got to know me." Then a white woman yelled, "Yeah, you Nigger boy, go home and stay home." His peer, Elizabeth Eckford, sat on a bus stop bench hoping someone would come to her rescue. "What are you doing, you Nigger lover. You stay away from that Nigger girl!" yelled the crowd as a white woman, Grace Lorch, escorted the high school sophomore to safety on a city bus. The adults yelling slurs at the teenagers, known as the Little Rock Nine, emboldened the white teens, including Hazel Bryan, a Central High student captured in a timeless photo shouting at Eckford: "Keep out of our school, Nigger. You can't come to our school."[50] A freshman named Paul McGinnes told a reporter, "I don't want to go to school with Niggers. They have their own school, haven't they? If I sit behind one of them I'll do everything I can to get them into trouble."[51]

On her daily commute to William Frantz Elementary School in the winter of 1960, six-year-old Ruby Bridges faced torrents of slurs. A group of 40 to 60 mothers going by the designation "Cheerleaders" gathered each day to demonstrate against the enrollment of Bridges into the school. "I don't think the niggers are equal to whites," said Antoinette Andrews, a 42-year-old Cheerleader, who was joined by one parent holding a burnt cross and another with a crude casket containing a Black child. "Their heads are too hard to learn what our [white] children can."[52]

When state troopers removed Charlayne Hunter and Hamilton Holmes from the University of Georgia campus under a proclamation of Governor Ernest Vandiver in order to "restore order" on campus in January 1961, a crowd estimated at 2,000 students and townspeople met them on the campus lawn with "Nigger Go Home" inscribed on a bed sheet while others waved Confederate flags.[53] Later that fall, James Meredith was met by a large crowd of University of Mississippi students yelling "Nigger, Nigger, Nigger! Go home, Nigger!" and Confederate flags as he was blocked by Mississippi Governor Ross Barnett from enrolling at the university.[54] The then 29-year-old Air Force veteran faced steady epithets when finally attending classes two years later. "Ignore the nigger with vigor," was the chant by the student body. In 1963, Meredith announced he could not endure the hostile environment at the college under the present circumstances.[55]

These acts, and countless more, have reverberated with many white Americans as seen in backstage behavior on college and university campuses throughout the second half of the twentieth century and into the twenty-first century. Colleges and universities—while also at primary and secondary schools with less media attention—across the United States exist as extensions of society-at-large. As shown in the work of Leslie Houts Picca and Joe Feagin, instances of white students wearing burnt cork and other racial stereotypes as costumes has been an "ongoing series of individual and team performances" of racist acts.[56] For instance, a series of photographs recently surfaced revealing white collegians in various stages of racist performance, unseen in real-time by Black audiences but designed as theater for white coeds. Among those culpable of this mode of racial affront includes Virginia Governor Ralph Northam. It was discovered that Northam once wore blackface to depict Michael Jackson at a college Halloween party. Moreover, his 1984 Eastern Virginia Medical School yearbook page features two men standing side-by-side, one in blackface, with darkened hands and raggedy clothing, the other dressed as a Ku Klux Klan member. When first discovered, Northam conceded before denying that he was the individual in blackface. Similarly, several images and video footage surfaced of Canadian Prime Minister Justin Trudeau wearing brown makeup to an "Arabian nights" party in 2001. The most disturbing discovery perhaps descends from the University of North Carolina at Chapel Hill. A photo discovered in the university's 1979 yearbook, *Yackety Yack*, shows two members of the UNC chapter of Chi Phi fraternity dressed in full Ku Klux Klan regalia pretending to lynch another man dressed in scruffy clothes and wearing blackface. A noose was tied around the man's neck. The photograph was reportedly taken at the fraternity's "Old South" party, a now defunct event that paid tribute to the antebellum and postbellum South.[57]

The civil rights movement's impact on society wasn't only an impetus for sophomoric backstage racist behavior. The movement affected performative changes in locales across the United States when the federal government decided to remove from maps and signs the names of all geographic features that used the N-word in its moniker. For instance, in 1966, the Casper Chapter of the NAACP successfully won its campaign to convince the general population and the federal government to change the racist names of several landmarks in South Dakota. A gold-mining town 20 miles southeast of Casper and located in the northern portion of the Black Hills had been named "Nigger Hill" after a group of Black miners that arrived in town in 1875 looking for a place to mine for gold. White miners directed the group to a barren hill as a prank, where, ironically, they struck it rich.[58] Nearby was "Nigger Creek." The main thoroughfare running in and out of town was called "Nigger Creek Road." A uranium mine in the Edgemont Uranium District in Fall River County was called "Nigger Gulch." In 1962, a federal edict from the Kennedy Administration's Department of Interior resulted in name changes for the four landmarks on all federal government maps. By 1966, agents in South Dakota accepted the name changes in a backhanded way. Oddly enough, in South Dakota and elsewhere, the race-based names were replaced with "Negro." Thus, the landmarks were thereafter called "Negro Hill," "Negro Creek," "Negro Creek Road," and "Negro Gulch."

The Board of State Library in Vermont failed to make the same decision in July 1966 when the trustees voted 4 to 1 to retain the names "Niggerhead Mountain," "Niggerhead Brook," and "Niggerhead Pond" in Marshfield's Groton State Forest on the state maps.[59] A second effort led by college students at the University of Vermont (UVM) and Goddard College in 1971 succeeded, but only after it was discovered that UVM owned 320 acres of land surrounding two-thirds of "Niggerhead Pond" and including the southeast portion of "Niggerhead Mountain."[60] Like what occurred in South Dakota, the names of each site were changed to "Negro Mountain," "Negro Brook," and "Negro Pond."

* * *

The opening chapters were difficult to write. They are more difficult to read. But to include different contextual uses of the word throughout those chapters is to demonstrate varying implications. Tracing its popular culture roots back to T.D. Rice's "Jump, Jim Crow," racist folk music, popular children's songs, and corporate brands shows how the N-word has damaged the souls and spirits of Black people while emboldening white people to inflict physical and mental pain.

These stories speak to what the Black community does in an unmeasured way: it forgives. Award-winning historian Isabel Wilkerson says it best: "The act of forgiveness seems a silent clause in a one-sided contract between the subordinate and the dominant."[61] The list is long and should be unforgettable—slavery, lynching, Jim Crow laws, voter suppression, mass incarceration, racist representation in popular culture, and, among other items, a colorblind school system. The white race in America has given Blacks every reason to hate them. And yet, Blacks have forgiven all of the crimes inflicted upon their ancestral and living kin. The history recounted in these pages is included to provide the fundamental reason why so many people in this current moment in history are offended when a white person says the N-word. Collectively, this is what people mean when they say that the N-word spoken by a white person is loaded with psychological and physical torment unmatched by any other word in the Merriam-Webster dictionary. For so long in American history, racist public sentiment and racist local prejudices were the standard of justice, and no state law or federal law could be enforced that was incompatible with local racist standards. The N-word and the act of physical and mental lynching were interwoven for over a hundred years because local prejudice, mainly in the South (though acts of lynching were also performed in the North), was in favor of the public murder of African Americans without a trial. This cruel and oppressive history is as much part of white America's inheritance as property, wealth, and privilege.

A reframing of the interplay between whites and the epithet, however, reveals that there is another factor at play. This is not just a matter of how Black Americans respond to a white person who says the N-word.

Considered also should be the unconscious feeling nested inside the person using the slur. Research on implicit racial bias has been conducted by leading social and clinical psychologists since the Fifties. Harvard psychologist Gordon W. Allport wrote in *The Nature of Prejudice* that people have a way of simplifying their world by categorizing everything, including other people.[62] Therefore, according to Allport, people have various automatic reactions that rear their ugly heads during verbal and physical altercations with persons of other racialized groups. Academics revisited Allport's thesis decades later when Mahzarin Banaji, Anthony Greenwald, and Brian Nosek created Project Implicit. This project allows people to measure their own implicit biases on everything from race and gender to age, weight, and political candidates. Results have shown that 75 percent of white respondents subconsciously favor white over Black, more than 70 percent of all respondents favor straight people over gay people, and about 80 percent favor young over old.

The studies also show that people of non-dominant racial and ethnic groups also favor dominant racial and ethnic groups.[63] Decades of scholarship on the topic show that explicit and implicit bias have roots in the normal human tendency to categorize everything, including in-groups and out-groups. Often antipathy toward out-groups are mentally cataloged by way of societal curriculum or stereotyped images observed during a lifetime of exposure to certain forms of media, peer groups, formal schooling, and disproportionate representations in popular culture (the focus of this chapter). As a result, unchecked racial biases are unleashed in the form of racist slurs during intense verbal exchanges between two or more people of different racial groups. In part, it explains why Michael Richards of *Seinfeld* so easily and flagrantly scolded a Black heckler with a flurry of N-words during a standup routine at The Laugh Factory in Hollywood on November 17, 2006. "Throw his ass out! He's a nigger! He's a nigger! He's a nigger! A nigger! Look, there's a nigger!" exclaimed Richards. When on the David Letterman show three days later, Richards rationalized, "I'm not a racist. That's what's so insane about this."[64] A friend, Black comedian Paul Mooney, who will be discussed in greater detail in Chapter Six, defended Richards' behavior. Mooney and Richards had known one another for 20 years before the incident. During that time, Mooney had no indication that his friend harbored such horrid feelings toward Black people. "He told me he didn't know he had that ugliness in him," Mooney said to the Association Press after the incident.[65] This case, and the stories about people of less fame who shout slurs at someone sitting in another car during a fit of road rage, is evidence of the very real process of lifelong socialization that matriculates in a racist society. Slurs that surface because of implicit prejudices stem from ordinary cognitive processes. A combination of the science and socialization that triggers racist behavior substantiates why Black people who hear the epithet exit the mouths of white individuals—including well-meaning teachers, journalists, or musicians—feel a terrible and torturous sensation underpinned by a dehumanizing historical legacy.

The remainder of this book will explore the history of the N-word debate through the lens of music. The afterlife of Rice's "Jump, Jim Crow" has always pervaded American vernacular culture. We have seen it in standup comedy. We have read it in literature, namely canonical books such as *Huckleberry Finn, To Kill a Mockingbird, Native Son, Invisible Man, I Know Why the Cage Bird Sings,* and *Tar Baby.* It is heard in music, from ragtime to hip-hop, and from bluegrass to rock 'n' roll. The word, largely due to "Jump, Jim Crow," has traveled fluidly with varied plots, giving heft to performative modes. The N-word spreads wide not only because of anti–Black racism. Music has often given the word new life and new meaning. And an excellent place to start this journey is to look at one of the most consequential voices in the history of music: John Lennon.

THREE

John Lennon's N-Word Moment

At 3 o'clock in the morning, Saturday, December 11, 1971, John Lennon appeared on stage with Yoko Ono at the University of Michigan's Crisler Arena. Dressed in matching purple t-shirts and black leather jackets, the couple appeared at the Free John Sinclair Rally, an event sponsored by the Rainbow People's Party and the Free John Sinclair Committee, to advocate for the release of political-poet, hippie leader, manager for the Detroit rock band MC5, and founder of the White Panther Party, John Sinclair. Two years earlier in 1969, Sinclair had been sentenced to ten years in prison for selling two marijuana cigarettes to an undercover police officer.[1] It had been his third conviction, and Detroit Recorder's Court Judge Robert J. Colombo issued Sinclair the maximum penalty of nine-and-a-half to ten years in state prison. Judge Colombo's sentence also denied bond, which would have allowed Sinclair to stay out of prison during the appeal process.[2] Starting at 7 o'clock in the evening on December 10, about 15,000 people showed up to rally in support of Sinclair's legal fund, which raised $26,000 as his appeal was currently before the Michigan Supreme Court.[3] Other notables at the rally were Yippie leader Jerry Rubin, Black Panther Party co-founder Bobby Seale, radical pacifist David Dellinger, musicians Stevie Wonder and Bob Seger, and poet Allen Ginsberg. Lennon and Ono were the headliners nonetheless. Lennon and Ono's planned joint appearance recognized the absurdity of Sinclair's prison sentence as one in a long line of inconsistencies in State actions.[4] Ironically, Lennon would soon be at risk of deportation from the United States for a 1968 marijuana possession conviction in London. The song Lennon performed as the event continued well beyond midnight was "John Sinclair." It was a previously never before heard number about the song's subject. In fact, with Ono on a bongo drum, Lennon performed three unreleased, politically inspired songs that cast a spotlight on the intersection of the American justice system with war, government surveillance, and race relations. His wasn't a fantastic performance; in fact, Lennon warned the event's sponsors ahead of time that he wasn't bringing a band. "I'm only here as a tourist," he said.

"...I'll probably fetch me a guitar, and I know we have a song we wrote for John [Sinclair] and that's that."[5]

Lennon and Ono performed at the concert as leading participants in a worldwide movement for peace. In a sense, they both sought to serve as witnesses to an ongoing historical drama they had actively shaped in their respective roles as musician and artist. "We're really thinking in terms of John Sinclair," Ono told reporters before the event, "and our friends, and our brothers and sisters who are in pain, and we really feel the pain with them."[6] So when it came time for them to take the stage during the early morning hours, amid clouds of marijuana smoke, Lennon sang lyrics that no one had ever heard before about his fellow peace lover: "If he'd been a soldier man / ... Breathing air, like you and me."[7]

Although their time on stage lasted just a bit more than ten minutes, Lennon and Ono were credited by, among others, John Sinclair for influencing the opinion of the judges that sat on the Michigan Supreme Court who went on to release Sinclair from prison three days after the rally. The same judges ruled the current law in Michigan that treated marijuana and heroin equally dangerous to be unconstitutional, which temporarily legalized marijuana in the Great Lakes State.[8]

Lennon, in 1971, experienced a remarkable political transformation. His pro-peace reputation swelled as the antiwar and anti-establishment movements he came to personify expanded beyond his full comprehension. His long-standing appreciation of the relationship between peace and social justice—what he would attempt to convey in his forthcoming album *Some Time in New York City*—remained thwarted by many in America who refused to commiserate with the high price of peace, love, and music. "So Flower Power didn't work," he told the audience at the John Sinclair Rally. "So what? We start again!"

Lennon's candid exculpation of State violence would rapidly escalate after the John Sinclair Rally, which he considered a trial run for a nationwide anti–Nixon tour, designed to bring rock 'n' roll together with leftist politics leading up to the 1972 presidential election.[9] Lennon hoped to end the tour in August 1972 with a giant protest rally outside the Republican National Convention in Miami on the night Richard Nixon was to be re-nominated.

Over the next six months, Lennon made final touches on *Some Time in New York City*. This double album alluded to many national and international political debates over the Nixon administration, State violence, race, and feminism. Lennon responded to the geopolitical landscape by writing songs about issues happening at that moment rather than universal themes that had come to define his musical genius. One song, "Attica State," is about the 1971 riot and heavily armed law enforcement raid of the Attica Correctional Facility near Buffalo. That event resulted in the deaths of 39 people after failed talks between inmates and prison authorities, including New York Governor Nelson Rockefeller, for better prison conditions.[10] The song "Angela" brought attention to the imprisonment of Communist Party leader and Black Panther Party sympathizer Angela Davis, who was standing trial for kidnapping and murder and had yet to be exonerated. Two songs lashed out at his native country by expressing sympathy for the Irish in "Sunday Bloody Sunday" and "The Luck of the Irish." Of course, "John Sinclair" exposed attempts by establishment authorities in the criminal justice system to suppress leading figures of the counterculture.

Returning to Lennon's performance at the John Sinclair rally, there is one line in "John Sinclair" that should have made listeners cringe: "If he'd been a soldier man / Shooting *gooks* in Vietnam." Lennon never received censure for using the slur against people of Asian descent. Nor did Ono, who is Japanese and was already on the receiving end of anti–Asian coverage in the press for being made out as the individual responsible for breaking up the Beatles. It is possible Lennon escaped reproach given that the song and the album were never popular. It may have also been because Lennon sympathized with the Vietnamese in the song. These are the same reasons that arguably granted a pass to Bob Dylan for calling African American boxer Rubin Carter the N-word in his 10-minute ballad "Hurricane," which addressed the wrongful imprisonment of Carter during the Sixties and Seventies. In Lennon's "John Sinclair" and Dylan's "Hurricane," empathy flows naturally through the heart of exposing illicit State-sponsored injustices to the world.

There is one song nonetheless that is at the heart of this chapter. The first single released from *Some Time in New York City* was "Woman is the Nigger of the World." Sticking the N-word in the middle of the song's title was a bold move indeed. Furthermore, while the word is sung five times throughout the track, Lennon sang about the global oppression of women, "the women's problem," he said, while saying nothing about the subjugation of African Americans or the violence committed against African-descended people anywhere on the planet.[11] In today's climate, this song would leave Lennon in ruin, rightly or wrongly a victim of cancel culture. But in the Seventies, the N-word was marginally acceptable. Musicians often exploited the trauma and self-loathing that exists in the history of that word.

Few in our current moment ever criticize Lennon for taking this risk with his music. Still, the sad truth is that he understood only surface-level interpretations of gender and racial oppression. He also never expressed knowledge that racist language is not limited to the vocabulary of skinheads and Ku Kluxers, but is also deployed by educated and progressive whites like himself. It is clear that he was wrapped up in using his immense platform to speak out on several causes; yet, when intersecting the public figures he spent his time with in 1971 and 1972 with the titles of his songs on *Some Time in New York City*, one hears the words of Ono, Abby Hoffman, Bobby Seale, John Sinclair, and Jerry Rubin. More to the point, while Lennon's overt sexism and racism are not the culprits here, we can see how Lennon reproduces the stereotype of white liberals who are unable and unwilling to recognize their own sexism and racism.

In 1960, at a time when Lennon was just 19 years old and in his third year with the Beatles, Martin Luther King, Jr., said to an interracial audience at the annual National Urban League conference in New York City that no person "can afford to be apathetic about the problem of racial justice." Racism, he said, "is a problem that meets every man at his front door." In a year that saw mostly college-age activists sitting in on a national scale to desegregate public lunch counters, King grew weary of white, liberal fence-sitters that feigned ire at national stories about some type of racial abuse but kept silent about the inequality and prejudice existing in their own backyard. King criticized white liberals for performing a version of polite racism, a parade of moral goodness instead of actually combating racial injustice. He spoke about the "pressing need" for a more vocal white liberal who "firmly believes in integration in its own community as well as in the deep South." The civil rights movement needed the white liberal to "not only rise up with righteous indignation when a Negro is lynched in Mississippi, but will be equally incensed when a Negro is denied the right to live in his neighborhood, or join his professional association, or secure a top position in his business."[12] This speech is so powerful and continues to resonate in American society because it goes to the heart of the white liberal problem: that most whites are blinded to their own prejudices. It also embodies the mistake made by John Lennon, who was shamed by the music industry and members of the public for writing and publicly performing the song "Woman is the Nigger of the World" in the spring and summer of 1972. Following the initial firestorm, Lennon made the public cringe further as he appeared on radio and televised talk shows to defend his use of the N-word. Similar to King, critical race scholar Shannon Sullivan sardonically uses the term "Good White People" for those whites like Lennon who draw clean ontological lines between overt white racists and antiracist whites, while skipping over white liberals stuck in the middle that actually cause more harm in less spectacular ways.[13] Even Lennon would admit years later that he was neither a feminist nor an antiracist despite the meaning behind the song in question.

His false rhetoric about purporting to be a progressive yet owner of sexist and unchallenged implicit racial views of Black people is centered by white male virtuousness. Though feigning feminist and antiracist empathy in his music, Lennon was incapable of giving up heteronormative and white-skin privileges that would have challenged the established power structures he attacked so ferociously in his music. There is a romanticized perception of Lennon's genius that pervades the consciousness of peace-loving people that has long been misconstrued. Lennon's bed-ins in 1969 and his musical career were grandiosely performative toward sociopolitical awareness and signaling peace-loving values. And yet he missed how his off-stage actions hurt those who were close to him. Though willing to give up a certain amount of privilege when performing in front of audiences—a way to feel righteous—he was actually a paragon of the white liberal problem. While willing to call out a grave violation of humanity that occurred on an international scale, he all too often remained silent about his own privilege, never taking notice of the injustices that infiltrated his most intimate spaces. Lennon was abusive to his first wife, absent from his older son, suppressive and suffocating to his second wife, and unconscious to the world's racist structures by assuming racism was limited to the actions of individuals, whether it appeared in a white robe and hood or settlers on indigenous soil.

Placing Lennon in a framework of the white liberal problem would, I claim, greatly assist discussions about social justice. Instead of focusing exclusively on "race," Lennon's actions would otherwise avert attention toward white privilege, colorblindness, sexism, and white-savior performative behavior. The idea for this approach is to rope white people into a discussion about white supremacy as the real issue, not whether they have love in their hearts for people of color, or whether they believe in equality with women. Once one understands that they are tied to privilege, racial and sex discrimination is, in one uncontroversial sense, linked to vested interests. In 1963, Malcolm X cautioned about the white liberal who "poses as the friend of the Negro." He told an audience, "The white liberal differs from the white conservative in one way. The liberal is more deceitful and hypocritical than the conservatives. Both want power. But, the white liberal has perfected the art of posing as the negro's friend and benefactor.... The American negro is nothing but a political football and the white liberals control this ball through tricks, tokenism, and false promises of integration and civil rights."[14] At the moment, Malcolm X spoke about the perpetuity of racism in America and around the globe despite the outcomes of various civil rights demonstrations that occurred the year he made these remarks. Displeased by what he perceived as tokenism by way of performative gestures of whites self-righteously signaling virtue while positions that lacked power and authority were the ones desegregated, Malcolm railed against the way Martin Luther King, Jr., and other African American leaders allowed white liberals to exploit the freedom movement. History has shown that the major determinant of white attitudes on civil rights issues is their perceptions of collective group interests, of how, in other words, their group will be affected by whatever public policy matter is up for debate.[15] Critical race theorist Derrick Bell would later call this "interest convergence," a theory describing "temporary peaks of progress" and "short-lived victories" as a result of white liberal policymakers recognizing a peculiar benefit by advancing a civil rights cause. Put simply, whites refrain from supporting efforts to improve the lives of people of color until it is in their interest to do so. Through performative acts of "wokeness," laws might change but institutional authority and racist ideas will always be controlled by the system of white domination.[16] White perception of a vested group interest in advancing a progressive cause can then be understood as the primary motivator of white liberal behavior. White liberal Barack Obama voters who subsequently casted ballots for Donald Trump in 2016 or the Hillary Clinton voter who spat racist malice toward an African American bird-watcher in a public park in 2020 act in such a way because most people who are white are inundated by economic, political, educational, and professional organizations that remain white institutional spaces. Put differently, racist ideas are baked-in. If there is not a concerted effort to learn about and resist unconscious biases, discriminatory behavior will surface. John Lennon's actions in the early 1970s tell us everything about the paradox of being a white liberal.

On April 24, 1972, "Woman is the Nigger of the World" became the first single from *Some Time in New York City* that Lennon released to the public. Within a week, Lennon became predictably immersed in a public relations imbroglio trying to protect his reputation. He expressed to television host Dick Cavett that there is no way he could be a racist because he had Black friends. That line of self-defense is still all too common for white progressives that knowingly or unknowingly perpetuate racism. Lennon was not capable of drawing a distinction between an individual racist who has no problem calling African Americans the N-word from whites who read all the right books and donate to the appropriate causes while tolerating the racist structures that keep people of color in the margins of society. Lennon, like most whites, was conditioned by societal curricula to think of racism as individual acts of explicit bigotry. Unwittingly, since he was involved in the anti-war movement and other freedom revolutions, he possessed a sense of exemption from the benefits bestowed to all white people by the system of white supremacy.[17] That is, many white progressives, then and now, fail to see that they have been shaped by a worldview that normalizes and values whiteness while corroding all racialized Others.[18]

* * *

In the reaction to the proceedings of Brett Kavanaugh's confirmation hearing to the United States Supreme Court in October 2018, singer and actress Bette Midler made headlines for a Twitter post directed at condemning the patriarchy's apparent influence over at least two branches of the American government, including the judicial branch to where Kavanaugh would eventually be confirmed, and the executive branch, where President Donald J. Trump had skirted ethical limits to nominate an individual accused of sexual misconduct. She offered sharp criticism of Kavanaugh's alleged rape allegations along with warnings that his confirmation could lead to reproductive rights rollbacks. Midler's post describing women as the most oppressed group in the United States included the euphemism "N-word." For the most part, Midler's Twitter controversy—in mainstream media, at least—was eclipsed by Kavanaugh's inevitable confirmation. And although this was not an occasion of a white person saying the full iteration of the N-word, it did amass a storm of acrimonious responses calling her racially illiterate and the Twitter post ill-mannered toward the Black community. Some critics saw the tweet as the blanketed undoing of the racialized terror overcome by Black women in America's long history of racist ideas, racist policies, and racist actions. Midler claimed white women endured the same level of sexual abuse and racial oppression as their Black counterparts. The post stated: "'Women, are the n-word of the world.' Raped, beaten, enslaved, married off, worked like dumb animals; denied education and inheritance; enduring the pain and danger of childbirth and life IN SILENCE for THOUSANDS of years[.] They are the most disrespected creatures on earth."[19] It took just three hours of public shaming before Midler deleted the tweet. In a public redaction she said, "I gather I have offended many by my last tweet. 'Women are the ... etc.' is a quote from Yoko Ono from 1972, which I never forgot. It rang true then, and it rings true today, whether you like it or not. This is not about race, this is about the status of women; THEIR HISTORY."[20]

Midler attempted to expose and relieve the pain women have endured, the feeling of invisibility in a country that had elected an accused sexual assaulter who just gave another man accused of sexual misconduct a seat on the Supreme Court amid a placated FBI investigation into a sexual assault accusation. In doing so, she was actually quoting the song by John Lennon titled "Woman is the Nigger of the World."[21] Ono's first utterance of the expression, followed by Lennon's rendition of the phrase, invited people to see life through the eyes of women. In Midler's case, it was in 2018 the old viewing of society through the eyes of a Baby-Boom feminist. All three contended that men should trade places with women and that men should experience life as defined by women. The important element here is the N-word nonetheless.

Why had the discourse over Bette Midler—or for that matter, John Lennon and Yoko Ono—using a racial slur in the context of calling to conscience the oppression of women become characterized as an unthinkably insensitive gesticulation deserving of public ridicule? This quandary is the premise of this chapter. The answer, however, does not warrant a simple response. For this reason, I crafted this chapter as an examination of John Lennon's forgotten song "Woman is the Nigger of the World."

Lennon, one of the most complex and puzzling musicians ever, wrote song after song that has stood the test of time. Since his tragic death in 1980, Lennon's life has increasingly acquired mythic stature. The scholarship includes award-winning biographies as well as titles having to do with his final days, his musical genius, and his New York years. Documentaries have focused on his anti-war activism, his contentious relationship with the American government, and the making of his incomparable *Imagine* (1970) album.[22] Along with Paul McCartney, Ringo Starr, and George Harrison, Lennon is a member of a pantheon of mid-twentieth-century musical prodigies. Perhaps the most important figure of that era exceeding Lennon's global popularity was not a musician but heavyweight boxing champion Muhammad Ali. Unlike his Beatles mates but somewhat similar to Ali, Lennon's rise to fame was both aided and complicated by his desire to politically incentivize his professional career. Like Ali, Lennon found himself in the crosshairs of the American government.

Lennon's ideas of politics and peacemaking were shaped in the waning years of the Beatles, after he met and married Yoko Ono, an avant-gardist raised in Japan but influenced into activism during her time in the United States. As an artist interested in the ways of the Fluxus group, a community of Dada-inspired artists that engaged in unconventional forms of art, Ono spoke out against hegemonic authority. In May 1968, even before his divorce from his first wife, Cynthia, Lennon recorded songs with Ono for an album that eventually became *Two Virgins*. After the divorce, Ono became pregnant, but suffered a miscarriage in November 1968. They were married on March 20, 1969, in Gibraltar and spent their honeymoon in Amsterdam, where the couple held the first of two week-long Bed-Ins for Peace. Between March 25 and 31, Lennon and Ono laid in bed from 10 o'clock in the morning to 10 o'clock at night. "If everyone stayed in bed for a week there'd be no killing," suggested Lennon.[23] He later told David

Wigg of BBC Radio-One's "Scene and Heard" that he and Ono intended to bring countries to a standstill. "Imagine if the whole world stayed in bed," he said with ire about the war in Vietnam. "There'd be peace for a week and they might get to feel what it was like."[24]

Lennon's life after meeting Ono went from stylistically popular to political. Taking on a personal crusade for world peace was at the forefront of his professional career. Before returning to London, the couple spoke to the media inside body-sized bags as part of a "Bagism" protest in Vienna designed to speak out against the war in Vietnam. They also sent two acorns each to world leaders as part of their "nuts for peace" idea meant to get the heads of state to plant them and grow trees as peace symbols.[25] Lennon referred to himself and Ono as "peace nymphs" for their creativity and dedication as nonviolent antiwar activists.[26]

The Lennons staged another Bed-In at the end of May.[27] While the couple hoped to conduct the demonstration in New York City because, as Lennon put it, "We're starting with America because of all the violence going on [there]," the U.S. Department of State denied the couple entry due to a 1968 marijuana conviction that took place in London.[28] The Bed-In was then planned for the Bahamas, but one day in the 80-degree heat ultimately forced the couple, traveling with Ono's five-year-old daughter Kyoko, to make Montreal the site for their public demonstration. Montreal was also closer to the American border, which was important for Lennon to, in his words, encourage, "all peace-lovers to join us in our campaign, but they can do it in their own beds."[29] But not everyone stayed in their own beds. In fact, during the Montreal Bed-In, which lasted from May 27–June 1, the Lennons received visits from scores of celebrities, journalists, and students. Lennon used the occasion to write the song "Give Peace a Chance." On May 31, the last full day of the Bed-In, Lennon, Ono, and all of their visitors, including Tommy Smothers of *The Smothers Brothers Comedy Hour*, singer Petula Clark, poet and philosopher Allen Ginsberg, and former Harvard University professor and LSD advocate Timothy Leary, recorded the song from Room 1742 at the Queen Elizabeth Hotel.[30] "Give Peace a Chance" became the anthem of the antiwar movement. The couple then chronicled their entire Bed-In and Bag-In experience in "The Ballad of John and Yoko," which is credited to the Beatles though never appearing on a full album released by the band.

There was a firestorm of disapproval for Lennon that had been stoked during that final year of the Sixties. The marijuana arrest, his nonconforming shoulder-length hair, the steel-rimmed glasses, his nudity on the cover of *Two Virgins* with Ono, fan loyalty to Lennon's first wife, Cynthia, the gradual disintegration of the Beatles, and the political stunts following his nuptials to Ono were too much for many people in America. Ono's race and ethnicity had something to do with it too, as she was referred to as "his Japanese wife" and "ugly" in American newspapers.[31] The criticism was worth it to Lennon and Ono nonetheless. During the late Sixties, enormous changes occurred rapidly throughout the United States in regard to Vietnam, the Cold War, race and gender relations. The combination of the Black power and anti-war movements influenced the Black Left on more than 250 colleges and universities across the country to demand campus climate and curricular changes by occupying administrative buildings and striking from class. The most noteworthy of the Black campus disruption movement was the takeover of Willard Straight Hall at Cornell University on April 16–17, 1969. After 36 hours, about a hundred Black and other non–Black students of color walked out of the building, some holding rifles and wearing bandoleers, once Cornell's administration made promises to make curricular changes and to reform campus culture. Self-determination rhetoric coming from the Black Panther Party inspired other power movements, including the Young Lordz in Chicago, the American Indian Movement in San Francisco and South Dakota, and the Yellow power demonstrations in California. Those radical trends, coupled with new feminist publications, also ignited the second-wave feminist movement.

Though criticism existed in certain sections of the public, Lennon was seen by many as the face of the counterculture. His music in 1970 and 1971 leaned heavily on drawing contrasts between what he viewed as corruption in the military industrial complex, vis-à-vis the American government, and the redemptive message of peaceful salvation proffered by peaceniks like himself. He relentlessly spoke and sang about the virtue of peace even as he denounced political radicals that refused to negotiate with establishment figures he called "squares."[32] America was his muse. This is why his eventual relocation to New York City in August 1971 enabled him to produce some of the most provocatively written political scores that unmasked the pains, agonies, and frustrations of an American people ailing from a political machine that was seeming unaware of the cost of war, racism, sexism, suppressed free speech, or the sensitivities of the Baby Boomers.

These were topics Lennon wanted to write and sing about. So, he made an album in 1972 called *Some Time in New York City* that resembled a real-time political treatise aspiring to address some of the larger social justice subjects of that year. It was a double album collaboration joining Lennon and Ono with the New York City bar band Elephant's Memory. As previously mentioned, the album includes songs about the Attica Prison riots, the jailing of Angela Davis, the civil war in Ireland, the Leftist writer and founder of the White Panther Party John Sinclair, and second-wave feminism.

For his good intentions, the one song on the record that got Lennon into trouble was the album's first single, "Woman is the Nigger of the World." In it, Lennon called for unity with women, whom he intimated through the title as the world's most marginalized and victimized group of people. The thesis of the song was not what bothered the public. It was the choice of using the N-word that got the song banned from most radio stations in the United States and the United Kingdom. Owing to the consequential promotional problems of *Some Time in New York City's* signature song, the album eventually tanked. It almost tanked Lennon's musical career too.

What we learn from Lennon's use of the N-word and the reaction that followed says a lot about what we learn from every unfortunate episode the epithet is uttered by a white person. It is true, the word carries a stronger—more taboo—meaning in our current era than it did in 1972, but the arguments have always been the same. A 2018 YouGov poll shows that a slight majority (53 percent) believe the N-word spoken by anybody and in any context is racist. There is a rather large divide between Democrats (73 percent) and Republicans (45 percent) that find the word offensive. African Americans who feel the word is offensive slightly outnumber their white counterparts, 59 percent to 55 percent. The same poll asked participants to indicate if they felt a white person using the N-word to refer to a Black person makes them a racist. Americans were split on this question: 38 percent responded yes to 26 percent that said no, while 36 percent of participants felt indifferent about the question.[33] This survey is important for one particular reason: it shows that Americans stand divided on this issue. For all of the debate, there still is no clarity on who can say the word, when they can say the word, and why they can or cannot say the word.

Fisticuffs over the N-word is arguably the biggest indicator of frustrations with America's racial dynamics. A half century ago, John Lennon was a pseudo member of the Black, Indigenous, and People of Color community according to some Black celebrities and activists. What gave him quasi Black membership? He was outspoken for Angela Davis and the inmates at Attica Prison. He spoke at rallies alongside Bobby Seale and attended at least one Black Panther Party meeting. He joined indigenous peoples in the fight for land sovereignty. His wife was a Japanese woman. He patterned his music after 1950s and 1960s Black rock 'n' roll artists. As his good friend and Black comedian-activist Dick Gregory would say about good-intentioned white liberals, Lennon "thought black."[34] None of that mattered, however, when he spoke the N-word out loud. While some famous members of the African American community like Gregory would come to his defense in 1972, no pass was granted. It is this story that gives us a glimpse at the precarious terrain of the N-word.

✳ ✳ ✳

Several years ago, I was introduced to the music of John Lennon. As I made my way through his anthology—the Beatles albums, then *Plastic Ono Band*, and later *Imagine*—I purchased his political record titled *Some Time in New York City*. Lennon described the album as a "pop-rock record" that he collaborated on with Yoko Ono. The songs he and Ono wrote were about "subjects we and most people talk about," he explained in a note accompanying the album. "[I]t was done in the tradition of minstrels" or singing reporters, he said, "who sang about their times, and what was happening."[35] The cover of the album is creative. It looks like the front page of a newspaper. On the top right is a photoshopped picture of a naked Richard Nixon dancing with China's Mao Zedong, who also bares all. The album's many song titles are used as headlines for the various news stories found on the album cover. The lyrics of each song make up the stories. At the center is one image of a devilish looking man sexually assaulting a woman. This grotesque depiction of rape is accompanied by the headline of the album's feature song: "Woman is the Nigger of the World."

In the music world, most songs that stand the test of time are the ones that touch upon the zeitgeist, the intellectual, moral, and cultural climate of an era. No one emblematizes this fact more than John Lennon, whose musical compilation was as inspiring as it was turbulent. (The exception might be Bob Dylan, the purported "voice of a generation," according to rock 'n' roll fans.[36]) In a rare interview with Tom Snyder in 1975, Lennon spoke insightfully about why he politicized his music after the 1970 breakup of the Beatles. In referencing his musical partnership with Yoko Ono, he explained, "We knew anything we did was going to be in the papers … so we decided to utilize the space we would occupy anyway … with a commercial for peace."[37] His era is shaped by some of the most noteworthy moments of the century: the civil rights and Black power movements, assassinations of world leaders, the conflict in Vietnam, Watergate, and, the issue he was probably less familiar with, the feminist movement. Nearly every solo musician paid lip service to one of these topics, although Lennon's hit song "Imagine" seemed to be especially symbolic for the era. Dylan's "Blowin' in the Wind" and "The Times They Are A-Changin'" along with Joan Baez's performance of "Birmingham Sunday" in 1964 encompass lyrics that reflected on the civil rights movement and America's escalated involvement in Vietnam, while Buffalo Springfield's anti-war tune "For What It's Worth" roared through radio waves in 1967. Neil Young challenged President Richard

Nixon in the 1970 protest song "Ohio," and a year later Marvin Gaye's pulsating "What's Going On" took on police brutality. These were not the trailblazers of protest music. Billie Holliday's performance of Abel Meeropol's "Strange Fruit" in 1939 and Woody Guthrie's 1945 "This Land is Your Land" were explosive renderings of what was wrong in American society. It is now common to see musicians of every musical genre perform tracks that examine problematic elements of America just as academics do, ranging from Green Day's 2005 affront to President George W. Bush in "Holiday" to Kendrick Lamar's 2015 anthem to the movement for Black lives, "Alright."

Lennon's labor in protest music started in 1968 as a Beatle with the B-side hit to "Hey Jude," the anti–Vietnam war song titled "Revolution." But Lennon's relevance to the protest canon is due to his unapologetic intersectional approach to full dissidence. Writing as a solo artist, though still a member of the Beatles in 1969, Lennon released the anti-war movement's anthem "Give Peace a Chance," and later its kin "Happy Xmas (War is Over)" and "Power to the People." The song "Working Class Hero" exposed the global manipulation of class divisions in his 1970 album *John Lennon/Plastic Ono Band*. As dissent became central to his life upon his relocation to the United States and the release of his *Imagine* album, both in 1971, topics of his singles varied. Although "I Don't Want to be a Soldier" was another thrashing of the war in Vietnam, Lennon found an intersectional formula in "Gimme Some Truth," a song that weighed in on war, Nixon, and sexism. His marriage to Yoko Ono and new influences in America that included Jerry Rubin, Abby Hoffman, and Bobby Seale shaped his inclination to protest war and injustice with grand oeuvres. His capstone project, he hoped, would be *Some Time in New York City*, released during the summer of 1972, with the album's featured song being "Woman is the Nigger of the World."

"Woman is the Nigger of the World" is actually profound, reflective, and politically incisive. By invoking the N-word, Lennon appealed to an intersection of race and feminism that he didn't quite understand, that the patriarchy and white supremacy normalized gender domination and racial oppression through social, economic, and political mechanisms. The woman, he sang, "is the slave to the slaves." The line, Lennon would indeed acknowledge, originated from Irish revolutionary leader James Connolly, who is credited with saying: "the female worker is the slave of the slave." With lines like, "We tell her home is the only place she should be / Then we complain that she's too unworldly to be our friend," Lennon identified himself as an advocate of feminist work, speaking out against domesticity, body shaming, and women's acquiescence to men. Lennon was likely alluding to female targeted advertisements, like Virginia Slims cigarettes that were "tailored for your hands—for your lips ... slimmer than the fat cigarettes men smoke." Women were told by Massengill Powder to "Be confident of your daintiness." *Collectors Weekly* ran a chin reducer advertisement for a product that "Gives the flesh the resilience and freshness of youth" and "prevents double chins."

Lennon didn't take his use of the N-word lightly as time and again he offered justification for why he felt righteous in saying it. But embedded in his argument were promotion and record sales. Upon the single's release on April 24, 1972, seven weeks ahead of the complete album *Some Time in New York City*, some 300 radio stations across the United States refused to play the song. In Chicago, only two stations, WCFL-AM and WDAI-FM, dared to give the single airtime. Both stations took the song off the air by the first week of May.[38] One AM station that boldly put "Woman is the Nigger of the World" on rotation for a sustained period was KDAY of Los Angeles, which reported its communication office received more than 500 calls about the single. "Lots of black, some whites, took offense," said the station's program director Bob Wilson. While with Ono in California on a search for her daughter, Kyoko, who had disappeared with her ex-husband, Anthony Cox, in the middle of an ugly custody fight, Lennon took advantage of a free moment to call into the radio station's news director Lew Irwin.[39] He told Irwin, "Anyone who denies the fact that women are having the worst of all worlds is obviously not seeing things clearly."[40] He recounted the hardships endured by his mother, Julia, who married an absentee father and made the consequential decision to have John raised by her sister, Mary Smith, also known as Aunt Mimi.[41] Lennon told Irwin:

> If a man is brutalized, he brutalizes his wife. Being from the working class, I know what that's about. A man comes home from work, sick to death of the whole business and doesn't know how to express it any other way than to take it out on the woman.[42]

The call-in to KDAY was an attempt to change the public's attitude in southern California.

As for the rest of the country, Lennon needed a larger outlet to make his claim and save both his reputation and forthcoming album from tanking. In May, a month after the single was released in the United States, he appeared with Ono on the *Dick Cavett Show*. Lennon fervently maintained to host Dick Cavett that those who were still reacting indignantly to the song were "mostly white *and male*," he emphasized. Sure, there is no evidence that he used the epithet outside of this song, though his childhood friends certainly did. And, he alleged, those defending him were his "black friends who feel I have quite the right to say it." Why, he contended? "'[C]ause they understood where it was comin' from."[43] And yet, the oppression of African Americans was not the crux of the song; rather, he placed the song's implications on women's liberation. He described, albeit falsely, that the single was "actually the first women's liberation song that went out."[44] While just a few years earlier Lennon was, in his words, "more of a chauvinist than I am now," his Yoko Ono–inspired gravitation to feminist theory existed at the song's core. While explaining both the origin and the meaning behind the song to Cavett, Lennon used Ono's feminist sensibilities as an object to rationalize his use of the racial slur. He recounted a story about Ono's 1969 cover story with *Nova* magazine when she told journalist Irma Kurtz that women were the most mistreated and oppressed beings among all racialized and minoritized groups on earth. "Yoko was well into liberation before I met her," he explained. "She had to fight her way through a man's world. The art world is completely dominated by men." Ono in that *Nova* exposé used the phrase "Nigger of the world" to amplify her pull to feminist work. Those words were later stamped on the magazine's cover along with a picture of Lennon and Ono.[45]

On this score, Lennon advanced his defense to Cavett when he read a statement about the N-word from African American U.S. Congressman Ronald V. Dellums of California. Though the Democratic representative gives a damning and biting disavowal of white supremacy, Dellums' statement falls short of directly attacking the patriarchy.

> If you define a nigger as someone whose role in the society is defined by others, whose justice is determined by others, whose mobility in the society is limited by others, whose humanity is defined by others, you suddenly realize that you don't have to be Black to be treated like a nigger in American in 1972. …
> [T]here are Black niggers, Brown niggers, Red niggers, anti-war niggers, ecology niggers, student niggers, long-hair niggers, women niggers.[46]

It is not difficult to see how Lennon rationalized his argument in his own head—he had Black friends and they told him it was okay. His reasoning aside, quoting Rep. Dellums was noticeably amateurish; so was his follow-up commentary. "I think the word *nigger* has changed. It does not have the same meaning as it used to," he delineated to Cavett, who later conceded that Lennon's performance of the song on his show caused a "flap" with the producers at ABC.[47]

Lennon was on to something when he said the meaning of the word had changed. His analysis, however, was inaccurate. In the decades that followed, the N-word evolved from impolite in Lennon's time to profane in the 1990s to inexcusably taboo in the current era and often no longer spelled out in print. The change is due to an academic shift toward Critical Race Theory in the 1980s, which grew out of a field that utilized the law to redress racial injustice before becoming a topic that includes cross-disciplinary methods related to ethnic studies, American studies, gender studies, and educational theory. In the public discourse, however, progressive attitudes about race evolved after the 1992 Los Angeles uprising following the acquittal of four police officers captured on camera beating Rodney King and, more importantly, journalistic sensitivities applied to the coverage of the eleven-month O.J. Simpson murder trial that spanned 1994 to 1995 (discussed later in Chapter Ten). Wary of how the bigoted language used by Los Angeles Police Detective Mark Fuhrman would influence the jury's verdict, journalists substituted the racial slur with its euphemism thus fixing into the American vernacular the coded descriptor "N-word."[48] Since that moment, educators and journalists find themselves treading water as there is certainly a need to push the envelope with the aim of educating the general public. The risks often result in firestorms.

None of this excuses Lennon's decision to place the N-word in the track's title and to make it the buzzword of his song. He was certainly aware that something was wrong with it or else he wouldn't have gone to such great lengths to defend himself. Lennon's exploitation of Dellums' words was part of a strategy aiming to justify his use of the word in the context of art. A short time after the appearance on the *Dick Cavett Show*, he and Ono promoted the song to the largest Black publication of the day, *JET* magazine. An advertisement for the single along with Dellums' statement appeared in the weekly publication's June 1 edition. This was, mind you, about two months after the release of the single. Dellums' statement was used to defend Lennon and the song, which still received little to no airplay on many radio outlets in America and none in the United Kingdom for fear that listeners would find the title and the lyrics offensive.[49] However, included in *JET's* Dellums' quote was the affirmative: "I agree with John and Yoko.... Women are the niggers of the world." If Dellums explicitly sat quietly by after Lennon's performance in front of a white audience at the *Dick Cavett Show* a few weeks prior, the line in *JET* triggered a response. Dellums wrote of his dismay in the magazine's June 15 "Readers Rap" section, asserting he made no such endorsement of Lennon's choice of words. "To set the record straight," Dellums wrote, "I have never made any such statement [in condoning the Lennons], either publicly or privately." The congressman claimed to be "victim of some over zealous promoting company's efforts to capture a portion of the Black music market."[50] The clever response should have warranted a greater discussion about Lennon's ulterior motive: was the former Beatle more concerned about his reputation as a peace and justice crusader or was he worried about the bottom line? The media failed to investigate Dellums' accusation.

Dellums' defense nevertheless was contingent upon word-play. "To the issue of women as niggers in *this* society"—with the emphasis placed on the word "this" versus any attempt to allude to "the world" as Lennon's title suggests—it is possible to accept his rationale. He wrote, "In a white male-dominated society that sees the role of women as bed-partners, broom pushers, bottle washers, typists and cooks, women are niggers in THIS society." This final statement, however, did little to help advance in either direction understanding around the N-word. Nor did it really clarify the congressman's position on whether it was okay that a white musician could use the N-word in a song about any form of oppression. Dellums' letter was only to defend himself so as to not be seen defending a white individual who uttered the slur.

One thing became clear in the ping-pong match that was Lennon's media blitz and how the public actually responded to the song: there was no way Lennon could sell people on the argument that he possessed good intentions when using the epithet without winning over the Black community. His May appearance with Ono on the *Dick Cavett Show* only served to stir up "tense moments" at ABC, according to newspaper reports and the host Dick Cavett.[51] Moreover, his strategy of sending a press release to *JET* with Dellums' words did not yield the results— more airplay—he had hoped. So, in October he and Ono joined African American comedian and justice warrior Dick Gregory on a visit to *Ebony* and *JET* headquarters in Chicago. On the surface, the visit to the office of the sibling publications was so Lennon could explain that Black stars inspired his brand of music. Consciously aware of the audience, Lennon praised the influence of Black musicians for shepherding his career. There was no real purpose for Gregory to accompany the Lennons except to get them into the building. In a cover story exposé, *JET* put Gregory on the cover with Lennon and Ono, and the story included a photo taken of the three together in England months earlier; however, the comedian is not quoted a single time in the article. With two people of color in Gregory and Ono literally and figuratively standing by his side, Lennon was able to credit the likes of Little Richard and Bo Diddley and Chuck Berry and B.B. King for inspiring his musical style. Lennon claimed, "Black music is my life."[52]

In reality, Lennon was on the offensive during his sit-down with *Ebony* and *JET*. By appearing with Gregory, who years earlier used the N-word as the title of his first memoir, *Nigger: An Autobiography*, Lennon could draw a favorable reaction from Black Americans. He and Ono in Gregory's company at the Black media epicenter held symbolic power that music, comedy, and other forms of performance art have a way of using the N-word in a redemptive context to undo white supremacy. And this is how he spun his narrative in the *JET* cover story. "I'm still based in Black music. I still feel it," he told *JET's* editorial board. Then, as he placed a recording of "Woman is the Nigger of the World" on the coffee table, he said, "Listen to this record." The gesture was a plea to *JET's* readers. He wanted them to see the influence that African American culture had on his frame of mind. "All I talk about [is] when I heard 'Long Tall Sally,' when I heard 'Johnny Be Good,' when I heard Bo Diddley." That music, he said, was the reason he "dropped out of school [and] got me a guitar."[53]

Writing in her memoir three decades later, Julia Baird, Lennon's sister, recounted the performers that influenced her brother's music. She credited Elvis, Bill Haley, and, of course, "his hero" Buddy Holly.[54] Not one African American artist is mentioned in her chapter on this moment of Lennon's life. While Baird's insight might not reflect all of those who shaped Lennon's gravitation to rhythm and blues artists and ultimately to make a life out of rock 'n' roll, she was present when her brother rehearsed in the bathroom of his home and performed with his first band, the Quarrymen, in the early 1950s at a fee of 15 shillings.

For all intents and purposes, Baird would not have the final say. In fact, it seems more like an intentional omission because Lennon has documented his own admiration of Little Richard as early as 1956. As a young rocker, he struggled to come to grips with the fact that anybody— let alone a Black artist—might be better than "The King of Rock 'n' Roll," Elvis Presley.

> When I heard ["Long Tall Sally" by Little Richard], it was so great I couldn't speak. You know how you're torn? I didn't want to leave Elvis. Elvis was bigger than religion in my life.... I didn't want to say anything against Elvis, not even in my mind. How could they be happening in my life, both of them? And then someone said [to me], "It's a nigger singing." I didn't know Negroes sang [rock 'n' roll].[55]

On February 16, 1972, months before the release of "Woman is the Nigger of the World," Lennon fawned over African American artist Chuck Berry on *The Mike Douglas Show* like he was one of the obsessive fans that once groveled over the Beatles. "I think he's the greatest," he told host Mike Douglas before performing two numbers with Berry: "Memphis, Tennessee" and "Johnnie B. Goode," as backup vocalist and electric guitarist. "I really love him. It's an honor to be here backing him [up]," Lennon said of the purported "Father of Rock 'n' Roll" before he started reading from cue cards to introduce Berry to the show. In a now famous line credited to Lennon, he said of Berry, "If you tried to give rock 'n' roll another name you might call it Chuck Berry."[56]

In one of his last televised interviews, an appearance on *The*

Tomorrow Show with Tom Snyder, which aired April 28, 1975, Lennon reflected on his early career dating back to those days at Quarry Bank High School and the contrast between rock 'n' roll and the music of an earlier generation. In doing so, he spoke more insightfully on the fusion of what he called "black-blues" and rock 'n' roll. "People have been trying to stamp out rock 'n' roll before it started," he told Snyder. "I always thought it was because [rock 'n' roll] came from black music. And the words had a lot of double entendres in the early days. And it was sort of, you know, our nice white WASPs are going to go crazy with all this moving their bodies." This was a genuine moment that found Lennon speaking with ease rather than with the complex and coded "double entendres" he placed in his music about the level of influence African American artists bestowed upon rock 'n' roll musicians like himself and his ex-mates in the Beatles who had released extended play records that included covers of Chuck Berry's "Roll Over Beethoven" and Little Richard's "Long Tall Sally" in the early Sixties. He minced few words in illustrating the appropriation of African American rhythm and blues styles: "You know the music got to your body and the Beatles carried it a bit further, made it a little *more white*," said Lennon.[57] If by "more white" Lennon meant more accepted by society as the normative genre of music, he is certainly correct. Music historian Elijah Wald emphasizes this point: "A generation of black musicians remembers the Beatles' arrival as an apocalypse, the moment when rock 'n' roll became white and they were banished to a lower-status ghetto labeled R&B or soul."[58] One of his fellow Beatles, George Harrison, validated that point when he told a film crew from the Smithsonian Channel in 2015 about the band's admiration for one of the early blues artists, Lead Belly. "If there was no Lead Belly, there wouldn't have been any Lonnie Donegan. No Lonnie Donegan, no Beatles. Therefore," Harrison explained, "no Lead Belly, no Beatles."[59]

JET's 1972 cover story on Lennon and his admiration of African American musicians was actually not the first time the weekly magazine wrote about the ex-Beatle's veneration for the "brown sound." In a July 1965 editorial titled "What the Beatles Learned from Negroes," *JET* reported that during the Beatles' first appearance in the United States, their objective, "aside from making dough," was to meet many of the African American artists "upon whom they had drawn so heavily, in absentia, for inspiration and guidance."[60] All four Beatles along with Motown singer and top female vocalist award-winner Mary Wells, whom the band had met in 1964, appeared on *JET's* cover. Wells, a young African American artist who had recently been selected as the top female vocalist in the rhythm and blues field, and the Beatles ended up touring together for five weeks in Europe.

Perhaps we have not given him sufficient credit because Lennon scholars have done little in dissecting his interplay with race. The bias for Lennon as an artist won't allow either the public or scholars to see that one of the most complicated aspects of his life was his grappling with race. Lennon proved his musical mettle and pedigree as a wordsmith through the sophisticated use of vocal fluctuation and refined songwriting. He proved his resolve for social activism by arguing persuasively for peace in a highly politicized time. He also indicated that he was willing to grow out of his sexist underpinnings by his willful acquiescence to Yoko Ono's feminist work. Lennon not only enthusiastically embraced the use of visual and performance art to shape the public consciousness, but he did so while wrestling with his identity as a drug addict, a misogynist, an absentee father, and a dishonest husband to his first wife, Cynthia, in the pursuit of an existence defined by social betterment and peace-making.[61] If scholars missed Lennon's misinterpretation of race, perhaps it is because they insist on explaining his musical elegance, his adept understanding of war and peace, his willingness to appear alongside Black leaders, and his clever deconstruction of American political leadership. They end up doing, ironically enough, the very thing most white liberals are guilty of: sticking to well-meaning intent rather than giving a below-the-surface take on how Lennon should have viewed the intersection of race and gender.

There is, too, the grappling with how blindly Lennon followed Yoko Ono. So much so that in the instance of "Woman is the Nigger of the World," he felt it was pardonable for him to use the N-word. By this point in his career, Lennon was no longer just a rock 'n' roll singer. Marrying Ono in 1969 made him "like her, an *artist*," according to biographer Ray Connolly. Lennon was wrapped up in the life of being part of the avant-garde intelligentsia, accompanying Ono to universities and art shows, along with the desire to acquire admirers that were politically engaged rather than the "teenybopper fans" that once followed the Beatles everywhere. In his acclaimed biography *Being John Lennon: A Restless Life*, Connolly describes Ono as a student of Yonkers' Sarah Lawrence College and as the New York "sophisticate" that helped Lennon "reinvent himself and his life." As Lennon began describing himself as "an artist" on television and radio interviews, he fancied the idea of collaborating with Ono on music, artwork, film, and other unconventional politicized projects.[62] *Some Time in New York City* was just the undertaking that the born-again John Lennon coveted: an album that would reflect the timeliest news stories of the day that dabbled in counterhegemonic symbolism. One song about the violent uprising that occurred inside Attica Correctional Facility over the course of four days in September 1971 was certainly a brash attack on a racialized carceral state. Two weeks after a prison guard killed an inmate at San Quentin State Prison, Attica prisoners rebelled by taking control of the prison. The inmates also took 41 correctional officers and civilian employees hostage before issuing 28 demands that addressed better prison conditions. Upon the order of New York Governor Nelson Rockefeller on September 13, 1971, the New York State Police used tear gas to enter the prison yard. They then shot smoke into the courtyard for two minutes, injuring 128 men. The raid resulted in the deaths of 29 inmates and eight hostages.[63] Lennon wrote another track for Black Panther Party advocate and communist party member Angela Davis. In 1972, Davis stood trial on kidnapping charges and for conspiracy to murder. She was eventually acquitted of all charges. Another song on the album called for the release of John Sinclair, founder of the White Panther Party, who had been sentenced to 10 years in prison for selling two marijuana joints to an undercover police officer.

These songs were in addition to the headliner, "Woman is the Nigger of the World." Lennon's audaciousness to proactively go into the public defending his use of the epithet and to perform the song on daily talk shows is indicative of how much his music had been manipulated by his wife and others within his social circle in 1971 and 1972. Those lyrics were Ono's, only they were sung by Lennon. Like Connolly, the *New York Times* bestselling biographer Philip Norman claims "Woman is the Nigger of the World" is the working example that illuminates the "full creative partnership" between Lennon and Ono as the song's title was her "pioneering feminist slogan."[64] One can further see Ono's power in a solemn note written by Lennon on an early draft of the song: "Life style is defined by others, opportunity is defined by others, role in society by others ... you don't have to be black to be a nigger in this society ... most people in America are niggers."[65]

Lennon's submission to Ono was also detailed in a memoir written by his first wife, Cynthia Powell. "I was stunned," she wrote, of her ex-husband's behavior around Ono. She equated Lennon to a "haughty child" and "sulky boy with his tail between his legs," while likening Ono to a "controlling parent." Cyn, as she was affectionately called by Lennon and others close to her, shuddered, "John had given Yoko a vast amount of power over him." In her book, Cyn explains why. She saw Ono as an extension of Lennon's childhood caregiver, his Aunt Mimi, who raised him during his adolescent and teenage years. When a young child, Lennon's biological mother Julia gave him to Mimi for the comfort of a stable home. Although Julia visited her young son whenever possible, it was Mimi who was both disciplinarian and provider. Then, when Lennon was 17, Julia died as she was struck by a car, leaving Mimi as his sole caregiver. Beatles historian Mark Lewisohn called Mimi's parenting style, "tough, rock-solid, firm."[66] Cyn's insight is key to this argument, as she began dating Lennon in 1957. This perspective afforded her the chance to witness much of Lennon's emotional growth as well as his musical development before they were married on August 23, 1962. "John had grown up in the shadow of a domineering woman—it was what he knew and was most familiar with," she explains. Cyn conceded that she offered the "devotion and loving" that Lennon needed when his mother died but it was Ono who "offered the security of a mother figure" that he once had in Aunt Mimi "who always knew best."[67] As a matter of fact, Lennon would eventually use the moniker "Mother" as his nickname for Ono.

To return to an incident discussed earlier in this chapter, there are no signs that Dellums' sudden rebuke of Lennon's use of the N-word changed the mind of the public. It is also unclear if Lennon's *JET* interview in the company of Gregory helped preserve support from his fans, the white public, at least. In fact, how much did it really matter if African Americans took offense to the song? The overwhelming majority of people buying Lennon's albums were white. Without falling prey to cancel culture in white America, the song would eventually spend five weeks on the *Billboard* Hot 100 chart, though never reaching higher than number 57, and sold no more than 164,000 copies.[68] Lennon biographers usually cite that fact to criticize the single for not living up to the artist's talent. British music retailer and Beatles historian John Blaney writes that Lennon's work on this song was "hollow at best."[69] Lennon biographer Ray Connolly seemed to be more critical of the album *Some Time in New York City* rather than the single "Woman is the Nigger of the World," which he called "the best song" on the record.[70] Geoffrey Giuliano, a Lennon biographer looking at the ex-Beatle's eight-and-a-half years in America, including an exhaustive examination of 1971 and 1972, finds *Some Time in New York City* a package of "political clichés" hastily recorded over "nineteen stoned days." As a result, the album is deservedly remembered as "an effort doomed to almost universal critical, commercial, and artistic failure" because of Lennon's weak and overly fraught "ham-handed" lyrics.[71]

It is true, the track does not rate in Lennon's upper tier of musical numbers. But despite what the detractors say, it was hardly a flop when you consider the single wasn't released in the United Kingdom, where Lennon and Ono tussled with a copyright dispute, and that the song was banned from most radio stations in the United States. Rock 'n' roll author Johnny Rogan calls it "one of his greatest political songs," claiming that Lennon had pulled "away a veil of false conditioning to confront the world's appalling treatment of women."[72] His marketing tactics ensured that his most devoted fans and members of the media were aware of the song's existence. "It's such a beautiful statement," Lennon claimed. "You can talk about blacks, you can talk about Jews, you can talk about the Third World, you can talk about everything but underlying the whole thing, under the whole crust of it is the women and beneath them the children."[73] The quandary he levied upon his fans, nonetheless, is the subtext of the drama that played out in the summer of 1972: would white people really sing along during live performances of a song with the N-word in the refrain?

Just two radio stations, WMCA and WNEW-FM, in Lennon's new locale of New York City gave the song airtime. Contrary to the explicable decision to not broadcast the single, lack of rotation on the radio did little to keep that era's music critics from issuing out approbation. The *Austin American's* Denny Delk wrote, "If you didn't hear it.... It is a pity that the truth is so controversial." Music columnist Robert Hilburn of the *Los Angeles Times* praised the song as "a stinging view of the brutalization of women in society."[74] Al Rudis of the *Chicago Sun-Times,* emphasized, "The words are simple, but they ring true." And *Chicago Tribune* rock critic Lynn Van Matre made an explicit reference to the song in a June 1972 column about the feminist movement. "Have you ever felt discriminated against because you are a woman?" she asked readers in a piece titled "Women Speak Out on Their Status." The majority of women who responded to the query, according to Van Matre, "did so out of a sense of frustration over subtle and overt indignities they believe they are forced to suffer because they were born female, the 'woman-as-nigger-of-the-world' place society has put them in."[75]

As it turned out, the song's appeal to the feminist movement won him and Ono the New York Chapter of the National Organization for Women Women's Equality Day special citation award that August, albeit with some help from another song on *Some Time in New York City,* one sung by Ono called "Sisters, O Sisters."[76] Glossing his mother's personal story of the working class rat race; showing his vintage sense of the zeitgeist; drawing on the political wave of the era to make a point about sexism; countering male chauvinism with melodic gesticulations of dissent; linking hegemonic oppression with the question of respect to women; and highlighting, even appropriating, a degree of emotional injury to justify the use of the racial slur won him favor in the white feminist crowd. There is no doubt Lennon saw the advantage of Ono's political experience. Hilburn wrote that Lennon described Ono as his "artistic catalyst" always "questioning, discussing, [and] challenging" him intellectually and morally on his stance about the woman's problem.[77] For those that stood at the intersection of socialist feminism and anti-colonial feminism, Lennon's single made him a prominent ally in the cause.

The National Organization for Women (NOW) was not a racially exclusive organization. Several of its founding members were people of color, namely civil rights attorney and former member of John F. Kennedy's Presidential Commission on the Status of Women, the Rev. Dr. Anna Pauline "Paulie" Murray and Aileen Hernandez, who served as NOW's second president between 1970 and 1971. Another notable founding member was the first African American woman to serve in the U.S. House of Representatives, Shirley Chisholm, who was also the first woman to run for president of the United States in 1972 as a member of the Democratic Party. Despite NOW's justly celebrated effort to become an interracial group of women, frustrations did exist over prevailing racial inequities within the feminist movement as a whole. White feminist organizations including NOW were bent on consciousness-raising around sex discrimination, especially in education and athletics, child care, bodily autonomy, abortion rights, sexuality, alternative lifestyles, the Equal Rights Amendment, and other seemingly race-blind private and political commitments. The belief in an ostensibly universal and color-evasive gender system alienated Black women and other women of color whose challenges were deepened by racism and whose lives did not mirror those of white women in the gender politics of abortion, sex life, sharing housework with men, and sexuality.

Recent scholarship has described second-wave feminism as composed of varying groups of activists that were organizationally distinct from one another, split mostly along lines of race and ethnicity.[78] Historian Winifred Breines tell us in *The Trouble Between Us: An Uneasy History of White and Black Women in the Feminist Movement* that tensions between white and Black second-wave feminist activists date back to the civil rights movement. In her view, African American women were less concerned about challenging domestic roles, instead focusing their activism on economic survival—a topic that was front and center in the era's Black power movement, which coincided with the founding of NOW and the acceleration of second-wave feminism. White feminists failed to see an intersectional relationship among sexism, systemic racism, and white-skin privilege. Equally important to Breines' scholarship on second-wave feminism is the work of Benita Roth. In *Separate Roads to Feminism: Black, Chicana, and White Feminist Movements in America's Second Wave*, Roth says that Black mothers, in particular, were under attack by government publications such as the Moynihan Report[79] in addition to the public perception that social welfare programs were *blackening* because of the civil rights movement. Roth says white women possessed race and class privileges that were not utilized to create an interracial sisterhood that could collaborate to defeat both the patriarchy and structural racism.[80] While white women complained about lives that were far easier to cope with than what women of color were experiencing, Black and

Brown feminists desired jobs that paid enough to meet the cost of living. As NOW's president in 1971, Hernandez, who also possessed an extensive background in labor politics, tried unsuccessfully to amalgamate the interests of Black members into the national organization.[81] Consequently, Hernandez, other feminists of color, and some white allies formed autonomous organizations like the Black Women Organized for Action and the National Black Feminist Organization that worked through the matrix of domination, namely the intersections of gender, race, and class, without most of their white counterparts from NOW.

The honor, nonetheless, was bestowed to the Lennons after consultation with a very small number of women of color. It was not awarded by the national NOW group located in the District of Columbia. It was conferred by the New York City NOW (NYC NOW) chapter, its "largest and most politically radical chapter," according to historian Kelsy Kretschmer.[82] NYC NOW possessed a considerable amount of autonomy from the national organization. Noted feminist and author Kate Millett was a member of NYC NOW and was a friend to Yoko Ono.[83] Months earlier, during the winter and spring of 1971, Millett, Lennon, and Ono collaborated in England for the exoneration of Black Muslim revolutionary Michael Abdul Malik, also known as Michael X, who had been arrested for extortion and later executed on the gallows for the murder of his cousin.[84] Millett introduced Lennon and Ono to NYC NOW's president Jacqui Ceballos shortly after the couple moved to New York City in the summer of 1971. The Lennons would meet at least once with Ceballos and NOW's national president, Wilma Scott Heide, Hernandez's successor, to persuade NOW to come out against the war in Vietnam. Ceballos and Heide disappointed the Lennons when they said NOW could not compromise its feminist interests by taking up the anti-war crusade. "Yoko must have been upset," recalled Ceballos years later, "but she accepted our reason graciously."[85] A relationship was nevertheless established between the Lennons and NOW's leadership. In 1973, Ono would accompany Heide, Hernandez, NOW's founder Betty Friedan, and 300 of other feminist activists from 28 countries to the First International Feminist Planning Conference organized by NOW and held at the Harvard Divinity School in Massachusetts. Lennon and Ono provided entertainment for the attendees during one evening of the conference.[86] Minutes of that inaugural international gathering of feminist workers have not been unearthed. It is only imaginable that the song the Lennons performed was "Woman is the Nigger of the World," as it had become an anthem for NOW during that time.

All of this is to say that the fact that NYC NOW gave the Lennons an award for their song, one that aimed to cast a spotlight on global conditions that kept women in a state of inferiority whether it be in New York City or Swaziland, was not just a coincidence. Ono was among the trailblazing artists who used her work to advocate for the cause of women's liberation. The song in question contained her words sung by Lennon. To honor the couple was an important consequence of their commitment to challenging injustice wherever they saw it.

Lennon would release his ultimate album *Double Fantasy* just weeks before his December 8, 1980, assassination. During the promotional tour for the album, which includes numbers such as "Woman" that touch upon feminist motifs, Lennon admitted "Woman is the Nigger of the World" was a conciliation to Yoko Ono rather than a treatise on his feminist views. "I accepted intellectually what we were saying in the song," he said, "but I hadn't really accepted it in my heart."

This revelation is disturbing, especially knowing in hindsight the measures he took to defend the song and the homage paid to him by the National Organization for Women. He explained, "It wasn't a matter of whether I accepted Yoko's opinions—or any woman's—I didn't even consider them." Lennon conceded that his five-year hiatus from making music (a period spanning 1975 to 1980) had an educative effect on his ability to emphasize with women. That time was shaped by his assumption of the traditional mother role in the family. Lennon spent those years as a "househusband," he would say, staying home, taking primary responsibility for tending to his and Ono's son, Sean (granted, with help from a nanny and a cook). "I didn't just intellectualize about [feminism] or go to a meeting or write a song," he said. "I shut up and learned how to cook and be with the baby and allow the feminine side of myself to exist rather than crush it out in fear or insecurity that I wasn't manly enough. I cut through all that macho ritualism that we all go through."[87]

There are several moving parts to John Lennon and his 1972 song as discussed in this chapter. But ultimately, this book examines the fine line between compassion and exploitation that has been a prime area of skepticism in white social justice work for decades. The response Lennon should receive for this song is pity: that is, sympathy tied to disappointment, and shame fixed with empathy. In the process of using his musical talent to confront the patriarchy, Lennon made two grave mistakes. The first was his refusal to listen to others who told him that the N-word coming out of a white person's mouth would be taken as a racist affront to Black people while also signaling to whites they too can say the pejorative. The second gaffe was his attempt at playing the game of measuring discrimination between racial and gender groups while not acknowledging the injustices that both Indigenous and African people endured in the United States and around the world at the hands of whites, including white women. Lennon made these mistakes wholly because he didn't believe what he was saying about women and that directly obstructed his views of racial oppression, diminishing structural and private racist violence afflicting African Americans.

Debates over language matter. But they are seldom, if ever, conclusive regarding deeply felt and sharply contested disputes over the N-word. They commonly trigger a conversation but never resolve the matter as there are important nuances within each debate. More powerfully than most cases, therefore, the circumstance surrounding John Lennon and his 1972 song—with undertones of white virtue, race consciousness, sexism, and performance art—represent the greatest debate over the word when uttered by a white individual: Is there ever a time when a white person can say the word?

FOUR

Interlude

Diverse Opinions

When John Lennon first performed "Woman is the Nigger of the World" on the *Dick Cavett Show,* he faced a potent deluge of criticism that would have been career ending for the average musician. The traditional arguments enveloped the controversy: that the N-word exists to defend white interests and identities; that the epithet has morphed both in how it is spelled and what it means; of whether the word needs to be policed by African American intellectuals and other intellectuals of color along with white liberal allies; and that a new nationwide dialogue must take place to enlighten people as to how to navigate the word. Half a century has passed. Opinions have been provided by the best minds in America, ranging from critical theorists to historians to philosophers to linguists. A safe option does exist for whites: choose never to say the word. But the world is more complicated than that. If the rise in hate crime violence against individuals as shown in multiple FBI Uniform Crime Reports since 2017 as well as viral recordings of police and vigilante violence on communities of color in 2020 and 2021 are any indication, color-silence and color-evasiveness in the white community on any issue pertaining to race is not the road to travel.[1] What are teachers to do about the N-word when it is found in textbooks? What are artists to do as they could offer the world something profound from which to learn? What are journalists to do when the N-word is part of the story?

White Americans are left with several options; however, choosing wrongly could run the risk of losing a job, suspension from work, and scorn from the public. There are those who insist only African Americans can say either form of the N-word. Others argue African Americans can say the version of the word that ends in an "a" because, owing to its contextual definition of "dear friend," it doesn't share the same meaning as the word with a hard "r" at the end. Then there are those who feel no person can say either version. A small number of people believe the policing of the word must stop; that all people, whites included, can say any version of the word in proper context.[2] These people perhaps have the most experience studying words, like linguist and Columbia University professor John McWhorter. Then there is the dilemma of the slur pervading school curricula, where the debate roils among three groups: those that want the word banned from school texts; those that believe the word can be said aloud by teachers as long as they are reading directly from a text; and those that feel the N-word cannot be spoken audibly by the teacher though it may exist in a text.

"Racism, we are not cured of it," then president of the United States Barack Obama said to Marc Maron, host of the podcast "WTF with Marc Maron" in June 2015. Early in the interview, Obama established his central thesis: that his presidency was not a sign that America moved into post-racialism, or, for that matter, post-racism just because he served two terms as America's only mixed-raced president. He could have stopped there, but he continued on anyway: "And it's not just a matter of it being polite to say *nigger* in public."

There it was—the atomic bomb of English words. It hardly mattered what Obama said next, which was rather insightful, especially since he offered a complex narration of America's persisting race problem just days after the shooting at Emanuel African Methodist Episcopal Church in Charleston, South Carolina, that resulted in the deaths of nine people. "[The N-word is] not the measure of whether racism still exists or not," Obama continued. "It's not just a matter of overt discrimination. Societies don't, overnight, completely erase everything that happened 200 to 300 years prior." Obama's comments served to distinguish between individual acts of anti–Black racism, racial disparities, and the larger structure of racial disparities embedded within America's institutions. Instead of talking about what lies behind structural forms of racism in the military industrial complex, or the prison industrial complex, or the public education system, or in elections; instead of debating legacy aspects of institutional racism: slavery, Jim Crow, housing segregation, genocide, reservations, boarding schools, occupational segregation—topics that could conceivably enlighten the public on the difference between private and structural forms of racism in the context of the mass shooting that just occurred—the talking heads in the media focused on the N-bomb the sitting president just dropped.

One of the most explosive exchanges about Obama's decision to use the N-word occurred between CNN anchor Don Lemon, appearing as a guest on Wolf Blitzer's show *The Situation Room*, and legal analyst Sunny Hostin. Hostin, the former trial attorney in the U.S. Department of Justice's Antitrust Division and award-winning federal prosecutor, began the segment by reproaching the president for using language that "now opens up the field for others using it."[3] On the contrary, Lemon argued that instead of "sanitizing" the word, it should be "used in context of a story.... I encourage people to use it ... historically." He then said the epithet on air, causing Hostin to explode. "We shouldn't use it at all!" she exclaimed. The debate lasted less than five minutes, and one can only imagine what was said off camera. This was a time of enormous frustration, just one week after the Charleston church shooting and calls to remove the Confederate flag from the South Carolina capitol building. Hostin was not alone in her derision of both Obama's intentional use of the term and of Lemon's belief that the word can be spoken aloud in the context of education, art, and journalism. Some of Hostin's allies in deriding the president included NAACP president Cornell Brooks and Mark Morial of the National Urban League. In contrast, one unlikely source defending Obama was the editor at the conservative online news outlet *National Review*. Charles C.W. Cooke championed Obama for using the N-word with the traditional hard "r" at the end rather than the evolved iteration ending in an "a" because the forty-fourth president of the United States spoke in the abstract about race and language. In other words, according to the publication's editor, Obama mentioned the word in an edifying context.[4]

This debate highlighted the argument that had taken hold across the United States—an argument ignited by the persistent mistreatment of African Americans, the well-intended but often hurtful efforts of white liberals, and uninformed persons of every race, ethnicity, and creed inflaming racial discourse. Obama was in mourning at the time of the WTF interview over those who were killed at Emanuel African Methodist Episcopal Church. In fact, the last 18 months of his presidency had been defined by racial turbulence ranging from tense and unpredictable Black Lives Matter demonstrations, the rhetorical rollercoaster that was the forthcoming presidential election, and mass shootings seemingly orchestrated by lone wolf shooters possessing white nationalistic sympathies. But in short order, Obama roused debate over the N-word that actually enlightened the public about the multifaceted meaning behind the different versions of the N-word that rarely come about in classroom discussions about texts like *The Adventures of Huckleberry Finn* or anything written by James Baldwin.

Not too long after, Obama's successor in the White House brought the N-word back into public discourse in a less erudite way. There always existed curiosity if recordings exist of Donald Trump using the racial slur. This inquiry predates his 2017 inauguration, when, during his candidacy for the presidency, actor Tom Arnold alluded that outtakes to *The Apprentice*, "where [Trump] says every bad thing ever, every offensive, racist thing ever," were in his possession.[5] Later in August 2018, when Omarosa Manigault-Newman threatened to release recordings of Trump saying the N-word shortly after her very public split from the Trump Administration, the president's supporters hardly seemed to care. According to a survey of 1,500 adults conducted by YouGov and *the Economist* that August, just 18 percent of Trump voters believed using the slur made him or anybody else a racist, while 58 percent of his supporters did not find the term offensive. More than 70 percent of those who voted for Trump two years earlier—which included just five percent of eligible Black voters—indicated they would still cast their vote for a political candidate even if they said the N-word.[6] An interesting point is that the firestorm that followed Obama's utterance of the word in the context of a discussion on racism in 2016 did not greet Trump in 2018 as his apparent use of the word to degrade Black people living in places such as, say, Harlem, where Trump owns property, was a matter of discourse. In fact, the closest thing resembling the verbal quarrel between Don Lemon and Sunny Hostin over Obama's history lesson on racism was an unassuming exchange between CNN's Victor Blackwell and Georgia State Senator Michael Williams on the network's *New Day Saturday*. Blackwell became bewildered when the representative said he saw no problem if Trump used the word "years ago when he was not our president [and if so that] doesn't mean we need to continue to berate him because he used it."[7]

A different kind of challenge is presented when comparing the ways and the particular context in which these two American presidents used (or may have used) the N-word. Why did the media make a bigger deal out of Obama's mention of the N-word? How was it fair that Obama, an individual identifying as Black, could say the word but Trump could not? Would fragility have anything to do with the uproar after Obama's 2015 use of the slur? If so, where was the anger in 2018? What was missing from the deliberations over Trump's racial intimations in 2018? Were most people not concerned that the forty-fifty president of the United States had a history of expressing views about ethnic minorities that echo some of the most rudimentary and antiquated stereotypes: Black Americans are "low IQ"; Latinx people are dirty and "rapists"; Asians carry diseases? John Lennon's case fits in between. Similar to Obama, Lennon used the epithet in his art to drive home a point about the global oppression of women. By joining a word associated with domestic terrorism inflicted upon the Black community with the international liberation of women, and the fact that he is white, Lennon crossed a line. And yet his career endured the next three years before voluntarily taking a five year interval from music and his eventual death.

The remainder of this chapter will explore this quandary by

examining the diverse perspectives of ten race critics—Randall Kennedy, Neal Lester, Jabari Asim, Michael Eric Dyson, Cornel West, John McWhorter, Elizabeth Pryor, Imani Perry, Tim Wise, and Joe Feagin. Collectively, this group of voices will debate this question: Why is there never a contextual right time for whites to say any version of the N-word? In correlation with that query, the work of these intellectual scholars will be used to respond to the rectitude of John Lennon titling a song "Woman is the Nigger of the World." With arguments vacillating between "the N-word should be banned from the English language" to "only Black men can say the word," in addition to several arguments middling between why white people can't say the word and why do white people want to say the word, this chapter will argue that whites should be granted very limited leverage to voice the N-word audibly, and only in dramatic performances that include on-stage productions, film, and television dramas that advance the cause of racial justice. There are too many risks for other white social and cultural archetypes like musicians, educators, lawmakers, and journalists to verbalize the epithet in their songs, lesson plans, policy statements, and reporting, respectively. But what about the altered version of the word ending in an "a"? The general presumption is that this endearing iteration of the racist slur is Black English. These two words are related but distinct from one another. In-group membership means that the transformed term can be uttered only by African Americans. Linguists, on the contrary, might grant some leeway for some whites of a particular sociocultural upbringing to say the friendly iteration because we are actually dealing with two different words in the Standard English form. But it will take the remainder of this chapter to explain this nuanced take.

Voice No. 1: Randall Kennedy

In 2002, Harvard law professor Randall Kennedy wrote *Nigger: The Strange Career of a Troublesome Word*. Within a few weeks of publication, the book went to press nine times and reached as high as No. 8 on the *New York Times* bestseller list. Kennedy got the idea for the book during preparatory work for one of his law courses at Harvard. Typing the N-word into the search engine of the LexisNexis legal database, hundreds of references to the term appeared. He used that initial search to track the usage of the epithet through the American judicial system. After that point, Kennedy compiled a legal history of the pejorative noun and placed the word in his book's title, causing a jarring reaction from critics that, as he predicted, accused him of "giving cover to people who are thoughtlessly using this word or malevolently using this word." A Princeton graduate and Oxford University Rhodes scholar, Kennedy uses mostly historical methods to contend that the word's current taboo nature is "an important, positive development in American culture."[8] However, a nod at the book's subtitle reminds us that the word has certainly endured a strange career.

Kennedy acknowledges that the American language is "dotted" with many varieties of racial, ethnic, gender, and religious slurs. But he calls the N-word the "paradigmatic racial slur," one that remains the "gold standard" for Othering members of non-dominant cultural groups.

> The young Jewish kid running from a gang of thugs saying "kill the kike" is likely to be as terrified and for good reason as a black kid running from a gang of thugs saying "kill the nigger." But from a macro level, nigger is quite special … it is the only epithet I know of that has generated other epithets. So for instance when people want to heap contempt upon Native Americans they call them "timber niggers." When they want to heap contempt upon the Irish they called them "the niggers of Europe." When they want to heap contempt on Arabs [it's] "sand niggers."[9]

He says the word was not always taboo, nor has the word always been pejorative. During the Atlantic Slave Trade, the word was more descriptive and bereft of derogatory connotation, though carrying a derisive subtext. In 1619, Virginia settler John Rolfe described a shipment of enslaved persons from Africa to Virginia as "negars." Others in the seventeenth century used different spellings: "nigguh," "niggor," "neger," and "niger" are some examples Kennedy shares. The word's meaning took an "ugly turn" during the 1830s. The decade came at a peak point when thousands of free-Black persons lived together with whites in northern states that had enacted gradual abolition statutes. In addition, as noted in Chapter One, blackface minstrelsy emerged as a popular cultural phenomenon that glorified anti–Black caricatures like Jim Crow and Zip Coon, and later the Mulatto Wench and Mammy.[10] Kennedy (as well as two other voices discussed later—Jabari Asim and Elizabeth Pryor) offers Hosea Easton, an African American minister from Hartford, Connecticut, as the individual who gave the first explanation of the word's shifting connotation. (I claim in Chapter One that David Walker was the first voice on this topic in his 1829 *Appeal*.) In *A Treatise on the Intellectual Character and Civil and Political Condition of the Colored People of the United States: and the Prejudice Exercised Towards Them*, written in 1837, Easton said the word became "an opprobrious term, employed to impose contempt upon [blacks] as an inferior race."[11]

Though admitting that the word is not "a routine part" of his vocabulary—Kennedy declares he typically refers to it as "that word" or "the N-word"—he has laughed at comedians like Chris Rock making light of the pejorative. And while he told the *Washington Post* upon the release of his book that he prefers his children not say the word "for purposes of basic safety," he is not an adherent to banning the word.[12] In fact, the 400-year history covered in *The Strange Career of a Troublesome Word* ultimately sets forth the argument that it is fine for any person—Black or white—to use the word in the proper context. He also says that it should never be used as a pejorative by people of any race.

There are two arguments at the center of Kennedy's work on the N-word, which also includes an article in *The Journal of Blacks in Higher Education* titled "Who Can Say 'Nigger'? And Other Considerations." One of those arguments includes a handful of vocal critics of the N-word at the turn of the century, such as Bill Cosby, Tipper Gore, C. Delores Tucker, E.R. Shipp, and the individual once leading the charge to remove *The Adventures of Huckleberry Finn* and *To Kill a Mockingbird* from school curricula, John Wallace. This collection of voices will hereafter be referred to as Group A. Group A argues that the word should be stricken from the English language, which would accordingly result in its indiscriminate removal from texts, music, and film; from the mouths of schoolteachers and journalists; and from comedians, screenwriters, and playwrights. The fundamental motive for Group A is aimed at preventing white people from saying the word. If Group A can prevent Black people from saying any variant of the epithet in the first place, then surely white people will stop saying it. Kennedy warned that this potential "bowdlerization" would eliminate great works in America's cultural landscape. He lists Ralph Ellison's *Invisible Man*, Richard Wright's *Black Boy*, Malcolm X's *Autobiography*, and Martin Luther King, Jr.'s "Letter from Birmingham Jail." But there are others.[13] Classics by Zora Neal Hurston, Langston Hughes, James Baldwin, Maya Angelou, and Toni Morrison would fall victim to a ban. So would Norman Rockwell's portrait of Ruby Bridges, "The Problem We All Live With." Kennedy's work would be eliminated too, as would much of the hip-hop and film industries.

The other argument Kennedy adjudicates comes from Group B, a legion of advocates that want the word forbidden from contemporary American culture yet preserved as a relic for the public to study. In other words, Group B would allow the N-word to remain in school textbooks and in the performing arts of the past where it can be exhibited as "a linguistic fossil but absolutely nothing more."[14]

Kennedy opposes both options. While he prefers that no person of any race say the word in a casual greeting or conversation, he is not in favor of a ban. This position distinguishes him from Group A that wants total removal. While Kennedy and Group A agree that nothing empirical justifies why African Americans can use the term but makes white usage intolerable, they disagree on the word's wholesale eradication. On the other hand, Kennedy's disagreement with Group B's argument is that this cohort only finds it permissible to allow the word to be uttered in historical context as "an inert linguistic fossil."[15] Kennedy argues that the word spoken in the present should be permissible. There are "socially useful purposes," such as satire, comedy, the game of Scrabble, social criticism in the field of education that should belay the language police. If one racial group can say the word as "a term of affectionate salutation," he says, that means another racial group should also receive a pass when it is said in a context that condemns white supremacy. He expounds on this in the Afterword of his book:

> By insisting that *nigger* does not signify only one thing—a term of racial abuse—and should not be forced to mean only that one thing, I necessarily open the door to uses of *nigger* about which people will disagree—a situation of ambiguity that some racists will probably exploit.

But for those who are white, Kennedy offer this caution: "Simple prudence would dictate that you use this term very carefully, if ever."[16] In sum, Kennedy's argument throws support behind John Lennon's song, "Woman is the Nigger of the World," though he would have advised against it if consulted in 1972.

Voice No. 2: Neal A. Lester

"Any debate over the N-word is not a matter of free speech."

"There is no difference in meaning no matter what version of the N-word one uses."

"Yes, other slurs exist, but the N-word is the most potent word in the English language."

These stances are held by Arizona State University English professor Neal Lester, who specializes in African American literature and cultural studies. In addition to his work on cultural aspects of Black life in America, Lester is known as a leading scholar on the N-word. During the presidential candidacy of Barack Obama in 2008, which led to the "proliferation" of the N-word on social media, Lester designed a course to investigate alongside his students the term's generational and linguistic dynamics.[17] He has since written and spoken extensively on the various changing aspects of the word, including an essay on the "presence/absence of the word 'nigger' in children's texts," in which he argues against using evasive terminology, like the pejorative's euphemism, "N-word." He contends that children's books should be used "as tools to combat violent language."[18] If children's books have historically been used to explain sensitive topics such as death and dying, disease, bullying, and physical disabilities, and if they today are used to engage children in conversations about skin color, hair texture, divorce, and gay parenting, then these texts can exist as a resource to educate children on how to respond to racist behavior. Ignoring the slur does not make it "go away" from the real world. "Erasing the word from dictionaries or airbrushing it ... does not remove its social and historical association with blacks," he says, adding, "Removing the word from print does not erase its public use."[19] Candid and honest use of the slur in children's books can help Black parents speak proactively with their children about forms of verbal violence that awaits them. Furthermore, Lester argues, welcoming children's books that include the slur "might also educate white children to the harms of the word despite their adult racist environments."[20] A study to test this claim is certainly needed.

The course he used to instruct at Arizona State, "The N-Word: An Anatomy Lesson," guided students through the standard debates: whether a double standard exists in the Black and white use of the word; hip-hop's investment in the word; Black vernacular pronunciations and spellings; the word in context of the history of anti–Black racism, including slavery, reconstruction, and Jim Crow culture well into the twentieth century. Lester also looks at the word's appearance in popular culture, including parody and stand-up comedy, sitcoms, porcelain figures, household dolls, children's music, and minstrelsy. What was unique to his course is the transnational scope of the study. Among many things, his students spent time looking at the word's use in other countries. The global scope has become a regular talking point—similar to that of Randall Kennedy—as Japan and Australia are two of several countries guilty of using the word in casual conversation and throughout their respective media outlets. It is worth noting that the word's use in those countries predates the globalization of rap music. After all these years, Lester has determined "as long as black/white American racism exists, the need and desire for such a focused study of language is important and necessary."[21]

Lester is resolved to the notion that the N-word is all about "identity." Pushing back against popular opinion, he argues that the way the word is defined has very little to do with only a person's behavior, sexual orientation, gender, age, or class. He states, "It's about an identity [of] People that were uncivilized, unable to be educated, and buffoonish." While there are disparaging words specific to other racial, ethnic, religious, gender, age, and class groups, along with body type, those slurs don't cross intersectional barriers like the N-word. "It is an equal opportunity slur," says Lester, who argues a sharp distinction with insults like the B-word, which fixes on gender, or "white trash," which emphasizes white racial class hierarchy, or "porker" for someone that is overweight, and, among others, more age-specific (old-timer, old bag, Pop) or ethnic-specific (wop, dago, greaser, Guido) insults. The N-word carries an unparalleled sting, according to Lester, simply because it crosses diversity intersections: in addition to teenage and adult Black men, Black infant and adolescent children are commonly called the epithet, as are Black women. White people fighting for racial justice are often called N-word-lovers. Lester recognizes that the word is used to wound any person of color at any spot on the globe. So, it punctures trans-racially and trans-ethnically.

Lester speaks candidly about the Black use and white use of the word. He contends that it would be best if the word was eradicated from congenial conversation between persons, no matter the race of the user. His work is driven by the goal of making people think about the language they use—to not take words for granted. "It's not whether the words hurt you," he tells listeners, "it's whether you understand the words that define you." Words predict and speak to behavior. Like anyone calling for a moratorium on the N-word, Lester maintains that using any deviation of the word leads to self-defeating behavior. "Nothing about that word changes when you change the end of the word," he says. "In fact, the root of the word, 'N-I-G' stays there."[22] There are rules to the N-word that Lester has begun to push back on. Those rules suggest it is all right for Black people to say the word, but not for white people. There are some Blacks who feel it is all right for whites to say it as long as those whites attain the status of honorary Black. Yet, if those same whites mistakenly use the word outside their circle of Black friends, there will likely be a physical price to pay. He asks, "If it's like friend and like brother, what's wrong with [saying] those words?"[23]

For as much blame as hip-hop has endured, rappers shouldn't become the scapegoat for this perplexing problem. Sure, Lester recognizes that rap artists have complicated the discourse by peppering songs over the last 30 years with several variations and contextual uses of the epithet. He even recognizes "a song is never about that word" and then questions whether the violent, misogynistic, and self-defeating messaging deriving from rap songs are compounded by the use of the word. And yet, the word has endured. Why? Lester attributes that to an existent generational and cultural detachment between proponents and opponents of the Black use of the word in any form of casual conversation. "There is a disconnect of the history that is present and also the history that is in the past," he believes, while adding, "…it is much easier for those who are part of this generation of hip-hop to believe that their history is in the last 30 years."

Complicating the matter further has been the belief that many in America believe society had reached post-racialism when Barack Obama became the forty-fourth president of the United States. For a time after that moment, it became really cool to say the word, Lester suggests. For a white teenager to say to his Black friend, "Well, we are friends and I don't see [your] color," makes it easy for white and Black youth to not think about the ugly legacy underpinning the racial slur. "That becomes very dangerous when we don't think about these words," he says, adding that eventually the interracial friendship between those peers will fracture due to mistrust.[24]

John Lennon, then, would not receive a pass from Neal Lester. For that matter, neither would Barack Obama's 2015 use of the word on the WTF podcast with Marc Maron as described at the beginning of this chapter. Why not? According to Lester, words have too much power. Could Lennon have made his point without using the word? Could the same be said about Obama? Lester contends that the word should remain in texts in an educative context but should not be spoken out loud by anyone, even if used to make a point about America's oppressive legacy and what that means to the emotional development of Americans of all colors. While free speech of all people is protected from legal ramifications, there will still be social consequences. "And social consequences," posits Lester, "have nothing to do with free speech."

Voice No. 3: Jabari Asim

Like Randall Kennedy's legal history of the N-word and Neal Lester's comprehensive study of the appellation, Jabari Asim is another academic who has published on the epithet. His 2007 book *The N Word* carries the subtitle *Who Can Say It, Who Shouldn't, and Why*. Critically speaking, Asim examines white supremacist policy, popular culture manifestations of the N-word, and presidential racist behavior while doing little to respond to the three questions in his brilliant subtitle. But by the book's end, readers can infer Asim's opinion about who can say it and who shouldn't. All told, Asim argues that the word in any iteration should not be used in casual conversation because its original meaning was meant to degrade and terrorize people of African-descent by means of enslavement. "I don't believe the word has a place in polite speech," he says on the record.[25] He nevertheless concedes there are instances in which the use of the word is proper. Asim contends that the word in either form can be spoken by popular culture figures, namely African American comedians and some hip-hop artists, whose intentions are to "progress African American identity and culture." Many in hip-hop culture would not fit his metric however. A profound point in Asim's scholarship is his critique of the comedian Richard Pryor, who stands out as the "yardstick" for appropriate and effective use of the N-word. He says, "If you are using racist language to satirize or expose our racial neurosis, our racial preoccupations, then you are advancing the culture."[26] This is what Pryor did with his comedic invention of 1960s and 1970s black hero characters that quarreled with white racist attitudes (more on Pryor in Chapter Six).

Asim speaks little about white usage of the term. Then again, a look at his defense of Quentin Tarantino and the films *Jackie Brown* and *Django Unchained* against a torrent of criticism from Spike Lee gives the impression that white screenwriters receive a pass for including the term in movie scripts as long as the context depowers the slur, and, in doing so, moves society closer to racial harmony.[27] Despite this one example found in *The N Word*, Asim warns white people that "attempts to tinker with the N word" will lead to "unpredictable consequences." His warning reaffirms the cautionary statement given by Kennedy, that white people should "use this term very carefully, if ever," no matter the vocation.[28] In homage to the early twentieth-century linguist Ludwig Wittgenstein, who called language a "labyrinth of paths," Asim tells well-intended whites to consider the risks before jumping into this rabbit hole: "Where will it lead [you?]," he asks. The unpredictable maze might find a humorous or even a favorable landing, but those instances will be very rare. More often, choosing to say the word either as a positive appellation or to inform others about America's racist history will most likely result in indignation, shock, ugliness, and plenty of "unexpected encounters."[29]

Voice No. 4: Michael Eric Dyson

During his 2005 book tour for *Is Bill Cosby Right? Or Has the Black Middle Class Lost Its Mind?*, intellectual icon Michael Eric Dyson garnered attention for his unapologetic use of the N-word at speaking events and televised appearances. Asserting, "I have been quite explicit about my belief that [the N-word] was a term of endearment, not a racial epithet," he called complaints about his frugal usage of the expression "nitpicking and trite and petty."[30] Dyson came under fire for an unhinged explication of the N-word while serving as a panelist during the 2005 State of the Black Union (SOBU) in Atlanta. The SOBU was an annual event beginning in 2000 and organized by Tavis Smiley for the purpose of challenging the landscape surrounding the cultural diversification of political commentary in mainstream media. The free public event, which eventually ended in 2010, aired each year on C-SPAN. At the SOBU event in question, Dyson joined other thought leaders, politicians, and political analysts like Cory Booker, Donna Brazile, Keith Boykin, and the Rev. Jesse Jackson on a panel designed to discuss the role of Black religious, political, and intellectual leaders and to define the most pressing issues for the Black community in 2005. When fielding a question on whether the American government was wrong to engage in torture, Dyson went off on global oppression befalling people of color namely in the Global South. He made the case for transnational solidarity by those who are similarly degraded. The way he presented his argument, however, rubbed many elder civil rights warriors the wrong way. He said, "We got to understand *nigga* is a global phenomenon. And you are a *nigger* wherever you are. This is why I use the term with promiscuity. I understand, if you are a *nigger* in America there are *niggas* throughout the world. Can we connect through our core *niggerdom* to understand the vicious ways for which we have been subverted?"[31] While the crowd erupted in laughter and applause—an energy that was most certainly encouraging—the remarks made Brazile, who was sitting pensively at his left, shudder. The comment also annoyed the Reverend Jackson, who later cornered Dyson about the remarks at the funeral for Johnnie Cochran. Since then, Dyson only uses the word publicly when he has an opportunity to explain himself. "When I can explain it," he said, "I will feel free to engage in its use."[32] Elucidations about the word, both in its original racist form and the sociable variant, have become central to many of his books since then, most notably *Tears We Cannot Stop* (2017) and *What Truth Sounds Like* (2018). For this approach, Dyson has given the public—namely people who are white—a chance to ponder the appellation's usage in various contexts.

Dyson's scholarship—a total of 23 publications as of 2021— is peppered with his thoughts on the N-word. He has long claimed the N-word is a *for-blacks-only* term of endearment.[33] This argument began in 2006 with his book about Tupac Shakur, a 1990s rapper who used his platform as one of the world's most popular hip-hop artists to redefine two words: Thug (The Hate U Give) and the endearing form of the N-word (Never Ignorant, Getting Goals Accomplished). White individuals born into Generation X, the Millennial Generation, and Generation Z have since been perplexed by how loosely the word is thrown around in mixed company and how rappers like the late Tupac liberally use the term in their lyrics. Dyson explains in *Holler If You Hear Me: Searching for Tupac Shakur*, "Even if white youth understand the word's wretched history and are savvy about its complex use by hip-hop artists or their black friends, the use of the word by even 'hip' whites evokes an unspoken history of racial terror." In an era following the Los Angeles riots and later the O.J. Simpson trial, storied and contemporary history of racially incentivized violence has produced a "durable double standard," he says, that "Blacks could call each other 'nigga,' but whites were universally forbidden the privilege."[34] For Dyson, there is never an appropriate time that a white person can speak the word out loud. He has yet to address how he thinks about white actors and actresses reading from scripts; however, educators and journalists receive no pass. Neither do white hip-hop artists or white people singing along to a rap song. Not only does the meaning of the word change when it is spelled differently, but any version of the word's meaning also changes by the racial identity of the user. Dyson says that white people who wish to use the word in its most endearing form are typically the individuals that refuse to learn about Black life and culture.[35] The basic argument behind the Black use of the term has everything to do with the freedom struggle in American history. "For a long time we couldn't make you stop using it so we gave it a go ourselves," he writes in *Tears We Cannot Stop*.[36] Dyson argues that behind the word is self-determination, self-identification, and self-expression "that all black communities have historically waged," and therefore it exists as a malleable term passed down through generations, whether by way of hip-hop lyrics or casual conversation.[37] This is an aspect of African American culture that white people are not welcome to enjoy.

Dyson has effectively clarified his argument over the course of about 20 years. His is a treatise that speaks to the discourse within the Black community as well as explanations for why whites should never use the word. As portions of this book concentrate on the white usage of the word, here is a straightforward summary of Dyson's fundamental case. In our current moment of history, white people cannot predict how a Black person listening to a white person say the N-word will react, even if used in an assumed proper context. Therefore, the utterance of the N-word by a white teacher or even a white person with Black friends will most likely be taken the wrong way. Moreover, the attempt to accuse African Americans that say the N-word of perpetuating the legacy of inequality is a "vicious ruse." Fundamentally, it is a way of refusing to accept responsibility for willfully enabling racist policies and racist ideas. While Randall Kennedy and Jabari Asim grant some leverage to someone like, say, John Lennon, to include the epithet in his music because the intentions are good, Dyson would hit back: "That's the risk of all great art. You can make it, but you can't determine how it gets interpreted."[38]

Voice No. 5: Cornel West

The intellectual rival to Michael Eric Dyson in the current generation is the Princeton Theology professor and author of the acclaimed 1993 book

Race Matters, Cornel West. For many reasons, it has been intellectually stimulating to see these towering race scholars debate one another on a public stage over issues including presidential politics, Barack Obama's interest in Black political matters, the meaning of Langston Hughes' writing, and, in particular interest for this book, the N-word. West has remained reticent when it comes to writing about the slur, compared to his Vanderbilt University counterpart who sees the use of the N-word part of Black linguistic creativity aimed at taking something meant to be vicious and turning it into a term of endearment. West respects Dyson's perspective, namely for his colleague's unwavering defense of hip-hop culture, which evolved from a relatively obscure subculture in the Bronx at the end of the 1960s into a universal industry criticized for its violence, sexism, and homophobia by the turn of the century. He told PBS host Tavis Smiley in 2007, "You can never put limits on human creativity."[39] Redefining the word with the help of hip-hop artists consisting of Tupac Shakur, Dr. Dre, Easy-E, Ice Cube, and Snoop Dogg was certainly something inventive. However, West, like the aforementioned Neal Lester, elucidates that the real challenge that must be addressed in any debate over the N-word should be to do what is best to regenerate the Black consciousness—to create a racial awakening free of commandeered and reformed language, so to speak—that enables young African American men and women to see injustices in housing, law enforcement, the education system, and voting as racist structural forces that unendingly degrade and demoralize the Black psyche. "I know that 'nigga' as opposed to 'nigger' is a term of endearment," he told the *Washington Post* in 2007, adding, "But the history of 'nigger,' with its connotations of self-hatred and self-disrespect, needs to be acknowledged."[40] West once called for a moratorium on the word, a verbal holiday that affords the chance for intellectuals and racial justice activists to discuss the slur's various usages. That time, he believes, should be spent in national discourse over the saga of the freedom struggle, the origin and continuance of the N-word, and the evolving meaning behind the word. West's call for a freeze on the word's usage occurred during a period where the nation's leading civil rights organization, the National Association for the Advancement of Colored People, held a symbolic funeral for the N-word in Detroit, Michigan, in July 2007. West and his allies in the moratorium movement were concerned that young Black people who find themselves using the word will eventually fall victim to a form of stereotype threat that often leads to underperformance in school, behavioral problems, and criminality. While West calls Dyson's contention that the N-word is an expression of love "troublesome," it becomes more problematic when the word reaches millions of African-descended people around the globe. He argues this is when "self-hatred is then more deeply internalized because they have not engaged in the kind of discipline to elevate themselves to the same moral and spiritual level that so many of our freedom fighters have." West also believes the real challenge over the word is due to corporations that have exploited its use: it is overly used in hip-hop and has become permissible to play on many radio and television stations. The word even in its most familial form is interpreted differently throughout the United States. Consequently, West alludes, people outside the Black community feel comfortable saying the word. Young whites, in particular, casually say the word "without any thoughts about the history of violence and malevolence" inflicted upon Black people.[41]

This is to not believe Professor West thinks white people have a right to say the word in an appropriate context. That, in fact, is not among West's principal worries. While appearing on Al Jazeera's social media program "The Stream" in 2013 with, among others, the white antiracist crusader Tim Wise, West gave Wise the right to say "any word he wants 'cause he's in the legacy of John Brown." It may have been a warm gesture made out of respect for the antiracist work for which Wise is justly celebrated, but the nod was nevertheless given. West added, "But I appreciate him not using it."[42] West is most concerned about the socioemotional development of Black youth, which, he believes, ruptures still when non–Black people of color and white people engage in flippant uses of the word; accordingly, he would like a freeze on the word so that the Black public can discuss when it can be said and by whom. "[W]e need a renaissance of self-respect, a renewal of self-regard. And the term itself has been associated with such abuse," he says. "It associates black people with being inferior, subhuman and subordinate. So we ought to have a moratorium on the term. We ought not to use the term at all."[43] West, who once carried a distinction at Harvard University that allowed him to lecture at any school on campus, suggests, "Most importantly we're trying to keep track of human beings. We're trying to track the suffering. We're trying to make the world a better place so we have got to *de-niggerize* our way of being in the world, which is [to] humanize our way of being in the world and that is true in every corner of the globe."[44]

If West could give a pass to Tim Wise in 2013, would he have done the same to John Lennon in 1972? There is no clear answer here. Lennon was only relatively proven in his work for Black people, though he was among the world's antiwar leaders, which included frank and forthright public declarations for the well-being of Black and Brown people living below what is called today the Global South. West falls somewhere in between Randall Kennedy's forbearing temperament and the less forgiving disposition of Michael Eric Dyson.

Voice No. 6: John McWhorter

John McWhorter is a linguist who often performs his work in line with social historians. He views language as a common currency, evidenced by popular adaptations and improvisations to words throughout the course of history: brother versus brotha, gangster versus gangsta, fellow versus fella, girl versus gal, and vegetables versus veggies.[45] To him, there is no language on earth quite like English. It is what speakers of Chinese, Arabic, and Russian speak when they communicate across cultures. English is also the top language filling content on the World Wide Web. McWhorter is part of a large group of linguists that see the progression of the English language headed toward a fracturing into a family of dialects, or collection of Englishes, much like many fluent Spanish speakers in the United States are already familiar with.[46] No one can deny, McWhorter acknowledges, the general public and linguists see speech very differently.[47] This is actually a big part of his work as of late, to get the general public to see Black English as something that is *in addition* to Standard English, and not as something *separate* from Standard English.

A Critical Race Theory skeptic, McWhorter wishes to get Americans to look beyond explicit and implicit biases and the doctrine of antiracism to see that people talk in varied ways at different times depending on the contextual setting. Sometimes that includes casual language that gets passed off as slang or bad grammar. Even Stokely Carmichael addressed this in a famous Freedom School lesson given to teenage students in Mississippi during the summer of 1964. In his memoir *Stokely Speaks: From Black Power to Pan-Africanism*, Carmichael illustrates one lesson on speech where he addressed cultural differences in style and grammar. At the start of the lesson, he wrote eight conflicting sentences on the blackboard. The sentences were written in two columns. The column on the left indicated broken English. The column on the right was the designation for Standard English.

"I digs wine"	"I enjoy drinking cocktails"
"The peoples wants freedom"	"The people want freedom"
"Whereinsoever the policemens goes they cause troubles"	"Anywhere the officers of the law go, they cause trouble."
"I want to reddish to vote"	"I want to register to vote."

Carmichael's goal was for the students to see that the majority of people in the United States, including whites, speak in a casual and broken way most of the time as shown in the left column. But it was a powerful minority that spoke all the time in a Standard English form. He asked his students, "If the majority speaks on the left (broken English) … Why do we have to change to be accepted by the minority group?"[48]

Likewise, McWhorter asks the same question in *Talking Back, Talking Black: Truths About America's Lingua Franca*: "Why would it be that in so many places, casual language is an alternative to the standard one, treated as perfectly normal [but] while here in the United States, the casual speech of millions of people is thought of as a degradation of the standard form, rather than simply something different?"[49] In this case, McWhorter compares Black English to ultraviolet light's association with skin cancer. He says, "Scientists (linguists, in this case) discuss it, but for almost everybody else it is an unperceived abstraction despite permeating our very existence."[50] All of this is to say, understanding McWhorter's approach to language is important to accept his view on whether or not it is safe for whites to say the N-word.

No matter his position (I will get to it shortly), it is quite indicative through his scholarship that McWhorter is frustrated by the never-ending deliberation about the N-word's meaning and who can say it. He calls the discourse over whether or not a person should say the word "a hopeless debate" that "endlessly swirls."[51] Here is where the linguist and social moderate in him grows frustrated (he describes himself a "cranky liberal"): the original spelling of the word with a hard "r" at the end is Standard English while the version ending in an "a" is Black English. Since Americans have no graceful way of referring to Black English (Ebonics is usually the term used), the public can't intelligently engage in discussion about the N-word. However, if people could see Black English as a category *within* Standard English, that could be the game changer. He says, "*Nigger* is a standard English slur. *Nigga* is a word in a different dialect, used among black people themselves, usually men, to mean 'buddy.' It emerged from a common tendency … to use mockery and joshing as an expression of affection."[52] This idea is what draws white people, usually the youth, to use the word in their circle of friends. Oftentimes African Americans are included in that circle of friends who grant a pass.

Using the linguist's disposition, these are two different words in the English language that unfortunately sound similar. He says, "*Nigger* is dead [but] Long live *nigga*." This statement is why McWhorter defends white people who use the "friend" version of the word. Simply put, McWhorter would suggest no one say the slur in its original spelling, except in an educational context. "This word has legs," he writes in his 2021 publication *Nine Nasty Words*.[53] As a linguist, he finds it okay for anybody to say the endearing derivation. Why? Because the endearing version is a completely different word, with a different definition, than the word ending in a hard "r." McWhorter, and perhaps Randall Kennedy as noted earlier, find that the attempt to make either rendering of the word taboo has a paradoxical effect of actually empowering the word in its racist power. He recognizes nonetheless when a white person, raised in the same social-contextual environment and who listens to hip-hop artists, who uses the term as an endearment will end up using the word quite frequently in casual conversation. Take someone like rapper Eminem—who has largely lived up to a public vow to never say the N-word, and would, in Cornel West's words, likely receive a pass from his peer group because he's in the legacy of John Brown—it would only be common that he would grow comfortable using the word in casual conversation. That word has effectively been part of his social environment and emotional development.

Where would John McWhorter stand on John Lennon's use of the N-word? Lennon's upbringing was nothing like that of Eminem. Working-class backgrounds, sure. But along lines of race and diversity, not even close. When Lennon heard his friends say the N-word, it was used to demean. When Eminem heard the N-word, it had a welcoming connotation. Though not familiar with "Woman is the Nigger of the World" when contacted for this book, McWhorter's scholarship exists as a contemporary defense to Lennon's decision to center the term in the song. Lennon used the epithet, employed with the hard "r," in the context of art, which aimed at casting a spotlight on a level of unbridled chauvinistic oppression heaped upon women across the globe. "[I]n Lennon's time," McWhorter did explain, "the word was not yet taboo the way it is now. Thus [Lennon's] impressions [about the word] are now antique." Because of that, those living in the current era should not hold him to the same standard of political correctness that white musicians, artists, and educators are held to at present.[54] In fact, McWhorter has taken strides to argue on behalf of white educators that refer to the word in the course of a lesson plan as long as instructors are not "directing it at someone." In 2019, he wrote an article in *The Atlantic* in support of honest white teachers mentioning the word in class. The piece was composed as a reaction to the suspension of Laurie Sheck at New York's New School for repeating the N-word in a class discussion about James Baldwin's work (more on this in Chapter Ten). He called the preoccupation with policing the N-word "less with matters of morality than with matters of taboo."[55] In an earlier commentary following President Obama's utterance of the N-word on the WTF Podcast in 2015, McWhorter called the fact that a euphemism now exists as a proxy for the real word a "fake, ticklish nicety that seems almost designed to create misunderstandings." Obama, he argues, should not have to use the euphemism "N-word" when delivering a history of racism in America. He says white people "shouldn't have to either."[56] In the end, he says, the N-word is, "in all of its menace, filth, scorn, teasing, warmth, love, and interracial outreach," absolutely "marvelous."[57]

Voice No. 7: Elizabeth Pryor

It seems fitting that Elizabeth Pryor, the daughter of the iconic comedian Richard Pryor, would grow up to dedicate several years of her professional career researching the N-word. Though she understood that her father once used the N-word in a way that was "divisive and defiant" to anti–Black discrimination, her scholarship on the topic has mostly concentrated on the etymology of the word. Both her book *Colored Travelers: Mobility and the Fight for Citizenship before the Civil War* and academic article "The Etymology of Nigger: Resistance, Language and the Politics of Freedom in the Antebellum North" argue that the word ending in a hard "r" should be seen as a homonym; Pryor believes the words are spelled the same and sound the same, but have different meanings because there are two origin stories. Black abolitionists during antebellum used the word to unify African-descended people across the diaspora. Whereas, whites before and after the Civil War used the word as a pejorative to label Blacks as subhuman. The white version of the word was crafted during moments of history when Africans in America obtained social mobility, first with gradual abolition and later after emancipation, and were thus threatening to the social, political, and economic power of whites.[58] These points are also made by the aforementioned Randall Kennedy and Jabari Asim. The gap in scholarship filled by Pryor, however, is the conceptualization of the word as a social marker originating among free Black laborers. Saying the word—at least in written form—was usually done in quotation marks as if the speaker was quoting racist whites. In that context, the word was used in an effort to become, according to Pryor, "categorized as part of the immutable social class out of which they aspired to rise."[59]

Whether or not, as Pryor suggests, African Americans built their own meaning around the word or, like her contemporaries have contended, the Black usage of the word has become damaging to social identity, she reveals, at the very least, that whites were flummoxed upon hearing the word exit the mouths of Black people. Whites were bemused as if something was stolen and flaunted in front of them, and there was nothing that could be done about it.

Much in line with Kennedy and John McWhorter, Pryor's research shows that the post–O.J. Simpson trial taboo nature of the N-word has created an atmosphere in which people, young and old, can't move beyond the varied contextual uses of the term. It has become the norm to exploit real pain and anger in order to levy charges against white educators for verbalizing the word in class. The three scholars empathize with teachers whose reputations and, in some cases, careers, are damaged through this discourse. They express sympathy for teachers who are not the enemies.[60] Pryor blames this on a lack of race conscious education. She likens it to the natural reaction to sex before sex education. When sex comes up, adults typically become "squeamish" and shush their children. Students are going to encounter the N-word, like sex, during their formative years. Both issues saturate music, comedy, television, and movies. Talk of sex and the utterance of the N-word play out in school hallways, locker rooms, and on social media channels such as Instagram and Twitter. As a result, students pick up information about both topics from colloquial sources and misinformed friends, which has been proven by statistics released through the Centers for Disease Control and other authorities to be harmful to personal morality and health. Sex and race are central in the lives of young people as American popular culture makes it inevitable that students will encounter both before the age that schools offer formal instruction on the topics.

Consequently, young people don't know how to think about sex or the N-word. This is why Americans have so many explosive encounters when it comes to these subjects. Specifically speaking of the N-word, a teacher getting in trouble for saying the word out loud during a lesson is not an issue of freedom of speech, Pryor believes, although it often appears that way in the media fallout. She says the fiery discourse that typically follows a student complaint comes down to a matter of a lack of education. As it stands at present, the discourse has reached an impasse. The most current study conducted on public opinion about the N-word, provided by the Pew Research Center in 2019, indicates 70 percent of adults in the United States believe it is "never acceptable" for a white person to say the word.[61] By avoiding difficult conversations about the N-word for the last 25 years, the education system has helped turn this word into America's quintessential taboo. It becomes more reasonable to see why classroom encounters between students and teachers over the N-word often lead to distressing results. Every person, Pryor contends, has a moment of encounter with the N-word. And yet few schools afford students and teachers the space to talk about these "points of encounter."[62] If given the leeway to discuss the word freely, what should be taught? Pryor wants people to know that conversations need to go beyond who can and cannot say the word. She says, "It's just not a racist word. Fundamentally, it's an *idea* disguised as a word: that Black people are intellectually, biologically and immutably inferior to White people. And that ... inferiority means that the injustice [Blacks] suffer and inequality [Blacks] endure is essentially [their] own fault."[63] While nobody has to verbalize the word in class, teaching the N-word, like sex education, is something that cannot be avoided. The solution for educators who teach the N-word, in her estimation, is to frame the lesson around individual "points of encounter" with the word. This enables everyone to come to class prepared to talk about their experiences while not having to say the N-word out loud.

Although Pryor would not want John Lennon to use the N-word in his music, her scholarship thus far suggests she would offer an ambivalent nod at the way the word was used in context with the feminist struggle: the word has always been an assault on freedom, mobility, and aspiration. These concepts become "points of encounter" in some fashion for every person that has had the N-word hurled at them. Therefore, the question must be asked, how did Lennon accomplish the proper contextual use through his music? The themes existent in "Woman is the Nigger of the World" that dismantle the patriarchy are consistent with points of encounter between African Americans and anti–Black racism. Lennon's lyrics focus on body shaming, spousal submission, domesticity, intelligence, rape, and liberation. In view of that, there are aspects of the 1972 song that Pryor would support. However, using the actual N-word is something she would condemn. Lennon's decision to use the N-word risked opening up wounds previously created by a complicated history of racism.

Voice No. 8: Imani Perry

Although Imani Perry's scholarship has not focused on the N-word, her role as the Hughes-Rogers Professor of African American Studies at Princeton University, combined with the publication of *Prophets of the Hood: Politics and Poetics in Hip Hop* (2004), makes her voice among the most valuable in any discussion centered on coded language, particularly given how the N-word has moved into mainstream parlance by way of hip-hop. Instead of musing over its white usage, her scholarly reflections on the epithet pivots around the hip-hop genre and how the word has been embraced as a cultural expression within the Black community. And yet Perry's voice illuminates for ingenuous persons a history of both how the word has been appropriated in Black vernacular and why it has moved beyond the privacy of Black households, where the word carries a more gregarious and distinctive meaning, and into the mainstream, causing discomfort and bewilderment in the white population. She calls the appropriation of the term and its ascent into the populace "tricksterism par excellence."[64] What she points to in her work on hip-hop vernacular are some of the truths that have resulted from the N-word's incorporation in recorded music. Once the Black usage of the word became public, she says, it crossed a "frightening boundary" into a juncture where anti–Black racism meets white desires to re-appropriate the Black linguistic connotation.

Hip-hop, today, is the leading reason why whites are so confused over why they cannot say the term. Perry's point is very similar to the way Black blackface minstrel and ragtime performers whose lyrics included the word and other anti–Black stereotypes empowered and reassured whites that it was fine to name everything under the sun the N-word during the late nineteenth and early twentieth centuries. This viewpoint does not mean Perry believes whites who say the term deserve a pass. In fact, in at least one interview with the *Philadelphia Inquirer*, she made it quite clear that there is never a time when white people should use the word in casual conversation. "If a white person calls me the n-word, supposedly out of some hip-hop kinship, I can't dissociate that from being called that by white kids in the suburbs of Boston when I was a child," she said. "It's not about rules, it is about history. We have a history of white people using the word and backing it up with violence and mistreatment."[65] This comment alone leaves open the possibility of other contextual uses: the classroom, in particular. I doubt, nonetheless, she would exempt John Lennon and his music in any scenario. In her short yet poignant book *Breathe: A Letter to My Sons*, Perry pleads to a society that has historically beleaguered Black children (specifically Black boys) to treat them with humanity. She writes of her experience as a 10 year old seeing *Ten Little Niggers* in the card catalog as "[d]isappointing and yet so unsurprising." But also, as a lover of literature, how demoralizing it was to read the phrase "nigger-eye berries" in Sylvia Plath's poem "Ariel." The phrase is a metaphor for blackberries. But the N-word itself, she contends, is a racial category joined with white supremacy and deadly violence.[66] It is a "distasteful metaphor," she says.[67] This is why the simple fact that Lennon fails to address the oppression of Black Americans in his song is disqualifying. What is more, there is nothing in Perry's scholarship, which includes six academic books, that suggests it would be fine for a white musician to use the N-word to describe any form of racial or gender oppression. To her, the word is taboo.

Voice No. 9: Tim Wise

"Beyond Diversity: Challenging Racism in an Age of Backlash." That was the title of a lecture Tim Wise, antiracist author and host of the podcast

"Speak Out with Tim Wise," used to give when invited to speak about white privilege and white denial in the first decade of the twenty-first century. His presentations traditionally have been known to rip into white behavior regarding the ways Black people are stereotyped and dehumanized by the "white gaze," to borrow a phrase from philosopher George Yancy. Wise's critique on anti–Black racism is based on the presumption that whiteness is eroded by the presence of Blackness. He would typically issue polemics to white audiences about racially provoked social encounters in order to expose the "false sense of security [perpetuated] by media representations of crime and violence that portray both as the province of those who are anything but white like us."[68] In the white mind, he often theorizes, the presence of Black bodies is a warning sign for criminality.

In communities that are changing in color, studies show that the trend is now for white people to find locations along the peripheries of suburban neighborhoods. By studying more than 200 metropolitan areas in the United States, sociologist Daniel T. Lichter exposes a modern white flight pattern featuring walled-in housing communities along the fringes of the urban countryside.[69] Lichter's research shows that Wise's argument comes down to one thing: white people avoid living in communities alongside Black and Brown people because of the perception of crime. The result has been the reaffirmation that most spaces in the United States are owned and controlled by white people. This concept became all too familiar for the Black community in the second half of the 2010s and into the 2020s as stories such as BBQ Becky, Permit Patty, Amy Cooper, and other so-called "Karens" and "Kens" went viral on social media and were covered by cable news programs. Those who see an African American driving a nice car and instantly think "drug dealer," or assume a Black jogger in a predominantly white neighborhood is a burglar, are triggered by racial animus perpetuated by the lack of comfort with race and ethnic diversity[70]; that the only exposure white people have to people of color occurs when watching the crime report on the evening news or when viewing professional basketball and football where African Americans make up more than 70 percent of the athletes. It also means that white people have little sense of racial dynamics as they play out in real time. A stark example of this is in Tim Wise's book *White Like Me: Reflections on Race from a Privileged Son.*

During a third-grade encounter with two Black friends, Wise found himself literally in the middle of a game of monkey-in-the-middle that taught him something profound about the history of the N-word. At recess one day, Wise stood between his two Black friends who were passing a football over his head. His task was to intercept the ball, and he did so with seeming ease. But each time he pulled in the ball, one of his friends would say, "My nigger Tim!" Thirty times this went on, each with a friend proclaiming "My nigger Tim," not the variant of the term ending in "a," but the slur. At that moment, Wise believed his friends were applauding his athletic skills. The joke was on Wise however. He was made into the clown, the white boy that didn't realize he was being used, made to dance, to be the butt of the joke. Years later, Wise recounted this incident:

> I was overcome with a profound sadness, and not because I had been tricked or played for a fool; that's happened lots of times, usually at the hands of other white folks. I was saddened by what I realized in that moment, which was very simply this: even at the age of nine, [his friends] had known what it meant to be someone's nigger. They knew more than how to say the word, they knew how to use it, when to use it, how to contextualize it, and fashion it into a weapon. And the only way they could have known any of this is because they had either been told of its history and meaning, had been called it before, or had seen or heard a loved one called it before, none of which options were a lot better than the others.[71]

The message that comes from this experience has become a signature point of his antiracist work: that white people fail to see racism, not because they are thoughtless or naturally insensitive, but because they don't have to see it. He says, "Even when a white person is closely tied to African Americans, that white person is often living in an entirely different world."[72]

Wise's efforts to take on white privilege in order to interact with the reality of pain and suffering caused by anti–Black racism has remained indispensable to the antiracist movement. Michael Eric Dyson has extolled Wise as "one of the most brilliant, articulate and courageous critics of white privilege in the nation."[73] One of those battles Wise has unflinchingly waged is against the white usage of the N-word. He firmly believes there is no contextual setting where a white person can use the term because "that word has never had mixed meaning coming out of our mouth." Furthermore, Wise centers his attention on the arrogant presumptuousness of white people who use the N-word. In one of his many appearances on *CNN Tonight* with Don Lemon, he spoke about a deeper issue entrenched within the white defense of using the N-word. He explained, "Whenever people of color bring up the issue of racism in their lives, … [white people] say, 'Oh, you're hypersensitive … what that amounts to saying is that, 'You black people are so irrational, so illogical, so unintelligent that you can't even be trusted to interpret your own life so let me and my whiteness interpret your reality for you."[74] There is a "third grade logic," he believes, that might settle the debate: while I can talk about my momma, you better not talk about my momma. This argument rests on situating oneself *in the family*. Black people can use the N-word any way they want to use the N-word because it was historically used against them in a degradingly violent manner. Such slurs volleyed against various racial, ethnic, religious, and gender-oppressed persons can be used in any fashion those identity groups choose them to be used. He once explained this rationale to Lisa Fletcher of *Al Jazeera's* "The Stream."

> I'm from the South and I don't much like the term Redneck because I know it's a class slur against, frankly, my people. But that said, when other white folks like Jeff Foxworthy the comedian use that term, even though I don't like it, [and] I don't think he's all that funny, but nonetheless because he's in the family so to speak, I cut him a little bit of slack…. I know he has love for the people he's talking about. Now if Jerry Seinfeld does 20 minutes of Redneck jokes the way that Jeff Foxworthy does we might have a problem because he's not in the family…. In that regard, I think white folk should refrain from using the word regardless of what Black folks do with it.[75]

With this "in the family" mentality, Jewish comedians commonly get away with telling jokes that mock Jewish people. Members of the LGBTQIA+ community have reclaimed the Q-word in recent years while denying the press the privilege of saying it. By this logic, Wise believes there is no proper context in which white members of the media, or the school system, or the music industry, or any other profession can vocalize the N-word. John Lennon, then, cannot be absolved of his choice to use the word in his 1972 song. Influential white figures like Lennon serve as culpable proxies for whiteness, emboldening other white people to use language that could perpetuate racial trauma. Wise leads the wing of the movement that forbids white people from ever using the word, even in the most innocent of ways. However, he is not calling for a ban on the word; instead, he is insistent on keeping white people out of the conversation as it pertains to how the word is used in the Black community. Not just a musician like John Lennon whose full intent was to raise awareness about oppression, but educators who believe it is tolerable to pronounce the word out loud when quoting from a text, even though they run the risk of inflicting pain on African American students. This case, in particular, is an example of those subtle yet daily pokes and prods commonly called microaggressions that have the potential of gradually giving microaggressed victims race-based traumatic stress injury. As noted earlier, if there were one white person who would get a pass for saying the affectionate iteration of the N-word, it would likely be Tim Wise, but he never would. The fact that he understands the history, pain, and emotion associated with that word is what sets him apart from other white individuals who wonder why they can't say the word.

Voice No. 10: Joe Feagin

While Joe Feagin might appear to be the random voice among those I have selected to center this narrative, he is a critical whiteness scholar with more than 40 years invested in antiracist scholarship. A professor of sociology at Texas A&M University, Feagin has written more than 60 books on anti–Black racism. Although he has not written specifically on the N-word, nor has he isolated the term in his public lectures, his insight on what he calls the "White Racial Frame" (WRF) is invaluable for framing the N-word in the ongoing debate. The WRF not only encompasses cognitive stereotypes and articulates what is valuable or valueless, but it also casts a spotlight on biased and anti–Black, anti–Brown and anti–Other nonlinguistic elements such as racialized emotions, images, and even smells. Altogether, these various elements of the White Racial Frame act as a categorizing principle: the ideas, images, feelings, dispositions, assumptions, perspectives, and worldview about race are used to interpret social reality. In other words, these principles are used to make sense of relational roles and responsibilities, to understand whose lives are valued, why certain lives are devalued, and who has power. Fostered constantly by white social archetypes in education and media, in addition to peer groups, color-evasive child rearing, places of worship, the workplace, and other cultural institutions where ideas are transmitted, the WRF has a deep and inescapable influence on how people see the world. Feagin argues this is due largely to the fact that 82 percent of America's history has seen some form of structural anti–Black racism: the enslavement of African-descended people along with genocidal oppression, land theft, and forced assimilation through boarding schools that amounts to about 60 percent of American history while *de jure* segregation in the form of Jim Crow legislation has occupied 22 percent of the country's history.[76] Feagin says, "The white racial frame is so institutionalized that all major media outlets operate out of some version of it."[77] This dominant frame shapes the thinking and actions of white people in everyday situations. Whites as well as people of color absorb perspectives, assumptions, dispositions, and values of the WRF in ways that they don't recognize. Where and when people find it appropriate, they consciously or unconsciously use this frame in accenting the privileges and virtues of white supremacy while devaluing the lives of Black and non–Black people of color.[78] John Lennon making the N-word the fundamental element of his 1972 song is an example of one of those privileges.

Feagin's WRF is not a condemnation of white people or white culture; rather, he explains it as "a summing up of an ideology or worldview that holds white civilization as the essential definition of what must count as virtuous, innately and universally good, along with preeminent rights and privileges—to rule and to be the universal standard of correctness." His theory constitutes a hierarchy of ideas that privileges those who create that pecking order and its ideas, beliefs, values, assumptions, expectations, interpretations, and appropriate feelings about a person. Although it might be hard to comprehend, the WRF is not solely about the white race. It is about "a belief system" that is learned over time through socialization and enculturation. He says, "A person of any 'race' can hold to a 'white-framed' worldview or even a white supremacist worldview."[79] By understanding Feagin's WRF, a window is opened, allowing one to see how a word like the N-word has become forbidden for whites to say.

In one sense, a white teacher who uses the word as part of a lesson, or a white journalist who says the word when covering a story, is a performance of white virtuousness. That behavior is a display of white moral hubris. In this case, the culprit perceives themselves as a good and decent person. Feagin calls this an "accented view of white virtue" that "overrides the actual reality of racist performances."[80] Put differently, to say the N-word in an innocuous way is still a microaggressive act that levies pain and frustration on an African American individual who is forced to hear it; it is an act that denies the compounding harm already afflicting entire families and communities. In reference to John Lennon's 1972 song, Feagin would be perplexed by the employment of the N-word. Even in the Seventies, Lennon as a white progressive should have understood how negative stereotyping underscores the word. When a white person unknowingly commits a racist action, Feagin writes in *The White Racial Frame: Centuries of Racial Framing and Counter Framing,* that individual still sees himself as an altruistic individual. He says, "The dominant racial frame not only provides the fodder for whites' racist performances, but also the means of excusing those performances." Such actions, he argues, which get passed off as harmless, later generate behavior that perpetuates anti–Black discrimination within the institutions of American society. Feagin calls choices like the one John Lennon made in 1972 the "muscles and tendons that make the bones of structural racism move."[81]

Conclusion

Figure 4.1 is a chart explaining in simple terms the conclusions about each of the voices in this chapter. Variety about whether whites can say the N-word is found among the African American male perspectives, while the white and African American female critics believe that white people cannot say the word out loud in any contextual setting.

Figure 4.1: How the Voices Feel About the White Use and Mention of any version of the N-word

	Kennedy	Lester	Asim	Dyson	West	McWhorter	Pryor	Perry	Wise	Feagin
Believes white people can say the N-word with a hard "r" in historical context *and* can say the friendly iteration of the N-word						X				
Believes *only* Black people can say the word				X						
Believes white people can use the N-word *only* in historical context	X		X							
Believes that as long as iterations of the N-word exist, white people who prove themselves as allies can use the N-word					X					
Believes in a total ban of the word										
Believes the N-word (including the version ending in "a") should be removed from casual conversation although artists may use it (comedians, playwrights)			X							
Believes white people cannot say the word in any context							X	X	X	X
Believes no one (Black nor white) should say the word, but it can remain in texts, books, and film as long as it serves an educative purpose		X								

FIVE

Philosorock

John Lennon, Bob Dylan, and Other
White Musicians Who Sing the N-Word

One of the most memorable musical events of the twentieth century was the Woodstock festival, a free concert that unfolded on a 600-acre dairy farm owned by Max Yasgur in Bethel, New York, from August 15 to August 18, 1969. The crowd at Woodstock—estimated between 200,000 and 400,000 people depending on the source—was largely white. Most newspapers of the day called it the "biggest event of its kind ever held."[1] It was long believed that the festival's few performers of color, such as the weekend's opening act folk-singer Richie Havens, Sly and the Family Stone, Santana, and the headliner Jimi Hendrix, failed to bring in a large delegation of Black attendees. There were certainly many famous Black performers at the time—James Brown, The Temptations, Smokey Robinson & the Miracles, Chuck Berry, and The Foundations, to name a few. These artists maintained a large following of white fans to complement their base of Black listeners, but performing at Woodstock did not interest them. A concert lasting three days with 32 acts but lacking in representation begs the question: why weren't the performers at Woodstock more racially diverse? While musicians in the Sixties are known for unabashed commitment to peace and justice, the reality is that there was a clear line of racial segregation when it came to those consuming the music. White artists who wrote socially conscious music, like Bob Dylan and Joan Baez, unwaveringly promoted justice yet failed to garner a loyal Black following. One reason for the lack of representation at Woodstock could be the existence of a free, multi-weekend festival already taking place 100 miles south of Bethel, at the epicenter of African American culture and life.

Over the course of six Sunday afternoons in July and August 1969, including the weekend of Woodstock, the biggest names in Black music, comedy, and politics performed or gave speeches at an outdoor event in Harlem's Mount Morris Park on 124th Street. Officially dubbed the

"Harlem Cultural Festival," the event, which has also been called "Black Woodstock," drew a combined audience of 300,000 people and featured comedian George Kirby, the politician The Rev. Jesse Jackson, and musicians Nina Simone, Stevie Wonder, Fifth Dimension, B.B. King, Gladys Knight and the Pips, Abbey Lincoln, the Edwin Hawkins Singers, and the only band to perform at both Woodstock and Harlem, Sly and the Family Stone.[2]

If there was one band in the Sixties and Seventies that represented the democratic promise of a multi-racial and multicultural United States, it was Sly and the Family Stone. Founded in 1966 at San Francisco, the band consisted of Black and white musicians, and both male and female members. Its front man was Sylvester "Sly" Stewart, a child of rock 'n' roll and fan of the emerging psychedelic rock. Working as a radio disc jockey in nearby Oakland, Sly's show featured a diverse illustration of music: rock, soul, funk, rhythm and blues, and psychedelics. He would weave this same mixed-bag of musical genres into his new band—a multi-racial, multi-gender, and multi-genre group that represented everything America said it was on paper. Songs like "Everyday People" and "Dance to the Music" became Top 10 singles in both the United States and the United Kingdom. Right before Woodstock and the Harlem Cultural Festival, Sly and the Family Stone released its fourth and most successful album, *Stand!*, which would reach platinum in sales and become one of the bestselling albums of the Sixties.

The second track on *Stand!* carries a shocking title: "Don't Call Me Nigger, Whitey." The subject and meaning of the track were not a deviation from previous songs written by the band, as Sly's lyrics often offered commentary on the war in Vietnam and anti–Black racism in America. However, the explicit way in which Sly's band chose to decry the era's unraveling of race relations was driven by the public condemnation of the Black Power movement, including attacks on the Black Panther Party for Self Defense, founded by Huey P. Newton and Bobby Seale in Oakland around the same time in 1966 that Sly organized his band and not too far from Sly and the Family Stone's home in San Francisco. In addition, the assassination of Martin Luther King, Jr., and urban upheaval that ensued strained race relations further. Compounded by Black campus activism in the late Sixties with antiwar crusading, one would think today that there is nothing surprising about a song titled "Don't Call Me Nigger, Whitey." And yet it was a shock to many in 1969, as it was the angriest song the band placed on an album. Indeed, Sly and his record label Epic chose not to release the song as a single. Accordingly, it did not elicit the same level of intense scrutiny levied upon future songs using the N-word.

"Don't Call Me Nigger, Whitey" told a story about America's dark side, a reaction to racial unrest of the late Sixties. It also forecasted what was to come in America: a massive race riot in Miami in 1980 that left 12 dead following the acquittal of four police officers accused of beating to death Black motorcyclist Arthur McDuffie; the violence that occurred in Los Angeles in 1992 when over 50 people were killed after the similar acquittal of another four police officers caught on a homemade video using excessive force against Black motorist Rodney King; and the advent of the Black Lives Matter Movement in the wake of the 2013 acquittal of self-proclaimed neighborhood watchman George Zimmerman, who was accused of killing 17-year-old Trayvon Martin a year earlier. Music journalist Hardeep Phull writes that the song "captures a protest at how divided black and white people had become by the end of the decade."[3]

The song, which would become one of Sly and the Family Stone's "most critically celebrated works," according to Phull, received a powerful rendition at Lollapalooza in 1991. Perry Farrell of Jane's Addiction went head to head with Body Count's gangsta rapper Ice-T in a remade modification of "Don't Call Me Nigger, Whitey." "Perry pitched me this idea of doing a cover of the Sly Stone song 'Nigger/Whitey' for this video they were doing called *Gift*," recollects Ice-T in his memoir *Ice*. The film he references, *Gift*, was eventually released in 1993 as a docudrama about Jane's Addiction and the beginning of Lollapalooza, a one-day concert featuring seven bands representing the alternative, punk, heavy metal, and hip-hop genres and bearing witness to the most diverse, culture-crossing crowd ever witnessed. Farrell and Ice-T's rendition of "Don't Call Me Nigger, Whitey" was the last song featured in *Gift*. It shows the two front men inches from one another's faces trading verses. "I'm going to sing it at you, then you sing it at me," Farrell told Ice-T in advance of the performance, "I don't like you, you don't like me."[4]

"Don't call me Nigger, Whitey!"
"Don't call me Whitey, Nigger!"

The Jane's Addiction–Body Count performance adds several more uses of the N-word than what appeared in Sly's original. Also included in the remake is the refrain, "I'm proud to be a…. Say it loud," as Farrell held up the Nazi salute contrasted with Ice-T's Black Power fist. The music industry was shocked that Farrell and Jane's Addiction performed the song. "It's a joke, right?" was the reaction from Metallica's James Hetfield. "You can't say nigger, especially whitey."[5] Despite any condemnation Farrell received from Hetfield or any other critic, he maintained that Sly was among the most influential musicians of his generation. Like Sly, Farrell was never one to shy away from critiquing what he considered to be a morally and culturally insufficient society. He spent zero time defending himself to public critics.

Farrell is not the only white musician to challenge this line of demarcation. In 1993, the Swedish rap-rock band Clawfinger released "Nigger" as a declaration that the word is and always will be a racial slur, and that Blacks on any continent should refrain from saying it regardless of the connotation. In the song's opening line, front man Zak Tell says, "Goddamn my man you see I can't understand / Why you wanna say nigga to your brother man."

As for social critics in our current time, there are plenty. There are those like John McWhorter and Randall Kennedy who might see the decisions by Farrell and Tell to sing the N-word repeatedly as a justified method of enlightening the public about the horrid history of anti–Black racism and a plea to Blacks to give up the word, respectively. They may argue that Farrell's reprisal of Sly's song and Tell's original lyrics are quintessential examples of the degree of violence behind the words— that words can wound. Words can leave the type of psychological scars that Michael Eric Dyson calls "slow terror," which leads to self-defeating behavior.[6] This particular violent word can lead to physical scars—the beating, murder, and maiming of Black Americans. On the contrary, minds like Jabari Asim, Cornel West, and Neal Lester might contend that the point of the two songs could be made without the use of the slur, that the safeguard of being an artist doesn't protect one from the consequences of shouting the pejorative time and again. Other critics, namely Dyson, Imani Perry, and Tim Wise, would rather a white musician not be the one to pronounce it.

And yet, the judgment confronting Farrell in 1991 and Tell in 1993 over their performances was nothing in comparison to what John Lennon encountered in 1972. In fact, quite a few white musicians representing a cross-section of musical genres willfully waded the dangerous torrent that comes with the decision to use the slur. To examine this obscure aspect of musical history, let us begin by looking once again at the legacy of John Lennon. Before the conclusion of this chapter, we will circle back to many of the white musicians who use the N-word in their songs.

✳ ✳ ✳

John Lennon's assassination transformed him from a man with unquestionable musical genius, who also possessed egocentric sexism, to the archetype of altruism. On December 8, 1980, when Mark David Chapman pulled the trigger five times in front of The Dakota, the Manhattan apartment building where Lennon and Yoko Ono resided, the narrative about the ex-Beatle's life was once again changed. For

Generation Xers, Millennials, and a few Generation Zers, Lennon would become the superlative of love and peace. The hope for world peace that defined Lennon in his days after the breakup of the Beatles was forever stamped on his legacy.

Truth be told, Lennon had come a long way from the man he was 10 years earlier. After the Beatles, Lennon slipped further into drug use while inconsistently acting as a father to his first son, Julian. His first born was not the only one abandoned by Lennon; so were his fans and family back in England. Lennon would never return to Liverpool after departing his 60-acre estate at Tittenhurst Park in Ascot, Berkshire, with Yoko Ono for New York City on August 13, 1971. For a time, he tried to help Ono kidnap her daughter, Kyoko.[7] This was why the couple moved to the United States where Kyoko was living with her father, Anthony Cox. In New York City, Lennon and Ono quickly connected with leaders of the counterculture, namely hippie leaders, Abby Hoffman and Jerry Rubin, and Rock Liberation Front member A.J. Webberman. It is uncanny that while two years earlier Lennon and Ono were bedding down together and sending acorns to world leaders as gestures of world peace, they had become leading figures in revolutionary politics. Lennon never showed signs that he favored violence. And yet he had no misgivings about supporting those who did. In 1971, Lennon paid bail for London's Black Power leader Michael X, also known as Michael Abdul Malik and Michael de Freitas, who was on trial for extorting a commune in London called the "Black House." Michael X was later charged and executed for the murder of his cousin at the London commune. Lennon had paid for Michael's defense attorney during that trial.[8] Also that year, Lennon aided an Irish Republican Army (IRA) member smuggling hashish into the United States to purchase guns and bombs for Ireland's war against the British. He then went on to support the Northern Irish Aid, a front for the IRA in New York City.[9] On *Some Time in New York City*, an album scolded in the press as a "Leftist screed" and "a letdown album," he wrote "Sunday Bloody Sunday" and "The Luck of the Irish" to condemn the January 30, 1972, massacre of 26 unarmed Irish civilians by British soldiers in Derry, Northern Ireland, and the long history of British colonialism of Northern Ireland. Although Lennon and Ono walked away from all of this under sobering scrutiny, it liberated Lennon from his pop star prestige.[10] Lennon began to walk in the shoes of the New Left, to talk about their stories in his music, and to awaken the public about the dispossessed in America, Ireland, and throughout the world. If he had learned anything from his transplantation to New York, it was that, whether he wanted to or not, he had to use his platform to refocus the public's hearts and minds on millions of oppressed persons.

It was Ono's influence that caused him to write "Woman is the Nigger of the World" and to make it the signature song on *Some Time in New York City*. She strove to teach Lennon to see gender and sex as more than just how America's social norms expect men and women to behave but to see the patriarchy as the moral rot at the heart of global bigotry. One of the first things Ono did when she and Lennon arrived in New York was to stage a sham art exhibit at the Museum of Modern Art, which was advertised in local newspapers as a "one-woman show." When art enthusiasts and fans of the Lennons arrived at the museum, nothing was there. Instead, Ono had released flies on the museum grounds and hung a sign at the entrance instructing viewers to track the insects' movements across Manhattan. Ono said she did this to protest the lack of female artists at the museum. On October 9, the day marking John Lennon's thirty-first birthday, she opened a one-woman art exhibit titled "This Is Not Here" at Everson Museum of Art in Syracuse, where she displayed interactive conceptual art stations, including corner portraits, a "Cut Up" display asking viewers to cut up a piece of art and restore it into something new, and a "Shadow Painting" urging guests to outline their shadows as they are cast on a blank canvas. The purpose of her exhibit was to inspire amateur artists to produce works of art that could reframe the struggle for world peace.[11]

Though always an advocate for women's liberation, it was her signature performance "Cut Piece" in 1964 before she met Lennon that affixed her art to the feminist movement. Sitting alone with a pair of scissors on the floor, she invited audience members, mainly males, on stage to cut off her clothes. As men trimmed away her clothing, she sat powerless and expressionless. With each slice of her clothing, more of her body was exposed to the audience. Ono sat unresponsive. She was a victim, a feeble concession to sexual assault. The men cutting off her clothes were naively prevailing in their domination. Her aim in "Cut Piece" was to provoke the audience into discomfort. She wanted onlookers to become angry at her for making them feel uneasy.

It must be stated that Ono's approach to feminizing her husband was flawed for two reasons. First, Lennon admittedly was not ready to see women as equals to men. To his credit, he tried for her. And Ono knew it. "In the beginning it was hard for him to realize that women can talk back and have a 50–50 relationship," she said in a September 1971 interview.[12] Despite joint appearances on countless talk shows, art shows, and concerts, their relationship suffered problems that led to an almost two-year separation between 1973 and 1974 that was due much to Lennon's inability to grant Ono the degree of independence she desired.

A second problem with Ono's line of attack was how she took

advantage of Lennon's musical platform and longing for world peace to persuade him to prematurely speak out on feminist issues that he didn't understand. Ono and Lennon found common ground in their respective advocacy for human rights and respect of citizenship. Their joint ventures in politicized music between 1969 and 1972 illustrate their shared belief that experimental art could transform the world. While Lennon's commitment to nonviolence has had an enduring influence that continues to inspire peace movements, his willful amalgamation of his personal conviction about global tranquility with Ono's sharp criticism of sexism exposed a problematic area of the couple's avant-garde art. To include the N-word in the song "Woman is the Nigger of the World" was Ono's doing. This is not to say that Ono didn't have a right to work with Lennon on his music. Nor is he exonerated of any responsibility in making that decision. The problem is that Lennon tried very little to understand the issue he was singing about, nor did he care to obtain more than a cursory education about feminism and racism at this moment in his life. The song's title and its lyrics—as well as Lennon's resultant defense of his use of the epithet—demonstrated a lack of nuanced and empathetic knowledge about the oppression of African descended people. It also inclined Lennon to weigh the levels of cruelty and violence committed against women and African Americans, a competition over who suffered the worse persecution, in a manner of speaking.

This is not to say that Lennon was full of flaws; that he never moved beyond his nescient ways. After he and Ono got back together in 1975, Lennon made what appeared to be a responsible decision about becoming a stay-at-home father to his newborn son, Sean. Responsible is the operative word since some reports claim his five years out of the spotlight were occupied more with an eating disorder and sustained drug use than househusband duties. Upon the release of *Double Fantasy* in 1980, Lennon would admit that some of his music and life decisions during the early Seventies should have destroyed his career. He was referring to a string of inconsistent albums between 1972 and 1975: *Some Time in New York City* (1972), *Mind Games* (1973), *Walls and Bridges* (1974), and *Rock 'n' Roll* (1975). At least *Mind Games, Walls and Bridges,* and *Rock 'n' Roll* each obtained gold certifications. It was *Some Time in New York City* that nearly annulled his career. It was clear by his actions in 1972 that Lennon struggled to find a balance between who he once was as a Beatle and the person he wanted to be as a solo artist. The twist of fate is that "Woman is the Nigger of the World" was at the center of his public behavior during that disconcerting period.

None of this is to say that Lennon alone is guilty of such musical insensitivities. The N-word is not the only word that was at one time marginally acceptable only to later become socially taboo. The hit song "Money for Nothing" by Dire Straits is one example. Though released in 1985, it took until 2011 for the Canadian Broadcast Standards Council (CBSC) to ban the song from Canadian radio stations for its repeated use of the word "faggot" in one sequence: "See the little faggot with the earring and the makeup / Yeah buddy, that's his own hair / That little faggot got his own jet plane / That little faggot he's a millionaire." It is a refrain that has been a matter of contention for more than a quarter-century, though seemingly had passed the tolerance test when it was first released. The song is sung in the third person. Singer-songwriter Mark Knopfler sang in the character of a "real ignoramus," he said, who resents the amount of fame and fortune conferred to rock stars.[13] Oddly, the criticism toward Knopfler's lyrics falls concurrently with Dire Straits' attempt to blast those who disparage rock stars. The song brought instant notoriety to Dire Straits. It then becomes very interesting to note how the band responded in a way that protected their brand after their newfound fame. Dire Straits chose to perform an edited version of the song at live concerts by replacing the F-word with "Queenie." Knopfler also chose not to embark on a media blitz to defend the lyrics as Lennon had in 1972, which ran the risk of bringing unwanted negative attention to the group. For these reasons, plus the fact that the slur was not included in the song's title, which would have drawn added scrutiny to the single, "Money for Nothing" eventually won the Grammy Award for Best Rock Performance by a Duo or Group with Vocal in 1986.[14]

The decision to ban the song in 2011 caused an instant controversy. One Canadian columnist, Chris Selley, called the CBSC ruling "idiotic bureaucracies caving into the whims of a tiny number of people."[15] Dire Straits' keyboardist, Guy Fletcher, called the ban "unbelievable" and said, "Canada could ban about 75% of ALL records ever made." Two classic rock stations, K-97 in Edmonton and Halifax's Q14, played the unedited version of the song for one hour in protest.[16] All of the dissenting voices claimed the ruling was a censorship violation. Oddly enough, Lennon hardly used the word *censorship* in his debates with media personalities 40 years earlier. Lennon's defense was over whether people would see him as a racist. In contrast, the argument about Knopfler has never been whether he is a homophobe. But the plea for a censorship violation in this case is a problem of whether private radio stations working under the ethical policy of a private council—the CBSC—wishes to air a song that includes a word that destructively impacts the emotional well-being of LGBTQIA+ people who already cope with bigotry inflicted trauma. Restrictions were never enforced preventing Dire Straits from performing uncensored renditions of "Money for Nothing" during live performances. Canada's Prime Minister Stephen Harper said, "The [CBSC] is a private body that works with broadcasters [and it] makes its own decisions."[17] The radio prohibition was therefore a position taken by CBSC to declare it wanted to play no role in extending pain to Canada's lesbian, gay, bisexual, transgender, queer/questioning, intersex, and asexual community. It was not a wholesale abolition of the song.

One may ask, with the focus on taboo words in music, what about Bob Dylan's use of the N-word in his 1976 song "Hurricane"? "Hurricane" is about the wrongful conviction of African American middleweight boxer Rubin Carter, who spent almost 20 years in prison on charges of triple homicide in Paterson, New Jersey, in 1966. After learning that the key witness against the boxer, Alfred Bello, recanted his story, and after the publication of Carter's memoir *The Sixteenth Round* in 1975, Dylan penned this 10-minute ballad explaining how the still-incarcerated Carter was falsely convicted of three murders. The lyrics call the investigation and subsequent trial a sham. Dylan uses the N-word only once in the song to argue that the narrative spun by the prosecution attorneys fractured African Americans over how to feel about Carter's innocence. He sings: "And to the black folks he was just a crazy *nigger* / No one doubted that he pulled the trigger."

As the lyrics are read, it appears as if Dylan needed to find a word that rhymes with "trigger." The N-word became a convenient solution. But the lyrics selected by Dylan were not a matter of convenience. Rather, his choice was strategic, similar to Mark Twain's intentional use of the slur throughout *The Adventures of Huckleberry Finn*. For Dylan, "Hurricane" serves two functions. The first is to render a powerful condemnation of Carter's conviction, one that would certainly enlighten his fans about the boxer's unjust incarceration. Following the song's release, there were reports about the sale of Free Hurricane t-shirts and bumper stickers.[18] The other lesson conveys a peculiar point about the White Racial Frame. White hegemonic structures have the ability to blind Black and other people of color to prevailing racist ideas just as much as whites. The way Dylan placed the N-word in "Hurricane" ostensibly implies intra-racial class and cultural prejudices: an idea that assigns generalized inferior qualities to some people within a racial group. This practice would later become central to a controversial Chris Rock comedy routine: "I love black people but I hate Niggaz." It is also a question—why can't people of color be racist?—that race scholar Ibram X. Kendi has spoken about for years. Kendi disagrees with the standard notion that racism is limited to an institutionalized power system that privileges one racial group (whites) over all others. While this is certainly part of what it means to be a racist, the definition of racism has nuanced gradations. The prompt and predictable response from whites who face criticism for saying the N-word or are accused of other racist actions is, "I'm not a racist." Similarly, when African Americans are reproached for racist behavior, "I can't be a racist" is as much part of the plea as "I'm not a racist" is when it comes from whites engaging in racist behavior. To deride a cultural group within a socially constructed racial group is an act of "racializing that group," he says.[19] It is as much an act of cultural racism when African Americans scoff at Black Southerners as it is an act of behavioral racism when middle to upper class whites blame poor whites, or "White Trash," for making all white people look bad. This is the same erudite take on intragroup racism undertaken by Bob Dylan, a man who clearly wasn't concerned about the repercussions of singing the N-word. The combination of time and increased antiracist scholarship have proven Dylan's knowledge on the topic to have been astute.

What happens when musicians not as famous as Lennon and Dylan write songs that include the racial epithet? In 1971, the Virginia Mountain Boys, a vintage bluegrass band relying heavily on banjo-picking that had performed for audiences since the 1940s, released the song "Nigger Trader" on the album *Country Blue-grass from Southwest Virginia.* The song is not a reprisal of minstrelsy. Rather, the Virginia Mountain Boys wrote the song as an original to provide commentary on how enslaved persons were torn away from their families through the domestic slave trade. It is a somber and poignantly written number: "Lord, a Nigger Trader has bought me…. Lord, a Nigger Trader has bought me / Well they gonna take me a way down yonder." In a society with diverse experiences with racism, is it possible today for a song titled "Nigger Trader" performed by four white men strumming instruments and singing in the view of an enslaved African to be accepted no matter its meaning?

In different ways, two Seventies-era punk artists released songs that used the N-word. In 1978, Patti Smith released "Rock N Roll Nigger," a semi-autobiographical number on her album *Easter.* According to the artist, the epithet conveys feelings about social issues that white heteronormative and Christian culture normally would not allow women to express. While Lennon used the slur to mean *suffering,* Smith's contextual definition denoted a *rebellious outsider.*[20] In Smith's song, she *is* the N-word. On the contrary, Lennon's song does not highlight the perils endured by any single woman. In an interview with *Rolling Stone,* Smith told a reporter that she had redefined the slur to mean "an artist-mutant that was going beyond gender."[21] She explained further that she was raised with Black people. "It's like, I can walk down the street and say to a kid, 'Hey nigger.'" The purpose of the song was to explain life as an outsider, not to provide a commentary on racism. No matter how Smith spun the meaning of the song, its fate was similar to that of Lennon's "Woman is the

Nigger of the World." Radio stations refused to give it airtime.[22] Despite the radio blacklist, Robert Hillburn, one of the foremost music critics of the Seventies, praised the "Rock N Roll Nigger" as "the most powerful" number on Smith's album.[23]

Lennon, the Virginia Mountain Boys, and Smith featured the N-word in both the titles of their songs and used it repetitively throughout their singles. The punk band Dead Kennedys, a group known for writing music possessing a warped sense of humor about depravity in the world, was guilty of the same transgression. In "Holiday in Cambodia," the San Francisco–based band unleashes a verbal skewering of college students and former anti–Vietnam war protesters for their collective silence on war crimes committed in Cambodia, where the communist Khmer Rouge, led by Pol Pot, orchestrated a genocide of a quarter of the country's population between 1975 and 1979. In the song, lead vocalist Jello Biafra suggests former hippies and leftist hipsters, some who would identify as being *woke* in our current age, go on vacation to Pol Pot's oppressive state. The lyrics read: "On your five-grand stereo / Braggin' that you know / How the *niggers* feel cold / And the slum's got so much soul."

One music critic writing for the *Los Angeles Weekly* called the song, "one of the most scathingly hilarious pieces of social commentary ever written."[24] Another columnist called it a "frenetic, churning rocker" that became an instant "punk classic."[25] And in those days before political correct consciousness of absurd bluntness, the Dead Kennedys' critique of white liberals about performative do-gooding for those that live in the "slums," as the song suggests, was an expression against a social structure which they considered corrupted by politicians, corporations, and an American public that refused to do anything about the killing of Black and Brown people in America and throughout the globe.

The same year "Holiday in Cambodia" hit the airwaves, Elvis Costello released "Oliver's Army" in the United Kingdom. Written in response to The Troubles, a decades-long ethno-nationalist skirmish between Irish national paramilitary groups and Ulster Protestant forces in Northern Ireland, the song became an instant hit. Containing a melody sounding similar to "Here Comes Santa Claus," "Oliver's Army" includes the phrase "white nigger," a common pejorative used by working-class British soldiers to describe Catholic Irishmen deemed non-citizens in the British-held nation of Northern Ireland. Costello penned the song as a result of his first visit to Belfast in 1978, where teenage boys walked around in military uniforms while brandishing automatic weapons. He said "Oliver's Army" is based on the premise that imperialistic states, like the British Empire, "always get a working class boy to do the killing."[26] The lyrics read: "Only takes one itchy trigger / One more widow, one less *white nigger*."

The song never released in the United States because Costello refused to remove the line that included the N-word. He told reporters that the phrase "was the aim" of the song. Much like Patti Smith and John Lennon, he used the word as a general attribution of an oppressed identity rather than a pejorative directed to or about the world's Black people.

While the intent is believable, Costello's racist presumptions were revealed a few months after the release of "Oliver's Army." During a tour of the United States in 1979, Costello called Ray Charles a "blind, ignorant nigger" and James Brown the same racial slur. Following a concert at the Agora Night Club in Columbus, Ohio, Costello found himself in a verbal spat with Bonnie Bramlett of the Stephen Stills Band. Costello, Bramlett, and a bunch of Stephen Stills Band roadies were in the hotel barroom at the city's Holiday Inn. Stills and his band had finished a show at nearby Veterans Memorial Auditorium and agreed on a late-night rendezvous with Costello. During drinks, Costello and Bramlett got into a heated exchange about American musicians. Costello said American musicians are "just a bunch of greasers and niggers." When Bramlett protested, Costello said, "Fuck Ray Charles. Fuck niggers. And fuck you." She slapped Costello across the face for those comments. Costello countered by calling her a slut. One of the Stills' roadies responded by punching Costello, knocking him to the floor.

"I'm not a racist," Costello protested at a press conference the following day. "If they'd been art fans I'd have said Toluose Lautrec was a dwarf," he rationalized, adding, "If you use emotive words in song or conversation, and somebody misquotes you, it can make you look like an angel or Adolf Hitler."[27] After saying he had nothing to apologize for, he said, "I don't want to leave America with the last thing in the minds of Americans being that I'm a racist. I want to be remembered for my songs."[28]

Costello's apathetic feelings about America would show the remainder of the tour. At his last performance in Seattle, his set lasted no more than 40 minutes before he walked off the stage. One music critic called him "one of the music industry's most irresponsible, immature, smart-assed phonies [who] flaunts his Muhammad Ali mouth with his Suzanne Somers intellect to abuse his fans, which gains media coverage, which in turns boosts album sales...." Costello earlier that year had headlined a London concert "Rock Against Racism." But in America, one drunken barroom argument exposed his racial bias and couched view of racial superiority—a feeling so often felt when Black people hear white people say the N-word in any connotation.[29]

There are plenty of songs by white musicians in the final three decades of the twentieth century that illustrate the raw sting that follows in the word's wake. One example is by the punk band X, which released

"Los Angeles" in 1980 about a racist white woman who desires to leave the title city for a less cosmopolitan environment. Vocalist Exene Cervenka explained that the song was indeed written to be a "racist song." The featured character in "Los Angeles," she said, "hated every negro and other people too." The song begins: "All her toys wore out in black and her boys had too / She started to hate every *nigger* and Jew / Every Mexican that gave her a lotta shit."

While there is no getting around the fact that Cervenka attacked several historically marginalized groups in "Los Angeles," the N-word is what elicited attacks. When asked why she didn't write "negro" instead going with the derogatory slur, she responded, to be "truthful about the character [and] because she didn't hate negroes she hated niggers."

Unlike X's offensive song, rock musician Randy Newman's "Rednecks" was temporarily banned from airplay by radio stations in Boston during the racial turmoil over school busing in 1974 and 1975. Newman, a self-identifying Northern liberal with Southern roots who voted for George McGovern, wrote the song from the perspective of a Southerner identifying as a "redneck." While mocking Southerners like Lester Maddox, a racist restaurant owner who once refused to serve Black customers in violation of the 1964 Civil Rights Act turned one-term Governor of Georgia (1967–1971), the thesis of "Rednecks" is to deride holier-than-thou Northern white moderates and liberals for self-righteousness. The song jabs constantly at the condescension of Northerners who think they have moral authority over whites in the South.[30] "Now your northern Nigger's a Negro.... Yes, he's free to be put in a cage in Harlem in New York City / And he's free to be put in a cage on the south side of Chicago / And he's free to be put in a cage in East St. Louis."

In interviews, Newman said he "winces at the prospect that blacks will misunderstand" his use of the epithet. "If you were a black person and heard some white guys singing that word, you might not get past it. It's an awfully ugly word. I don't feel that it's okay for a white person to use it. I did it because I had to in the song. I'm not comfortable with it. Never. I never will be." His body language showed just that when performing "Rednecks" at concerts by commonly slurring the pronunciation "Nih-uhs." Conceding that Black Americans haven't taken kindly to the song, he said, "I haven't been asked to go on 'Soul Train.' I devoutly hope it causes no trouble to anybody."[31]

Then there was Frank Zappa's "You Are What You Is," a song that offers a musical complement to social and psychological assumptions about W.E.B. Du Bois's theory of double consciousness wherein Black Americans endure struggles of identity and code-switching in the United States. The song's fury over racial stereotypes, condemnation of Black

Americans who try to conform to whiteness, sympathy for those who mask identity in certain circumstances so as to survive in America, and the sentence, "I ain't no *nigger* no more" got the music video banned from MTV.

From 1988 to 1991, Axl Rose, the lead vocalist from Guns N' Roses, underwent a surge of criticism for his defense of racist lyrics in "One in a Million," from the album *G N' R Lies*. "One in a Million" is a warning to young, presumably white, entertainers struggling to make it in the music industry. It begins with Rose saying: "Police and niggers, that's right / Get outta my way / Don't need to buy none of your gold chains today." The song includes subsequent homophobic and xenophobic lines. Though released in 1988, one year later the title appeared on a *Hollywood Reporter* advertisement under a headline reading, "The new sound in music: Bigotry."[32]

Vernon Reid, lead singer of Living Color, an all-Black band that toured with Guns N' Roses, told the press, "If you don't have a problem with gay people, don't call them faggots. If you don't have a problem with black people, don't call them niggers."[33] Living Color then backed out of future performances with Rose's band. Arsenio Hall, popular late-night talk show host between 1989 and 1994, called Rose "an ignorant racist" for writing and performing the song. Hall said, "And Guns N' Roses' attitude points out the very danger in using it. Because ignorant white people like Axl Rose are going to get the idea that it's OK to use it too."[34]

Discourse over "One in a Million" resembled the White-Black double standard debate that so often plays itself out in our current moment. Rose, then in his late twenties, asked Del James of *Rolling Stone*, "Why can black people go up to each other and say, 'nigger,' but when a white guy does it all of a sudden it's a big put down?" Citing the popular 1980s rap group NWA (Niggaz With Attitude), Rose said, "I mean, they're proud of that word."[35]

Hall provided his opinion on that last remark: "The difference is very clear. NWA uses it in a very figurative way, whereas Guns N' Roses uses it in a negative, derogatory way—as a white slave owner would use it."

Rose then dug a deeper hole with his own definition of the N-word: "I use the word nigger because it's a word to describe somebody that is basically a pain in your life, a problem…. When I use the word 'nigger,' I don't necessarily mean a black person. I don't give a crap what color you are as long as you ain't some crack-smoking piece of shit." The statement, however, is a difficult one to accept when looking at the lyrics, "don't need to buy none of your gold chains today."[36] Nothing about that line suggests Rose insinuated he was speaking about anybody but a Black person.

In the midst of this period, which coincides with the arrival of rap music and the recurring appearance of the N-word in hip-hop, alternative rock, and punk music, arguably the most racist and vulgar song in modern history, "Nigger Fucker," originally recorded in 1982 by erotic country music artist David Allan Coe, was brought to the attention of many in the public. The song is about a white woman who left her husband and child for a Black man, and includes the line, "How any decent girl could ever fuck / A greasy nigger" and "'Cause there's nothing quite as worthless / As a white girl with a nigger." Despite the actual lyrics, the song wasn't a racist song to Coe, who fell back on his experience serving time in prison where he claimed to have received permission from Black inmates to write songs containing the N-word. He defended the song: "Anyone that hears this album and says I'm a racist, is full of shit."[37] Coe, the self-proclaimed antiracist, released the song on an album titled *Triple X*, which sold in the underground market to white adults only through biker magazines.[38] Coe released other songs that dehumanized Blacks with the slur. In "If That Ain't Country," Coe sang, "Tryin' like the devil to find the lord / Workin' like a nigger for my room and board." Coe rarely performed the songs in public but sold the records at his shows.[39]

Coe's music experienced a resurgence when Detroit-based rocker Kid Rock invited the country artist to open for him at the Blossom Music Center in Cuyahoga Falls, Ohio, in August 2000. According to a *New York Times* investigation on the matter, white college fraternity members had already taken to Napster to download his sexually explicit and racist music. The appearance with Kid Rock at the peak of the rap-metal performer's career buoyed Coe's popularity with the college audience while serving to complicate matters on a few campuses across the country.[40]

All of this allows us return to the question: why is Dylan's decision to use the slur in "Hurricane" pardonable but not so for Lennon's "Woman is the Nigger of the World"? If an answer can be formulated, then we have a resolution to why or why not white musicians can sing the word. Every page thus far has argued that there is no proper time that a white person can say the word audibly unless it is spoken by a character in a dramatized performance aimed at educating the public about anti–Black racism. So why might this iconic musician be treated the same as John Lennon? Dylan sang the word, as Jabari Asim might suggest, to critique white supremacy in order to advance Black culture. Contrary to Dylan's credo, the N-word in Lennon's 1972 song was not about race. It was about the state of perpetual oppression. That argument alone is problematic because many will find it as an attempt to pit one group's history against another. This fundamentally erases how and why the word was originally invented. This is a revisionist approach at redefining a word that carries too much cultural and institutional violence. Sure, while the logic behind this redefinition carries practicality, it also exists as an erasure of the

Six

Black Demystification, White Bewilderment

*Transformation and Numbing
in Black Comedy and Black Music*

History is a road map for addressing bigoted language. History helps those who live in communities insulated from racial stress understand and sequentially challenge behavior that perpetuates racist epithets. Most importantly, history creates a shift in consciousness so that nuanced matters that subsist in the debate over racist appellations can be appreciated.

If we take another glance at history, there is one story that hit the press on February 25, 1965, that allows us to re-litigate the history of violent language and the racist acts it precipitates. On that date, just a few days after the assassination of Malcolm X as he spoke to about 500 people inside the Audubon Ballroom in the Washington Heights section of Harlem, law enforcement disclosed a plot to kill Martin Luther King, Jr. Detectives found 1,400 pounds of stolen dynamite and a collection of small arms, several bazookas, a 60-mm mortar, and several cases of ammunition inside the apartment of 27-year-old Keith D. Gilbert, a gun dealer already awaiting trial for the charge of attempting to murder a Black man in September of the previous year. An informant told authorities the weapons were going to be used to "blow up every nigger Black Muslim temple in [Los Angeles]" and "blow up that nigger Martin Luther King," who was scheduled to speak at the Hollywood Palladium.[1] If there was a time that the N-word was more benign, less derogatory but more illustrative, it would be reminders like this that told generations of people that racist whites created the word and used it to debase, to castrate, and to reduce African and African-descended people to something less than human.

Engaging in this kind of wordplay is not uncommon to other nativist terms like "infest" used to describe undocumented immigrants in the

United States or "infestation" used by Nazi-sympathizing Germans to persecute Jews. Government propaganda during the two world wars dehumanized America's enemies. During the Great War, the Germans were the first to fall victim to nationalized media efforts, followed by Japanese and Japanese Americans after the Empire of Japan's December 7, 1941, attack on Pearl Harbor. These campaigns desensitized the public to the wholesale mistreatment of racially and ethnically Othered American citizens. For instance, wartime propaganda portrayed Japanese Americans as un–American and inferior beings who participated in an international conspiracy for global domination. The effort resulted in the internment of citizens and residents of Japanese ancestry for more than three years during World War II. The pushback against the internment camps was meager. Six of the nine judges on the United States Supreme Court even cosigned the Roosevelt administration's systemic relocation of Japanese Americans into concentration camps. "A Jap's a Jap," said John DeWitt, the Army general in command of executing President Roosevelt's internment order: "They are a dangerous element, whether loyal or not … he is still a Japanese and you can't change him…. The Japanese race is an enemy race."[2] Perhaps the most glaring moment in recent history when terms were used to dehumanize and desensitize a public to the ongoing slaughter of racial or ethnic Others occurred when the Hutu called Tutsis "cockroaches" and "snakes" during the genocidal civil war in Rwanda. These examples all happened in the twentieth century. People of a majority class have historically used such debasing metaphors to numb the masses to atrocities that afflict non-dominant cultural communities that are so often deemed less-than in a social caste.[3]

The white use of the N-word was once so entrenched in American culture that speaking it was as casual an act as blinking. For instance, when one reporter traveled the Commonwealth of Pennsylvania in 1865 asking residents if they agreed that African American men should receive the right to vote, one man, Ed Seull said, "Niggers should have a vote … niggers [should] have all the rights of white men." Another respondent expressed concern over the coming of "nigger judges, nigger jurors, nigger governors, sheriffs and magistrates."[4] As noted in Chapter One, Black performers in the nineteenth century were commonly called "nigger minstrels." Nighttime was called "nigger daytime." Dogs with dark fur were called "little niggers." When asked to give an explanation for the rise in lynching cases in Monroe, Georgia, in 1946, one witness presented a tone-deaf response: "Every time a white man kills a nigger, it's self-defense and he goes unpunished. Yet in all the time I've been living there, all the trouble I've seen between niggers and whites, I don't believe I know of a single time when the nigger started it." The school superintendent of

Monroe, J.M. Williams, spoke sympathetically about the plight of Blacks that resided in his school district. He admitted that Black schools were "mere shacks, usually without electricity or water," and the lowest salary of Black teachers was $28 a month in 1946 compared to $45 a month for white teachers. And yet, in the same statement, Williams impulsively tacked on the slur as a noun: "Our niggers don't get much education. They just can't take it—or they won't."[5]

The N-word was a frequent guest in the courtroom during the trial of Roy Bryant, 24, and his 36-year-old half-brother, J.W. Milam. The two men were on trial in Sumner, Mississippi, for murdering 14-year-old Emmett Till in 1955. Tallahatchie County Sheriff Clarence Strider was the individual most known for using the slur unrepentantly during the four-day hearing. "We never had any trouble until some of our Southern Niggers go up North and the NAACP talks to them and they come back home," he told the national press. When passing African American Congressman Charles Diggs of Michigan, who had traveled to Sumner to see firsthand the hearing, and an assemblage of Black reporters sitting at a small table in the courthouse, Strider greeted them with "Hello Niggers." One of the reporters, James Hicks of the *Amsterdam News*, failing to secure a seat, was approached by a deputy: "Where you going, Nigger?" Before Hicks could finish explaining that he was given a pass from Congressman Diggs, another deputy approached his colleague and said: "This nigger said there's a nigger outside who says he's a Congressman."

"A nigger Congressman?"

"That's what this nigger said."

Sherriff Strider interjected, "I'll bring [Diggs] in here, but I'm going to sit him at your niggers' table."[6]

During her sworn testimony, Caroline Bryant claimed that Till was the "nigger man" who grabbed her hand and waist before asking "How about a date, baby?" and later whistled at her.[7]

In similar instances, the slur was in the air. When asked to respond to the opinion of Chief Justice Earl Warren's corollary to *Brown v. Topeka Board of Education*, known as *Brown II*, declaring that schools must desegregate at "all deliberate speed," Mississippi Governor Hugh White said, "We've got just as good nigger schools in this state as white schools. We got a dandy nigger college right here—Jackson College, that is—with 700 to 800 niggers."[8]

After the deaths of Cynthia Wesley, Carole Robertson, Addie Mae Collins, and Denise McNair, victims of the 16th Street Baptist Church bombing in Birmingham, Alabama, on September 15, 1963, white supremacist The Rev. Charles Conley "Connie" Lynch reportedly said they "weren't children. Children are little people, little human beings, and that means white people. They're just little niggers and there's four less niggers tonight."[9]

In the 1970s, the disreputable racist joke—"How do you tell a good nigger from a bad nigger?" Answer: "You understand a good nigger when talking"—evolved from being a punchline into cool conversation dividing Black people by class and education.

After the election of 38-year-old Kenneth A. Gibson as mayor of Newark, New Jersey, a local bartender said, "[His election] don't make him less a nigger."[10] It was the Federal Communications Commission that ruled the 1972 campaign ad titled "Nigger, Nigger" by J.B. Stoner, candidate for U.S. Senate from the National States Rights Party of Georgia, was not a violation of FCC rules. Stoner, an attorney for James Earl Ray, convicted assassin of Martin Luther King, Jr., says in the political ad, "I am for law and order with the knowledge that you cannot have law and order and niggers too. Vote white." When asked by telephone to comment on the FCC's decision, Stoner responded, "God has heard my prayers and blessed me. I'm very happy that they've voted in favor of freedom of speech. I think it should apply to Niggers and Jews too but it's overdue for us poor whites."[11]

Although President Ronald Reagan signed a bill announcing the federal Martin Luther King, Jr., holiday in 1983, it wasn't until three years later that the day was actually celebrated in 17 states. That year, 1986, marked the birth of the racist expression "Happy Nigger Day."

"Our N-words" was a phrase that reinforced already-dismantled white supremacist institutions, an articulation reminding the public who has control over Black people despite the collapse of *de jure* segregation. The use of the phrase was a very casual, ordinary pattern of speech, a natural part of the conversation. The phrase subjected Blacks to the prolonged tentacles of slavery. While the slave system and its offspring, Jim Crow, were no longer visible, the phrase caused fury and manipulated passion for the sake of maintaining an unseen hierarchy. The phrase made superior the white race, rendering valued the person speaking the language. The Black race, then, was the scorned, the lot rejected as paltry objects worth nothing more than a house pet. While commonly spoken by men in power, the masses grew entrenched in racist presumptions and accordingly worked tirelessly to maintain segregated facilities—whether by *de facto* or *de jure* means—as long as possible. History has shown that whites enslaved, lynched, and segregated people that were called that slur. That phrase—"Our N-words"—was the lynchpin in indoctrinating the white populace.

* * *

Blues music sprung up similar to minstrelsy and ragtime. It started as melancholic folk music in locales populated by Black Americans in the South during the period of Reconstruction. Blues then became more popular at the turn of the century and into the Progressive Era when African American musician William Christopher "W.C." Handy, credited by music historians as "Father of the Blues," taught budding artists at Alabama Agricultural and Mechanical College for Negroes during the 1890s. In addition to serving as music instructor at Alabama A&M, Handy earned a "fat salary" working as musical director of the Mahara's Minstrels, a troupe made up of Black singers, dancers, choruses, and comedians. The troupe also included a concert band and an orchestra. A review appearing in the *Parsons Weekly Globe* (Parsons, Kansas) called it "the most classical and most richly costumed company ever organized."[12] It was a job that made him thought of as the "Colored Sousa," a reference to American composer John Philip Sousa, author of the official national march of the United States, the "Stars and Stripes Forever" (1896).[13]

Handy is among the first to write compositions of the folk, spiritual, and minstrel songs that were part of Black folk life.[14] His music drew on the sadness and yearning expressed in the folk songs of Black Americans trying to survive economic oppression and domestic terrorism of the postbellum Deep South. Handy was able to fashion the ragtime, syncopated sound with a melancholic tempo to produce the blues. By way of "St. Louis Blues," "Beale Street Blues," and other "immortal compositions," as one reviewer put it, his music was widely disseminated throughout the country at the turn of the century.[15] Because of Handy, blues would go on to affect every form of American music, including bluegrass, jazz, gospel, rhythm and blues, rock 'n' roll, and country. Music scholar and educator William T. Dargan said because of Handy, music culture today "rests, in large measure, upon the blues aesthetics."[16]

Naturally, white artists capitalized on Handy's new blues sound. In 1913, white minstrel performer Leroy "Lasses" White copyrighted a song that historians believe originated among Black blues artists in Dallas, Texas. White originally called the song "Negro Blues," but upon publication, had changed the title to "Nigger Blues." Three years later, Columbia Records contracted ragtime artist George O'Connor, a white lawyer-musician already popular for his musical impersonations of the Black dialect and cover titles of several "coon songs" (see Chapters One and Two), to record the "Nigger Blues" for national syndication. O'Connor's rendition of the song was a smashing hit for the remainder of the decade.[17]

By the Great Depression, blues had become the national genre of gloom—its truth and bleakness, its straightforward pain, and, as more listeners were pulled into the sound, its unvarnished hollowness reflected the soul of America. As the music flourished during the 1930s, Black artists used the blues to push back against both the Jim Crow treatment of Black citizens and the appropriation of rural Black blues music. One such artist was Lead Belly, who used his songs to introduce new irony to the use of the N-word. Among his most popular blues numbers was a diss track aimed at his hometown, Washington, D.C., titled "Bourgeois Blues." Lead Belly sings about his daily experiences with overt racism in the nation's capital: "Well, me and my wife we were standing upstairs / We heard the white man say'n I don't want no *niggers* up there.... Well, them white folks in Washington they know how / To call a colored man a *nigger* just to see him bow."

Lead Belly's contemporary, Tommy McClennan, recorded "Bottle It Up and Go" for Bluebird Records in 1939. The song draws on the N-word when speaking about a Black man's fear for his life after beating a white man in a game: "Now, the *nigga* and the white man / Playin', set 'em up / *Nigga* beat the white man / Was scared to pick it up."

While white people hung onto the slur to maintain a grip on their superiority in the social caste, Black people found ways to demystify the epithet, to dull the sharp edges of its racist meaning as the nation moved toward the dismantling of Jim Crow. Lead Belly and Tommy McClennan highlight the increased use of the N-word in the Black community during a time period stretching from the Great Depression to the Double Victory campaign of World War II and the civil rights movement a decade later.[18] Their use of the term—with dual spellings—was much different than early twentieth-century African American blackface performing artists who used the term in a self-deprecating fashion according to members of the Black musical community of the era. Black musicians and comedians from the ragtime and blues periods had engaged in wordplay over how many different contextual definitions the word could take on. Dating back to dual-threat ragtime performer and comedian Ernest Hogan, there have been three connotations of this explosive term. A contextual use aimed at *irony* has precipitated the practice of Black Americans using the N-word as a pronoun to speak of themselves in the third person, or by calling someone else N-word in a friendly manner. A second contextual use aims to *injure* another person with a violent and profane deployment of the word. A third contextual use aimed at *redemption* employs the N-word to mock systemic racism, the racial caste, institutional oppression, and anti–Black racists. When it comes to Black comedians whose careers coincided with the conclusion of the civil rights movement and the ascent of the Black power movement, these three contextual uses have been fully noticeable—and have remained fully noticeable ever since comedians Richard Pryor, Dick Gregory, and Redd Foxx shook up the entertainment industry by means of habitual use of the word in standup routines and on record albums.

Legal historian Randall Kennedy notes, the N-word has always existed as a protean word, especially for Black Americans.[19] This is due to the systems of oppression: enslavement, Jim Crowism, residential segregation, educational injustice, police and vigilante violence, mass incarceration, and a 200-year history of demeaning African American stereotypes, from lighthearted "Sambo" to the animated "Mammy," and caricatured images presented in storybooks, calendars, postcards, cartoons, and children's songs. In each despotic system, there has been an attempt to "rob the word of its essential viciousness," writes Michael Eric Dyson. "For a long time," he adds, "[Black people] couldn't make [white people] stop using it so [Black people] gave it a go ourselves." Kept as subjugated persons, Black people have always made ironic and redemptive attempts to make the word opposite of its original definition. Dyson writes, "Powerless people often fight power with their words."[20] The notion of "reclaiming" the word as defended by Dyson and Kennedy is misunderstood by a large percentage of the population. This is due to the fact that whiteness, or systemic forms of racism, is something unseen by white people. For that reason, when the word is used by whites, it will continue to conjure pain because those who are white still benefit from how this word was originally used while African Americans still suffer from the remains of those oppressive systems.[21] The pain of this word is not just passed down in families of color, but getting called the N-word is often the first memory in the racial timeline of an African American individual.[22]

This history creates a sense of honor misunderstood by the white community. As it happens, African Americans dating back to the antebellum period used the N-word for redemptive purposes in public lectures and ironically in casual conversation. Historian Elizabeth Pryor (the daughter of comedian Richard Pryor) calls the word a "verbal symbol of U.S. racial repression" commandeered by the Black labor class in her study of African American travelers before the Civil War.[23] Instead of thinking nineteenth-century African Americans appropriated the N-word merely to imitate Standard English, Pryor suggests the word transformed into a social identity marker for Black laborers throughout the world who endured the same humanitarian abuses: slavery along with physical and psychological violence with widespread traction due to minstrelsy entertainment. Those of African descent created a Black derivation to counter the white version of the word. David Walker, Frederick Douglass, and countless other Black American racial justice warriors transformed the word into a "viable identification that imagined a community larger than an individual's immediate social network and extending throughout the Atlantic world and across the diaspora," writes Pryor.[24]

Put another way, Black intellectual leaders of antebellum and postbellum America achieved a transnational connotation for the word meaning brotherhood. Henry Highland Garnet once told an audience of African American civil rights leaders, "I have often been called a *nigger*, and some have tried to make me believe it; and the only consolation that has been offered me for being called a *nigger* was that when I die and go to heaven, I shall be white. But, if I cannot go to heaven as black as God made me, let me go down to hell and dwell with the devil forever."[25] Once, Frederick Douglass was approached by a conductor inside a Massachusetts train for sitting in a car reserved for whites. Looking at Douglass reluctantly, the conductor asked him "[Are you] Indian?" With hardened resolve in his voice, Douglass unapologetically responded, "No. Nigger!"[26] Garnet and Douglass offer a contextual change to the word; a redemptive modification of its meaning to spite white supremacy in its various institutional and cultural forms. These two iconic nineteenth-century antislavery champions captured the tension in Black America. They stole hatred from the word while taunting the purveyors of racism. Hip-hop artists are criticized in our current era for doing something similar (more on how hip-hop artists present this argument in the next chapter).

Among those first postmodern cultural trendsetters was the comedian Richard Pryor. Originally a performer who modeled his early routine after Bill Cosby, Pryor's career hit the American mainstream with a televised Broadway appearance at about the same time in 1964 that John Lennon and the Beatles first appeared on the *Ed Sullivan Show*. Like Lennon and the Beatles' music during these early years, Pryor's approach to his stand-up comedy was pure, focusing most on cracking jokes about can openers and riding the subway. Biographers David Henry and Joe Henry said Pryor's jokes insipidly resembled "pitch-perfect mimicry of Cosby's rapid-fire delivery, right down to the elongated vowels."[27] The nearest thing to race Pryor joked about during that first televised comedy show had to do with where he lived: "My mother's Puerto Rican, my father's Negro, and we live in a real big Jewish tenement building in an Italian neighborhood. Every time I go outside the kids say, 'Get him, he's all of them!'"[28] Like Lennon, Pryor was 23 years old at the time of his first small screen appearance. Similar to Lennon's shift to politicized songwriting, Pryor's comedy routine took a turn to socially relevant material in 1967 that was described by *Washington Post* reporter Henry Allen as "street-wise, street-filthy, cut-to-the-marrow style." It drew on his formative years in a Peoria, Illinois, brothel operated by his grandmother and where his mother was a prostitute.[29] He thereafter spiked his stand-up bits with obscenities, especially the N-word.

Pryor told the public his decision to use the epithet was to demystify the word. In 1968, he added to his monologue the character "Supernigger" that "could see through everything except whitey."[30] He released a Grammy Award–winning album in 1974 titled *That Nigger's Crazy*. In 1975, he created the "New Niggers" monologue, which identified Vietnamese immigrants as the new group at the bottom of white supremacy's pecking order. The skit signified Pryor's condemnation of the American tradition that finds new ways to dehumanize racial and ethnic minorities: "White folks are tired of our ass. They getting them some new niggers: the Vietnamese." He also titled his 1976 Grammy-winning album *Bicentennial Nigger*, an apparent dig at a series of celebrations paying tribute to the birth of the United States 200 years earlier while overlooking the nation's history of oppressing African Americans.

The fact that his audiences diversified during the Seventies indicates that his profane, comedic turn offered a new attitude about the casual verbalization of the N-word. In his early career, he performed in front of predominantly white audiences. But in the Seventies, when the N-word became a staple of his humor, that once loyal white audience grew uncomfortable. This shift proved that not only was the sting taken out of the word from the point of view of Black America, but it presented a conundrum for whites who became uneasy, guilty, and even angry and defensive while sitting in a racially-mixed audience. Pryor consciously provoked these feelings so white people could reckon with the Black experience in America. One of the best ways he dealt with this level of discomfort was on *The Richard Pryor Show*, a sketch comedy series that addressed sociopolitical criticisms much like *Chappelle's Show* did between 2003 and 2006. *The Richard Pryor Show* lasted just four episodes in the fall 1977 before it was pulled from NBC's lineup for its controversial content. One sketch particularly spoke to the ways that whites become frustrated, defensive, and angry when confronted with the reality of racist ideas and institutionalized discrimination. In a sketch titled "President Pryor," Pryor holds a press conference in the White House briefing room where he fields a range of questions from the White House Press Corps that includes geopolitical topics such as Mideast peace and atomic weapons, as well as the unemployment rate. It is during the unemployment rate question that President Pryor works race into the answer: "Well as you know the 5% [unemployment] level pertains mostly to, if I may say, white America. In black America and minority situations the rate is as high as 45%. We plan to with all of our efforts to lower that rate to about 20% in the black areas, and of course it will be lower in the white areas." [Laughs]

Then President Pryor takes a question about his decision to increase funding for NASA in order to recruit Black people into the space program: "I feel it's finally time for black people to go to space. White people have been going to space for years and have been *spacing out* on us." [Laughs]

A subsequent question from a *JET* magazine correspondent probes President Pryor about who he is considering to nominate as the next Director of the Federal Bureau of Investigation. The *JET* reporter asked if he would consider nominating the cofounder of the Black Panther Party and FBI target, Huey P. Newton. Pryor salutes the reporter and then says, "Yes, I feel Huey P. Newton is best qualified. He knows the ins and outs of the FBI. And he'll be an excellent director." [Laughs]

Peering beyond white reporters with arms extended, Pryor then calls on "Brother Bell" of *Ebony* magazine. Wearing a fedora and U.S. Army green buttoned-up shirt, Bell greets Pryor with the closed fist Black power salute and says in Arabic: "Assalam alaikum, brother." [Laughs]

To which Pryor responds, "Alaikum assalam," as the press pool shudders. [Laughs]

Bell asks, "Brother, about blacks in the labor force. I wanna know what you gonna do about having more black brothers as quarterbacks in the National Football Honky League?"

Pryor responds, "I plan not only to have lots of black quarterbacks, but we gon' have black coaches and black owners of teams. As long as it's gon' be football, it's gon' be some black in it somewhere" [Laughs]. He continues his impassioned statement about African American quarterback James "Shack" Harris who had been recently cut from the St. Louis Rams as the white reporters in the room are visibly annoyed. When a reporter with a southern accent from the *Mississippi Herald* stood to interrupt the president and ask a question, Pryor, visibly upset, asks, "Yeah, what?"

The reporter responds, "[I'm] Mr. Bigby, *Mississippi Herald*"

Pryor: "Sit down!" [Laughs]

The follow-up question came from Mrs. Fenton Carlton Macker of *Christian Women's News*: "Mr. President, since becoming president, you've been photographed in the arms of white women [Oohs from the press corps]. Quite frankly, sir, you've been courting an awful lot of white women. Will this continue?" [Laughs]

Pryor pauses mischievously, then says, "Only if I can keep *it* up" [laughs]. Snickering with pride as he looks at the Black male reporters in the room, "I mean, why do you think they call it the White House?" [Laughs]

The sketch hit its high point with a final question from a white man in a blue blazer. Pryor looks at the man and asks, "What's your question about?"

"My question is about your mother if you want to be frank!" the reporter responds, at which point the press room explodes as Pryor and Black members of the press pool anticipate a "Yo Mama" joke. [Laughs]

"It's okay," Pryor said. "The man has a right to ask a question. Please let's have some kind of decorum."

The reporter then asks, "Your mother was a maid in Atlanta [before you were elected president]. Now after your tenure, if your mama goes back to being a maid, *will your mama do my house!*"

Pryor: "Aw, Shhhiiitttt" [Laughs]. The press room goes ballistic again as Pryor leaps forward to attack the reporter. A fight breaks out between the white and Black reporters, and the press conference ends abruptly.[31]

A large body of antiracist thinkers deftly scrutinizes the defensive posture that whites take when challenged racially. Contextually speaking, Pryor was the capstone figure that used art to both deflate the air from the N-word and to generate uncomfortable circumstances that forced white people to ponder their lives in privilege and entitlement. Pryor was indeed naming racism, and it aggravated white people.[32] Life in white America has always been deeply shaped by racial isolation. But in a decade following the victories of the civil rights movement along with the influence of the Black power movement, one of America's greatest popular culture figures seized the opportunity to appear on television screens and on radio airways to deluge whites with race conscious material. No longer could white Americans remain totally isolated from racial stress.

At the same time that Pryor's career took off as a trend-setting, profanity-laced funnyman, John Lennon tried to politically restructure his music. The album *Some Time in New York City* was the start, and "Woman is the Nigger of the World" was supposed to distinguish him as a champion of the downtrodden. Like Pryor's art form, Lennon's song was a call to conscience, and, most importantly, consciousness in his like-minded male counterparts. Like Pryor's use of the N-word, the design behind Lennon's use of the pejorative was to be a generative idea; a vision that could inspire people to think more deeply about how women fall prey to the patriarchy. His use of the word was nevertheless problematic. So was his insistence on television and radio that he had been vindicated because he had approval from his Black friends. Award-winning historian Ibram X. Kendi once argued that the desire by whites to say the N-word is "a defense mechanism"; that the dispute over the right to say the epithet has always been an effort to maintain "dominion over everything ... to dominate whatever they want, whenever they want."[33] Self-assured as Lennon was, he also propagated an oppressive legacy, emboldening the people who continue to use it in its racist meaning.

In 1979, Pryor publicly renounced the N-word, something that Lennon never did. In a routine called "The Motherland," he explained the change of tune was due to a visit to Kenya: "A voice said [to me], 'Do you see any niggers?' I said, 'No.' You know, because there aren't any. It hit me like a shot.... I've been [in Kenya] three weeks and I haven't even said it. I haven't even thought it. And it made me think I've been wrong.... I ain't ever going to call another black man nigger. You know because we never was no niggers. That's a word that is used to describe our own wretchedness."[34] Later in an *Ebony* magazine cover story, Pryor expressed his regret, revealing that his trip to Kenya freed him of the expression, that the causal impact of his influence as a celebrity had heightened internalized self-hatred within the Black populace.[35]

If comedy is central in popular culture, it is also made a scapegoat for the proliferation of the N-word in Black life. The Richard Pryor stand-up comedian of yesteryear is certainly maligned in the media for using the N-word to perpetuate Black oppression, with some critics claiming he is at least partly responsible for opening the door for the white usage of the word in ways beyond racial malevolence. But Pryor is not the only comedian who once made the N-word a staple of comedy only to disavow the word later in life. Comedian Paul Mooney, who got his start as a joke writer for Pryor during the Seventies and later for Redd Foxx, shares a sharp comparison. Mooney represents an intriguing twist. At the time when stand-up comedy tangled with the emergence of gangsta rap, Mooney was able to articulate both sides of the argument over whether anyone is justified in using the word as a form of art. In 1993, Mooney released his comedy album titled *Race*. Half of the titles on the album contain the N-word, including routines called "Nigger Vampire," "1-900-Blame-a-Nigger," "Niggerstein," "Nigger Raisins," and "Nigger History." Pundits compared Mooney with rising gangsta rap artists Ice Cube, Ice-T, Tupac Shakur, Wu-Tang Clan, Dr. Dre, and Snoop Doggy Dogg, all of whom used the N-word as a racially blunt and in-your-face street expression of Black art. In fact, Mooney's standup routines are said to be as important for comedy as rap is to music. Columnist Robert Weider wrote that Mooney's material was "topical, pointed, incisive and, for some, uncomfortable."[36] Of course it was uncomfortable; here is how he delivered some of his jokes:

> "It's a good thing Paul Revere wasn't black. Riding up to white people's houses at night to wake them up; they'd've shot him! 'The nigger stole that horse'!"
>
> "Clarence Thomas got a nigger's American dream: a big dick, a white woman and a lifetime job."
>
> "Thank god the Titanic only had white folks. 'Cause they'd have blamed the niggers. 'They were singing while we were sinking.'"

Like Pryor's material at the peak of his career, Mooney's routines exhibited the form to poke and prod his white audiences. Weider said Mooney's material "reads as if it were designed to get white people moving to the exits." In point of fact, Mooney often told his white fans, "Some of you aren't gonna make it [to the end of the show]."[37] And yet, his white audience kept returning to his shows, and they kept purchasing his albums. When asked early in his career why he said the word unapologetically, Mooney responded, "I say nigger 100 times every morning. It makes my teeth white. Nigger, nigger, nigger, nigger, nigger, nigger, nigger, nigger, nigger. I say it. You think, 'What a small, white world.'"[38] He insisted on the publicity tour for the release of *Race*, "White people don't want me to say nigger. Well, why'd you make it up?"

It is a fair response to a question posed to him by white reporters. However, it really wasn't white people who wanted Mooney to stop using the slur. Mooney's most loyal supporters were whites who seemingly found entertainment in bits debasing his fellow Black Americans. Rather, deliberation over Mooney's ironic, injurious, and redemptive usages of the N-word transpired in the Black community. One of the biggest influencers in Mooney's eventual change of heart over the word was the Rev. Jesse Jackson. When the white comedian Michael Richards used the N-word to harangue a Black heckler at The Laugh Factory in 2006, Mooney vowed never to say the word in public again. "[Using the word] was so destructive," he told the Associated Press, a point of emphasis often delivered by The Reverend Jackson, "it was created by whites to hurt and destroy—and we [Pryor and myself] were trying to defuse it, trying to desensitize people to it…. Then I saw the tape [of Michael Richards] and I had an out of body experience. It was so ugly, so horrible. I hadn't heard [the N-word] like this—from someone I knew. I was able to look at it not just through my eyes but through the eyes of the world. I had always thought it was endearing. It's NOT! It's not an equal opportunity word. I don't want everyone running around saying it." When asked if his comedy would suffer now that he vowed to never use the word again, Mooney responded, "I'm an n-word alcoholic and I will not be drinking from the n-bar. I will say 'black' or I will say 'African American.'"[39]

Despite the bewildering repudiation of the N-word given by several exemplars in the field of comedy, the word would never wane as a new generation of comics emerged. Younger, even more rebellious, Black comics of the Nineties were either not alive yet or were very young during the peak moments in the careers of Dick Gregory, Pryor, Foxx, and Mooney, four men whose careers straddled the civil rights era. The generational split between veteran comedians and the Nineties newbies— Chris Rock, Bernie Mac, Dave Chappelle, and Kevin Hart, among many others—is a way to see how the vanguard, those traditional comedians, reached a point where the N-word became unmentionable, while their Generation X counterparts sustained the word's use because the new generation was too young to be affected in the same way. The division pitted civil rights–era comedians against post–civil rights beneficiaries who maintained the belief that comedy offers a protective shield against social ostracism, rendering the word useful in stand-up.

No matter the generation, Black comedy has always been used as a tool to resist white supremacy. Chris Rock, from Brooklyn's Bedford-Stuyvesant district and whose career peaked during the two decades that surrounded the new millennium with his own show *The Chris Rock Show* and appearances on big and small screens, performs a type of comedy that is married to the biting insights into politics and society offered by his predecessors. But in the Nineties, he faced an inflection point where Black reporters challenged him for composing material catering too much to stereotypical depictions of Black people that so often entertained white audiences in American comedic history. With jokes claiming, "Books are like Kryptonite to a nigger" and "When I go to the money machine at night, I'm not looking over my shoulder for the media. I'm looking for niggers," Rock buttressed racist beliefs dating back to T.D. Rice's antebellum minstrel performance "Jump, Jim Crow," Ernest Hogan's ragtime hit "All Coons Look Alike to Me," and Robert Allen Cole's *A Trip to Coontown.* "I'm a clown," he told Tracii McGregor, a lifestyle editor at the rap-oriented magazine *The Source,* when questioned about appearing on the cover of *Vanity Fair* in whiteface. "I have no agenda at all but to make the people laugh … do you want me to become Dick Gregory? Nobody likes that."[40] At that moment, Rock defended comedians' rights to "play the fool." However, in 1996, during his unforgettable and controversial routine, "Niggas vs. Black People" from the HBO special *Bring the Pain* and later appearing on the 1997 album *Roll with the New,* Rock introduced a whole new level of discourse on the N-word.

> There's like a civil war going on with black people, and there's two sides. There's black people, and there's niggas. And niggas have to go. You know what the worst thing about niggas is? Niggas always want some credit for shit they're supposed to do. Niggas will say shit like, "I take care of my kids." You're supposed to, you [idiot]. What kind of ignorant shit is that? "I ain't never been to jail." What do you want? A cookie?[41]

As an artist, he hardly cared about the criticism generated by this skit. Indeed, the performance won him two Emmy Awards.[42] "I don't think race," Rock once said. "I just think funny."[43] Funny aside, the routine has never left the public discourse over how people of any race or nationality can use the word. Rock's routine even appeared in NBC's *The Office*, season 1, episode 2, titled "Diversity Day," which aired March 29, 2005. The episode featured lead character Michael Scott, a white branch manager of a paper company called Dunder Mifflin, who found himself in trouble with the corporate office for entertaining his employees with a rendition of Rock's stand-up routine. While "Diversity Day" didn't offer *The Office* fans much of a message to ponder, instead only truly corresponding with Rock's "I just think funny" dictum, the comedian himself said that this act was the beginning of his effort to incorporate the N-word into his routines to draw a distinction between educated, motivated Black people versus those that engage in mischievous behavior. The routine conveyed an in-group form of racial bigotry that so many opponents of casual, comedic, and musical uses of the N-word have opposed.

Rock defended the sketch to Oprah Winfrey: "Our young people are using [the word] to justify ignorance. So I pointed out that the people who use the word, people that are embracing the word are truly ignorant." His attempt to defend the skit on *The Oprah Winfrey Show* did little to mitigate the firestorm that the routine ignited. Critics said Rock's use of the N-word perpetuated self-image issues in the Black community while, in the words of biographer Marty Gitlin, "oversimplifying a complex and deeply rooted societal problem for laughs."[44] The routine, critics like Oprah claimed, also granted an opening to racists who continued to use the slur as a way to characterize Black people as less than human, as slaves, and a racial group to devalue.

Though never removing the word from his standup routines or his films, Rock grew from the experience after becoming irked when seeing too many white people laughing at the famous joke. "Nigger is a heavy-duty word," he would later say. "You better have a good reason for using it." He explains that singing along to rap lyrics is not one of those reasons, especially for whites. He offered an allegory on this point in his 2001 film *Down to Earth*. In the movie, Rock's character, Lance Barton, is a comedian who is killed before his time on earth is supposed to be up. A guardian angel gives him another chance to return to earth and live out the remainder of his life. His soul, however, has to enter the body of a white man named Charles Wellington III, a capitalist who had just been murdered by his wife and his personal assistant. During one moment in the movie, Wellington, whose body is now assumed by Rock's character, finds himself rapping along to DMX's "Ruff Ryders' Anthem" while in a sub shop with almost a dozen Black customers. After rapping the N-word repeatedly, a patron punches Wellington (Rock) in the face, knocking him out. The scene represents something Rock would also say about the N-word: "It's exclusively ours." He added, "The thing with 'nigger' is just that white people are ticked off because there's something they can't do. That's all it is. 'I'm white, I can do anything in the world. But I can't say that word.' It's the only thing in the whole world that the average white man cannot use at his discretion."[45]

What we see with Rock, along with Pryor and Mooney, is a level of self-reflection that transcends the art form. Each comedian experienced his own come-to-Jesus moment with the word, which resulted in different outcomes. Rock's case is the most peculiar because he didn't reject the word outright like his precursors had. He came to believe that there was something gravely problematic with the injurious use of the word. Like his comedic forbearers, he discovered that the word created a social identity hierarchy of Black people. Some of his routines engaged in spreading racist ideas among the populace in the same way once perpetuated by the ragtime performer Ernest Hogan had 100 years earlier. And it was reflective of the way The Frogs' refused to allow Hogan and other Black entertainers of the early twentieth century into their social circle for using anti–Black stereotypes to entertain a white fan base.

While many comedians have come to rival Chris Rock, Donald Glover and Dave Chappelle have charged head-on into the N-word controversy more than anyone else. In 2011, the then-22-year-old Glover, who worked as a writer on NBC's hit show *30 Rock*, tackled the issue in an uncensored Comedy Central performance titled "Who can say the N-word?" Glover's routine is quite entertaining. He first uses his cellphone as a stand-in for a member of an out-group calling him the N-word. "I was writing the N-word [in my iPhone] and my iPhone goes, 'Did you mean niggardly?' And I was like, 'No, iPhone. I meant Nigger.' But then, like two weeks later, I was writing Jigga, short for Jay-Z … and my cellphone goes, 'Did you mean Nigger?' and I go, 'Whoa, iPhone! You do not get to do that.'"[46] He also made jokes—some very crude—about a light-skinned Armenian woman and a white sign language interpreter that said the N-word in various contextual settings, granting passes to both. He even granted a pass to the actor Charlie Sheen for calling his girlfriend Denise Richards the racial slur in a leaked 2005 voicemail. Young people in the Black community, he suggests, had grown numb to the word. "I hate it when Black leaders be like, 'We're getting rid of it. Everybody's got to stop saying it.' Rappers will still say it because you told them not to," he teased. The solution, he proposed, "Everyone's got to start saying it. Everyone, like white people, you guys have got to start saying it." After a pause, he delivered a punch line: "We will lose some of you in the process. Not all of you will make it home." His point was to assert that policing the N-word will never end. That whites should just let it go because it doesn't matter if Black people are saying the word or not. "Saying the N-word doesn't help me," says Glover. "It doesn't help Black people." There should be no reason that whites even discuss the existence of a double standard. He reinforced that point on his 2012 album *Royalty*, published under the rap name Childish Gambino. The compilation features *30 Rock* teammate Tina Fey on the album's final track, "Real Estate," which has himself and guest vocalists Alley Boy and Swank rapping the N-word 19 times. Fey, a white woman, raps the song's outro: "This is the part where most people would say something crazy and drop the N-word after it / Not going to. Not gonna do that. Don't feel comfortable! I'm out!"

Long before Glover's stand-up routine and music there was Dave Chappelle, a District of Columbia native who never shies away from testing his audience with slurs and sociopolitical comedic content. A raw and unapologetic comedian, Chappelle's "The Niggar Family" (2004) sketch from season 2 of *Chappelle's Show*, a skit that convinced critic Tony Norman to call the show "hilariously dangerous," offers a weighty, ironic interpretation of the word's usage. Norman said our society is lucky that "there isn't a lot of water cooler chatter" about the half-hour sketch comedy airing on Comedy Central. "The Niggar Family," spelled with an "ar," is a parody-sketch of a 1950s sitcom that revolves around a racialized double entendre—a white family saddled with the surname that sounds like the racial slur. White people in the skit, which include members of the Niggar family; the family of a love acquaintance of the family's son, Timmy; and the host at a fancy restaurant all avoid discussing the surname (until the final seconds of the sketch when a Mexican family named the Wetbacks appears at the family's front door). Chappelle, however, plays a milkman who is quite aware of the N-word homonyms. "Good morning, Niggars. This is my favorite family to deliver milk to, the Niggars," Chappelle's character shouts at the beginning of the sketch. Various Black American stereotypes are applied to the family, ranging from athletic ability, facial features, and wealth. Near the end of the skit when Chappelle encounters Timmy Niggar at a restaurant, he says, "I'll bet you'll get the finest table a Niggar ever got in this restaurant." His last line, uttered while clutching his chest and laughing passively, Chappelle says, "Oh Lord, this racism is killing me inside."[47]

For anyone following Chappelle's career since the beginning, a sketch like "The Niggar Family" should come as no surprise. As a 19 year old, fresh from a role as Ahchoo in Mel Brooks' comedy *Robin Hood: Men in Tights* and appearances in *Undercover Blues* and *Getting In*, Chappelle was appreciated by fans for his uncensored performances. One critic called him "funny and unsparing to black as well as white audiences." Right after the violence that followed the verdict acquitting four police officers who beat motorist Rodney King in 1991, Chappelle took on police brutality.

"Any police officers here tonight?" he asked his audience. "Tough job eating all those doughnuts." After laughter, he said, "I'm just kidding, man. Just kidding. You don't want to mess with me anyway. I got a camcorder in the car." And since the beginning of his career, Chappelle has addressed racial paranoia surrounding racial slurs. In a 1993 interview, he said, "I like to do stuff about hanging out with white friends when I was growing up, and how they didn't know black people like to talk in the movies, or how black people like to call each other 'nigger' in endearing ways but when a white boy wants to be endearing, and imitates us and says, 'Hey nigger, how you doing?' he gets himself beaten up."[48] Admittedly, Chappelle's comedy derived from "pain and insecurity," and that is what made it easy for him to talk about the N-word.

In 2020, the N-word still appeared in Chappelle's comedy bits. While appearing on *Saturday Night Live* on November 7, just four days after the contested presidential election between incumbent Donald J. Trump and Democratic challenger and eventual winner Joe Biden, Chappelle gave a startling 16-minute monologue addressing the impact of COVID-19 on the Black community, Trump's personal battle with the coronavirus, and an assertion that the election illuminated the emotions harnessed by angry white people which he feels constantly as a Black man. When speaking of Trump's use of the phrase "kung flu" to describe a global pandemic that, at the time, had killed more than two million people worldwide and more than 250,000 in the United States, he said, "[Trump] you racist, hilarious son of a bitch!" The phrase "kung flu," which existed as a racialized slur against all people of Asian descent in the United States during the pandemic, was not the only controversial word used by Chappelle during the performance. In fact, he would say the N-word three times on live television that evening. He introduced the slur in his sketch when talking about COVID-related stimulus checks, whites' refusal to work during the pandemic or wear masks, and rampant heroin use in white America: "Stimulus checks, the heroin, while the rest of the country is trying to move forward, these white niggas are holding us back…. Black people, we are the only ones that know how to survive this [pandemic]. Whites, come, hurry quick. Come get your nigga lessons. You need us. You need us to save you from yourselves."[49]

Similar to what Randall Kennedy said in his groundbreaking book on the N-word, if the word only represented an "insulting slur and was associated only with racial animus," an examination of how comedians and other social influencers use the word would not exist. But because of the fact that Black entertainers are first among the social archetypes to offer new contextual framings of the word, we now find ourselves in this quandary: do we concentrate our energy on identifying and eliminating racist actions powered by the slur or should we agree that the N-word connotes inferiority any way it is said?

That question takes this narrative back to those minstrel and ragtime performers who were chastised by Black intellectual and corporate leaders for profiting from humiliating Black people. Such stories are important for illustrating the context that shrouds the debate over the word within the Black community, where people wrestle with the question: Is it right to profit from a word that has historically debased and stereotyped Black people while entertaining white people? Every comedian included in this chapter offers a unique lens into the interchange between how the N-word is used. We see the various N-word connotations: irony, hate, and redemption. These inferences aren't limited to any one comedian. Their comedy stretches across circumstances and throughout generations. They do, nevertheless, help us see how the N-word has evolved from its original existence as a slur and into a popular culture reference and finally into casual conversation. There is one fundamental individual who enables us to transition the slur out of the field of comedy and back into the realm of music.

That person oddly enough is Muhammad Ali.

SEVEN

Muhammad Ali, Rap, and That Word

The interchange between the N-word's ironic, injurious, and redemptive usages was on full display through the vernacular habits of the three-time heavyweight boxing champion Muhammad Ali. The prolific boxing icon used the word often enough when speaking to the press throughout his superlative and unrivaled career. Exercising liberties to use the word in casual conversation so publicly when at the peak of his athletic career has bewildered many people. In fact, he may very well have aroused every deeply felt emotion with varying uses of the word before any comedian or rap artist. As it turned out, he was someone that exuded semantic diversification. Out of one corner of his mouth, Ali called himself a "bad nigger" in an expression of redemption to seize the word from racist hegemony. When speaking of his white critics, Ali would say, "I liked being the 'bad nigger,' being the different black man. Black people weren't supposed to act so proud, so confident. Everything in this country made them feel inferior. I like being the 'cocky nigger,' 'the loudmouth.'"[1] In this context, the Champ behaved in a manner that was both funny and provocative. Using the word in this way riled whites and some traditional Black Americans. Those in the media who refused to call him anything other than Cassius Clay were also in a state of confusion over understanding whether the N-word was off-limits to everyone. But this is a case of an iconic figure robbing the word of its viciousness while reshaping its use to stuff its inhumanity back in the face of America's blood-stained racist history. Ali contrarily and intentionally enraged a large swath of white America when he announced his refusal to answer a draft call because, as he explained, the Viet Cong "never called me nigger."[2] Building a full head of steam, Ali articulated his redeeming feelings along a track that put into plain words the history of the N-word: "They never lynched me. They never put dogs on me. They never robbed me of my nationality; never raped or killed my mother and father." In both examples, Ali linked vitriolic racist hatred (redemption) with comedic savvy (irony) about Black suffering, thus underscoring the point that there is just too much evidence that many Black people in America have been subjected to psychological and physical maiming.

Like boxing, when it came to the ironic employment of the word, Ali is also considered the Champ. During the week leading up to the National Football League's Super Bowl in 1971, Ali made an unannounced appearance at the league's press headquarters in Miami, site of the upcoming title game between the Baltimore Colts and Dallas Cowboys, to talk about his upcoming fight against Joe Frazier. Ali, who had just won his case against draft evasion charges in the Supreme Court of the United States, was still training at the Fifth Street Gym near South Beach owned by his manager Angelo Dundee. "I know what's going to happen the night before the fight," Ali told the press pool. "That Joe Frazier, he's gonna get telephone calls and telegrams from folks in Georgia and Alabama and Mississippi saying 'Joe Frazier, you be a white man tonight and stop that draft-dodging nigger.'"[3] While visiting with inmates at a federal prison at Milan, Michigan, in 1976, the heavyweight champion, in the beginning stages of preparing for a bout against former British heavyweight champion Richard Dunn, said "I'm Muhammad Ali, the baddest nigger there ever will be."[4] Later that year, while fielding questions about a potential fight that never transpired against 1976 Olympic champion Teofilo Stevenson of Cuba, Ali described himself as, "Just another nigger trying to get bigger."[5]

Ali also used the word to injure. He regularly decried Joe Frazier as the N-word during pre-bout trash talking events with the press. Except for Angelo Dundee, he called members of his entourage, namely Bundini Brown and his brother, Rahman Ali, the N-word when they would needle him about the need to increase the rigor of his training.[6] He also used the slur to attack his critics. "You niggers give me more trouble than whites!" Ali said to about one hundred Black students at Muhlenberg College in Allentown, Pennsylvania. The hecklers, many wearing African dashikis and professing to be militants, criticized Ali for buying a $75,000 home in the predominantly white Philadelphia Main Line. "Sit down! You're nothing but a nigger! Be quiet boy, before I knock you down!" Ali proclaimed.[7]

At times, Ali said to white sportswriters, "Niggers can call each other niggers, but you can't." And yet, his view on this issue became puzzling to those that followed his career when, many years after retirement, Ali came to the defense of one of his white friends caught in a quagmire over the word. In 1988, Ali defended Happy Chandler's use of the word. Students at the University of Kentucky, and later elected officials and community leaders, called for Chandler's resignation from the institution's board of trustees when he said the word at an investment committee meeting. "You know Zimbabwe's all nigger now. There aren't any whites," Chandler said. He spoke the slur during a discussion about the university's 1985 decision to liquidate its investments in the apartheid country of South Africa. Chandler, age 89 at the time of the incident, was a former governor and U.S. Senator representing Kentucky, as well as a retired commissioner of Major League Baseball (1945–51) who oversaw the Brooklyn Dodgers' acquisition of Jackie Robinson. He found valued support from Ali: "I say 'nigger,' all the blacks I know say 'nigger,' many of you whites say 'nigger.' So what's so different?"[8] Receiving backing from Ali only emboldened Chandler in his position that his intent should not have caused a public uproar. He contended that the term did not offend his Black friends when he used it growing up in western Kentucky.[9]

This contextual examination of Ali's verbal habits allows us to explore the music industry. Hip-hop, gangsta rap and, now, mumble rap, conscious rap, and hip-hop R&B, in particular, have long been imbued with the pejorative. With nuanced omissions of The Jubalaries and Pigmeat Markham, music journalists and cultural critics like Touré usually cite Muhammad Ali as the "father of hip hop."[10] Ali epitomized virility. "His idea of masculinity," writes Touré, "bold, brash, fully aware of its own genius, certain of its beauty—became the hip-hop generation's ideal." He was the paragon of Black manhood. Ali was also a manipulator of attention, imitated by rap artists years later who flaunted gold chains, flashed 100-dollar bills and scantily dressed women while showcasing classic Chevys and fancy sports cars. After winning the gold medal at the 1960 Olympic Games in Rome, Ali—fighting then as Cassius Clay— became known throughout the sports world as the "Louisville Lip," a nickname that characterized him among the best wordsmiths, according to historians Randy Roberts and Johnny Smith, authors of a dual biography about the Champ and Malcolm X. Ali was known for regularly "spouting poetry" and "belittling opponents" while "advertising himself" as the greatest boxer of all time.[11] Roberts and Smith write of Ali as "a self-made product." He was among the most charismatic self-promoters on earth and made a name for himself by composing diss tracks before they were called diss tracks. He called Sonny Liston "too ugly to be world champion" and warned the media, "I predict that [Liston] will go at eight to prove that I am great. If he wanna go to heaven, I'll get him in seven. He'll be in a worse fix if I cut it to six. And if he keeps talking jive, I'll cut it to five." Before his first bout with ex-champion Floyd Patterson in November 1965, Ali said, "I'll beat him so bad, he'll need a shoehorn to put his hat on." During pre-fight trash talk in 1967 with Ernie Terrell, who still refused to call him by his Muslim name, Ali called him an "Uncle Tom," and said, "I'm going to whup him until he says my name." During the fight, Ali shouted incessantly, "What's my name?" He later pulled no punches by calling Joe Frazier a "gorilla."

While Ali indeed executed provocative rhymes and taunts to promote his upcoming fights, there is no denying that Black performing artists drew inspiration from his verbal punches. "He (Ali) was able to engage his social surroundings into his whole persona," says Public Enemy's Chuck D. "That's what hip-hop was able to do—to be an antenna for social reflection."[12] Indeed, Ali's trash-talking rhymes spoke more about his opponents than social injustice; however, contemporaries and historians alike find many of his public comments about race, imperialism, religion, and politics to be poetic. Ali "was important to the early rap artists and DJs," says Chuck D. Darryl McDaniels of Run DMC calls Ali's "Fight like a butterfly, sting like a bee, your eyes can't hit what they can't see" the "most famous rap lyrics ever" (though that passage should be credited to cornerman Bundini Brown).[13]

Like Touré, race, law, and literature scholar Imani Perry, author of a seminal book on hip-hop culture, *Prophets of the Hood: Politics and Poetics in Hip Hop*, sees the correlation between hip-hop's founding and Ali's style and brashness. Perry calls Ali "part of the foundation for the explosion of hip hop."[14] Boxing is the perfect metaphor for hip-hop, she argues, "Not only because both foster a diverse group of bragging personalities with aggressive styles but also because they are strategic competitions."[15] She speaks of the relationship with how Ali boxed George Foreman, saying,

> Hip hop is poetry that shifts styles of defense and offense, moving between grace and bull-like forward barreling. It dances, it leans back, and then it attacks. It uses the broadest allegory to discuss the individual moment of confrontation. In the so-called "Rumble in the Jungle," the 1974 Muhammad Ali–George Foreman fight, Ali threatened to match Foreman's crushing power with dance. When the actual impact of Foreman's power became apparent, Ali responded with strategy, first surprising Foreman with an insulting right hook, then faking him out for three rounds, using up Foreman's energy, and coming back in the final rounds with new vigor.[16]

Never before had an athlete—Black or white—relied so heavily on poetry to market himself and galvanize the public. Ali's bombast and rhyming saved prizefighting in the mid–Sixties at a time when its popularity was in decline.[17] Similarly, hip-hop would save a community in the Bronx besieged by poverty and gang violence. The genre would then become a conduit of social progress for rap artists in the Seventies and beyond. As young Black rappers became an increasingly important part of American culture, the N-word paradoxically continued simultaneously to become more accepted in the industry. In fact, the word would eventually become indispensable to the genre. As noted earlier in this and other chapters, the word long before hip-hop had evolved into separate meanings with separate spellings—this of course is assuming that we still see the word with a hard "r" and the variation ending in an "a" as the same word (John McWhorter would disagree). As seen through the behavior of Black social archetypes ranging from Henry Highland Garnet to Frederick Douglass and from Richard Pryor to Muhammad Ali, Black Americans historically use the word to lampoon past oppression and to reclaim a sense of bodily autonomy.

One would think, until the Millennial Generation and Generation Z, that the word, by its very definition, could only be used by Blacks. The word's second definition is an expression of irony: people calling themselves the N-word in the third person, or calling friends the N-word in an endearment. The third definition channels hatred. This word, by its very definition, is used in the antiquated way of volleying a verbal missile in the direction of its intended target. For many years, that word said in a wounding context could be used only in white society. This has changed, as an analysis of rap lyrics will show in the next chapter. All of this is to say that everyone is increasingly exposed to the N-word. It has caused a resultant discomfort in every community of the United States and perhaps delivered us to a point of no return. And yes, rap music is only partly responsible.

One of the first great rap groups called itself "Niggaz Wit Attitude" (N.W.A.). Its final album in 1991 included a title that covertly used the N-word: it was titled *Efil4zaggin* or backwards *Niggaz4Life*. In his first studio album, titled *2Pacalypse Now* (1991), award-winning rapper Tupac Shakur included a song titled "Crooked Ass Nigga." That album, along with his second, *Strictly 4 My N.I.G.G.A.Z.* (1992), reframed the word with an acronym meaning, "Never Ignorant Getting Goals Accomplished." In his 1995 record *Me Against the World*, the song "Young Niggaz" told his listeners "to put down the guns and have some fun nigga, the rest'll come nigga." On the album *All Eyez on Me* (1996), which would reach number one on the Billboard 200, the 25-year-old rapper included a song titled "Ratha Be Ya Nigga." Posthumously, Tupac released songs previously recorded during the Nineties: "Definition of a Thug Nigga" on *R U Still Down?* (1997), "Made Niggaz" on *Gang Related: The Soundtrack*, "Fuckin wit the Wrong Nigga" and "Niggaz Nature" on *Until the End of Time* (2001), and "N.I.G.G.A." on the album *Loyal to the Game* (2004).

Rap has evolved significantly since Ali's trash-talking prose of a bygone generation. Accordingly, it is essential to point out that Ali is not responsible for the N-word's proliferation in rap music from the late-Eighties to the current moment in history. And yet, hip-hop in general, and rappers more specifically, have offered sociopolitical commentary since the days Ali held the titles of world heavyweight champion boxer and trash-talking lyricist. For many bad reasons, that word is foundational in the social and political experiences Ali addressed with his rhymes many decades ago. It is, therefore, reasonable to see how the use of the word has reached a state of numbing normality since those earliest days of rap— even to the chagrin of many thought leaders, social archetypes, caregivers, parents, and grandparents. Thus, one cannot address how the N-word has advanced through rap music without acknowledging the genre's first internationally known initiator, Muhammad Ali.

✳ ✳ ✳

In 2009, talk show host, television producer, actress, and philanthropist Oprah Winfrey confronted rapper Jay-Z about his regular use of the N-word. In response, the artist also known as Hova unremorsefully said, "What we did, we took the word and took the power out of that word. We turned a word that was really ugly and hurtful into a term of endearment." Jay-Z was earnest. He expressed an idea that has since been delivered by every proponent of the word's usage. The problem is not the word, he maintained, "The problem is racism."

Oprah wasn't having it. "I am where I am because there was a generation before me that fought for civil rights, and that word carries such a sense of hatred and degradation.... I think about black men who were lynched and that's the last word they heard. That's what comes from my generation."[18]

Their exchange played out for 90 seconds on *The Oprah Winfrey Show*; however, the conversation continued in the pages of *O Magazine*, where Oprah asked Jay-Z if he believed using the N-word was necessary. The rapper's response touched upon the generational claim delivered by Oprah on her show: "Nothing is necessary. It's just become part of the way we communicate. My generation hasn't had the same experience with that word that generations of people before us had. We weren't so close to the pain. So in our way, we disarmed the word. We took the fire pin out of the grenade."

"I was once at a Jay-Z concert," Oprah pivoted to another disturbing development with the word, "and there was a moment when everybody— including white people—was screaming the N word. I gotta tell you, it didn't make me feel good."

Jay-Z: "You know, hip-hop has done so much for race relations, even with its ignorance—which, by the way, we do have to take some responsibility for. But even without directly taking on race, we've changed things just by being who we are. It's difficult to teach racism in the home when your kid loves Jay-Z. It's hard to say, 'That guy is beneath you' when your kid idolizes that guy."[19]

The exchange between Oprah and Jay-Z unleashed a rhetorical debate throughout the country in 2009. The host maintained no secret that she disliked rap music for its violent language and misogynistic lyrics. She was also very forthright in her position on the N-word. Years later when filming *The Butler*, she famously convinced director Lee Daniels to stop saying the word.[20] She is also known for scolding former-Beatle Paul McCartney for collaborating on the song "All Day" with Kanye West, who uses the N-word 38 times. Talking about Black people using the word was one thing. Referring to white people who use the word because rap music offers a medium to do so was something altogether different. Letting that become something that slipped into popular vernacular was beyond the pale for the Queen of All the Media.

The discourse in Black America over Oprah's firm position was heated. Black social media was at bitter odds over Oprah's harsh attacks on the word, supporting or lambasting her with equal passion, especially when it came to the reprieve she granted to Black comedians, like Chris Rock and Dave Chappelle, who appeared on her show without the hot-seat drilling endured by Jay-Z. Despite the backlash on social media, Oprah's conversation with Jay-Z exposed one of the unwritten rules in Black America: the word is not to be uttered in mixed company, especially around white people. Hip-hop's popularity in white America granted currency to the word far beyond the Black community. This particular episode underpins the content of the next chapter, which scrutinizes the position taken by white people who draw an equivalence between various usages and spellings of the word and who try to establish fair rules about what Blacks and whites should be able to say. Oprah stated she doesn't want the word used by anyone. To her, Black people who use the word in any context, whether it be casual conversation or as a form of art, disrespect those who paid with their lives to ensure the current generation's rights and privileges under the law. In a pragmatic sense, she also believes that eliminating its use in the Black community will prevent whites from saying the word in public. Jay-Z, on the other hand, thinks that the word's mutation to a more congenial spelling and directed at other Blacks in an endearing way offers a sense of liberation from verbal violence of the original slur. Jay-Z and likeminded advocates such as his biographer Michael Eric

Dyson believe white people should be smart enough to abstain from repeating any rendering of the word.[21]

Dyson contends that the permissible use of the N-word by Black people is an "individual reparation" owed by the country for its history of racial violence. While the Vanderbilt sociology professor will never accept white people saying the word, he admits rap music has radically complicated the matter: "Part of the problem with hip hop music is that Redd Foxx, he was saying it on a party record in your basement. Now, Snoop Dogg is saying it in the world. Japanese people that don't even know the internecine squabbles among black people in America and white folk, about those struggles, [they] talk about 'my nigga.'"[22]

The positions held by Jay-Z and Dyson are "nonsensical," claims social critic Neal Lester. Reaffirming Oprah's point, "This word is unlike any other in the English language" and "You can't take back anything that you never owned," he says, refuting Jay-Z's ultimate point made as a guest on *The Oprah Winfrey Show*. The term of endearment argument is "so ridiculous," says Lester, "because [slave] masters used those same terms with their slaves endearingly." Why are people claiming "endearment" when there are so many other ways that the word has "had and continues to embody discrimination and violence and history both present and past?" He asserts, "...to think in a few years of hip hop that you can flip a switch and make it somehow nicer and make it smell better is absurd ... you can't take it back if you never owned it. And I can't find anywhere in history where Black people owned the word."[23]

The narrative provided thus far suggests there is no right time or place that the word should be spoken by white people. This argument gets muddied when looking at the relaxed and recurring use of the word—and its various deviations—in hip-hop, in particular. The objective here is to not pass judgment on the Black use of the term. Other more qualified scholars offer insight on that debate. Rather, my point is to say many white people, for some ungodly reason, argue that the frequent use of the N-word by Black rappers (and other social archetypes, comedians, on-air personalities, and social media influencers) exists as evidence for why whites should be able say it without repercussions. What is good for the goose is good for the gander, they argue. This expression is all too common in debates over fairness or arguments over whether someone is in violation of a social and cultural norm. If women can wear long hair to work, why can't men? If men can have more sex partners, why can't women? If members of one political party can obstruct a presidential administration, why can't those of the other? While the goose/gander binary is a principle that one is no better than the other, I challenge readers to see it as a reminder that an individual's sense of privilege is often misplaced. This angle is why the idiom's meaning doesn't afford equal access to whites when it comes to the privilege of saying the N-word, just as it wouldn't grant privileges to straight people who want to say the F and Q words, or to men that flirt with using the B-word.

EIGHT

A Hip-Hop Icon

In a local Nashville, Tennessee, newspaper, an obscure writer named Rick de Yampert called the N-word "a hip-hop icon." Nineties rap icon Ice-T reinforced de Yampert's assertion. "I wear that term like a badge of honor," he wrote in his memoir *The Ice Opinion.*[1] Historian Robin D.G. Kelley echoed the rapper's sentiments: "Nigga is frequently employed to distinguish urban black working-class males from the black bourgeoisie and African Americans in positions of institutional authority. Their point is simple: The experiences of young black men in the inner city are not universal to all black people, and, in fact, they recognize that some African Americans play a role in perpetuating their oppression." And English scholar Sheila Smith McKoy said rappers' use of the N-word is "true to the African American oral tradition [and] politics of subversion," citing the example when the word "bad" became "good" as an example of verbal mutation. She explains, "The hip-hoppers aren't the first ones to use the word in that way. It has been part of street culture since the days of slavery. And that term has always been reinvented within the context of the African American community." While these voices vary in how they go about justifying the use of the word in Black communities, it would be difficult to deny that some Black Americans have contended that the word has become an iconic symbol of brotherhood found in Black subcultures throughout American history. Following a pattern of Black social archetypes in the form of vaudeville theater, sociopolitical activists, comedians, and athletes, it happens now that hip-hop is the latest variation of Black popular culture making regular use of the word.

While the N-word's regularity in casual conversation, comedy, and rap lyrics has had a numbing effect in fractions of American society, a majority representing Black and all non–Black populations detest the use of the word. The internet-based research and analytical firm YouGov found that most Americans find the use of the N-word offensive no matter who is saying it, which includes 59 percent of the Black population and 55 percent of the white population. When broken down by political affiliation, 73 percent of Democrats believe the word is offensive in any context, while 43 percent of Republicans and 45 percent of independents believe this is the case.[2] Academics and hip-hop stakeholders likewise share differing opinions. "There is no socially redeeming use of the word...," said Ray Winbush, former director of the Race Relations Institute at Fisk University. He elaborated, "It shows how effective white supremacy and racism have been in getting the victim of it to say there's nothing wrong with the victimization."[3] In contrast, hip-hop producer Alvin Williams argues, "It just depends on what environment you come from, and where you are in public." Williams' colleague in the industry, Reavis Mitchell III of the rap group Utopia State, rationalizes the word as "used as a term of endearment." Public opinion poll numbers along with the contentious debate between public intellectuals and those who have a personal investment in the hip-hop industry certainly warrant the question of why rap music has complicated discourse over vulgar language, slurs, and what society now considers to be taken as racist behavior. Hip-hop producer Harold Durrett yielded, "If we use it all the time, then can we really fault anyone else for using it?"

The same polls show Americans divided over whether N-word usage makes a white person racist. While there are many different contextual ways whites can "use" and "mention" the word, overall, nearly half (48 percent) of Blacks questioned in the survey said any utterance of the word does in fact make the white user a racist. A smaller portion of whites (37 percent) agree with that sentiment. More than half of Democrats (59 percent) felt that saying the word exposed suppressed racist beliefs, while just 26 percent of Republicans and 30 percent of Independents agree. While it is necessary for all non–Black people to confront the word's history as well as its contemporary meaning and impact on Black people, the sheer fact that many Blacks feel that whites know that the word is taboo but willfully choose to use or mention the word anyhow is an affront to mutual respect.

A portrayal of the quandary just described once played out in season two, episode six, of the CBS All Access series *The Good Fight*, where African American attorney Adrian Boseman, played by Delroy Lindo, offers a profoundly moving performance in which he appears as a guest on a U.S. news talk show called "Review of the Day" to discuss the partisan debate over the existence of a racist double standard. During the 40-second scene, Boseman first listens as two white men, the anchor and a guest on the panel named "Chuck," discuss "racism against white people every day" before he is challenged on fairness over the fact that his African American law firm receives no-bid contracts. Chuck asks, "As a white lawyer, what am I supposed to make of that?" To which Boseman pithily replies, "I don't know."[4]

The host of the show interjects a comment, "I think Chuck is pointing out a double standard here. Take hip hop. We've talked about this on the show before. You have African American rappers saying N-word this and N-word that, but a Caucasian can't."

Boseman has trouble looking up at the other panelists. He even rubs his eyes and winces as the broadcast's host employs the predictable claim that whites should be permitted to say the N-word since it is widely used in hip-hop: "So, say it," a visibly irritated Boseman says. "Say the word you want to say."

The host and Chuck object to saying the N-word. "I'm not saying that I want to say it, I'm just saying that I can't," says Chuck.

"Sure you can. Say it right now," Boseman says. After a grimace and short pause, "I will say it with you...." He then pronounces the N consonant in an attempt to goad his melanin-challenged co-panelist to say the epithet before the scene cuts to commercial.

If the reaction to the scene on social media was any indication, Boseman's dismay was felt by much of Black America as Twitter users viewed the clip over five million times in less than 24 hours. In fact, many viewers had no idea that what they were watching was a prerecorded fictional streaming program. Many Twitter users thought they were watching a viral clip of a real news broadcast. Although this scene was only a subplot in the episode, the lesson is certainly reflective of the debate over the term. To whites, discussions about racism and abhorrent incidents where the N-word is used in racially charged behavior seem to occur infrequently enough that there is no greater meaning about the deep-seated nature of anti–Black racism. Meaning, it is easy for whites to be dismissive about racial topics that are otherwise consequential to Black people. On the contrary, Black America's frustrations over listening to rationalizations for the white usage was acted out in a series of poignant facial expressions and concise retorts delivered by Delroy Lindo's character Adrian Boseman in *The Good Fight*.

Those irritations (*Are you really more concerned about a racial double standard? Do you want permission to say the word without getting called a racist? Why is this issue important to you? Why do you want to say the word?*) were on display in real time during an interview between actor Samuel L. Jackson and former film critic Jake Hamilton in 2013 where white director and screenwriter Quentin Tarantino's film *Django Unchained* was the topic of discussion. In the film, which costars Jackson, the N-word is said more than 100 times, resulting in a public debate led by, among others, Spike Lee. "There's been a lot of controversy surrounding the use of the N-word in this movie," said Hamilton, who was then cut off by Jackson.[5]

"The word would be [what]?" asked Jackson.
   Feeling pressure, Hamilton said, "Oh, I don't want to say it."
   "Why not?" Jackson asked again, turning himself into the interviewer.
   Hamilton: "I don't like to say it."
   Jackson: "Have you ever said it?"
   "No, sir." Hamilton responded.
   Jackson: "Try it! … We are not going to have this conversation unless you say it."
   Silence penetrated an awkwardly long pause. "Do you want to move on to another question?" asked Jackson.
   Hamilton: "Okay. Awesome."

Though patient and affable in this moment, it was apparent Jackson wholly resented the question. Fury often materializes at the infinite feeling that racial ignorance and racial indifference could only vanish if whites as a racialized group undergo an awakening. Philosopher George Yancy writes about his cynical hope that this might happen in his book of essays and interviews *Across Black Spaces* (2020). Yancy believes there must be "a process of un-suturing that would bespeak both white vulnerability and a form of white forthrightness to admit to the white racist toxicity to which [whites] have given birth and have nurtured," thereby possibly identifying the racism that exists within themselves, even if they must go through stages of denial and guilt.[6] The relationship between racist behavior and the N-word is poignant. Hip-hop music has exposed this because it is the only genre of music that widely uses the expletive and is the paramount reason the N-word is debated today.[7] This is not to say that the N-word wouldn't exit the mouths of racist whites. More exactly, it is to say that any attempt to rationalize the white usage of any derivation of the word in any context exists solely because of rap music. If it weren't for rap's well-known use of the word, what other reason could there be for white people to wish to say the N-word beyond a classroom or journalistic setting? How else could whites claim a racist double standard?

Heavy irony comes with the habit of placing the N-word in rap lyrics. As white Millennials and Generation Zers commonly listen to the form of music, many now long to say the word as they rap along to the lyrics. Some consequently partake in the habit of calling friends the appellation. This must aggravate some white grandparents and parents in the Baby Boom and X generations knowing that their grandchildren and children now call each other the N-word as a congenial greeting. As professor and scholar Imani Perry notes, the N-word in hip-hop has created a state of great trepidation, "a line in the sand which the [rap] artists continually ask their listeners to cross, enticing and challenging. It marks a provocative irreverence with potentially large but unknowable consequences."[8] The popularity of hip-hop means that the term has become common in American vernacular culture regardless of one's social-contextual environment. The genre has created a significant generational fracture with those under 40 years of age distantly removed from the ugly history of that word.

The musical and generational gulf that Perry speaks about has produced fraught and, at times, pugnacious exchanges between Black and non–Black people. In the fall of 2019, trouble followed actress Gina Rodriguez's utterance of the N-word as she rapped along with The Fugees' "Ready or Not," a song she claimed to have listened to growing up. The *Jane the Virgin* and *Annihilation* actress posted on Instagram a video of herself singing the expletive as she was getting her hair done. After facing a tsunami of online criticism, Rodriguez made a public apology that fell flat—"I'm sorry if I offended anyone." Her Instagram post and the credulous apology that ensued yielded a *New York Times* Op Ed by freelance journalist Gary Suarez who claimed, "Many of us [Latinx people] assume our proximity to black people makes it O.K. for us to say the word. It's not [O.K.]."[9] The case was similar to the 2001 dispute that put a mark on Jennifer Lopez for singing the endearing form of the N-word in her 2001 hit "I'm Real," sung alongside the rapper Ja Rule.

In January 2020, William Wolf, a little-known white battle rapper, was punched in the face for working the N-word into one of his freestyles. While facing off in a rap battle against an African American opponent, Wolf said, "I ain't like these other battle rappers / They talk too much / Saying I can't use the 'n' word in this battle / My nigga." No one knows if there was supposed to be more in that last bar, but Wolf certainly wasn't endearingly using the term, given the extent of insults that traditionally occur during rap battles. It was at the very moment Wolf crossed the line that he was struck. While there are not many white professional rappers, it is essential to note that they usually come from Black communities and can adopt accent, grammar, and a vocabulary drawn from Black vernacular English.[10] In many ways, white rappers can also communicate shared lived experiences in lyrics. And yet, white and Black hip-hop artists do not share a common history of surviving enslavement and an apartheid state. This is why, aside from one slip up from Eminem in the 1990s, professional white rappers have kept the expression out of their music. Therefore, the question regarding whether white people have a right to voice the N-word while rapping along with a song does not apply to professional rappers. Instead, this has mainly become an appeal of white lay persons. As such, then, one must examine ugly disputes over whites verbalizing the N-word while singing along to rap music.

Rappers maintain a complicated relationship with the public. While rap music is made largely by Black people with content about Black people, whites have always been the largest group of purchasers of rap music dating back to a 1993 United States Senate subcommittee investigation into gangsta rap, a subgenre of rap music. Under the leadership of Carol Moseley-Braun, Democrat from Illinois, the subcommittee found 53 percent of those purchasing rap music at the time of the study were white.[11] That number has remained constant over the last 30 years. When his album *Doggystyle*, which features the N-word 112 times and includes a song titled "For All My Niggaz and Bitches," received criticism from several federal lawmakers, including Moseley-Bruan's subcommittee, for its language and sexually suggestive album cover image, Snoop Dogg issued a clap back to an older generation of critics: "I know you hate me. But your kids don't."[12] That was certainly true in white households. Most white listeners of rap music grow addicted to the rhythmic beats. Others like to hear tales about the Black experience in America without having to live it. The N-word, then, complicates matters because, as listeners routinely sing lyrics that overuse the term, saying the word in conversation often becomes a tendency that is no different than casually uttering curse words.

To be clear, there are two things at play in this particular discussion. Should a degree of tolerability be granted to someone who is white who says the popular use of the word ending in an "a" versus its evil cousin ending with a hard "r"? And, should Black Americans who say the word in mixed-race company be held responsible for the actions of white people who mimic the language? This chapter reflects on these two questions. In the pages that follow, I will provide anecdotes along with journalistic commentary defending and attacking habitual and artistic use of the pejorative in rap music through four decades. As counterintuitive as it may seem, the information herein is provided for readers to form their own opinion on the matter, to carry on, so to speak, the debate that played out between Oprah Winfrey and Jay-Z in the fall of 2009 as described in the previous chapter.

Of course, there are moments when you would think there is no question that the white usage of the word needs no debate. Take, for instance, what happened at the University of Oklahoma (OU), where two variations and contextual uses of the word were at the center of a firestorm involving a predominantly white fraternity. In March 2015, white members of Sigma Alpha Epsilon were seen in a nine-second video suggesting they would rather see a Black student lynched than become a member of their fraternity. They chanted, "There will never be a nigger at SAE [clap, clap]. You can hang 'em from a tree, but he'll never sign with me. There will never be a nigger at SAE [clap, clap]." Their use of the appellation carried the baggage of centuries of violence and oppression, along with a history of exclusion felt by OU students of color for generations. The incident resulted in a Twitter hashtag #SAEHatesMe and an uproar on campus demanding university administrators take stern action against the fraternity. Two of the students leading the chant were eventually expelled, and the national SAE headquarters closed the chapter at the University of Oklahoma. Within a week, a second video surfaced of the SAE chapter's white house mother, Beauton Gilbow, repeatedly using the N-word while singing along to "All Gold Everywhere" by Atlanta-based rapper Trinidad James.[13]

James, who commonly performed at fraternities, eventually responded to the incident, saying he was less concerned about Gilbow repeating his lyrics than the chant from the fraternity brothers. "It's hard to ridicule someone for something that you continue to use in your music," James said, who sounded very similar to Muhammad Ali defending Happy Chandler in 1988. "If we don't want the word used and the word holds such a negative connotation, then we shouldn't use it at all, period."[14] Not everyone agreed with James's position giving Gilbow a pass. A few days later, social media outcry forced James to issue a qualifier. Regarding Gilbow, he said, "I think she comes from racism. She's 79 years old. Seventy-nine years ago, whatever year that is, she has seen tons and tons and tons of racist acts. Going off her age and seeing that right there, I don't think that when she was doing that she was doing it to be a protest or anything. But it tickled her because she knows where she came from." He tried to settle this incident one last time during a one-on-one interview with CNN's Don Lemon: "I am not defending her."[15]

James's instant take on whether white people have a right to sing along with rap lyrics that include the N-word gives credence to the argument that the rap industry has marketed and promoted the word in a way that has not been done to the LGBTQ+ and Jewish communities. One rapper, Turbo B, committed professional suicide after incorporating anti-gay lyrics in the 1990s. Puff Daddy's line "You should do what we do, stack chips like Hebrews," in the song "It's All About the Benjamins" was removed by the record label.[16] The only rapper who has endured despite constant criticism for using homophobic and anti–Semitic lyrics is Eminem.

During the shared uproar over Gilbow's unrestricted and mocking use of the slur, Don Lemon raised the question on his show *CNN Tonight* of whether rap artists profit from the N-word. On his panel were Trinidad James, conservative commentator Ben Ferguson, and then-CNN progressive commentator Marc Lamont Hill. Ferguson, who is white, was the first to respond to the query. He said, "I think you [James] know that we should probably get rid of the n-word, but in reality, I think many rappers are afraid they will lose out on money and sales and street cred if they stop using the word."[17]

To which, James replied, "I'm making money off of doing music and being creative, sir. I'm not making money just because I use the n-word. Nobody goes to buy an album because it's full of the n-word."

Ferguson retorted, "Trinidad, you wouldn't be on this show tonight if it wasn't for using the n-word in your rap music. Let's be honest."

"No, no, no," Hill chimed in. "He wouldn't be on the show if a white woman hadn't said the n-word on a tape. White people have been saying the word long before Trinidad was born." He continued,

> The n-word isn't divisive. White supremacy is divisive. Slavery was divisive. That's the problem. And maybe, just maybe, it's not white people's position to tell Black people what to say. I might see Trinidad James on the street and call him "my nigga." You know why? Because he is "my nigga." The difference between Trinidad James and you is that Trinidad James has to deal with the same oppressive situations. He's born into a world where anti–Black racism prevails. He lives in a world where police might shoot him on the street no matter how much money he has. We share a collective condition known as "nigger." White people don't. I'm not saying it should be illegal for white people to use it. I'm saying white people shouldn't want to use it given everything that has happened after 400 years of exploitation and institutional racism.

Included also in the debate was the show's host, who has never skirted from a debate over the appellation. Lemon pushed back on Hill's position by arguing that anyone should be able to say the word in a proper context, and it is only through a visceral reaction by a victimized individual that empowers the word. He asked, "Should we just not get so upset about the use of that word and that will help take the power away?"

The segment offered no clear resolution on the matter. Rather, these four voices bring to light the unending inconsistency of N-word debate. Each individual in discussion with Lemon offered a different take on who can say the N-word, who shouldn't, and why. Ferguson, the white conservative, wished to ban the word from curricula and popular culture. More specifically, he wanted to remove the word from music. Trinidad, the rapper, proved reluctant to take a position and ultimately called the debate "a two-sided thing" wherein rap artists share responsibility for the white usage. Hill, the progressive and professor of media studies, found no problem with Black people calling one another the word, even going as far as citing a moment when Martin Luther King, Jr., called his aide Andrew Young "Little Nigga." What this episode shows is that the word will always mean different things to different people. What white people should take into account, then, is that for all of the Trinidad James voices that offer passes to white people who say the word, whether it be quoting from a text while teaching a class or singing along to rap music, it is virtually impossible to know how someone will respond to the word's utterance. And there will be consequences. Hill said, "You cannot divorce words from the history despite the context." That is why it is so problematic when whites say it. That is why white people like Ben Ferguson could lose jobs for mentioning the word in any context. What do we make of whites who claim they should be able to say or mention the word without any repercussions? It would be fair to consider absurd any argument claiming white people are the ones being treated unfairly. The issue is whether whites should have a voice in determining whether Blacks can say the word. And of course, they should not.

There have also been times in recent memory when Black authorities have attempted to both literally and figuratively legislate the N-word. In 2007, New York's City Council voted unanimously to ban the use of the N-word. Motivated by the proliferation of "rap's favorite epithet" on the radio and the big screen along with the subsequent debate over offensive language in casual conversations, the 51-member council, comprised of 25 Black, Latinx, and Asian members, and 26 white members, enthusiastically voted to remove the slur from the vocabulary of local rappers and, by extension, young New Yorkers.[18] The measure's key sponsor, Leroy Comrie (D–Queens), who is Black, explained his position: "We're not looking to start a trend to eliminate words or try to turn into book-burning types of people. There's been an attempt to reformat this word … to use it as a word that means affection or friendship. We're saying that doesn't work."[19] Although it was called "commendable" and "laudable" by New York's *Daily News*, the ban carried no weight. It was a performative gesture designed to encourage New Yorkers to "voluntarily eliminate the word from their vocabulary," according to media coverage, although Comrie publicly called for a national ban on the word and asked Black Entertainment Television (BET) to stop giving airtime to music videos that included the word in the lyrics. Comrie, who would later fill a seat on the New York State Senate, also asked the National Academy of Recording Arts and Sciences to no longer give Grammy awards to artists who use the word. Ironically in 2007, the year of the city council's symbolic ban on the word, Clifford Joseph Harris, Jr., who goes by the stage name T.I., won the Grammy for best rap solo performance for his song "What You Know." The song's lyrics contain one reference to the N-word: "Give every ho a hug / Nigga don't show me mugs / Cause you don't know me cuz."

The winner of best rap performance by a duo or group was Hakeem Seriki, better known by the stage name Chamillionaire, and Anthony

Henderson, also known as Krayzie Bone, for "Ridin'" from *The Sound of Revenge*. The song includes the passage: "Nigga see if they can see me lean / I'm tint so it ain't easy to be seen / Nigga like who is dat producing / That the play n' skillz when we out and cruising."

The loudest voices expressing disdain over the council's moratorium were members of the public, who shifted focus away from ugly language and toward systemic problems in New York City. "The 'N' word is not obscene," wrote one concerned citizen, "but here are a few that are: poverty, unemployment, uninsured, illiteracy, gangs and drugs." Another New Yorker wrote, "Here was an opportunity to ban the murder rate, drug dealers, gangs, teen pregnancy, single parent households and the high dropout rate, which all have a greater negative impact on the black community." One letter to the editor expressed concern over other slurs: "What about the racial slurs that refer to people of other ethnicities? Are these to be considered less serious or offensive?"[20] To this end, the same city council later in the year failed to move forward a ban on two misogynistic words, the B-word and "Ho." Democratic councilwoman Darlene Mealy from Brooklyn acknowledged that the two words lacked the "historical weight, significance and capacity to wound," according to a *Daily News* editorial, but deservedly belong in the discourse over the N-word. The local press criticized Mealy's efforts, saying a resolution of this nature would "unfortunately cheapen" the accomplishment of passing the performative ban on the N-word.[21] Bearing in mind, no metric was provided to rate the success of the council's original moratorium on the N-word. The entire affair yielded one last comment from the public: "If the City Council bans the 'h' word, will Santa Claus be allowed to yell 'Ho, ho, ho!' as he and his reindeer fly over N.Y.C.? And what about the Jolly Green Giant?"[22]

Mealy's efforts aside, those on the New York City Council fought hard to start a movement that would, in view of social critic Cornel West's hopes, as discussed in Chapter Four, issue a nationwide moratorium on the N-word. The council's measure to legislate offensive language preceded actions undertaken by the National Association for the Advancement of Colored People (NAACP) during the summer of 2007.

On July 9, Julian Bond and leadership at the NAACP, along with hundreds of onlookers, symbolically laid to rest the N-word in a burial held during the organization's national conference in Detroit, Michigan. Honorary pallbearers were hip-hop artist Kurtis Blow, Rhythm and Blues singer Eddie Levert, general president of Alpha Phi Alpha fraternity Daryle Matthews, former NFL player Olrick Johnson, Jr., and NAACP delegates from around the United States. They marched from Detroit's Cobo Center to Hart Plaza. Two Percheron horses pulled a coffin, decorated with fake black roses and a solemn ribbon, meant to contain the N-word's remains. The day's orators, including Detroit Mayor Kwame Kilpatrick, the Rev. Otis Moss III of Trinity United Church of Christ, and Bond, collectively admonished rappers for using the word as much as they criticized comedian Michael Richards of *Seinfeld* and radio host Don Imus, both white men under intense scrutiny at the time for calling Black audience-goers the N-word and the women on the Rutgers University basketball team "nappy headed hos," respectively. "Today, we're not just burying the N-word, we're taking it out of our spirit," said Kilpatrick, while adding, "We gather burying all the [terms] that go with the N-word." To which, Bond later declared, "While we are happy to have sent a certain radio cowboy back to his ranch, we ought to hold ourselves to the same standard. If he can't refer to our women as 'hos,' then we shouldn't either."[23]

No one at the event expected an abrupt halt to the word's usage; rather, as one newspaper editorial described, the N-word "will continue to rise to the surface, sort of like a dead man floating, before it starts to fade away."[24] However, the tactic evidenced arguments from those like the aforementioned Ben Ferguson that a double standard exists in the discourse that enables Black people to get away with using the N-word while white people cannot. The NAACP's symbolic burial declared loudly that no one of any skin color should verbalize any derivation of the word. Leadership of the NAACP situated the organization in the corner of total, without qualification, eradication of the word from the cultural landscape in general, and Black artistic expression more particularly, on the grounds of respect for Black ancestors. When it comes to rappers, Blow, one of the forerunners of hip-hop culture, said at the symbolic funeral, "I'm living proof that it's possible to rap or do hip-hop and not offend anyone."[25]

The NAACP's mock funeral for the N-word was two generations too late. Over 50 years earlier, on April 3, 1955, the same organization held a funeral ceremony in Baton Rouge, Louisiana, that placed "Jim Crow" in a casket. Although the service honored the legal victory in *Brown v. Topeka Board of Education* that occurred almost a year earlier, civil rights advocates believed it was time to give Jim Crow segregation its last rites. The NAACP declared the casket would be buried by 1963, the hundredth anniversary of the Emancipation Proclamation.[26] The organization offered a vision of championing civil rights that inspired every like-minded organization for which to strive. It presented a hope that the Supreme Court had handed Jim Crow a fatal blow with the desegregation of public schools. This was no time for freedom workers to take their foot off the neck of Jim Crow. But before Jim Crow took his last breath, there would be a series of back-and-forth victories and defeats: the lynching of Emmett Till, the Montgomery Bus Boycott, the lunch counter sit ins, the Freedom

Rides, the marches in Albany and Birmingham, and gubernatorial stonewalling of court-ordered desegregation at Little Rock Central High, William Frantz Elementary, the Universities of Alabama, Georgia, and Mississippi; to name a few. However, by the target date, every Black American could gain citizenship with the unmitigated enforcement of the Fourteenth and Fifteenth Amendments. This level of prudence was not on display in 2007. Julian Bond and others in the NAACP believed the N-word's symbolic burial and abrupt erasure could do the job.

Though not as strong an argument as many presume, there are clear differences in how the N-word is perceived between generations. It is not difficult to understand why varying prohibitions on the N-word cause unpredictable combustions of confrontation; rap music is an easy target. Its ascent and the varying genres expose why disagreements in a culture exist among several generational lineages. Consider first that the proponents of placing moratoriums or bans on the word—baby boomers mostly—have typically failed to result in cultural or semantic changes in hip-hop. The list of top-five rappers with the most Grammy wins in any category includes Jay-Z (22), Kanye West (21), Eminem (15), Kendrick Lamar (13), and Lauren Hill (8). Not in the top five, but ranked high on the list of most decorated rap artists are Dr. Dre (7), Outkast (6), Lil Wayne (5), Childish Gambino (5), and Drake (4). Excluding Eminem, every artist on the list is Black and is known for regular use of the N-word. In other respects, in 2018 Kendrick Lamar became the first rap artist to receive the Pulitzer Prize for *DAMN*, an album that uses the N-word 31 times.

Social critic and Columbia University linguist John McWhorter sympathizes with the artists. "I know their hearts are in the right place," McWhorter says of those that are trying to enforce a halt on the N-word's usage. "But they're not listening to the language with young ears. They're hearing it in a way that is not intended."[27] According to McWhorter, language is something that cannot be legislated. Society chooses in each generation how a word is modified (fellow to fella, brother to brotha, what's up to 'sup) and whether or not its use will carry on. While individuals like Oprah Winfrey and Cornel West, and groups like the New York City Council and the NAACP, may hope particular offensive words will die off because of disuse, the N-word in contrast to other slurs directed at Black Americans, such as coon, darky, jigaboo, and Pickaninny, happened to catch on in popular culture at a moment when saying the word could get an individual into hot water. Additionally, the N-word's popularity coincided with rap's explosion in American culture in general through popular programs like MTV's *Yo! MTV Raps* and BET's *Rap City*. As a result, that particular word's various deviations have remained in the public conscience. McWhorter says, "If 'coon' had been the term of choice then, I suspect it would now be the term decorating rap."[28]

Yo! MTV Raps, in particular, permeated white living rooms as much as Black living rooms. After a maligned beginning in August 1988, the program hit the airwaves six days a week within two years. A story at the time was about President George H.W. Bush's grandchildren who were regular viewers of the program and had become fans of its hosts Fab Five Freddy, Ed Lover, and Dr. Dre. In one episode of *Doogie Howser,* a medical drama about a teenage physician that aired on ABC from 1989 to 1993, Doogie Howser, played by Neil Patrick Harris, wore a *Yo! MTV Raps* t-shirt. Teenagers commonly rushed home from school by 4 o'clock to catch the show. Waking up on Saturday mornings for the 10 o'clock program also became a teenage obligation. Occasionally, viewers inserted a VHS tape into the VCR to record rap videos for on-demand viewing. Although this was MTV's first program dedicated to Black music and culture, the network believed a large percentage of *Yo!'s* audience were white holdovers from the preceding heavy metal show *Headbangers Ball.*[29] While rap was always a Black medium, white middle-class teenagers were drawn to the novel genre's "raw beats," reported the *Detroit Free Press.* The music's messages, often pro–Black, sexually explicit, political, anti-police, and profanity-laced, were not the draw that many critics presumed. MTV, at the time, was one of the very few television outlets one could turn to hear rap, as radio stations, even Black FM stations, chose not to give rap artists much airtime.[30] Music sellers at the time, particularly those from Detroit, a city with a rich musical legacy, claimed it was white customers who enabled NWA's album *Straight Outta Compton* to go platinum in 1989 and helped *Efil4zaggin* (Niggaz4life spelled backward) reach number one on the billboard charts in 1992.

From NWA to the Geto Boys to Tupac Shakur to Snoop Doggy Dogg, young Black men committing acts of violence were readily available in a wide variety of entertainment formats. *Yo! MTV Raps* and other programs on MTV, BET, and VH1 offered white households depictions of Black rap stars flashing wads of money, hanging out with girls dressed in bikinis, driving souped-up cars, flashing handguns, and sometimes holding a blunt while brazenly gesticulating at the camera. While rap music was proportionally more popular among Blacks, its primary market audience was suburban whites. History shows that rap's shift from an insurgent street genre that sprung up during the upheaval of the Bronx's gang wars in the late Sixties, originally featuring happy party music such as its first great hit, the Sugar Hill Gang's 1978 "Rapper's Delight," to the mainstream with edgy lyrics celebrating street warfare, drugs, sexual exploitation, and money, points to the dispiriting conclusion: like the Seventies-era blaxploitation movies, the more the rap industry packaged Black rappers as violent criminals, the bigger their white audience grew. Rap's appeal to whites—at least the appeal of many of rap's most popular artists, excluding Run DMC, LL Cool J, Salt-N-Pepa, MC Lyte, and DJ Jazzy Jeff and the Fresh Prince—during the late Eighties and throughout Nineties rested in its recreation of an age-old image of blackness: a foreign, sexually charged, and criminal underworld against which norms of white society are defined. While rap music in the twenty-first century is largely made by Black artists for Black audiences, there was a time in the genre's infancy where record producers and the artists themselves capitalized on white stereotypes of Black people. McWhorter, who wrote *All About the Beats: Why Hip-Hop Can't Save Black America*, recognizes Grandmaster Flash's 1982 "The Message" with its chorus "It's like a jungle sometimes, it makes me wonder how I keep from going under," as the turning point where "rap took a dark turn." In the song, Melle Mel warns, "Don't push me, 'cause I'm close to the edge." To the dismay of Jeff Chang, author of *Can't Stop Won't Stop: A Political History of the Hip-Hop Generation*, who praises the hit song as a dig at the Reagan recession of the same year, McWhorter criticizes "The Message" for advancing the trope "that ghetto life is so hopeless" that "violence is both justified and imminent."[31] The next step in the transformation of rap music occurred when rap producers like Russell Simmons repackaged the genre away from "soft, unaggressive [and] the pop audience" represented by many Black mainstream artists of the mid–Eighties, namely Michael Jackson, Lionel Richie, Luther Vandross, and Freddie Jackson. "So the first chance I got," Simmons writes in his autobiography, "I did exactly the opposite."[32] Soon embedded in the music at this very early stage was a mix of hardened street hustler and the N-word. As stated earlier in these pages, rap music does not deserve sole blame for the use of the N-word in white or communities of color, but the contention that rap musicians and rap music have reduced its shock value in mainstream society as Jay-Z claimed on *The Oprah Winfrey Show* back in 2009, and as many do in our current era, is held by many as logical fallacy.

To examine the indictment of rap music levied by the likes of media mogul Winfrey and Neal Lester, one of the country's leading N-word gurus, one would benefit from an evaluation of the ironic, redemptive, and wounding usages of the N-word by some of the most popular rap artists of the Eighties and Nineties. Those two decades saw the propagation of the word's use through popular culture representations in music and film, namely *Boyz N the Hood* (1991), *New Jack City* (1991), *Juice* (1992), *Menace II Society* (1993), *Poetic Justice* (1993), *Above the Rim* (1994), *Crooklyn* (1994), and *Friday* (1995). Each film led up to the almost ten-month O.J.

Simpson trial in 1995, where media coverage wrote the N-word into its most taboo form (a topic discussed in detail in Chapter Ten). This way, readers have something to think about regarding some of the most consequential hip-hop artists who abetted in advancing the word's use in casual conversation.

In 1985, the first gangsta rap artist, Schoolly D, used the word repetitively in "P.S.K. (Park Side Killers) What Does It Mean?" A close reading of the lyrics shows that the N-word was used in no way other than to insult the song's antagonist: "A sucker-ass *nigga* trying to sound like me / Put my pistol up against his head / And said, 'You sucker-ass *nigga* I should shoot you dead' / A thought ran across my educated mind."

A Philadelphia native and Overbrook High School product on his way to Georgia Tech University for a fine-arts degree when he found rap to be a vehicle for creative expression, Schoolly D, born Jesse B. Weaver, Jr., developed a sinister character based on neighborhood gangs. His inspiration as a rapper was the "mean cats living their version of the black experience [that] no one in rap talked about.... Or lived it, for that matter," he said. And yet, his mother called him a "pretty nice guy ... a good student and serious artist, whose worst crime is that he doesn't like to do dishes." Schoolly D admitted in 1988 that he had a "pretty normal" upbringing in West Philadelphia. He created the gangsta rap identity because "half of America" was obsessed with cars, guns, drugs, and sex, which seemingly typified Black life. Without saying what he meant by *half of America*, he admitted that his artistic persona, which resembled a mix of George Clinton and Richard Pryor, was for a white audience who paid for the "packaged product."[33]

One of the most popular gangsta rap groups during this time was Houston-based Geto Boys. In 1990, the trio of Scarface, Willie D, and Bushwick Bill signed onto Def American Records, a Geffen Records–distributed label. But with the release of the group's second album, the self-titled *The Geto Boys*, that included a cover image resembling The Beatles' album *Let It Be* and compilation of crude songs, Geffen Records announced it would not serve as distributor of the new record. Geffen received criticism for the decision. After all, it was the same label that distributed comic Andrew Dice Clay's profanity-laced *The Day the Laughter Died* and the Guns N' Roses song "One in a Million," which contained epithets about Blacks and gay men.[34] Warner Bros. Records eventually released the album with a disclaimer on the cover announcing that its manufacturer and distributor "do not condone or endorse the content of this recording, which they find violent, sexist, racist and indecent." Naturally, the album sold like hotcakes within the first week of its release.[35] On its follow up album *We Can't Be Stopped* in 1991, the Geto

Boys released "Another Nigger in the Morgue," a song containing the lines "you'll just be another nigga in the morgue" and "That's 3 or 4 niggas left for dead." The single, along with the much acclaimed "Mind Playing Tricks on Me," helped the album go platinum.[36] It seemed the more unapologetic the group's lyrics became, the greater financial success it garnered.

The Geto Boys' gangsta message rap style was packaged for success at the turn of the decade. But when the group first debuted in 1988 as the Ghetto Boys (notice the alternate spelling) with original lyricists Ready Red, Johnny C, and Juke Box, the inaugural album *Making Trouble* contained lyrics self-described as "clean." *Making Trouble* was not a commercial success. As a result, Rap-A-Lot Records co-founders James Smith and Cliff Blodget suggested the group needed a hard-core edge. The label dropped Johnny C and Juke Box. The group's dancer, Bushwick Bill, was promoted to rapper; Willie D. and Scarface were added. Soon, Ready Red exited the group, which had now changed the spelling of its name to Geto Boys. The new trio bought into Rap-A-Lot's vision to present the group as deprived-ghetto-kids-turned-rappers from Houston's Fifth Ward. "Hard-core outsells [other styles] 10 to one," said Scarface, whose real name is Brad Jordan. Jordan once said his name Scarface was acquired on the streets because "I would have done anything to get mine no matter what it would take" in rough and tough South Village Park. However, Blodget explained later that his rap name comes from the Geto Boys' single "Grip It." Jordan wrote and rapped the song and fans began calling him Scarface, or Tony Montana, the movie character the song was based on. Jordan also was discovered to exaggerate his upbringing to play the role of poor ghetto kid. He once claimed, "[W]e had to boil water to bathe in." Many years later he said that his parents both worked white-collar jobs and admitted rap groups embellish their past for business purposes. "It's all about business," Jordan said in 1991. "They can scream … no sellout … and starve if they want to…. I'm down with the black movement, but to me it's a … waste because [black people] are going to do what they want to do."[37]

The year 1993 features some of the best rap music ever produced. Songs by Wu-Tang Clan ("Da Mystery of Chessboxin," "C.R.E.A.M.," "Protect Ya Neck"), Tupac Shakur ("I Get Around," "Hollar if Ya Hear Me," "Keep Ya Head Up"), OutKast ("Player's Ball"), A Tribe Called Quest ("Electric Relaxation," "Award Tour"), KRS One ("Sound of the Police," "Mad Crew"), Biggie Smalls ("Party & Bullshit"), Lords of the Underground ("Chief Rocka"), Snoop Doggy Dogg ("Who Am I [What's My Name]," "Murder Was the Case," "Gz & Hustlaz"), Digable Planets ("Where I'm From"), Queen Latifah ("U.N.I.T.Y."), Cypress Hill ("Insane in the Brain"), Onyx ("Slam"), and future Grammy-award winner Naughty

By Nature ("Hip Hop Hooray," "It's On") define a year considered by hip-hop historians as one of the greatest in rap's history. However, it was also in this year when one music journalist started to question whether the lyrical meaning of gangsta rap was much different from Nazi rock.

> When you see a Turk in a tram
> And he looks at you annoyingly
> Just stand up and give him a good punch
> And stab him seventeen times

This set of lyrics is from a 1993 song titled "Final Victory" by Endsieg, one of Germany's neo–Nazi rock bands. Endsieg's music was distributed through shadow right-wing organizations across Europe but rarely sold more than a few thousand copies each. In comparison, there are lyrics like these from Ice Cube: "So don't follow me up and down your market / Or your little chop suey ass will be the target / ... So pay respect to the black list / Or we'll burn your store right down to a crisp."

This song, "Black Korea," was a single released from *Death Certificate*, and was written after the 1992 Los Angeles uprising. More than 60 people died in the civil unrest that occurred that April and May. Forty thousand jobs were lost, 15,000 permanently, representing nearly 20 percent of South Central Los Angeles's workforce.[38] The song is as xenophobic as the aforementioned European neo–Nazi band, yet Ice Cube's music received approbation from critics as "street poetry." *The Predator,* Ice Cube's album released before *Death Certificate*, was the first rap album to ever debut at the top of Billboard's pop album charts, having sold 193,000 copies in the first week alone. Ironically, nearly 75 percent of all rap music sold in 1992 and 1993 was purchased by whites, most young suburbanites attracted by its anti-establishment posture. There was no secret that most record companies in the early Nineties that distributed gangsta rap were run by whites and produced by white men. Meanwhile, the harshest critics of Ice Cube's lyrics and gangsta rap, in general, were Black. *Village Voice* critic Stanley Crouch called gangsta rappers "spiritual cretins," "slime," and "vulgar street corner type clowns." *Boston Globe* columnist Derrick Z. Jackson said of Ice Cube, "Homicide is searing African Americans, and here you come with more assault rifles. With carnage like yours, who needs genocide?"[39] Pop Music columnist Leonard Pitts, Jr., said in 1993 that rap music turned right and wrong "inside out so that violence, bigotry, drugs and misogyny become enviable traits, and compassion is a weakness worthy of scorn and death."[40] Pitts's problem with gangsta rap wasn't that it simply reflected street violence—he conceded that Elvis, the Temptations, and Lou Rawls also reproduced it. But rather, "the gangstas endorse it. Only the gangstas make it romantic and seductive and cool."

Pitts's criticism of gangsta rap emerged at a time when there were signs that the music industry might eventually cold-shoulder artists who continued to use such vile language. As noted earlier, MCA and A&M Records refused to release some gangsta rap songs because of concerns over the content. Conscious rappers in 1993, like Arrested Development, challenged gangsta rap—albeit, while still using the N-word—by performing an Afrocentric and socially conscious subgenre of rap that sold four million copies in a single year, including the timeless first single off the album *3 Years, 5 Months, and 2 Days in the Life of ...* titled "Tennessee." The Rev. Jesse Jackson had spearheaded a campaign that flirted with a boycott of gangsta rap artists, and "anyone, white or black, who makes money calling our women bitches and our people niggers." In June 1993, the Rev. Calvin Butts of the Abyssinian Baptist Church in Harlem literally drove a steamroller over a collection of gangsta rap CDs and cassettes. Rather than call for government legislation that could control the genre's content, the Reverend Butts called for consciousness-raising.

> We're talking about trying to turn people's heads so they will realize how bad this stuff is. Most people fail to realize—particularly those of us who are insulted by this trash—that we, too, have freedom of speech. We, too, can say how we feel. We're not talking about censorship, but we can say to the record companies, "You say you are socially responsible, you say you are concerned about the nature of our society and what's happening to our children. *We* say, as long as you're doing this, you are hypocrites, you're lying, you're not telling the truth. You will do anything for money, even promoting bigotry, misogyny, homophobia, and violence. Most importantly, violence."[41]

Whether it be Revs. Jackson and Butts or Oprah Winfrey and Neal Lester, the contention is that rappers prey on and exploit the Black community, calling women names, referring to each other as the N-word, all for a dollar, "much like a drug dealer," said Butts.

Anyone would be hard-pressed to say that rap music of any era, but in particular, rap of the Eighties and Nineties, fell short of entertaining or failed to challenge its listeners. The music indeed enabled an older generation to see what young people were thinking. It also uplifted life experiences passed down in oral tradition and found in books by offering a window into seeing what life is like in urban America.

Despite rap music's explosive rage and controversy, the genre's popularity—much like minstrelsy had in the nineteenth century—eventually traversed the seas by the mid–Nineties. Accompanying rap music's popular beats and rhymes was also the ever-present N-word. As the word increased in acceptability, as often happens, it reared its head in Asia and Europe, where Black and non–Black people started to refer to one another as N-words in casual conversation. In January 1995, Paul George, a Black columnist at *The Guardian*, wrote a biting editorial in response to the word's frequency among the Black populace in England. He called the word an "ugly racial insult [that] carries all the aspects of the negative racial stereotypes constructed since the days of slavery." George did not blame rappers for making the word fashionable; rather, Black activists, or "radicals" from the Eighties, started using the word "in an attempt, they say, to reclaim it." It was then that gangsta rappers, like Snoop Dogg and Dr. Dre, whom George identified specifically, "who have flirted with the radicals [and] now use the word in their songs." According to George, the business model of "the more you shock the more you sell" yielded rap artists earnings not imagined a generation earlier. "So black American rappers happily 'trash' their 'own people' in order to shock and sell," he said.[42]

Soon after that, Clawfinger, an all-white rap-rock band from Sweden known for writing songs about racial conflict, class, and war, pleaded to Black people to stop using the N-word. In a single titled "Nigger," the band sang about how absurd and self-debasing it was for some Blacks to call one another a slur created by whites. The song's most striking feature is a chorus that includes redundant chants of the song's title. The lyrics include the stanza:

> Goddamn my man you see I can't understand
> Why you wanna say nigga to your brother man
> Talking black pride then you call yourself a nigga
> Don't bring yourself down 'cause it just don't figure

Not only was Clawfinger's plea largely ignored, but the band escaped criticism for performing the song. Described as an antiracist statement that attained massive success on radio stations in Sweden and Norway, the song failed to make waves in the United States.[43] Americans "misunderstood" the song, said the band's frontman Zak Tell: "I just started thinking about where the word was coming from. It was invented by slave traders. I'm telling people I can't quite understand why they would want to use such a word." Yet, Tell also conceded that it was naïve for four white musicians to raise the issue with loaded language. He explained, "When we wrote that song, we didn't even have a record contract. I realized afterwards that, 'Whoa, this is quite a lot of weight to carry.'"[44]

One rap artist of that era who did not care what anyone said about him or the rap industry was Tupac Shakur. Precisely because he offered a panoramic view of being young, black, and male in America, Tupac embodied the wildly conflicting meaning behind gangsta rap. His 25 years on earth was a case study in paradox: a poet and self-proclaimed thug; a champion of women and convicted sex felon; a chosen one with expectations to carry the mantle of the Black Panthers yet one who embraced the free market of entertainment capitalism; and an embodiment of racial uplift with an imperfect defense of the rap genre's defensive use of the N-word. He was born Lesane Parish Crooks; his mother was Afeni Shakur, one of the Panther 21, a branch of the Black Panther Party in New York, who was arrested and charged with more than 150 counts of conspiracy in 1969. A jury eventually acquitted Afeni in May 1971, a month before Tupac's birth. Afeni received help in raising Tupac from a gangster called Legs, who died from a crack-induced heart attack when Tupac was young. Mutulu Shakur and Elmer "Geronimo" Pratt, two high-ranking Black Panthers, also helped to raise Tupac. Afeni changed his name to Tupac Amaru Shakur at age one and eventually enrolled him in the Harlem theater group, the 127 Street Ensemble, when he was 12. One year later, he played Travis in a production of *A Raisin in the Sun* at the Apollo Theater. His family would eventually move to Baltimore. Tupac attended Roland Park Middle School and Paul Laurence Dunbar High School before he auditioned and was accepted to the Baltimore School for the Arts, where he studied acting, poetry, jazz, and ballet. At age 17, his family moved to Marin City, California, across the bay from Oakland. In those days, he listened to the Culture Club, Sinead O'Connor, The Cranberries, and U2 along with rap music.[45] He also enrolled in a poetry class taught by Leila Steinberg, who would become his first manager. Steinberg organized Tupac's first rap group, Strictly Dope, before getting him signed as a roadie and dancer with an alternative rap assemblage from Oakland called Digital Underground. In 1991, Tupac debuted on the single "Same Song," from Digital Underground's EP *This is an EP Release*. In the song, his only appearance on any Digital Underground track, Tupac expressed an attitude about fame: "Get some fame, people change, wanna live the life high / … I remain still the same, cause it's the same song."

Tupac's performance as an artist, of course, would not stay the same. Controversies—both by proxy and directly—changed his trajectory in hip-hop.

Later that year, Tupac broke through the rap industry when he released the debut solo album *2Pacalypes Now*. The record carried three career-boosting singles: "If My Homie Calls," "Trapped," and "Brenda's Got a Baby." Each hit song addressed individual struggles with inner-city life. And overall, the album is known as a paradoxically profane-laced yet conscious production full of messages about positivity and a window for outsiders to see into the world of Black youth. However, once a Texas attorney defending a client who had shot a state trooper rationalized the defendant's actions by claiming he had been listening to Tupac's music at the time of the altercation, controversy consumed the remainder of his life. Vice President Dan Quayle interjected an opinion in national discourse over the relationship between law enforcement and the Black community by implicating Tupac in any violence against the police. Quayle, who also attacked Ice-T's lyrics and challenged recording studios to blacklist artists "condoning cop killing" during his and President George H.W. Bush's failed re-election campaign in 1992, said an album like Tupac's "has no place in our society."[46] Though not what he intended—Tupac would say, "I didn't know that I was gonna tie myself down to just take all the blunts and hits for all the young black males, to be the media's kicking post for young black males"—the controversy helped sell half a million copies of *2Pacalypes Now* by the end of the year. The attention also made "Trapped" one of the most memorable songs of his decorated career. He would spend the remainder of his life—just five more years—immersed in media firestorms.

During the fall of 1991, Tupac sued the Oakland Police Department (OPD). That October, OPD officers had slammed him to the ground, beat him, and arrested him for jaywalking near the intersection of 17th and Broadway. Tupac brought a $10 million civil lawsuit against the OPD, which was eventually settled out of court for $42,000.[47]

He then completed filming the 1992 Hollywood crime thriller, *Juice*. Released with widespread acclaim, *Juice* told the story of four African American teenagers in New York who would rather attend late-night disc jockey competitions that high school. In the film, Tupac played Roland Bishop, a teen preoccupied with assuming power over his peers once he gets his hands on a pistol and robs a local convenience store. Many feel that Tupac never removed himself from the thuggish character. Others claim the role as Bishop actually sheds light on Tupac's authentic personality, as he was just 20 years old during the film's production, and the world was just getting to know him.[48] The lead in *Juice* was followed by similar roles as a troubled twenty-something in John Singleton's 1993 *Poetic Justice* opposite Janet Jackson and as drug-dealing Birdie in Jeffrey Pollack's 1994 film *Above the Rim*.[49] Tupac also starred in two posthumously released films *Gridlock'd* and *Gang Related*; both hit the big screen in 1997.

Although he established a budding film career in a short window of time, Tupac is remembered and celebrated for his music. His second album, *Strictly 4 My N.I.G.G.A.Z.*, was released in February 1993 at No. 24 on the Billboard 200 pop charts. By year's end, *Strictly* would sell over a million copies.[50] The album was a product of Tupac's two previous years in the spotlight, addressing the intersection of state violence and the bygone struggle for racial uplift. The album's first single, "Holler If Ya' Hear Me," released on February 4, uses samples from People's Choice's "Do It Any

Way You Wanna" and "Rebel Without a Pause" by Public Enemy, and became an anthem of resistance against poverty, police brutality, and the government. Featured on the album with Tupac are gangsta rappers Ice Cube and Ice-T, both of whom had recently released their own militant political albums. The trio collaborated on "Last Wordz," a song that fit a gangsta rap theme of the era—eff the cops and eff the white establishment, and to hell with Black lawmakers like C. Delores Tucker and political activist turned failed presidential candidate The Rev. Jesse Jackson, who had nothing positive to say about rap music. "Last Wordz" was an angry denunciation of how music critics treated Tupac in the media. He also used the long to condemn public figures, like Vice President Dan Quayle, who used his music as a scapegoat for society's problems that they failed to legislate. At the end of "Last Wordz," Tupac called for intergenerational unity: "One Nigga teach two Niggas, three teach four Niggas / And them Niggas teach more Niggas."

Strictly exposed the public to a different side of Tupac, who self-identified on the album as "Mr. Fuck-A-Cop." In his popular 2006 biography of the rapper, Michael Eric Dyson calls Tupac "a ghetto Dickens," one who, like characters in Charles Dickens' novels, represents hip-hop's best and worst times with haunting tales that examined poor and over-policed Black Americans.[51] He dramatically inspired young people with his revolutionary pavement poetry. Historian Kara Keeling describes him as a representative of "a hyper-commodified form of rebellion." Tupac was supposed to be representative of nostalgia for the Black Panther Party and of a new age Black revolutionary, but gave in, or sold out, to corporate movers and shakers who marketed Black delinquency to white fans who craved violent lyrics spoken in front of urban beats.[52]

Perhaps better than anyone before or after, he made several attempts to provide a hip and urbane new meaning to the N-word, just as the Black Panthers once did for black leather jackets, berets, and community programs. In "Words of Wisdom," a track on *2Pacalypes Now*, Tupac gives a monologue offering imagery about Black unity and triumph. "When I say niggas it is not the nigga we are grown to fear," he says. "It is not the nigga we say as if it has no meaning. But to me, it means Never Ignorant Getting Goals Accomplished." The song was the first of many that fused the political and personal with a Black nationalist lens. Like the poet Nikki Giovanni, who began her career as a member of the 1960s Black Arts Movement, Tupac's "Words of Wisdom" reflected the Generation X version of white-defying, self-reliant, Black pride rhetoric. Giovanni had composed a poem more than two decades earlier that Tupac drew inspiration from.

In January 1968, Giovanni wrote a complication poem replete with threatening rhetoric and violent images titled "The True Import of Present Dialogue, Black vs. Negro." The poem's first part is a call for Black people to kill "a honkie" and "the Man" by way of "drawing blood," "poison," stabbing, vehicular murder, and beheading. While taken as a call for bloodshed against white people of varying ethnic groups and religions, Giovanni, a founding member of Fisk University's Student Nonviolent Coordinating Committee at age 24, speaks figuratively about various forms of bloodshed emanating from white power, namely war and racial violence. The poem's final lines call for a psychological shedding of socially constructed identities that, in her view, plagued the Black community. She writes: "Can we learn to kill WHITE for BLACK / Learn to kill niggers [and] Learn to be Black men."[53] This poem was a bitter rebuke of racist white people and a call to conscience for Black people to resist colonized thinking.

> Can you kill your nigger mind
> And free your black hands to strangle

So much was happening in the lead-up to 1968: police and vigilante violence in Selma, the rebellions in Watts and Detroit, the shooting of James Meredith, the assassinations of Malcolm X and Medgar Evers. At the time of publication, the massacre at Orangeburg nor the assassination of Dr. Martin Luther King, Jr., had yet to occur. But when they did, Giovanni grew bitter with each event, going as far to say after King's murder, "What can I, a poor Black woman, do to destroy america [sic]? This is a question, with appropriate variations, being asked in every Black heart. There is one answer—I can kill. There is one compromise—I can protect those who kill. There is one cop-out—I can encourage others to kill. There are no other ways. The assassination of Martin Luther King is an act of war."[54] Those were incendiary words. Her unfiltered and unapologetic prose was akin to Tupac's lyrics in "Words of Wisdom."

Tupac's short-lived rap and movie career trumpeted Giovanni's poetry. Indeed, Tupac and Giovanni would each hold one another's work in high regard. Giovanni would eventually pay tribute to Tupac by inking "Thug Life" on her left arm after his September 1996 death, an homage to the rapper's tattoo across his abdomen (an acronym meaning "The Hate U Give Little Infants Fucks Everyone"). Returning to another acronym, Tupac included a second song on his *2Pacalypse Now* album titled "Violent." The song decries the trope that Black men are more fearsome and prone to violence. Tupac includes a passage that reinforces his novel meaning for the N-word: "'Cause I'm the nigga that you sell-outs are ashamed to be / ... I'm Never Ignorant, Getting Goals Accomplished."

Through the years, "Words of Wisdom" and "Violent" are now overshadowed by his Billboard 100 Hits, "How Do U Want It/California Love," "Dear Mama/Old School," "I Get Around," and "Keep Ya Head Up." Popular success notwithstanding, Tupac's effort at redefining the pejorative was an incredible leap from the word's original meaning. Giovanni appreciated his artistic expression of in-group love. Whether the public bought it is another story. Nonetheless, his effort was an attempt to use his art to transform the word to mean distinguished pride, Black pride, Black is beautiful. In 2017, during Tupac's posthumous induction into the Rock & Roll Hall of Fame, his collaborator at Death Row Records Snoop Dogg told a story that reflected the signifying meaning behind Tupac's acronym. Just before he died in 1996, Tupac had encouraged Snoop to get into acting. "He saw more potential in me than I saw in myself," Snoop explained. "And it's funny because after he passed away, I started to get a lot of movie roles. And I always felt 'Pac was looking out for his Nigga."[55] Several prominent rappers, including Ice-T in his single "Straight Up Nigga," reaffirm Tupac's argument about the word. Indeed, Ice-T writes in his book *The Ice Opinion*, "I wear that term like a badge of honor."[56]

Like Tupac, a large portion of Snoop Dogg's and Ice-T's record sales came from white America. Neither the trajectory of violence and violent language from Black rappers nor the volume of record sales from white patrons changed when many Black record executives like Sean "Puffy" Combs and Suge Knight took over recording studios in the mid–Nineties. White consumption of rap music has always been a form of voyeurism that produced record-breaking profits. The fantasies of street life captured what professor and philosopher George Yancy calls the "white gaze." In this context, crude sex lyrics and a distorted version of the Black experience captivated the white gaze. Speaking similarly about white listeners of rap in the early Nineties, historian Henry Louis Gates said, "What is potentially very dangerous about this is the feeling that by buying records [white people] have made some kind of valid social commitment" to racial justice.[57]

A more sustainable change in tone toward conscious, or political, rap occurred after the 9/11 terrorist attacks. The shift happened throughout all music genres when, after September 11, 2001, pop music artists weighed in with a series of tribute songs, benefit concerts, and charity albums. Country singer Alan Jackson, R&B singer Alicia Keys, and rock 'n' roller Neil Young all took part in patriotic recordings within the first eight months of that fateful day. However, as America's war in Afghanistan intensified in 2002 and as a war in Iraq seemed imminent, rap artists started to release songs that took a more contrarian stance on military action and praise heaped upon the New York Police Department. Among the scores of rap artists, the tune "My Country" by Queens-based rapper Nas, utilizing his marquee status, signaled a turn from gangsta rap to political hip-hop: "My country shitted on me / She wants to get rid of me." The September 11 terror attacks jump-started a new era of socially conscious agitprop rap. In his 2002 album *Stillmatic*, Nas attacked Jay-Z and Wu-Tang Clan, who seemingly bought into the jingoism of the political climate with raps about the World Trade Center and attacks on Osama Bin Laden, respectively. In addition to "My Country," Nas's "Rule" is a plea to the Bush Administration for global peace. "Stop acting like savages," he raps.

This is not to say an artist like Tupac was apolitical. Tupac had tracks on every album—even his posthumously released LPs—that took on serious issues: militarism, xenophobia, the treatment of women, police brutality, and poverty to name a few. Nevertheless, as scholar Kara Keeling points out, his music did not spark the revolution that many had hoped. His music, albeit among the best written and recorded, was more about ideology and attitude than action. Those that saw him as a new-age Black Panther who was going to use street poetry to spark the social revolution felt disillusioned when eloquently written songs in his body of work like "Keep Ya Head Up," "Dear Mama," and "To Live or Die in LA" were accompanied by "Wonda Why They Call U Bitch," "Hit 'Em Up," an erotic music video titled "How Do You Want It," and other misogynistic titles.

Tragically, Tupac died from wounds suffered in a drive-by shooting in September 1996 after just five years of producing music, starring on the big and small screens, and releasing poetry that has proven to age well in the decades since his death. His voice was missed after September 11. We can only project what he might have recorded in the weeks, months, and years following that tragic event. In his place, other rap artists offered a flood of political releases. Sage Francis's "Makeshift Patriot" is a fiery rebuke of blind patriotism, willful acceptance of the loss of personal freedom, and the media's role in galvanizing the public in support of the war in the aftermath of 9/11. Boston's Mr. Lif recorded a musing on President Bush's oil-driven war in "Home of the Brave." Hardly a critic can deny that every era of hip-hop is filled with messages of dissent, but during the George W. Bush administration, there was an apparent intolerance of war, the loss of free speech, and skepticism toward a government that was more willing to invest money into foreign wars than historically marginalized communities. "I understand these people died in the line of duty," said J-Live of the New York Police Department following the collapse of the World Trade Center Towers, "but that doesn't give them a pass to do whatever they want." In "Satisfied," he says, "Now it's all about NYPD caps and Pentagon bumper stickers, but yo, you still a nigga / It ain't right that those cops and firemen died / that shit is real tragic, … It won't make the brutality disappear, it won't pull equality from behind your ear."

At the time, conscious rappers were still on the fringes of hip-hop, albeit popular within rap circles.[58] It would take a few more years until the conscious rap style hit the mainstream. Kanye West became one of the leading artists. His 2005 "Diamonds from Sierra Leone" questioned the high cost of fashion of those involved in the African diamond trade. A year later, West's song and its message received a boost with the release of Leonardo DiCaprio's blockbuster *Blood Diamond*. Soon thereafter, Harvard University became one of a number of institutions in higher education to offer courses on various hip-hop topics. In February 2006, the Smithsonian introduced an initiative to research hip-hop and later launched an exhibition at the museum. The National Hip-Hop Political Convention, a bi-yearly conference that began in 2004, aimed to link hip-hop's roots with social conscious artists of the aughts. "I think hip-hop is innately political," said 2006 convention chair T.J. Crawford. "If I'm rapping about the ills I see in my community, how people are being treated halfway around the world or about regimes and policies I want to see changed, what do you do? Do you just keep talking about it? Or do you make all that talk a reality?"[59] At this time, the movement to bring conscious rap out of the periphery faced dime-a-dozen gangsta rappers. "In many ways," wrote *Boston Globe* columnist Michael Endelman, "hip-hop is its own worst enemy." New Orleans native rapper Juvenile collaborated with fellow New Orleanian Master P to raise money for victims of Hurricane Katrina. But his 2006 song "Get Ya Hustle On" suggested hurricane victims invest FEMA money into cocaine to turn a profit as drug dealers: "Ever since they tried to down a nigga on the eastbank / Everybody need a check from FEMA / So he can go and sco' him some co-ca-lina / Get money! And I ain't got ball in the Beemer."

Moreover, conscious rappers struggled to keep the attention of rap enthusiasts when rappers such as 50 Cent released Billboard Global 200 party-hearty hits such as "In da Club" (peaked at #1), "How We Do" (peaked at #3), "Magic Stick" with Lil' Kim (peaked at #1), "21 Questions" (peaked at #1), "Candy Shop" with Olivia (peaked at #1), "Hate It or Love It" with The Game (peaked at #1), and "P.I.M.P." (peaked at #3). The rebellious attitude, confident style, menacing beats, and synthesizer notes on display in songs like "Ni**as in Paris" by Jay-Z and Kanye West, two of history's most successful rappers, simply eclipse any argument made by neighborhood elders suggesting that a combination of ugly language and debilitating messages of Black life would be decried as racist if performed by artists of another color. The beat coating the lyrics is the decisive force behind the music's popularity.

Public intellectuals added to the skepticism about conscious rap in particular and rap music in general with the publication of varying viewpoints about the significance of hip-hop culture during the first decade of the current millennium. Existing as a call and response to the relevance of rap in American society, S. Craig Watkins's *Hip Hop Matters* duked it out with Jeff Chang's *Can't Stop Won't Stop*; while Imani Perry's *Prophets of the Hood* and Tricia Rose's *The Hip Hop Wars* explored the cultural issues underlying the polarizing claims about how rap represents Black American life. But it was John McWhorter's *All About the Beat* that drew fury from the aforementioned scholars for urging rap enthusiasts to see the genre simply as a violence-laced art form rather than a true reflection of Black society. Leaning heavily on data about crime, poverty, and education, McWhorter argued against the notion that rap offers Black Americans a blueprint for political activism. His point is not a complete resignation to rap's obsolescence. Instead, he challenges the genre's most loyal fans to ask themselves: despite some of rap's positive messages about Black uplift, does the music tell anyone how to launch a policy-reform revolution? And, do conscious rappers offer much more than a creative, even poetic way to say "Fuck you!" to the Man?

Conscious rap pressed on despite criticism coming from politicians, public intellectuals, and lawmakers. Lonnie Rashid Lynn, Jr., better known as Common, accepted an invitation to join Oprah Winfrey in an April 2007 town hall on the effects of hip-hop culture after radio personality Don Imus attacked the women's basketball players at Rutgers University. One of Common's earliest socially conscious songs that drew indignation from right-wing pundits was the George W. Bush–bashing "A Letter to the Law" (2007). A year later, he released "A Song for Assata" (2008), a nod to the convicted Black Panther political exile in Cuba.[60] The Obama and Trump administrations brought us three of the most decorated rappers in the history of the genre: J. Cole, Childish Gambino, and Kendrick Lamar. Lamar was awarded the Pulitzer Prize in 2017 for *DAMN*, an album that offers a portrait of modern African American life. The Pulitzer meant the genre had come a long way in terms of respect and social acceptance. Twenty-eight years earlier, in September of 1989, KRS-One organized a team of rap stars to collaborate on an effort to stem the tide of violent messaging in rap music. KRS-One called it the Stop the Violence Movement, a tribute to his friend and Boogie Down Productions group-mate DJ Scott La Rock, who had been shot and killed shortly after the release of their debut 1987 album *Criminally Minded*. Joining KRS-One on the initiative were MC Lyte, Kool Moe Dee, D–Nice, Doug E. Fresh, Heavy D, and Public Enemy. Together, they raised over $100,000 for the National Urban League. The artists also released a 12-inch single, "Self Destruction," and roused an explosion of positive-message rap records to counter the burgeoning gangsta rap sub-genre.[61] KRS-One shortly thereafter founded the Temple of Hip Hop, a ministry and school with the goal to promote positive hip-hop culture. The United Nations accepted the Temple of Hip Hop as a religion, since its mission called upon all hip-hop fans to create more socially-conscious songs.[62] In 2008, in preparation for the twentieth anniversary of the release of "Self Destruction," KRS-One revived the Stop the Violence Movement with two new songs: "Self Construction" and "Self Destruction 2009."

It would be interesting to see whether John McWhorter would revise the thesis of *It's All about the Beat* now that the country has borne witness to the presidencies of Barack Obama and Donald Trump and has arrived at the intersection of rap activist-art and the Black Lives Matter movement. Both presidential administrations were besieged with racial justice protests and new calls to consciousness following the police and vigilante killings of so many Black men and women throughout the 2010s. The Movement for Black Lives moved hip-hop artists, who would otherwise perform party songs, into producing socially conscious singles. Kendrick Lamar's 2015 "Alright" became the anthem of the Black Lives Matter Movement. Other conscious rap songs, including J-Cole's "Be Free" and Childish Gambino's "This is America," have kept the fire of protest burning. President Obama's embrace of hip-hop captivated many in the public. The 44th President of the United States publicly quoted Jay-Z. He offered yearly playlists to his followers on social media that included Nas, Chance the Rapper, and Mos Def. In 2011, he invited Common to the White House to read poetry. Big Sean, who at the invitation of the Obamas rapped alongside Ariana Grande during Easter weekend of 2014, is considered the first rapper to perform at the White House. At a 2016 concert celebrating the opening of the National Museum of African American History and Culture, Obama rapped along to Public Enemy's "Fight the Power." In 2018, Obama's successor, Donald Trump, hosted Kanye West in the Oval Office for a (bizarre) meeting that didn't have an agenda. Rap artists have always thought their music could function in the place of classroom teacher, speaking about cultural heritage, instilling racial pride, and bridging hegemonized neighborhoods across the United States. The accent placed on education and justice in contemporary rap is both inspiring and pedagogical. While revolutions are born in conversation, they are sustained in song.

And yet, there is still the pervasive use of the N-word in conscious rap which so many critics see as a cultural aberration to Black America.

It is also a word that appeals to white audiences that long for not just the compelling beats and deft rhymes, but also for the obscenity of hate, sexual bravado, and violence. Are those circumstances any different from the eras of minstrelsy and ragtime? The N-word, fundamentally, has always been a much-craved condiment for music in general. But for now, rap music is the provocative form of music that has a hold on nearly every community in America and beyond.

NINE

A Sensible Rule

A Case Study

To circle back to those cringe-worthy moments when white people say a derivation of the N-word while singing along to a rap song: it was not too long into the fall semester in 2017 when a group of sorority sisters from the University of New Hampshire (UNH) found themselves momentarily entrenched in a humiliating predicament for singing Kanye West's 2005 hit "Gold Digger." A social media uproar followed the discovery of a video showing white members of Alpha Phi sorority failing to censor their vocals when the song arrived at the N-word. The viral recording appeared on Snapchat and was later reposted on a student-operated injustice watchdog Facebook page "All Eyes on UNH."[1] As university officials announced they were launching an investigation into the sorority's behavior, a far bigger spotlight was cast on this episode when conservative *Daily Mail* opinion columnist Piers Morgan jumped into the fray, telling the world to "blame Kanye" and other hip-hop artists "for putting [the N-word] in their songs."[2]

Even before the event in question, Morgan acquired a reputation for speaking out publicly about the N-word. He has always been a reliable critic of the African American usage of the term. In 2013, he posted on Twitter: "The N-word is used 500,000 times a day on Twitter alone. Mostly by young black Americans. How does that help get rid of this hideous word?" Strangely enough, however, he also insisted in this same Twitter thread that whites who use the word ought to be imprisoned. But sometime between 2013 and the 2017 episode at UNH, Morgan had a change of heart. "I doubt any of [the sorority sisters] gave it a moment's thought when Kanye's song 'Gold Digger' began playing, and certainly not a racist thought," he wrote.[3] He no longer called to "jail" the white perpetrators. He was now on the side of allowing whites to say the word because it is used in the hip-hop industry.

To his credit, Morgan's point is persuasive: if the hip-hop industry has commercialized the term, effectively making it part of American popular culture and by default the cultures of numerous other global societies, then whites should have the right to sing along to Kanye West and others like him without self-censoring. The innocence of intent behind singing a song, according to Morgan and his supporters, is to simply do just that: sing a song. All of this suggests that white people rapping the N-word understand its vile history. But they don't because studies show that most white Americans have been conditioned to not think about it.[4] One such study conducted by Sesame Workplace in partnership with the NORC at the University of Chicago in 2019 shows that white parents and white educators still find color-evasive childrearing the best way to raise and educate white children. The report reveals that white parents and teachers fail at cultivating a healthy sense of identity in white children's psychosocial development. According to the study, just 10 percent of parents said they discuss racial identity "often" with their children, while 25 percent do so "sometimes." On the contrary, 34 percent "never" discuss racial identity with children, while 33 percent do so "rarely." The survey also shows that 53 percent of children are not aware that race and ethnicity impede or accelerate success. Meanwhile, the study indicates that teachers evade race discussions in the classroom as much as parents avoid speaking to their children about the topic. While 65 percent of the teachers surveyed feel prepared to teach about race, 61 percent believe race is an inappropriate classroom topic. At a rate of 72 percent, the teachers who participated in this survey also revealed that their schools either discourage or provide no guidance on discussing racial and ethnic identity in the classroom.[5]

Then there is the rare case when a white person tries rapping the N-word in front of a group of Black people. As the headliner of the three-day Hangout Music Festival in Gulf Shores, Alabama, hip-hop artist Kendrick Lamar called up to the stage a white woman to rap along to his song "M.A.A.D. City." Lamar stopped the woman, self-identifying as "Delaney," after she rapped the N-word repeatedly. The Pulitzer Prize–winning artist ended the song entirely. Many in the crowd stirred with rage over Delaney's decision to repeat the N-word without hesitation. Her bemused reaction to the abrupt halt to the concert was equally cringe-worthy. "Am I not cool enough for you? What's up, bro?" Delaney asked into the microphone. To which Lamar responded, "You gotta bleep one single word."[6] (More on this momentarily.)

Oddly enough, the Netflix original series *Dear White People* portrayed a similar incident a few months earlier. In season one, episode five, titled "Chapter V," African American student-activist Reggie Green, played by Marque Richardson, confronts his white friend, Addison, played by Canadian actor Nolan Funk, over the latter's unapologetic sing-along of a rap song that recurrently used the endearing version of the N-word.

"Man, don't say that," Reggie says, as the two dance shoulder to shoulder.

Addison replies, "What? You know I don't really use that word."

Reggie: "Yeah, man, I know, but I just really heard you say it, though." An African American female friend of Reggie's, Joelle Brooks, played by Ashley Blaine Featherson, interjects: "We all learned something today," as Joelle and Reggie go back to dancing, turning their backs to Addison and dismissing the matter in general. To them, the affair was over. Fragility kicked in for Addison nonetheless, who became so defensive that he couldn't let it go.

"Wait, so it's bad if I'm just repeating what's in the song?" Addison inquired without receiving a response. After a meditative gaze into the distance, he returns his eyes to Reggie and says, "But it's not like I'm a racist."

Joelle: "Never said you were a racist."

Reggie: "Just don't say 'Nigga.' Like, you didn't have to say it just then."

With the situation now turning tense, Addison retorts, "I guess it felt kind of weird to censor myself." Later he would ask, "What am I supposed to do? Hum?"

Reggie, who originally trusted his white friend not to say the word although they were both dancing and rapping along to the music, responded, "It felt kind of weird to hear you say it." Then, in a predictable hypothetical exchange, Reggie says, "I mean, how would you feel if I started rapping to songs that say 'honky' and 'cracker'?"

Chuckling, Addison says, "I wouldn't care at all."

"Exactly," says Reggie, "that's the difference. The fact that you don't care and I do." Though ambiguous at first, the jab contrasted with a color-evasive and color-conscious dichotomy; that those who are white need not be aware of the historic mistreatment of Black Americans and how any iteration of that word is centered in that history. The scene intentionally sends an introspective message because this particular topic is both deep and complicated. *For* the Piers Morgans of the world, it can be conveyed that Reggie overreacted; incidentally, the N-word was apparently in the song's title. Addison was "not some redneck," as he put it. However, *to* the Piers Morgans, the scene communicates two lessons. On one hand, Reggie made it clear to Addison that just because they were friends there would be no "Nigga dispensation." Another point is made about perspective and experience. The two collegians have lived different lives and, perhaps more importantly, were nurtured in separate households where racial values and racial history differed. Addison, who was more concerned about his own awkwardness about self-censoring than how Reggie would feel hearing him say the N-word, did not want to bear witness to Reggie's pain, nor was he encouraged to do so by his white friends at the party. A shoving match eventually erupted. When campus authorities arrived, a police officer confronts only Reggie: "Are you a student here? ... Son, I need to see your ID." The officer then pulls his revolver and points it at Reggie's head when Reggie indirectly calls him a "pig." This moment effectively makes the episode's ultimate point: Reggie is made helpless. He is the expendable one. The officer never uses the N-word, but his actions conveyed that expression.[7]

At the same time, Reggie's reaction to Addison's word-choice is a common example of becoming the victim of a racial microaggression, instances of intentional and unintentional racial abuses individuals endure at formal institutions like colleges, high schools, athletic locker rooms, and at social gatherings like weddings, picnics, and parties. In 1970, Harvard professor Chester Middlebrook Pierce gave language to the mental health problems experienced by African American students and other students of color at the university level. In this rubric, microaggression theory explains the deep psychological toll that verbal, nonverbal, and environmental expressions of prejudice have on non-dominant racial (and gender) groups. Likewise, clinical psychologist Monnica T. Williams has shown that African Americans have a 9.1 percent prevalence rate for post-traumatic stress disorder compared to 6.8 percent in whites.[8] The driving factor is race-based trauma experienced in the form of regularly occurring pokes and prods by way of racist jokes and overt racist behavior, both in which the N-word is central. Williams' research has linked race-based trauma to psychological distress, depression, anxiety, binge drinking, and eating disorders. One should add an aversion to predominantly white spaces.

While most studies like the one conducted by Williams concentrate on how racial invalidations and insults impact victims' mental health, attention must also be paid to white aggressors who are more likely to commit racial abuses. A team of psychologists from the American Psychological Foundation issued a report in 2017 that explored the rate at which white students from large universities in the South and Midwest self-reported their engagement in racially abusive acts. The report found white collegians who described themselves as possessing a racially colorblind worldview were "more likely to microaggress." Those same white students who claimed colorblindness admitted to holding "less favorable" and "less positive" attitudes toward people of color. The study measured white participants' attitudes toward racial and ethnic minorities ranging from zero degrees (extremely unfavorable) to 100 degrees (extremely favorable). Low scores on the race thermometer indicated explicit prejudice. With the lowest of scores, the most offensive comments white respondents admitted to saying were: "You seem more intelligent than I would have thought," "I have other black friends," "White privilege doesn't really exist," "A lot of minorities are too sensitive," "All lives matter, not just black lives," and "Racism may have been a problem in the past, but it is not an important problem today." The study further suggests that white students who deliver racist invectives are more likely to possess "negative racial attitudes and explicit underlying hostility" toward people of color. Overall, this team of psychologists believes it is possible to measure self-reported racial abuse scientifically. The report verifies claims that explicit and implicit racist acts are "related to prejudice" and "situated within the science of racism."[9]

Despite growing empirical data on the matter, there are many critics today who see the work on microaggressions as nothing more than the perpetuation of victimhood culture. In 2017, psychology professor Scott O. Lilienfeld called for a moratorium on microaggression studies until further research could be conducted to address the key domains of psychological science, including psychometrics, social cognition, cognitive-behavior therapy, behavior genetics, and personality, health, and industrial-organizational psychology.[10] But what if understanding can be shifted to see the cultural reaction that is at play? Since most people witness "black discourse from the outside," John McWhorter says, it becomes easy to "see the enshrinement of victimhood as the standard modus operandi."[11] For instance, readers may recall the story of Black model, Broderick Hunter, who expressed resentment toward a white woman who posted a TikTok video in April 2020 using a song with the N-word in it to fixate on his body. The four-second TikTok video shows the woman fawning over a shirtless photo of Hunter while female hip-hop artist Saweetie raps the line, "Rich nigga / Eight-figure / That's my type" from her song "My Type." Insulted by the post, Hunter responded with an unamused Twitter thread:

> "Wait—I'm sorry..[sic] rich what?"[12]
> "Idk what you YT girls take me for..[sic] but that ain't it."
> "Could've used Backstreet Boys, Blink 182, N'Sync, Pink, Avril..[*sic*]"

Some on social media came to the woman's defense, pushing aside the original intent to objectify Hunter by claiming she should be acquitted of racist behavior because she never actually said the N-word. The post illustrated two items. For one, since the post showed a white woman reducing Hunter to a half-naked Black man, and because the N-word is narrated overtop, it possessed inferences of white supremacist exploitation and control over the Black body that has occurred systemically in America for centuries. The second is that Hunter's interpretation of the post is the only one that should matter since he was the subject of the TikTok video. When Hunter responded to people on Twitter, he explained that context— her compliment of Hunter's appearance—and the fact that she didn't say the N-word made no difference. He tweeted: "'She didn't say it[?]' If that's the case. Go pull up one of Donald Trumps [sic] MAGA speeches and play it on a loudspeaker in a predominantly Black or colored neighborhood. See if you get your ass beat. While they're stomping you out. Just say 'I didn't say it' to see if that helps."[13]

If this incident demonstrates anything about microaggressions, it is not simply an occasion where the racial slur was centered but the chronic history of enduring one form of racial abuse after another. We should no longer frame Hunter's reaction to the TikTok post in terms of impulse behavior or *claiming to be the victim*. It is too ingenuous a contention of becoming an aggrieved party. It doesn't capture all or most racialized pain. The manner in which a microaggressed individual responds to a racial abuse means that, while some maintain decorum, many don't. Those who are sensitive to racial invalidations and insults respond in ways that maintain self-respect, unable to ignore slights for the sake of defending the honor of all Black people.[14] Therefore, when Reggie confronts his white friend who just verbalized the N-word, or when white battle rapper William Wolf was punched by his Black opponent, or when Black students at the University of New Hampshire become offended by a group of white sorority sisters singing the epithet, or when Broderick Hunter speaks out against the nature in which he was racially objectified, it is because there is no other effective preventative measure to halt those racial abuses.

To return to an earlier story, if any of the aforementioned examples prove a powerful illustration of the slur's full impact on African American people, the case of Kendrick Lamar at the 2018 Alabama Hangout Festival left a mystifying mark. Even among African American fans of hip-hop, the decision to bring the young white woman Delaney on stage to rap along to a song that uses the N-word 16 times looked like a set-up. Ruse or not, media outlets called for all rap artists to retire the N-word immediately following the incident. Several months later in the midst of another N-word firestorm, comedian Trevor Noah offered another alternative. While appearing on *The Breakfast Club*, a radio show hosted by Charlamagne tha God and Angela Yee, Noah suggested rappers make "non–Black people versions" of rap songs that either omit or substitute the N-word. "Everyone knows how to [censor themselves]," Noah said, "So, I don't get why people make it like it's [difficult]."[15]

One rap artist who actually tried Noah's suggestion was Fatimah Warner, known by her rap name Noname, though the effort was short-lived and futile since her white fans still sang the word at concerts. During a performance at the Pitchfork Festival at Chicago's Union Park in 2018, Noname rapped a censored version of a song that included the N-word. "I wrote this part so that you white people would have something to do, since y'all can't ever say that word," she told the crowd. But one year later, Noname informed the public that she was putting her career on hold over frustrations that not enough Blacks supported her music, which often left her to perform in front of majority-white audiences. She posted on Twitter: "When I go to work, thousands of white people scream the word nigga at me. and [sic] no I'm not changing my art so it is what it is."[16]

The reality is that there are still enough stories of whites engaging in racist tropes conjured up by the N-word. One example of contempt for African Americans as inferior beings occurred on April 16, 2020, when two Georgia teenagers posted a TikTok video showing them using the racial slur and mocking Black people with common stereotypes. The video presents two high school students, one male, one female, standing in front of a mirror offering viewers a recipe for how to bake a Black person. "Today," the girl begins, "we are making...." The boy interjects, "Niggers." The camera pans down at the sink where there is a piece of paper with the N-word on it. They then read from additional scraps of paper: "First, we have 'Black,'" the girl narrates as a cup of water representing an ingredient is poured over the paper. "Next we have, 'Don't have a dad.'" Written on other pieces of paper are: "Eat fried chicken and watermelon," "Rob people," and "Go to jail." One paper ironically states, "Make good choices," but the cup was empty and thus couldn't be used as an ingredient.[17] All so often, racist performances are set in a joking format, and they convey intimations about the value of White lives and, in contrast, the reduction of Black lives. It is the race scholar Joe Feagin who helps make sense of this type of racist performance: "We observe that the white racial frame prizes whiteness.... Racially framed notions and emotions that [purveyors of racist acts] have probably learned from their peers and previous generations have become the basis for extensive racist performances." Central to these contemptuous behaviors are selective stereotypes that bond 300 years of institutionalized white supremacy to the white-created epithet. From such stories, it becomes apparent that racist jokes are about much more than making others laugh. Feagin says, they intend to register "deep emotions, visual images, and the accented sounds of spoken language ... that included racial hatred, racial arrogance, and a sense of racial superiority."[18]

In a critique akin to Feagin's philosophical outlook on the White Racial Frame, Elizabeth Pryor says the utterance of the N-word during any racist action exposes the offenders as possessing anxieties about a decline to their privileged and normative rank. The high school these students attended is gradually diversifying. Of the school's 1,630 students, 47 percent are white, 29 percent are Black, and 17 percent are Latinx. Black ambition followed by achievement—an actual fracture to white domination—is the primary factor driving whites to engage the type of racist behavior displayed by those two Georgia teens who performed a racist cooking show.

As seen in this example, nothing in particular ignited the students' racist behavior. It was meant to be a joke with like-minded whites as the intended audience. Actions such as these matriculate due to exposure to racial scripts disseminated by social environs, begging the question, what destructive conduct and views are permitted to subsist? There are other instances where verbal altercations trigger N-word usage from the depths of one's hidden bias. Take, for instance, the case of a high school basketball announcer in Norman, Oklahoma, who called kneeling teenage girls the racial slur. In March 2021 during a live-stream, a hot mic twice caught 44-year-old Matt Rowan saying the N-word after growing upset that every player on Norman High School's women's basketball team took a knee during the playing of the national anthem. "They're kneeling? Fucking Niggers.... They're going to kneel like that? Hell, no.... Fucking Niggers."[19] Recurring stories such as these gives credence as to why the majority of the population feels that whites cannot repeat such language even in hip-hop songs. In such cases, there is no conflating the difference between wielding the slur versus referring to the word with either of these stories.

People like Piers Morgan contend that Black Americans should excuse white Americans for saying the word because it exists in rap music. His discounting of structural forces and his exclusive focus on one-sided responsibility ignore the persistence of entrenched racism. Michael Eric Dyson says it is "reasonable" to say that those younger whites who sing along to their favorite rap tunes "are ignorant of the history of violence against black folk that *nigger* suggests."[20] And while it is also possible that hip-hop artists are "poor historians too," the motivations are different. Eminem and about 20 other professional white rappers aside, rap songs today are usually made by Black artists and filled with content about the Black experience. Dyson asks, why is it so easy for the same people who insist they should be able to say the N-word refrain using the B-word around their mother? At some moment in life, people learn not to use the B-word in certain settings. Alas, Morgan suggests those at a party full of white people blasting hip-hop music as entertainment should be pardoned. Dyson would call Morgan's standard "hypocrisy." Though recognizably an unconscious wrongdoing without any malicious intent, he says, "It grows out of a culture that reflexively identifies that particular word with some heinous acts in history."[21] By way of illustration, take the case of Tiger Woods. As a freshman at Stanford University in 1995, Woods told the media he had already received letters calling him the N-word. This is the same Tiger Woods who, on his first day of kindergarten, a group of sixth graders tied him to a tree, spray-painted the N-word across his body, and threw rocks at him.[22] Stories like this should make plain that when Blacks hear whites say the word, it signals a reclusive reminder about personal and shared attacks on Black value, Black humanity, and Black American citizenship. Since such injuries are not visible, whites regularly take no notice of existing trauma.

Using the word hurts Black people, even if done unintentionally, because it evokes deep pain and reminders that white people still benefit from Black suffering, such as a lack of inheritable wealth, historic residential segregation, and even COVID-19 protections. While not agreeing entirely with Dyson's attitude on the topic, John McWhorter might find some common ground here. McWhorter would likely argue that those Alpha Phi sorority sisters at UNH had every right to say the N-word as long as intentions weren't to make Blacks out to be inferior. However, good sense practice, he believes, would apply to this particular example. "It isn't rocket science to understand that words can have more than one meaning, and a sensible rule is that blacks can use the word but whites can't," McWhorter says.[23]

In his 2011 book *Decoded*, Jay-Z calls criticism of rappers using the N-word "white noise," a distraction from systemic issues impacting Black people in America. The examples shared in the two chapters that follow give readers a lot to think about regarding Jay-Z's claim. Why is the discussion over whether rap music invites whites to say the word while also damaging the Black community a germane debate? Perhaps a look at how the word matriculates in other aspects of American society in the final chapters can help make sense of the dispute.

TEN

Inviting Destruction
Beyond the Music

There is an obvious reason why rap artists of any style in the Nineties felt unconcerned about dominant social conventions regarding the industry's profiting from the racial slur. The history of America notwithstanding, that decade alone was peppered with jarring episodes of anti–Black hate crimes wherein the antagonists uttered the N-word. Some of the most disturbing events occurred near the end of the decade. In 1997, four white police officers in New York brutalized Abner Louima, a man of Haitian descent. After Louima's hands were tied behind his back, the officers penetrated his rectum with the wooden handle of a toilet plunger while barking, "Take this, Nigger." They then shoved the stick into his mouth. That same year in Virginia, Garnett Paul Johnson, an ex-Marine, was doused with fuel, burned alive, and then beheaded. A year later, members of a white supremacist prison gang in Jasper, Texas, beat, chained to the back of a pick-up truck, and dragged 49-year-old James Byrd along a dirt road for two miles. A motorist later found Byrd's detached head and arm along the side of the road. These modern lynchings—though not as ritualistic as they once were—serve as signposts for a theme found throughout much of American history: that racist whites have used semantics to reduce Black people to bestial beings worthy of verbal abuse and physical torture. Implications of this theme were also made apparent in the O.J. Simpson murder trial, which placed the N-word into its most pernicious, sadistic, and taboo construct.

By the end of Simpson's murder trial, only one man would be charged with a crime. The court convicted Los Angeles Police Detective Mark Fuhrman of perjury, forced him to pay a $200 fine, and sentenced him to three years on probation. What was his crime? Fuhrman lied during sworn testimony claiming he had not said the N-word since 1985. His equivocation was a contention aimed at removing racial animus during his investigation of the murders of Simpson's ex-wife Nicole Simpson and her friend Ronald Goldman. But during the trial, audiotaped interviews between the detective and Laura Hart McKinny, a screenwriter working on a film about police, revealed Fuhrman's flippant use of the racial slur, as well as wildly sexist assertions and revelations of police brutality and evidence-planting within the LAPD. What did Fuhrman's racism have to do with whether Simpson was guilty of double homicide? McKinny's 13 hours of recordings opened an ugly underbelly of law enforcement, and a racist detective representing the LAPD became the central theme of the murder trial thanks to Simpson's dream team of attorneys led by Johnnie L. Cochran, Jr. One of the state of California's attorneys, African American prosecutor Christopher Darden, knew how deeply this word would impact that trial. "It will upset the black jurors," he told Judge Lance Ito during a preliminary hearing before the jury was selected. "It will issue a test: 'Whose side are you on, the side of the white prosecutors and the white policemen, or are you on the side of the black defendant and his black lawyer? ... Are you with the man, or are you with the brother?'" The detective's leisurely use of the N-word was so ugly and so frequent that, just as Darden predicted, it captured everyone's attention, implied racial animus, and carried implications that Fuhrman would intentionally plant evidence to frame Simpson. Cochran capitalized on Fuhrman's racist language and the LAPD's insidious history of racism, arguing that the racist attitudes captured on McKinny's recordings compromised the murder investigation. Simpson's lawyers turned the trial away from the ex-NFL star's guilt or innocence and toward the LAPD's chief investigator's racist pedigree. The media couldn't get enough of the story, especially after the defense team disclosed the audiotapes to the public.

"We got females ... and dumb niggers [in the department], and all your Mexicans that can't even write the name of the car they drive."

"Cmdr. Hickman ... should be shot.... He wanted to be chief. So he wants the City council and the police commissioner and all these niggers in LA city government—and all of 'em should be lined up against a wall and fucking shot."

"When I came on the job, all my training officers were big guys and knowledgeable. Some nigger'd get in their face, they just spin 'em around, choke 'em out until they dropped."

"I used to go to work and practice movements. Niggers. They're easy. And I used to practice my kicks...."

"Westwood is gone. The niggers have discovered it. When they start moving into Redondo and Torrance—that's considered—Torrance is considered the last middle-class white society. When that falls...."

"It's pretty clear-cut who the assholes are. You go to Pacoima, you got bikers and niggers."

"Niggers drivin' a Porsche that doesn't look like he's got a $300 suit on, you always stop him."

"How do you intellectualize when you punch the hell out of a nigger? He either deserves it or he doesn't."

"…anything out of a nigger's mouth for the first five or six sentences is a fucking lie. That is just right out. There has got to be a reason why he is going to tell you the truth."

"The only good nigger is a dead nigger."

"They don't do anything. They don't go out there and initiate a contact with some 6-foot-5 nigger that's been in prison for seven years pumping weights."

"We have no niggers where I grew up."

These are just some of Fuhrman's statements, pulled from the McKinny audio recordings, in which he said the epithet a total of 41 times. They show why the trial caused a "racequake," as Michael Eric Dyson once illustrated. Each opinion column, headline report, and evening news feature about Fuhrman augmented the N-word's bite. This collateral issue conjured vile images of enslavement, family separation, lynching, blackface minstrelsy, white robes, burnt crosses, and rape. The subtext had everything to do with a historically unjust justice system that time and again acquitted guilty whites for crimes where visual evidence existed; and vice versa, times when juries found innocent Black defendants guilty of crimes they didn't commit. Cochran skillfully rendered these sadistic and heartbreaking visions to the public, the Black public in particular. The Fuhrman interviews made this strategy easier to execute. It was no secret that Cochran's vivid portrayal of America's enduring racism aimed to win over persons of color on the jury and in the court of public opinion. While agitating white Americans, the strategy also drove a wedge through already frail and vulnerable race relations. *Chicago Tribune* associate managing editor, Reginald F. Davis, said the trial only confirmed what most Black Americans suspected: "A white male cop using racial slurs like verbs and nouns is no surprise.… Sadder still, many believe there is no white who is not racist." To them, Davis claims, Fuhrman is not the exception, "He is the rule." Moreover, media coverage of Fuhrman was enough to categorize the slur as the English language's most taboo word. The N-word materialized as the spark to enrage repressed emotions about racism. And those feelings exist into our present time.

The Simpson trial successively produced the euphemism "N-word." As the public transitioned from the slur to its coded alternative, the unspeakable disposition of those two syllables became even more precarious in the public conscience. This explicitly evasive maneuver semantically stigmatized the word all the more. White Americans, in particular, lost any leverage to say it. With generations growing up and hoping to keep the word in the closet of racist whites while concurrently making it "Blacks-only" in the mainstream after 1995, the N-word has catapulted beyond the proscribed reach of the B-word as it relates to women, smears directed at Jews, Muslims, Irish, Italians, Asians, Mexicans, and the Q and F words associated with the LGTBQIA+ community. The N-word now sits atop the pantheon of English's worst words thanks to Cochran, Fuhrman, Simpson, and the media. This explains why, at present, those who are wounded by its verbal articulation spring into World War III. In other cases, it makes clear why employers are pressured to issue suspensions or terminations to violators of this cultural standard.

This reckoning aside, in the postmodern era, Richard Pryor, Paul Mooney, and Muhammad Ali aided in making the word tolerable by African Americans in front of mixed company. All things considered, they were warm-up acts for the coming of rap in the Eighties, gangsta rap in the Nineties, and conscious rap of the 2000s and 2010s. Occurring concurrently, then, was the O.J. Simpson trial, which, with the help of the media's explicit decision to play along with Johnnie Cochran's stigmatization of the white use and mention of the word into its most pernicious form, ultimately cemented the slur's euphemism, thus awarding the word a degree of agency that has only become more dangerous over time. Consequently, that word uttered by whites in any context has thereafter felt like a cudgel, whether quoting from a text like *Uncle Tom's Cabin* or uttered by an evening news reporter reading from a teleprompter.

I am familiar with the famous Lenny Bruce and George Carlin comedy routines "Are there any Niggers here tonight?" and "They are only words," respectively. Both bits, coming about 25 years apart, share the opinion that the more power people give America's slurs, namely the N-word, the more dangerously taboo they become; that terms like the N-word are social constructs aiming to levy trauma at the intended target. But, if only the word were not censored, its viciousness might be suppressed. It was brave of Bruce and Carlin, two white men, to verbalize every derogatory word in the English language. Carlin, in particular, was equally as courageous to assert that slurs are "only neutral [words]" and "there is absolutely nothing wrong with any of those words in and of themselves," that "it is [about] the user," and that "it is the context that makes them good or bad." Carlin received enthusiastic applause from his white audience. I must say that I wonder how this routine would have held up in front of a Black crowd. I choose to call into question a Black audience instead of, say, a Latinx or LGBTQIA+ crowd because Carlin used the N-word more liberally in the skit. How would a predominantly African American audience respond when Carlin joked, "We don't care when Richard Pryor or Eddie Murphy say it. Why? Because we know they aren't racists [laughter and pause for effect]. They're Niggers!"

Likewise, historians and critics have lauded Bruce for his now-legendary routine on the racial slur. In the early 1960s, as the civil rights movement reached its zenith, Bruce used his comedy to suggest that everyone would become numb to the N-word if it became a norm in casual conversation. If President Kennedy went on television and introduced his Black staffers and cabinet members as N-words, Bruce said, the word would lose its meaning: "You'd never make any six-year-old black kid cry when he came home from school after someone called him" the slur. Bruce's bit roused Richard Pryor, Paul Mooney, and other Black comics to engage in shock-value comedy, where the N-word's unapologetic use became a signature feature of their routines. The thing is, people took heed of Bruce's advice—in music, on television, in casual conversation—but 60 years later, we find ourselves in a more perilous climate of fear surrounding the word. Bruce's hypothesis that public use of the word would usher in a new progressive step forward in race relations has been disproven.

Although Bruce and Carlin may have been right that a derogatory word is *only a word*, I am not speaking of those moments when the slur is scratched into a restroom stall or spray-painted on a Black church. The argument that if people proactively seek to demystify the slur would lead to fewer incidents of racialized trauma has been proven wrong time and again over the decades. To give this advice would lead people into troubled water.

To return to a point made at the end of Chapter Two, communities of color recognize that many white people possess a strong anti–Black bias. Several national polls have revealed that subconscious biases are not limited to explicit racists. In an Associated Press survey, even the most progressive-minded white individuals who took an implicit association test possessed unconscious negative feelings about Black people. The belief that prejudiced racial views are buried in a person's subconscious has support from the Pew Research Center. In August 2015, Pew's researchers facilitated an implicit association test designed to measure hidden bias by tracking how quickly individuals associate good and bad words with specific racial groups. The study of 670 single-race whites, 370 single-race Blacks, 603 white and Black biracial adults, and 404 single-race Asians and 470 biracial white and Asian adults found almost 75 percent of respondents in all five racial groups exhibited implicit racial bias by measuring differences in how quickly participants were able to correctly categorize positive and negative words or the images of Black and white or white and Asian men. In other words, due to a lifetime of disproportionate indoctrination by media representation and peer groups, public perceptions and attitudes toward African Americans, males in particular, not only foster barriers to advancement in American society, but also result in instances where verbal and physical assaults devalue Black lives. It is reasonable, then, to see that African American individuals coming from race-conscious households experience a heightened sense of frustration when listening to a white person say the N-word, even in the most innocuous case. It is, therefore, wise to forgo the argument to say the word out loud. Under present circumstances, keeping the word in texts while choosing not to speak the word is the best of the plausible options.

In a survey of educators conducted by the research firm the Equity Institute for Race Conscious Pedagogy in the fall of 2020, during a period when the public was still attentive to the racial awakening that followed the death of George Floyd and the Black Lives Matter protests of the previous summer, 81.3 percent of respondents said there is never an appropriate time for whites to say or mention any version of the N-word. When broken down by race and ethnicity, just 11 percent of Blacks, 25 percent of Hispanic, and 28.5 percent of those identifying as mixed-race felt whites could say the word in certain circumstances without indictments of racial insensitivity. Those participants only granted passes to those who read aloud a book after looking at the word in historical context, an actor reading a script, and when reporting the news. As we will see later in this chapter, even those heeding this advice found themselves in peril. Just under a quarter of white (20.7 percent) participants feel it is proper for whites to say the word in particular contextual situations. "[N]ot even in the name of literature!!" one respondent said. Another participant added a fascinating insight: "There is so much trauma in the N-word particularly coming from a White person, and in the era of President Donald J. Trump it's not appropriate. There are other ways to make the connection and explain the meaning behind the N-word." Like the commentary about the intensification of the N-word's impact on the receiver following the O.J. Simpson trial, this respondent hints at another turning point in the word's evolution: the Trump presidency. Donald J. Trump's four years in office were marked by deepened racial tensions and are largely responsible for the Salem Witch Trial–like unapologetic degree of word-policing on this issue. Indeed, as a result of his public statements on many high-profile events, Trump is culpable in widening distrust across white and all communities of color. His administration is bookended by the Muslim ban and the death of George Floyd, when, as protests wore on, Trump's public condemnation of the Black Lives Matter movement was followed by an executive order banning race and sex sensitivity training in federal jobs and a subsequent attack on Nikole Hannah-Jones and *The New York Times'* curriculum reframing American history titled "The 1619 Project." His administration's attack on the theoretical framework known as Critical Race Theory also undercut the longstanding work performed by diversity, equity, and inclusion officers and national organizations like the National Association for the Advancement of Colored People and the National Urban League, along with public intellectuals working to close existing gaps between whites and communities of color in education and the criminal justice system.

In 2019, the Pew Research Center showed that 56 percent of U.S. adults said Trump made race relations worse during his first three years in the Oval Office. The same study showed 65 percent of adults said it had become more common for people to express racist views. Black, Latinx, Indigenous, and Asian groups had reason to grow more impatient over racial progress as Trump failed to distance himself from white nationalist groups and when his administration used "Kung Flu" or "Chinese virus" to refer to the COVID-19 pandemic. In February 2021, the Asian American Bar Association of New York released a report showing more than 2,500 anti–Asian hate crime incidents within the first six months of pandemic-related stay-at-home orders. Yet conservative pundits portrayed Black Lives Matter activists as terrorists while remaining silent about the violent acts of pro-Trump activists. Examples include Trump-supporters who ransacked the Michigan capitol building in the fall of 2020 in an attempt to kidnap Governor Gretchen Whitmer in protest of COVID-related lockdown orders, others who drove a Biden campaign bus off the highway on Interstate 35 near San Marcos, Texas, a few days before election-day in 2020, and those who stormed the U.S. Capitol on January 6, 2021, in an attempt to kidnap the Vice President of the United States and several Congressional persons in order to subvert the results of the election. Taken together, the actions of the Trump Administration served to motivate antiracist activists to police N-word usage vindictively on college campuses, the corporate world, and in society-at-large.

The Equity Institute study mentioned above also reiterates many of the arguments presented by leading progressively-minded antiracist voices included throughout this book. As it pertains to the field of education, survey participants leaned heavily toward holding the position that classroom instructors should suffer some form of punishment even if reading the N-word from a class text. At a 65 percent to 35 percent rate, the study shows educators should refrain from reciting the slur when reading a book like *The Adventures of Huckleberry Finn*. A sizable share (67 percent) believe educators should not say the N-word if part of a class discussion on race and racism. The same survey looks at the question of a racial double standard. Participants overwhelmingly believe at a rate of 93 percent that whites cannot say any version of the N-word despite the fact that Blacks can. While many musicians are writing and performing socially conscious music, what John Lennon once called "philosorock," 92 percent believe that white artists cannot sing or rap the N-word for shock-value. Bringing this data down to nuts and bolts, the public feels that the person saying the word shows their unconscious and explicit biases. This is the reason why language-policing has become unforgiving.

Now, John McWhorter would call hypersensitivity to hearing a literature teacher say the N-word an act of "virtue signaling." While promoting his book that attacks progressive intellectuals whom he calls "The Elect," in the winter of 2021, McWhorter posited that an individual aggrieved by hearing the N-word spoken by a well-meaning individual "is seeking the cloak of victimhood because it gives them a sense of significance, a sense of group membership" to an ever-growing antiracist movement in academia and beyond. In one sense, McWhorter makes a strong point about pretense. He suggests that many of the individuals who would be the ones to submit a bias-incident report and call for the termination of the instructor would paradoxically go home and listen to rap music that repeats the N-word over and over again.

There are contingents representing every race who see no difference between the word's two variations. And it takes dialogue to move beyond the weeds. This survey's feedback illustrates a long drawn out "ambush," as Michael Eric Dyson says, of the N-word by Black people. Dyson and many of his contemporary progressives counter McWhorter's position as a matter of the word taking on the opposite meaning, also known as semantic inversion. To Dyson, the word's version meaning kinship can only be executed by the very people the word has traumatized for centuries. In his body of scholarship, Dyson invests ample time distinguishing between the two variations of the word. "Nigger is the white man's invention," he writes in *Tears We Cannot Stop*. "Nigga is the black man's response…. Nigger taps into how darkness is linked to hate. Nigga reflects self-love and a chosen identity. Nigga does far more than challenge the white imagination. Nigga also captures class and spatial tensions in black America. Nigga is grounded in the ghetto; it frowns on bourgeois ideals and spits in the face of respectability politics." Evoking the words of David Walker (Chapter One), Dyson, and his colleague in academia, Elizabeth Pryor, suggest Black antislavery activists well before the American Civil War were the first to use the N-word as political protest.[1]

A deep reading of that passage might surprise some people about the similarities in the positions held by Dyson and McWhorter. While framed in contrasting styles, they imply that the two versions of the word are independent of one another. McWhorter clearly states that the two words should be separate dictionary entries. In contrast, Dyson insists the two words are fraternal twins, but they possess unmistakably different meanings. There are generational distinctions that must be acknowledged, in much the same way that Dyson most likely never called his parents and grandparents that word. While the generational claim is not the be-all and end-all of the discussion, it is unequivocally placed at the forefront of the debate. The history of music has told us so.

✳ ✳ ✳

Harvard law professor Randall Kennedy called the N-word the "atomic bomb of racial slurs" in a 2016 interview with PBS NewsHour correspondent Charlayne Hunter-Gault, who faced a torrent of racial slurs when integrating the University of Georgia 56 years earlier. Kennedy's metaphor, whose book on the word carries the subtitle *The Strange Career of a Troublesome Word*, came at a combustible moment in American politics. Don King let the word slip while introducing Donald Trump at a rally inside a Cleveland church when trying to rouse Black voters for the Republican presidential candidate. Comedian Larry Wilmore used a colloquial version of the epithet when praising the first African American president of the United States, Barack Obama, at the 2016 White House Correspondents Dinner. There are scores of other stories since 2016 describing school teachers, students, celebrities, on-air personalities, and even YouTubers uttering the slur, costing some their jobs while others received unforgiving condemnation. Democrat or Republican, liberal or conservative, being of the dominant or non-dominant cultural group, it has become difficult to settle on an answer over whether there is ever an appropriate time to use the word. There is no point in the present quarter-century that alludes to a satisfying resolution on by whom and when the N-word can be said.

I was 12 years old when I first heard the word. My two friends and I were dancing to music playing over loudspeakers during halftime of one of my older brother's football games. My friends, an African American set of twins, were a year older than me. When we finally settled into our seats, an older white man approached us. Looking at me, he said, "Why are you dancing with these niggers?" Then he walked away. I froze, responding with nothing but a few "Ahs." I don't think he wanted me to respond. He just wanted to insult my Black friends. Honestly, I really didn't understand the power behind the word. My two friends did, however. Later that day, standing alone in their living room as they informed their parents about what occurred, I had a racial awakening. I had given little thought about my whiteness before that moment. I was sure they thought a lot about their blackness.

Like me, most white people know only a cursory history about the N-word. We know it was used by enslavers and later devotees to the Lost Cause. We understand that the word was hurled at Black Americans in every generation. We also realize that the word presents a dehumanizing sting. So, when the word pops up in the news, as it so often does, it seems like the same conversations repeat themselves. Many of the discussions occur at schools where the word is often loosely thrown around in the hallways, cafeteria, and at extracurricular activities. Classroom instructors and staff have also been guilty of using the pejorative, sometimes when demeaning a student, but mostly when teaching an assigned reading. The stories are ubiquitous enough to be found with any vocation and with people of any generation.

In 2002, *Boston Public*, a television drama broadcasted on Fox from 2000 to 2004, aired an episode that included substantial discussion on the N-word. In the episode, the topic was brought to the fore when a white student called his Black friend the N-word's endearing form. A fight ensues when another African American student eavesdropping on the conversation vocalizes his objections to the white teenager's language. A white teacher, Danny Hanson, played by Michael Rapaport, stops the fight, cancels the midterm exam scheduled for class that day, and chooses to use the confrontation as a teachable moment. During the class period, he shows the class Chris Rock's famous comedy routine about the N-word and then gives every student a copy of Randall Kennedy's 2002 book. He also facilitates a conversation about the word's meaning as the students debate one talking point to the next: Why can't whites say it if Black hip-hop artists saturate their music with the word? Why is it permissible for Black people to use the word as a term of affection? Should a ban be placed on the word? Can a white person say it to a friend who is Black? A problem arises when Hanson says the N-word when making a point about how the word is used as a substitute for "homeboys or buddies." The students in the classroom recoil in their seats. One student, Andre, admonishes Hanson. Another teacher, Marla, who is African American, later learns about Hanson's actions and reports the incident to the school principal, who is also Black. The next day in class, students insist they continue the conversation after having spent the evening before reading Kennedy's book. During the dialogue, the school's principal, Steven Harper, played by Chi McBride, enters Hanson's classroom to interrupt the lesson. In the next scene, Harper reprimands Hanson in his office. While Hanson felt it should be fine to discuss the word with his students, Principal Harper feels it is inappropriate for white teachers to broach the topic and threatens to fire Hanson. In a meeting with his union representative, Hanson discovers that context often gets overlooked during the fallout of an N-word controversy and realizes he crossed a line. Though he keeps his job in the end, the episode's final scene shows Principal Harper speaking with Hanson's students about the N-word.

I was in my first year of teaching during the initial broadcast of that *Boston Public* episode. It implanted some fear, I admit. As a white, 22-year-old rookie educator, I saw Hanson as a well-intentioned and learned instructor who did not shy away from the difficult conversation only to get pummeled by his colleagues and nearly lose his job. I was confused. But watching a rerun of the episode two decades later, it was the final scene where Harper guided the students through a discussion on the matter when I realized our society had reached a pivot point on the N-word debate. In the aftermath of the great racial reckoning of 2020, and because the history of anti–Black racism is so profound and enduring, both in the form of private acts of racial violence and institutionalized forms of discrimination where the N-word has been used as the mortar to hold up inequitable structures, context hardly matters. To the chagrin of the John McWhorter contingent, context hardly matters because there is no telling the degree to which racialized pain and suffering torment African American persons, no matter how young or old. Context hardly matters because there is a pervading sensation in the Black community that anytime the N-word rolls off the tongue of someone who is white, the ease with which the white person says the word indicates a degree of subconscious bias and feeling of superiority over African Americans. Context hardly matters because whites in general still benefit from the structural privileges that the word helped make possible. And context hardly matters because the public conscience has come to consider the word to be the most taboo subject in our society. After the racial turmoil of 2020, American society went through a very contentious debate. The two sides deliberated over how the aggrieved should respond to hearing the word versus whether or not the language police usurped too much power to decide what will be tolerated and how the consequence of said infraction should be distributed.

The second thing I observed from the final scene of *Boston Public's* N-word episode is how comfortable the students became when listening to Principal Harper ask questions and provide insight on the topic. In contrast, the conversation with their white teacher was more confrontational, perhaps because Hansen displayed moments of defensiveness and indifference to the Black conscience and the Black experience that often typifies racial discourse.

One of the first cases that brought my attention to this debate's seriousness after first entering the teaching profession occurred at a high school in Louisville, Kentucky, during the winter of 2005 through 2006. On December 2, 2005, Valley High School suspended Paul Dawson, a white veteran teacher, after he called a Black student the N-word. Wanting the student to sit down, Dawson shouted the N-word to capture the attention of the teenager.

It wasn't the newspaper accounts of the story that overly surprised me—the reports, at first, made it appear that the student said the pejorative first, and that Dawson only repeated the appellation as an unconscious reaction that emerged in the middle of a verbal squabble. (The investigation into the incident would eventually show that the student never said the N-word.) This incident became especially cringe-worthy watching Dawson repeatedly say the word when responding to questions on the evening news. Dawson erroneously attempted to rationalize his use of the word: the N-word ending in a hard "r" is a slur, while the version ending with an "a" is a different word, meaning "Hey, man" or "Dude." He said for as much as he dislikes the word, he still uses the slang version to feel more comfortable with Black students. "Yes, I use Niggah." After explaining that he puts the "h" on it for emphasis, he rattled off a series of examples when he says the word to his students: "Niggah this." "Niggah, please." "Can you lend a Niggah a pencil?" Because of the incident, Dawson received a 10-day suspension without pay and was forced to undergo diversity training. Upon returning to the classroom, Dawson organized a student protest of about eight students on February 6, 2006, who walked out of school to express disapproval for how he was treated. The school eventually removed him from the classroom. The entire affair ended with one final astounding claim from Dawson: "I'm the ultimate martyr."

For all intents and purposes, the word was burgeoning in casual conversation within the white community in those days, as it had been since rap music's nascent popularity. The presidential candidacy of Barack Obama in 2008 aided in complicating the matter when members of the public used the racial slur to describe the future president. After four years of hate projected at the 44th President of the United States, which included Tea Party marchers carrying signs depicting Obama as an African witch doctor and other crude, stereotypical imagery, plus several racist jokes gone viral, the slur made an unsurprising yet disturbing cameo in his reelection. During the 2012 election season, a troubling bumper sticker appeared in the American South. It read: "2012, Don't Re-Nig" with the caption "Stop Repeat Offenders: Don't Reelect Obama!" The bumper sticker designers were a married couple, Billy and Paula Smith of Ludowici, Georgia. When the media discovered they were its creators, the couple feigned: "We didn't mean it in a racist way." But considering that the word is properly spelled "renege," it is hard to reason that the Smiths had anything but racial animus in mind when designing the bumper sticker despite their public statement.

Controversy over the word's use moved away from the political arena and onto the gridiron shortly after 65 million voters reelected Obama to a second term. For several years, the National Football League and National

Basketball Association struggled to resolve its owners, players, and personnel's racist and casual use of the term. Starting with Commissioner Roger Goodell, the National Football League stepped forward as the first professional sports league to litigate N-word usage amongst its employees in the summer and fall of 2013. Mitigating N-word usage in professional football became an issue just days before the start of training camp in August when Philadelphia Eagle wide receiver Riley Cooper was forced to undergo racial sensitivity training after caught on video drunk at a Kenny Chesney concert vilifying a Black security guard and vowing to "fight every Nigger here." Later that fall, in November, the Miami Dolphins first suspended and later waived offensive lineman Richie Incognito after reports of his habitual use of the N-word followed the release of a voicemail recording berating rookie teammate Jonathan Martin as a "half (racial slur)." A few weeks later, the NBA's Los Angeles Clippers forward Matt Barnes was fined $25,000 for using the N-word in a Twitter post after receiving an ejection from a game. He tweeted, "I love my teammates like family, but I'm DONE standing up for these niggas! All this shit does is cost me money." He justified his use of the term to reporters: "The word I used is a word that's used on the court, used in the locker room, used amongst my friends and family; it's a regular word to me. I think my mistake was using it in a social manner, which I regret and I apologize for it. But you guys have to get used to it." He went on, "If you look at the particular way I said it, kids are seeing that through music, through their favorite artists, and probably some of their favorite movies and even on TV now. The word is not necessarily a racial slur." Another incident occurred that month when NFL lineman Trent Williams, of the professional team in Washington, called umpire Roy Ellison the N-word in a game against the Philadelphia Eagles. Williams denied the accusation.

Before Thanksgiving, Tony Kornheiser of ESPN's *Pardon the Interruption* and sports columnist Skip Bayless, both white, called for all professional sports commissioners to ban the word. Bayless called the word a "verbal evil." The Fritz Pollard Alliance Foundation likewise called for the abolition of the word. Named for Frederick Douglass "Fritz" Pollard, the first of two Black players in the NFL (1920) and the NFL's first Black head coach (1921), The Fritz Pollard Alliance Foundation refused to let the issue go. In a statement, foundation chairman John Wooten said.

> As former players (along with thousands of others) who have worked hard in different eras of the game to leave proud legacies for those who follow us, we are appalled and extremely disappointed to learn that the worst and most derogatory word ever spoken in our country is being used during games as well as casually in the locker room…. We are not asking players to point fingers or to report who said what when. We are simply asking that you respect

the dignity of your teammates, fellow players, officials, coaches, fans, and yourselves. Most importantly, we ask that you respect every man who has worn the uniform but especially those men who helped make the National Football League what it is today and have made it possible for you to follow in their footsteps. Refusing to use the N-word will show that respect.

The scenarios that played out in the fall of 2013 presented exciting case studies. While each NFL player caught in the firestorm was white, the case of Barnes, a mixed-race, Black-passing, Black identifying, professional basketball player, drew no such heat from several Black opinion columnists. Hillman Prize–winning journalist Ta-Nehisi Coates wrote in the *New York Times* that Barnes might have been "inappropriate" in his use of the term. Still, he argued, there is a difference between being inappropriate and being "violent and offensive." The *Atlantic* editor and author explained that the N-word with a hard "r" is a "signpost that reminds us that the old crimes don't disappear" and that the endearing version of the term, though built to make people uncomfortable, is a "marker of nationhood and community" among Black people. Coates' point—that there is a troubling distinction between the two words— is well-taken. However, his argument is a reminder that a consortium of people exist who wish to remove all variations of the word from Black vernacular simply to ensure white people have no excuse to say or mention the word in any context. While whites draw on rap music to raise a double standard, here, Coates says, Blacks present a separate case of two sets of rules, claiming that they are indicted as violators of civilized behavior just so that whites can be made more comfortable.

The NFL, nonetheless, was complicit in the effort to redact the word by penalizing Black players (the NFL is more than 70 percent Black) in an attempt to mitigate the white usage of the word off the field. Amid the Seattle Seahawks' playoff run in 2013–2014, Minnesota Vikings' special teams coach, Mike Priefer, was outed for his openly bigoted language against LGBTQIA+ persons. The organization's controversy started when head coach Leslie Frazier and Priefer took steps to waive Vikings punter Chris Kluwe for taking a stance in support of gay marriage. "I was fired by Mike Priefer, a bigot who didn't agree with the cause I was working for," Kluwe told the press. "... Priefer would use homophobic language in my presence. Priefer also said on multiple occasions that I would wind up burning in hell with the gays."

Just weeks after Seattle's Super Bowl XLVIII victory and days after the release of the 144-page Ted Wells report, a damning depiction of workplace misconduct within the Miami Dolphins organization following the Incognito scandal, the NFL's Competition Committee announced it was instituting a new rule to penalize players for using the N-word on the field. The rule enforced a 15-yard penalty for a first offense. If the same player was flagged a second time, he would be ejected from the game.

Pushback from many of the league's Black players and Black sportswriters, along with gay-rights advocates, convinced the NFL to include other bigoted terms in the new rule. That spring, Michael Sam would become the first openly-gay player in the NFL when the St. Louis Rams drafted him in the seventh round. The N-word, nevertheless, remained central to the new rule. Most saw it as an affront to the league's Black players. "It's not going to be white players using it toward black players," said retired-Pittsburgh Steeler Ryan Clark in an ESPN *Outside the Lines* interview with Bob Ley. The Black players, outspoken opponents to the new rule, protested that the regulation would exclusively penalize players of color. It wasn't until 2017 that the NFL announced a ban from stadiums for any fans caught using the word. Amid the league's deliberation over the issue, critics, including 10 members from U.S. Congress, couldn't help but point out the irony of the NFL taking such measures to ban offensive language while allowing the professional team in Washington to keep "Redskins" as its nickname. Comedians couldn't help but find humor in the NFL's performative behavior. Jim Florentine, who is white, performed a cringe-worthy stand-up routine in front of an all-white audience about the NFL's new rules, where he said the N-word on several occasions, including a moment of interrogation over how officials would not be able to distinguish the slur from the word "Niners," in reference to the San Francisco 49ers.

Just as music and sports exist as extensions of society's shared problems—and the debate about how to interpret those problems—schools share the same challenges over the wielding of violent language. The years spanning Donald J. Trump's term as president of the United States seemed like a highpoint in an era of stories about educators saying the N-word. The Madison (WI) School District saw a string of teachers resign or fired during the 2018–19 school year after "at least six incidents" occurred in which teachers and staff were "alleged to have used the N-word in front of students," according to a local newspaper account that interviewed a teacher involved in one of the incidents. In one of those cases, the school district disciplined a teacher after quoting the N-word from an approved curricular text. Another teacher chose to resign when controversy ensued in her school because she said to a student, "How would you like it if I called you nigger?" This teacher was attempting to compare the N-word to the word "cracker," which was a term hurled by one student to another.[2]

At another school district in Madison, an African American security guard was fired for saying the N-word when telling a student not to call him the N-word. That security guard was later reinstated after an uproar from the school community, which included a student protest, a petition that picked up over 15,000 signatures on Change.com, and a GoFundMe campaign that raised almost $12,500.[3]

In different parts of the country, educators found themselves in trouble for both problematic and perplexing reasons that involve the term. In 2019, Lucille Murray Brown Middle School in Richmond, Virginia, fired a middle school teacher for calling a student a "Nigglet."[4] A Nashville, Tennessee, high school English teacher was placed on leave and forced to undergo a disciplinary review for giving homework that asked students to "Write [a] one page [essay] on the term Nigger." The students were asked to reflect on how racist the term is, how it is used, how they hear it used, and how the term is both empowering and self-defeating. Inspired by a classroom discussion on the play and film "Fences," the assignment also asked students to reflect on why the story's main character used the term. Students at the Tennessee school started an online petition and conducted a walkout to support the teacher. The teacher eventually returned to work but was required to undergo diversity, equity, and inclusion training.[5]

A high school teacher in Des Moines, Iowa, faced protest from students and was placed on leave for saying the N-word in her classroom when asked to explain definitions of pejorative and derogatory. The teacher said the N-word in her explanation. She eventually returned to the classroom. The school district also formed a cultural advisory committee.[6]

While the difficulty played out in Des Moines, a school district in Mustang, Oklahoma, came into the public's eye over student complaints about a teacher who said the N-word repeatedly when reading *To Kill a Mockingbird* aloud to the class. A student recorded audio of the teacher reading passages out of the book. When asked by a student to stop saying the epithet because she was offended, the teacher replied, "Well, I don't care," adding later, "I've always said [the word]."[7]

On the same day, October 11, 2019, NBC News broke two stories of educators saying the N-word in incendiary ways while in the presence of students. At Willard School in Sanford, Maine, an elementary school principal called a nine-year-old student the N-word in a hypothetical lesson about name-calling. "What if I called you a Nigger and told you I was just joking around?" the principal asked.[8] The second story casts a spotlight on an already viral Facebook post showing a verbal altercation between a white teacher and a Black parent at Drexel Hill Middle School in Pennsylvania. In the exchange, the teacher proclaimed, "You're probably on welfare" and "Go back to your welfare and your section 8 house." When the parent responded that he owned "a 3,200 square foot home," she said, "Oh, you go fuck off, Nigger."

Several cases of college professors coming under fire for saying the N-word between 2018 and 2020 are worth noting. The first case occurred in October 2018 when Phillip Adamo, professor of history and medieval studies and the then-director of the honors program at Augsburg University in Minnesota, said the word in its fullest form during a class discussion on James Baldwin's *The Fire Next Time*. The story is complicated, and it actually involves students in two sections of his first-year honors seminar course. Adamo and his students came to an agreement at the end of each class that the word "was too fraught to use going forward," according to the online publication *Inside Higher Ed*. But later in the day, the professor sent all of his students an email suggesting they take a look at two articles, one by Andrew Perry and the other by Ta-Nehisi Coates, both African American authors who address the topic. Perry argues "good teachers use the N-word," while Coates' piece is less forgiving to whites who verbalize the epithet. The students determined that Adamo's motive for sending the links was to sway the consensus. How would that assumption be possible if he sent links for two counteracting voices? Perhaps the students presumed their professor was taking extra measures to protect his job, or perhaps the fact that Coates' article was a *New York Times* editorial which necessitates a subscription the students likely didn't have made them feel manipulated.[9] The *Inside Higher Ed* coverage of this story does a nice job explaining the turmoil that occurred at Adamo's ensuing class.

> … several nonenrolled students attended the next class session, saying they were there to observe, as leaders within the honors program. Students in the class then asked Adamo to leave to discuss the situation. Adamo suggested there was work to do, but he eventually agreed to step outside. One of the nonenrolled students began to film him discussing the word with the students. That recording, which is mostly audio, was shared online under the title, "Phil Adamo Justifying Use of N-Word." Adamo's tone throughout is deferential to students.[10]

Augsburg's administration handed Adamo a summary suspension from his teaching and advisory duties in October 2018 after students issued a formal bias report complaint.[11] In one post online from an Augsburg student, the grievance against Adamo was not as simple as his quoting Baldwin. The problem was "that he repeatedly said the word without any reason to be saying it," said one junior honors student of color that had Adamo as an advisor. Admitting she was not present in the class either as an enrolled or non-enrolled student, the commenter added, "This is not about a professor saying the Nword [*sic*], it is about a white male professor overstepping lines of cultural abuse and then both denying it, and passing blame on to other students of color…. This is not a violation of academic freedom, this is a violation of student safety."[12] In January 2019, the university provost and chief academic officer informed Adamo of his temporary suspension for the spring semester while officials conducted a "formal resolution process" concerning potential misconduct.[13]

In the professor's corner, however, was the American Association of University Professors (AAUP). In January 2019, the AAUP issued an open letter to Augsburg University president, Paul Pribbenow, stating that the "basic tenets of academic freedom and due process" existent at institutions of higher education across the United States are also included in Augsburg University's faculty handbook.[14] The administration, the letter's authors contended, failed to prove that Adamo presented a threat of physical harm to his students. And since the university's handbook set forth suspensions of faculty only pertaining to physical harm, both the suspensions from teaching during fall 2018 and spring 2019 were at odds with institutional regulations. Moreover, the AAUP maintained, Adamo's suspension was in violation of his academic freedom, as the administration's actions were based on the professor's classroom speech centering on *The Fire Next Time.*

Writing in *The Chronicle of Higher Education,* Harvard professor Randall Kennedy called the incident "a dispiriting farce," and asked, "Since when is reading James Baldwin out loud in class an academic crime?"[15] He wrote, "This is not a case of a professor calling someone 'nigger.' This is a case of a professor exploring the thinking and expression of a writer who voiced the word to challenge racism." Kennedy was touched by Adamo's defense when Adamo argued, "I see a distinction between use and mention. To use the word to inflict pain or harm is unacceptable. To mention the word, in a discussion of how the word is used, is necessary for honest discourse."[16] Adamo did indeed mention the word in a way that was supposed to advance his students' interpretation on Baldwin's view of American race relations. In light of his suspension from the university, it must be asked, was it worth it?

A second controversy involving another white college professor, James Baldwin, and the N-word occurred during the 2019 spring semester—this time at the New School in New York City. On this occasion, the text was Baldwin's essay "The Creative Process." Poet and novelist Laurie Sheck used the piece in a graduate-level creative writing course. Sheck designed her course syllabus so that the class "could experience and examine how writing and reading lead us out of complacency and into a fluid and sometimes volatile relationship with language, thought, and feeling." That approach caused her to include several books by African American authors that "painfully grapple with issues of racial injustice."[17] During an early semester class discussion, Sheck asked her students if they could explain why the 2016 documentary film on Baldwin, "I Am Not Your

Negro" chose to revise the title of Baldwin's speech, changing the N-word to "Negro." In the discussion, Sheck said the actual word. Then she asked two essential questions: "Does the alteration interfere with meaning?" and "If crucial aspects of the meaning are lost, are we really even reading that writer?" While two white students filed complaints against her before the semester concluded, Sheck retained her position and was pardoned of any wrongdoing.[18]

A third and fourth firestorm over higher education instructors and the N-word occurred at the beginning of the fall 2020 semester, a time when many colleges and universities chose to conduct remote learning or virtual classes while adjusting to meet the unique needs and circumstances caused by the coronavirus pandemic of 2019 through 2021. On September 5, a story broke when the University of Southern California replaced Marshall School of Business clinical business communication professor Greg Patton for speaking a word in Mandarin that sounded similar to the N-word during a virtual session. His August 20 lecture concentrated on non-lexical words during public speaking engagements. Patton explained to his students that "filler words" are culturally specific. In the United States, the fillers are "ums and errs," he said, adding, "Like in China, the common word is 'that, that, that.' So in China it might be 'nèi ge, nèi ge, nèi ge.'" The students felt something was nefarious about Patton's actions when he stopped the Zoom recording right before pronouncing the Mandarin word. That didn't stop students on the other end of the video conference from recording the session with their cell phones, as a video of his saying "nèi ge, nèi ge, nèi ge" went viral enough to catch the attention of the conservative publication, *National Review*, which published the story on September 3. Once students identifying as "Black MBA Candidates c/o 2022" reported the incident to the USC administration, the university pulled Patton from the course and assigned a replacement instructor while the incident underwent an investigation.[19]

The episode at USC raises questions about those who have faced stern punishments for using the word "niggardly," which means stingy or cheap. The stigma around the N-word has indisputably created an atmosphere where upper management has been positioned to enforce overly harsh punishments in order to evade charges of enabling racism. It has also produced a public that over-polices language, such as the outcry anytime an individual uses the word "niggardly." During the Democratic primary season in 2019, Bernie Sanders found himself in hot water after a 1986 video surfaced of him speaking as the mayor of Burlington, Vermont, in which he said, "I am not going to be niggardly about funding for daycare." In 1999, David Howard, aide to Washington, D.C., Mayor Anthony Williams and head of the District of Columbia's Office of Public Advocate, resigned after receiving condemnation for saying "niggardly" when referring to a public fund he oversaw. Upon Howard's resignation, Mayor Williams said his aide used "poor judgment," that there are better ways to discuss a limited budget.

The history that has led to the stigmatization of the N-word—and apparently anything sounding like the N-word—has resulted in troubling tendencies such as what transpired not just in the cases of Sanders and Howard, but also at USC during the fall of 2020. "He's a white American," said one Black USC student of Professor Patton. "He knows what it sounds like, right? It was distasteful because you know what it means to people. You know what it sounds like. And you didn't care how it came off to Black students in your class."

The incident matured into widespread debate that included comments from Patton's colleagues expressing concern about job security. "[When] I might make a verbal miscue," asked one professor, "is this administration going to support me?"[20]

Even Trevor Noah gave the story attention on *The Daily Show*. Noah asked his correspondent Ronny Chieng, who is Chinese, "If 'nèi ge is, like, just a thinking word, then isn't that confusing to you when you listen to rap music?" Chieng responded sarcastically, "Yeah, to be honest, Trevor, sometimes most rappers sound like they're really unsure of themselves."[21]

While the Patton incident at USC puzzled both liberals and conservatives, Duquesne University fired professor Gary Shank in October following an investigation after a video widely shared on social media and later reported by major news networks showed him repeatedly saying the N-word while licensing his students to say the word.[22] He asked his students, "What's the one word about race that we're not allowed to use? I'll give you a hint, it starts with 'N.'" When none of the students responded, he said, "It's even hard to say, OK. I'll tell you the word, and again, I'm not using it in any way other than to demonstrate a point."[23] He then spoke the N-word. He repeated it several times as he compared the term's use in his childhood to the current moment of American race relations, having just witnessed the George Floyd-inspired Black Lives Matter protests, the most widespread racial justice demonstrations in American history. Conceding that Shank acted with "extremely poor judgment," a faculty grievance committee at Duquesne appealed for his reinstatement, calling his behavior "misguided but not malicious."[24] The argument was convincing enough to have the professor reinstated, but only after serving a seven-month suspension without pay. Shank also had to attend diversity, equity, and inclusion training under the tutelage of Alvin B. Tillery, founder and director of the Center for the Study of Diversity and Democracy at Northwestern University. He was obligated to complete independent training on top of the sessions with Tillery and to submit to the university an extensive personal reflection.[25]

Here was a professor that brought trouble upon himself for a lapse of judgment. That same fall, a more abstruse story left even more people perplexed when the John Marshall Law School at the University of Illinois–Chicago temporarily barred law professor Jason Kilborn from campus after a student expressed distress when seeing "N*****" and "B****" on a Civil Procedure II exam. In support of the students, the law school decided that the slurs' heavily censored use was not protected by academic freedom, and Kilborn would face a penalty. A frustrated Kilborn, who had used the same question on the exam for close to two decades without complaint, joked to a student that he would turn "homicidal" if the dean cowered to calls for stern punishments. When that student reported the joke to the administration, the institution placed Kilborn on paid administrative leave until the investigation into "safety concerns" following the "homicidal" joke concluded in February 2021.[26]

Brown University social scientist Glenn Loury called this episode a "spectacle." The attack on Kilborn was caused by heightened and emboldened rhetoric following the racial reckoning of 2020, Loury claimed on his show, *The Glenn Loury Show*. Speaking of the actions of the student offended by the exam question, he claimed it was "a power move, a play for control" over enhanced language policing. "Is this really justice?" he asked.[27]

In a case that would complicate responses to Loury's question, in February 2021, *Slate* magazine indefinitely suspended its popular podcast host, Mike Pesca of "The Gist," for defending the mention of the N-word in some contextual uses. Earlier that January, following the breaking yet puzzling news about the termination of *New York Times* science and health journalist Donald G. McNeil, Jr., who had said the N-word while giving a history tour of Peru to students back in 2019, Pesca engaged in a debate with *Slate* colleagues via the business communication platform Slack over whether there was ever a time that people who are not Black could say or mention the slur.[28] Pesca took an unyielding affirmative position in his argument. Slate's spokesperson explained Pesca's firing was not caused by the "isolated abstract argument in a Slack channel." Reports proved that Pesca had a history of saying the N-word in backstage and frontstage settings, including during the recording of a 2019 episode about the slur. The incident upset Black employees, including the individual producing the show. Pesca was remorseful after recording the episode, which never aired. Therefore, the public never became aware of Pesca's frequent-enough use of the word in other settings.

If only for a moment, it is worth noting that other controversies about someone other than educators uttering the N-word in public, on social media, or in music have taken place in recent years. The first occurred in 2015 when Chester Hanks, a white rapper who goes by the stage name Chet Haze and is the son of actors Tom Hanks and Rita Wilson, defied social norms by defending his use of the N-word. Citing his association with hip-hop culture, Hanks, age 25 at the time, said, "If I say nigger I say it amongst people I love and who love me. If I say 'fuck yall hatin' ass niggers' it's because that's really how I felt at the time. And I don't accept society getting to decide what ANYBODY can or can't say." In a subsequent post, he said, "Under no circumstances would I go up to someone that I didn't know and just be like, 'Hey, what's up, my nigger.' It's an unspoken thing between people who are friends, who understand each other."[29] Three years later, Hanks expressed remorse for this behavior. In 2018, he presented Van Lathan, host of "The Red Pill" podcast, with a statement of regret 75 minutes into the episode. He said, "I was on a lot of drugs." It was a comment that made the podcast's host laugh out loud. He also admitted to seeking attention. "I just felt like I wasn't enough [and] I thought ... doing some crazy shit was going to like spark my career ... it was a decision [to use the slur] to just run with it."[30] In his discussion with Lathan, Hanks conceded he was on the wrong side of history.

Another white person forced to concede he was on the wrong side of history was the host of the HBO show *Real Time with Bill Maher*, Bill Maher. In 2017, Maher said the N-word while interviewing Senator Ben Sasse. During an exchange about Maher potentially visiting the Senator in Nebraska, Sasse said, "We'd love to have you work in the fields with us." To which Maher jokingly responded, "Work in the fields? Senator, I'm a house nigger!" Maher's casual exchange with a fellow white male was an unforced error resembling what race scholar Joe Feagin calls "backstage" racist behavior. Feagin argues that there are spaces or "arenas" occupied by white people who say "openly racist comments and jokes" away from people of color. The backstage is where whites generally feel their explicit racist thoughts stay "protected" from their peers of color.[31] Maher ended up issuing an earnest apology and underwent a televised intervention, or skull session, on his show that included the intellectual Michael Eric Dyson telling him to "own the mistake."[32]

Near the end of 2018, the resurfacing of a 2011 video of four comedians—Louis C.K., Chris Rock, Ricky Gervais, and Jerry Seinfeld— engaged in banter where the N-word was said in rapid fashion focused the attention of those that police the N-word in the comedy world. The first epithet dropped after Rock called C.K. "the blackest white guy I fucking know."

To which C.K. responded, "You're saying I'm a nigger?"

"Yes, you are the niggerest fucking white man I have ever met," Rock affirmed.

If Maher's error was a Freudian slip of the tongue, the case of C.K. and Rock exposes a different turn in the discussion over the derogatory noun. C.K., who is white, felt affirmed by a Black friend who offered validations that he might be part of the in-group, or as white antiracist activist Tim Wise phrases it, "in the family." C.K. admitted that he had a history of using the N-word in his comedy routines.

But C.K. is not the only white comedian to boldly cross that line in recent history. During the 2019 promotions of *Toy Story 4*, an old story resurfaced of actor-comedian Tim Allen defending to the *Tampa Bay Times* his use of the N-word in his comedy bits. "If I have no intent, if I show no intent, if I clearly am not a racist, then how can 'nigger' be bad coming out of my mouth," he said just before also claiming that to say the euphemism "N-word" is worse than the N-word itself.[33] Though Allen didn't say much about the online pushback he had received, he did appear on *The View* later that year where he fielded questions about comedy in the midst of, in then-host Joy Behar's words, "PC culture." Allen used the opportunity to take shots at the "thought police" and to vent about political correctness.[34]

These stories exist as a warning to all people. The climate as it currently exists is not one without confusion and fear. Whether some hope to police a fragile line where Black people can say any form of the word, or for those who wish the word were off-limits to all people, keeping watch over the word has prevented us from arriving at a much-needed solution.

Conclusion

Welcome to the Conversation, Country Music

The title of this conclusion is a bit misleading at first glance. Country music historians date the genre's origins to 1910. Its ancestral forms have been addressed already in this book. As it is known in the twenty-first century, with the exception of controversial country music artist David Allan Coe (see Chapter Five) who tried to make a living in the Eighties selling music with anti-black lyrics like "Some Niggers never die, they just smell that way," the genre has remained largely isolated from the other music fields facing difficulties of artists using bigoted language.

For generations, country has been perceived as an exclusively white musical genre. Its origins buoy the irony of this perception. The Father of Country Music, Jimmie Rodgers, learned to play both the banjo and guitar from Black railroad workers. His yodeling was a skill also taught to him by Black coworkers. Then there are the anomalies of the industry in nearly every decade of the century: DeFord Bailey in the 1920s, Clarence "Gatemouth" Brown in the 1950s, Charley Pride in the 1970s, Cleve Francis in the 1980s, and Darius Rucker and Cowboy Troy in the 1990s and 2000s, respectively. In this current moment, Carl Ray, Kane Brown, Jimmy Allen, and Mickey Guyton have hammered a crater-sized dent into the stereotype that country music is only for white people. Meanwhile, Nashville artists have stayed clear of any scandal surrounding the use of the N-word in lyrics during that entire time.

While there is no question that the N-word has largely remained out of country music songs, controversy abounds with Nashville artists and country fans (à la Riley Cooper, see Chapter Ten) wielding and mentioning the word in casual conversation and jokes. Writing in *Real Country: Music and Language in Working-Class Culture*, Aaron A. Fox concedes that in the absence of country music fans who are persons of color, derogatory terms, like the N-word, are often used by artists and white patrons in backstage settings.[1] For instance, on the evening of January 31, 2021, a doorbell camera captured 27-year-old recording artist Morgan Wallen calling a friend, who is white, a "pussy ass nigger."[2] Wallen's intentional use of the anti–Black slur was to equate his white friend to subhuman status caricatured in myths about Black Americans dating back to T.D. Rice's antebellum-era minstrel "Jump, Jim Crow." TMZ made the footage public on February 2. Within 24 hours, leaders in the country music industry began canceling Wallen. The liquidation began when the Academy of Country Music Awards barred his eligibility for the 2020–21 awards cycle for his 30-song *Dangerous: The Double Album*. Then the Country Music Association removed his digital content from their platforms. Falling third was his contract with Big Loud Records. Then his agency, Endeavor Holding Group, formerly known as William Morris Endeavor Entertainment, dropped him. More dominoes fell when the nation's largest radio network, iHeartMedia Inc., with close to 900 stations, removed his music from their rotation. The nation's second-largest radio network, Cumulus Media, with more than 400 stations, temporarily pulled Wallen's music nationwide. Finally, the country music TV network, CMT, removed his appearances and videos from all platforms. Wallen was contrite in the days after he had been outed by TMZ. He issued several apologies and met with Black organizations.

Unlike many of the stories previously chronicled in this book, the issue with Wallen is not one of the N-word appearing in the music. Instead, what makes this relevant to the book's argument is the fallout. Aside from general public commentary, the remarks coming from those within country music were most striking. The fire started when country music writer Lorie Liebig released a Twitter thread about "hate and disrespect [for] Black country artists" in Nashville. Earlier that year, Liebig had released a race-conscious spreadsheet after many colleges/universities, CEO, politicians, and professional sports teams issued public statements in response to the Black Lives Matter demonstrations following the May 25, 2020, killing of George Floyd in Minneapolis, Minnesota. Seeing an uptick in statements from musical artists representing genres traditionally producing music out of New York and Los Angeles, she conducted a content analysis of remarks made by country music artists. Her study exposed Nashville's silence, save a few examples like the Dixie Chicks who changed the band's name to the Chicks and released a social justice anthem titled "March March." Critics subsequently disparaged Liebig as a witch-hunter for shaming all country music artists who publicly refused to express support for the fight against institutional racism. Despite the pushback, when news about Wallen hit the news, she reminded her followers, "We know the [country music] industry needs to be torn down and rebuilt."

Likewise, country musicians of color shared opinions about Wallen on social media. Mickey Guyton, the first Black female solo artist to receive a Grammy nomination and who had recently released the socially conscious songs "What Are You Gonna Tell Her" and "Black Like Me," which address gender and racial inequality in the United States along with a coded rebuke of her colleagues in Nashville, asked her followers on Twitter to "just read some of the vile comments hurled at me on a daily basis." She continued, "I question on a daily basis as to why I continue to fight to be in an industry that seems to hate me so much."[3] Speaking directly about Wallen, she wrote, "This is not his first time using that 'unacceptable' racial slur and we all know that. So what are y'all going to do about it. [sic] Crickets won't work this time."[4] Though Guyton did not call for Wallen to be canceled, she said he should "feel the weight of his words."

Guyton's comments were not only a response to Wallen's behavior. While sharing her dismay with Wallen in a Twitter post, Black River Entertainment recording artist Kelsea Ballerini came to the defense of country music. "The news out of Nashville … does not represent country music," she posted on the evening of February 2.[5]

Yet Guyton had offered a rebuke to country's racial innocence. Guyton's condemnation found support in Maren Morris, a white country singer, who responded, "It actually IS [sic] representative of our town because this isn't his first 'scuffle' and he just demolished a huge streaming record last month regardless. We all know it wasn't his first time using that word. We keep them rich and protected at all costs with no recourse."[6] Similarly, Latina country artist Valerie Ponzio shared a story about one Nashville publicist who told her to stay silent about immigrant rights.[7]

While the commentary on social media exposed a rift in Nashville over the genre's racial troubles, oddly enough, Wallen's star continued to rise heading into the spring of 2021. His album, *Dangerous: The Double Album*, broke records atop the Billboard 200's charts.[8] And his hometown radio station in Knoxville became the first to play his music again later that spring. His lengthy apology, full of regret and ownership for his behavior, helped preserve his career. "The video you saw was me on hour 72 of a 72-hour bender, and that's not something I'm proud of either," he said in a YouTube video lasting 11 minutes and 13 seconds. After meeting with Black advocacy groups in the days after the incident, Wallen explained, "Our actions matter. Our words matter, and I just want to encourage anyone watching to please learn from my mistake."[9]

The Wallen incident gives meaning to the story used to open this book, when, in 1829, T.D. Rice released "Jump, Jim Crow," which became the conduit that welcomed the racial slur into the world as a term with loaded meanings. It was a dramatic moment signifying how readily popular figures from Morgan Wallen to John Lennon influence behavior, practice, and social relations in ways that regenerate harmful language used time and again to caricature Black people as subhuman, reckless, calculating, sadistic, and intellectually inferior. It is fitting to conclude with the spotlight on Nashville. Not because country is a form of music plagued with diversity issues (all music genres have this problem); instead, it shows that music doesn't occur in a silo. Rather than presume that all musical forms have little in common, all musical forms should be seen as intersectional manifestations of America's multiplicity with roots in the American South whether it be minstrelsy, folk, ragtime, the blues, jazz, rhythm and blues, rock 'n' roll, hip-hop, or country.[10] The artists and their lyrics are an extension of society-at-large. Therefore, the frictions existing in the general public get negotiated in the form of music. Residing at the center of that friction has always been coded language.

Music helps us to see how those two ugly syllables advanced generationally. Of course, the term was present first as a labor-class descriptor on slave ships and at slave auctions, and wielded often by slave owners, slave drivers, and lynchers. It was blackface minstrelsy and ragtime that helped the word enter society as a representation of Blacks, both enslaved and free. The word finally became part of the common language, reinforced by print media and various forms of entertainment. We see through music a peculiar dynamic playing out among white, Black, and other people of color. Music has always been there to keep the word alive, to help transform it, and to aid in normalizing it.

History has shown that firestorms over N-word usage often come down to the defense of free speech, whether used in music, education, jokes, or casual conversation. The examples herein, however, reframe the meaning of freedom of speech. Historian Elizabeth Pryor contends the framers of the Bill of Rights always intended for free speech to protect people's right to speak out against the government. It is the "lowly citizen's" right to speak out against an abusive power structure, including its elected officials, without the threat of state recourse. In the compulsion to use freedom to do and say anything, Americans have always been pulled to the insensitive and the malicious, the least worthy characteristics of what popular culture has told us to do. As that concept pertains to the atomic bomb of racial slurs, music has been instrumental in normalizing its use for many. Thus, music exists as a major barrier for those who have always attempted to police profane language.

✳ ✳ ✳

There is one question that every person with a degree of influence over other people should consider: What is the relationship between *power* and *words*? If one's job is to deliver the newspaper, there is minimal impact on human beings. But if one's job is to be an educator, journalist, lawmaker, CEO, comedian, or musician, a greater understanding of the meaning and power behind the N-word should instill a level of caution, sensitivity, and deference for those who wish for civility in how the public communicates. I cannot see any way that the newspaper deliverer would use the N-word except as the slur. Nothing will excuse that behavior regardless of its minimal impact on society. However, for those cultural figures who have a bearing on the masses' emotional growth, the content in this book explains how listeners will react to the word when spoken out loud, even if good intentions are behind the decision to say the word.

There are too many risks. Well-intended educators have received suspensions or lost jobs because administrators fear being tarred and feathered as racist if harsh punishments aren't levied. These zero-sum performative acts of virtue-signaling have done more damage to the public understanding of the term, while violating a very important restorative approach to equity principles. Language-policing has enhanced the word's inviolability because there are no clear rules on how to support people when they make this mistake. This will sound like a blanketed statement for a group of people that are certainly not a monolith, but the administrators who appear in such stories have not distinguished the line between those that use the N-word as a slur or merely refer to it because it is part of the lesson.

Those in entertainment have fallen victim to the same level of policing. In 2018, Netflix communication chief Jonathan Friedland lost his job for saying the N-word in a meeting with staffers when explaining his opinion about offensive words in comedy.[11] At the moment of this incident, Friedland was speaking to his team about standup comedian Tom Segura's Netflix special in which the word "retarded" is uttered. The crime was that Friedland actually said the full N-word in his remarks. He was trying to sympathize with the oppressed, not degrade them. According to a *Wall Street Journal* investigation four months after the firing, it was learned that Friedland had said the full explicative a second time in a meeting with Netflix CEO Reed Hastings, who forced the communication executive to meet with representatives from human resources and issue an apology. The apology did little to rectify the enduring hurt that he caused African American workers at Netflix. And he was consequently terminated.

That same year, the founder and namesake of Papa John's pizza chain, John Schnatter, resigned as the company's chairman after saying the N-word during an internal diversity training session when telling a story about KFC founder Colonel Sanders, who is purported to have called Black patrons the N-word. The fallout from this episode occurred in the wake of Schnatter's public criticism of the National Football League's inability to put an end to police brutality protests by ex–San Francisco 49ers quarterback Colin Kaepernick and other NFL players. Optics surrounding Schnatter were shattered further when Adrian Sol of the *Daily Stormer,* a white supremacist website, declared Papa John's the official pizza of the Alt-Right because of his public stance against "the anti-white NFL."[12] A picture of a pizza with pepperonis spread across the pie in the design of a swastika accompanied Sol's endorsement of Papa John's. Schnatter's resignation came one week after the audio of his use of the N-word was leaked to *Forbes.* "It wasn't a slur," Schnatter responded amid the fallout, "… I repeated something that someone else said, and said we're not going to say that."[13] When Schnatter's departure from the company was official, Papa John's CEO Steve Ritchie issued the following statement: "Racism and any insensitive language, no matter what the context simply cannot—and will not—be tolerated at any level of the company."[14]

Context doesn't matter is the lesson in the end. Consider the voices utilized throughout this book. Based on these examples, African Americans and white antiracist critics don't want white people saying the word because they understand that individual acts of anti–Black racism are byproducts of white supremacy held in place by a more extensive system of injustice. Central to those practices is the N-word. The utterance of it adds to issues of emotional distress and concerns about its targets' overall well-being while inflaming entrenched frustrations triggered by stomaching microaggressions and microinvalidations as well as evoking memories of white supremacist violence against Black people. This fact is no secret to anybody. So, therefore, I must ask, why do white people (and other non–Black persons) even want to mention the word? Why is it essential for white educators to read the word from a class text? Are there no other ways to teach students about racism, both systemic and interpersonal? Why can't students grasp the rhetorical power and visceral force assumed by this slur through learning about how power and systems of oppression are maintained? Is it so wrong that this be the one thing about which white people don't get to be the standard-bearers?

Putting aside the extent to which some whites want to say the N-word, the sad truth is that whites wish to wield or mention the appellation when in a space predominated by other white people. I equate this to the willful ignorance that transpires when white people dress up in culturally insensitive costumes, including blackface, for Halloween parties. One common response by an individual or a group of people caught wearing something racist to a party is the innocence of intent, that intentions were devoid of racist motives. Like the N-word's taboo nature, there is no secret that there is a debate playing out about white people wearing blackface. Stories about racist costumes appear annually every October and November on social media, in local newspapers, and on cable news outlets just as reports about some cultural figure using the N-word are covered in the press. Why would a bunch of fraternity brothers or sorority sisters not think about the potential backlash before putting on burnt cork or greasepaint before heading to a party? Every time I hear about a white person wearing a racist costume, I have noted that it occurs at a party predominated by other white people. Never have I read a story about a white person going to a majority Black and Brown party in something culturally racist. The crime, then, is one of willful ignorance, the obstinate refusal to see a racial framing grounded in a white supremacist mindset as the problem within the context of a racialized country. To put it another way, these culprits are aware that their costumes will offend people of color. The same applies to the N-word: teachers say it in a classroom filled with mostly white students, and members of the media use the word while looking into a camera or speaking into a microphone, often assuming they are speaking to white viewers. White comedians joke about the slur when performing standup in front of lily-white audiences. White corporate executives verbalize the word when speaking to board rooms predominated by whites. The White Racial Frame preserves white innocence through the logic of a racialized binary, where white is valued, and whiteness is the prevailing social norm. As James Baldwin once said, "People who shut their eyes to reality simply invite their own destruction, and anyone who insists on remaining in a state of innocence long after that innocence is dead turns himself into a monster."[15] Just like we inherit money, property, and privilege, we also inherit a system of oppression. But to view that system of oppression with indifference is a fundamentally dishonest enterprise, one that, we see through this debate, has brought society to a point of great rupture. Accordingly, we must pay heed to that system of oppression just like we do all of our most prized possessions.

Epilogue
Coda

Society is not short on N-word controversies. Just as I placed the final touches on this book, stories about teachers in Lee's Summit, Missouri, and Sacramento, California, along with a Tarrant, Alabama, city councilman, saying the N-word occupied mainstream headlines and social media feeds. Stories about uproars over both malicious and well-intended orations of the N-word will likely never cease to exist. Accordingly, I chose not to work those details into this book at such a late stage in the writing process. There was, however, a different dynamic to the N-word's contemporary history that got me thinking about the future.

In April 2021, the computer product design and manufacturing company, Intel Corp, announced the launching of a program to censor racist and sexist slurs in video games. Called Bleep, the software uses artificial intelligence processing on Intel-powered computers to remove insults and hate language before the gamers hear them. Using a sliding scale created by Intel's gaming solutions team, the designers made the new settings management system to grant gamers agency in filtering the offensive language. Categories include "misogyny," "swearing," "ableism and body shaming," "name-calling," "racism and xenophobia," and "white nationalism." While those stood as broad themes, the N-word received its own distinct category.[1]

Naturally, controversy ensued when metadata posts from the masses accused Intel of repressing its gamers. Comments ranged from the politically correct, "If you're offended by the language on a site you're visiting you probably shouldn't be going to that site," to the macho, "This will do nothing but make people weaker," and into the realm of irrationality, "100% was made for the Chinese communist party lol."[2] Luke Plunkett, a writer for Kotaku, said the software is "absurd," calling it a "waste of millions [of dollars] trying to use its own technology to combat deeply human problems."[3]

Intel's move to give gamers the option of removing the N-word and other offensive language when gaming on its platform is motivated, in part, by the Anti-Defamation League's (ADL) push to expunge hate images and hate speech from video games. In 2020, working in collaboration with Newzoo, a data analytics firm focused on video games and Esports, ADL surveyed 1,000 U.S.-based gamers between ages 18 and 45 to test whether video games emboldened harmful behavior in social interactions, attitudes, and behaviors emanating specifically from online multiplayer gamers. The survey found high levels of harassment in online multiplayer games. In 2020, 81 percent of adults surveyed "experienced some form of harassment." This figure increased from 74 percent as reported the previous year.

Additionally, the study showed that 68 percent of gamers experienced "severe abuse, including physical threats, talking, and sustained harassment." That figure was up from 65 percent in 2019. The ADL and Newzoo concluded that in games like *DOTA 2*, *Volorant*, *Rocket League*, *Grand Theft Auto*, *Call of Duty*, and *Counter Strike: Global Offensive*, roughly 78 percent of gamers experienced harassment in the form of hate speech emanating from the language utilized by characters and music in the games and expressed by way of in-game communication among the players. More than half (53 percent) of online multiplayer gamers felt targeted because of their race/ethnicity, religion, ability status, gender, or sexual orientation. One Black gamer explained that, while playing as a Black character in *Read Dead Redemption Online*, he has been "a target" of the N-word and other racialized slurs.[4]

The study exposed profound psycho-social outcomes for gamers. Almost 20 percent of gamers who experienced some form of harassment expressed that they grew less social. Among that number, just 12 percent took steps to reduce risks to their physical safety. Eleven percent shared thoughts about committing suicide.

The report caused concerns in the gaming industry over the economic consequences of allowing toxic language and slurs in online multiplayer games. ADL and Newzoo found that gamers who experienced racist, homophobic, religious, or disability slurs stopped playing. The organizations recommended that game developers "proactively reduce hate and harassment" and create new reporting systems in the gaming community. The report concluded, "The games industry should collaborate with civil society, educate it about the gaming community's unique challenges, and take advantage of civil society's expertise."[5]

Almost on cue, Intel announced Bleep to an uncertain public in the spring of 2021 after conducting its own study, which found that 22 percent of gamers quit due to harassing language. Intel's announcement of the Bleep software, in fact, cited both its study and the one conducted by ADL and Newzoo, expressing concern about players that shared personal anecdotes about quitting online gaming because of toxic encounters they had experienced. Roger Chandler, vice president and general manager of Client Graphics Products and Solutions at Intel, used the 2021 Game Developers (Virtual) Conference to tell stockholders, "We believe [Bleep] is a step in the right direction, giving gamers the tool to control their experience [and ensuring] a safe, positive, and welcoming experience."[6]

Intel's announcement prompted one distressed writer from *WIRED* to claim that it was time for Alexa, Google Assistant, and Siri to swear. "Voice assistants need to speak to us in the same way we talk to them," said journalist Jeremy White, positing that digital assistants should engage in natural conversations with humans that include a "smattering of what most would term as bad language."[7] Much like those who said recurring use of the N-word in casual conversation would normalize the word, thus dulling emotional reactions upon hearing those two ugly syllables, White's argument centered on numbing the public to toxic language, even if that included hate speech.

The fact that Bleep has a separate category for the N-word got me thinking about my own question. Is it possible that scholars will find themselves censoring the N-word as it falls within direct quotations?

In our present state, I find myself in a peculiar circumstance. My training in history gives me both sympathy and empathy for historical practitioners that use period vernacular. There is no surprise, then, that the toxic language will appear in not just oration, but most certainly scholarship. For this reason alone, we see why history teachers (and many English literature educators) find themselves in hot water for orating offensive language in a classroom setting. And yet, as of late, my attention and scholarship rest in the realm of contemporary social criticism. (I have written and edited several volumes about race-conscious teaching and educational criticism since 2019.) I am conscious of intersectional and cross-cultural sensitives. I communicate in spoken and written form accordingly. You may have noticed the word Black is capitalized throughout these pages. I do so to speak of this racialized color group as a noun. Descriptors for historically marginalized groups have been negotiated in each generation. The discourse has taught us that what we call people has power. Terms we use to label people are politicized. I don't speak solely about slurs, but words used to describe whole groups of people that certainly are not monolithic cultures. For instance, I agree that saying "enslaved persons" or "enslaved Africans" has a humanizing effect and that both scholarship and public discourse should move away from referring to

Black persons kept in bondage as "slaves," otherwise suggesting that those forced into bondage existed as subhuman, inanimate property.

But this book is about the pervasion of those two ugly syllables in music culture. Although I look into history to understand the world we currently occupy, I also look to the past to help forecast what is to come— dialogue overhearing the N-word, speaking the N-word, and seeing that the N-word will never disappear. And, frankly, the conversation over the word's various contextual uses and distinct meanings should continue well beyond our time. Not everyone is sentimental about this attitude. Already underway is an effort to amend the word in written form and where it appears in direct quotes (e.g., "N*****" or "N****r"). This linguistic turn, of course, could have a weighty impact on the music industry. We learn, then, that if musicians are censored in any way, profound transformations will occur in society, and I don't suggest silencing performing artists will improve our society. Music enlightens the public about culture, joy, humor, love, and, yes, oppression. Strong musicians can expose foul behavior and unjust institutional policy and thus inspire generations into action—even if only momentarily. It is in that quandary where this book ends, challenging others to answer my query.

Chapter Notes

Preface

1. Kevin Levin. "Civil War Memory: The Online Home of Kevin M. Levin." Accessed July 28, 2021. Retrieved from http://cwmemory.com/recent-confederate-monument-removals/

2. Letter from Frederick Douglass to Sydney Howard Gay, editor the *National Anti-Slavery Standard* "Mob at Harrisburg." Printed in *Anti-Slavery Bugle* (Lisbon, OH) Sept. 3, 1847.

3. John McWhorter. *Nine Nasty Words: English in the Gutter: Then, Now, and Forever.* New York: Avery. 2021. 174.

4. While written by Lennon and Yoko Ono, the song is credited to Lennon-McCartney. Giving song-writing credit to Paul McCartney was Lennon's way to thank his fellow Beatle for helping him record "The Ballad of John and Yoko." [SOURCE: Ian MacDonald. *Revolution in the Head* (2nd revised ed.). Pimlico, 2005. 358.]

Chapter 1

1. Frederick Douglass. "The Huchinson Family.—Hunkerism." *The North Star* (Rochester, NY). October 27, 1848.

2. Frank F. Patterson. "Looking back on the old Minstrels." *The Baltimore Sun* (Baltimore, MD). August 26, 1928. 16.

3. *San Francisco Chronicle* (San Francisco, A). "A Colored Magician." September 25, 1892. 1.

4. Elizabeth Pryor quoted in George Yancy. "White Journalists Are Still Using the N-word. This is an Intolerable Assault on Black Freedom." *Truthout.* February 27, 2021. Retrieved from https://truthout.org/articles/white-journalists-use-of-the-n-word-is-an-intolerable-assault-on-black-freedom/

5. Eileen Southern quoted in John Meacham and Tim McGraw. *Songs of America: Patriotism, Protest, and the Music That Made a Nation.* New York, NY: Random House, 2019. 79.

6. Patterson. "Looking back on the old Minstrels." August 26, 1928. 16.

7. Lenwood Sloan in Marlon Riggs. "Ethnic Notions: African American Stereotypes and Prejudice." California Newsreel Essential Collection. 1987.

8. *The Era* (London, Greater London, England). "The Christy Minstrels at St. James's Hall." April 4, 1869. 12.

9. *The Era.* July 7, 1867. 12.

10. Patterson. "Looking back on the old Minstrels." August 26, 1928. 16.

11. Frederick Douglass. "The Huchinson Family.—Hunkerism." *The North Star* (Rochester, NY). October 27, 1848.

12. *The Corpus Christi Caller-Times* (Corpus Christi, TX). "Part of White Audience Leaves when Paul Robeson Protests Jim Crow Seats." February 18, 1942. 7.

13. David Walker. *Appeal in Four Articles, together with a Preamble, to the Coloured Citizens of the World, but in Particular, and Very Expressly, to Those of the United States of America.* Boston: David Walker, 1830. 61; Elizabeth Stordeur Pryor. "The Etymology of Nigger: Resistance, Language, and the Politics of Freedom in the Antebellum North." *Journal of the Early Republic*, vol. 36, No. 2, Summer 2016. 208.

14. Frederick Douglass. "Letters from Frederick Douglass, No. V." *The Liberator* (Boston, MA). January 30, 184. 3.

15. David Blight. *Frederick Douglass: Prophet of Freedom.* New York, NY: Simon and Schuster, 2018. 149–51.

16. Blight. *Frederick Douglass.* 185–86; Frederick Douglass quoted in *Anti-Slavery Bugle* (Lisbon, OH). "Mob at Harrisburg." September 3, 1947. 1.

17. *St. Johnsbury Caledonian* (St. Johnsbury, VT). "The Black and White Douglasses in Illinois." October 28, 1854. 2.

18. *The Sydney Morning Herald* (Sydney, New South Wales, Australia). "Shall we refuse to admit the Chinese?" March 23, 1855. 3.

19. *Intelligencer Journal* (Lancaster, PA). "R.R.R. (Radical Relay Rally)." September 20, 1869. 2.

20. *Edmonton Journal* (Edmonton, Alberta, Canada). "Safety First" By Rhyme. October 27, 1917. 3.

21. *The Lancaster Gazette* (Lancaster, Lancashire, England). "Over Kellet." February 12, 1887.

22. *The Boston Globe.* December 10, 1905. 13.

23. Dennis Harrington. "Dear Miss Lee." *Fall River Globe* (Fall River, MA). April 9, 1910. 6.

24. *Wilkes-Barre Times Leader* (Wilkes-Barre, PA). "Elizabeth's Letters." February 29, 1912. 9.

25. S.C. "A New Version." *Wilmington, Dispatch* (Wilmington, NC). February 8, 1916. 2.

26. *The Corpus Christi Caller-Times* (Corpus Christi, TX). "Play Is Plagued by Title Trouble." July 3, 1965. 10.

27. *The American Israelite* (Cincinnati, OH). "'Mother Goose' Bigoted Poems Withdrawn by Xerox Corporation." April 17, 1969. P15; *The Wisconsin Jewish Chronicle* (Milwaukee, WI). "Mother Goose's Goose Cooked." April 26, 1969. 6.

28. *Kingfisher Daily Star* (Kingfisher, OK). "Inspiration for 'Shoo Fly.'" December 23, 1905. 3.

29. Robert Perloff. "Fixing the Stephen Foster Statue." *Pittsburgh Post-Gazette.* July 12, 2000. 15.

30. Joanne O'Connell. *The Life and Songs of Stephen Foster.* Lanham, Boulder, New York, and London: Rowman & Littlefield. 2016.

31. Steve Terrell. "Terrell's Tune-Up." *Santa Fe New Mexican* (Santa Fe, NM). September 17, 2004. 31.

32. *The Lancaster Examiner* (Lancaster, PA). February 10, 1915. 6; George T. Fleming. "Foster Family in Early City Life." *Pittsburgh Post-Gazette.* April 5, 1916. 2.

33. *The Morning Call* (Allentown, PA). "Uncle Ned's Banjo Stolen from Stephen Foster's Statue." December 27, 1937. 1.

34. Dean Root paraphrased in Perloff. "Fixing the Stephen Foster Statue." *Pittsburgh Post-Gazette.* July 12, 2000. 15.

35. *The Boston Globe.* "School Board Heeds Protest." November 13, 1914. 5.

36. Westbrook Pegler. "Fair Enough." *The Atlanta Constitution.* June 10, 1936. 6.

37. *The Bangor Daily News* (Bangor, MN). "New Talking Machine Records." July 15, 1916. 13.

38. Harry C. Browne. "Nigger Love a Watermelon Ha! Ha! Ha!" *AuthenticHistory.com.* Recorded March 1916. Retrieved from https://www.historyonthenet.com/authentichistory/diversity/african/3-coon/5-chickwatermelon/19160300_Nigger_Love_A_Watermelon-Harry_C_Browne.html

39. *Palladium-Item* (Richmond, IN). "Why Eenie, Meeni, Miney, Mo?" January 22, 1934. 9; Craig Conley. *Magic Words: A Dictionary.* San Francisco, CA and Newburyport, MA: Weiser Books. 2008. 252.

40. B. Fitzgibbon. *Word and Music.* "Eeny, meeny, miny, mo." F. B. Haviland Publishing Co. 1906.

41. *Herald and Review* (Decatur, IL). "Ragtime Music Doomed to Extinction says Composer." April 14, 1909. 8.

42. The juba is an African American folk dance that involves patting body parts (thighs, chest) or clapping to make percussion sounds.

43. James M. McLaughlin. "What are the Cause and the Effect of the So-called 'Coon' Song?" *Boston Globe.* March 24, 1901. 28.

44. *Herald and Review.* "Ragtime Music Doomed to Extinction says composer." April 14, 1909. 8.

45. Saron Ammen. *May Irwin: Singing, Shouting, and the Shadow of Minstrelsy.* Champaign, IL: University of Illinois Press, 2017.

46. Alan Dale. "Chilly Mame Melba and Magnetic May Irwin." *San Francisco*

Examiner (San Francisco, CA) January 17, 1897. 35; *Chicago Tribune* (Chicago, IL). "May Irwin, Star of the Stage Man Years, Is Dead." October 23, 1938. 20.

47. *The Philadelphia Inquirer.* "Auditorium—Coontown's 400." May 4, 1902. 27

48. *The Topeka Daily Herald* (Topeka, KS). "An Exposition Motif." January 24, 1902. 5.

49. *Sedalia Democrat* (Sedalia, MO). "Ragtime Music Was Born in Sedalia." October 16, 1960. 10.

50. *Herald and Review.* "Ragtime Music Doomed to Extinction says composer." April 14, 1909. 8.

51. *Ibid.*

52. Lester A. Walton. "Music and the Stage." *The New York Age* (New York, NY). May 27, 1909. 6; *The Anaconda Standard* (Anaconda, MT). "Sophie Tucker Talks on Ragtime's Origins." November 29, 1914. 10.

53. *The Butte Miner* (Butte, MT). "Ernest Hogan, Father of 'Rag Time Music." June 13, 1909. 16.

54. *The Honolulu Advertiser* (Honolulu, HI). "First Wrote Ragtime." November 7, 1901. 14.

55. Lester A. Walton. "The Frolic." *The New York Age* (New York, NY). August 20, 1908. 6; Reid Badger. *A Life in Ragtime: A Biography of James Reese Europe.* New York and Oxford: Oxford University Press, 1995. 36–38.

Chapter 2

1. Michael Nowlin. "James Weldon Johnson's 'Black Manhattan' and the Kingdom of American Culture." *African American Review.* The Johns Hopkins University Press. Fall 2005. 319–320.

2. Peter C. Muir. *Long Lost Blues: Popular Blues in America, 1850–1920.* Champaign, IL: University of Illinois Press. 2010. 28–36.

3. *The Tampa Tribune* (Tampa, FL). October 27, 1916. 3.

4. Lynn Abbott and Doug Seroff. "'They Cert'ly Sound Good to Me': Sheet Music, Southern Vaudeville, and the Commercial Ascendancy of the Blues" in David Evans (ed.) *Ramblin' On My Mind.* Urbana and Chicago: University of Illinois Press. 2008. 46.

5. *Indiana Herald* (Huntington, IN). September 23, 1881. 3.

6. *Boston Globe.* "Tricks in the Trade of an African Dodger." September 13, 1914. 8.

7. Lester A. Walton. "To Introduce Anti-African Dodger Bill at Albany." *New York Age* (New York, NY). February 8, 1917. 6; Lester A. Walton. "Race Unity Can Stamp Out 'African Dodger.'" *New York Age.* February 22, 1917. 6; *The New York Age* (New York, NY). "Gov. Whitman Signs African Dodger Bill." May 17, 1917. 1.

8. *The Kokomo Tribune* (Kokomo, IN). "Bunker Hill." October 31, 1953. 16; *Fort Worth Record-Telegram* (Fort Worth, TX). "Hit the Nigger Baby." May 5, 1926. 1.

9. *The Minneapolis Star* (Minneapolis, MN). "Cuban negro Slaps Way to Surprise Win." November 23, 1929. 1; Charles Gasner. "Oh Where, Oh Where can that Little Dave Be." *Los Angeles Evening Post-Record* (Los Angeles, CA). October 12, 1932. 1; Frank Ernest. "Quiz Whizzes and Press Secretaries." *The Journal News* (White Plains, NY). June 30, 1958. 12.

10. *Wisconsin State Journal* (Madison, WI). July 20, 1916. 9

11. Ralph and Terry Kovel. "Seashells valuable to tourists, collectors." *Kenosha News* (Kenosha, WI). October 8, 2003. C7; Nina Martyris. "Tainted Treats: Racism and the Rise of Big Candy." *The Salt.* NPR.org. October 30, 2015. Retrieved from https://www.npr.org/sections/thesalt/2015/10/30/453210765/tainted-treats-racism-and-the-rise-of-big-candy

12. *The Evening Sun* (Baltimore, MD). August 23, 1923. 9.

13. *The Post-Crescent* (Appleton, WI). "Nigger Toes. Brazil Nuts. We have about 200 lbs. of these nuts left." March 16, 1923. 12.

14. *Elizabethville Echo* (Elizabethville, PA). April 5, 1928. 2.

15. *The Sayre Headlight* (Sayre, OK). February 18, 1909. 3.

16. Bill Maxwell. "Worst of racial slurs also has a complex history and many uses." *The Times Recorder* (Zanesville, OH). October 26, 1997. 4.

17. Robert M. Denhardt. *Foundation sires of the American Quarter Horse.* University of Oklahoma Press, 1976; *The Daily Dunklin Democrat* (Kennett, MO). "Summer Races!" July 6, 1893. 1.

18. *The Brooklyn Daily Eagle* (Brooklyn, NY). "A Book of Animal Stories." December 1, 1900. 13.

19. *Visalia Times-Delta* (Visalia, CA). "Famous Play of Ages to be Given in Giant Forest Last of This Month." July 6, 1924. 4.

20. *Des Moines Register* (Des Moines, IA). "Jefferson council asked to Drop 'Nigger Shooter.'" September 10, 1969. 7; *The Caucasian* (Shreveport, LA). "The Nigger Shooter." March 11, 1890. 4.

21. *Coshocton Democrat* (Coshocton, OH). "Nigger in the Wood-pile." September 2, 1863. 2; *Delaware Gazette and State Journal* (Wilmington, DE); "Passed Slaves to Freedom." July 9, 1891. 8; Allan M. Trout; "Greetings." *The Courier-Journal* (Louisville, KY). December 31, 1952. 21.

22. Quoted in Frankie Y. Bailey. *Out of the Woodpile: Black Characters in Crime and Detective Fiction.* New York: Greenwood Press, 1991. 26.

23. *Reading Times* (Reading, PA). "Rapid Transit." June 15, 1901. 2.

24. *The Brooklyn Daily Eagle* (Brooklyn, NY). "Nigger in the Wood Pile." August 24, 1907. 11.

25. John McWhorter. *Nine Nasty Words: English in the Gutter: Then, Now, and Forever.* New York: Avery. 2021. 182; *Loony Tunes.* "Porky's Railroad." 1937. YouTube. CCCartoons. November 21, 2010. https://youtu.be/MzwxL6305Q4

26. *The Sunday News* (Ridgewood, NJ). "Ford Neglects Blacks, Union Leader Charges." June 22, 1969. 34.

27. *Fort Worth Star-Telegram* (Fort Worth, TX). January 23, 1933. 8.

28. Edwin C. Stein. *The Standard Union* (Brooklyn, NY). September 15, 1931. 11.

29. Dan DeLuca. "What's the story behind those Kate Smith songs with racist lyrics?" *The Philadelphia Inquirer.* April 22, 2019; *New York Daily News* (New York, NY). "God bless America! Kate's no racist." April 23, 2019. 24.

30. Thomas J. Davis and Brenda M. Brock. *Documents of the Harlem Renaissance.* Santa Barbara, CA: ABC-CLIO. 2021. 5.

31. *The Emmett Citizen* (Emmett, KS). "Cactus Leather New Product." August 13, 1908. 2.

32. *Osborne county Farmer* (Osborne, KS). December 12, 1901. 5; *The Randall News* (Randall, KS). "Storage Prices on Coal." August 29, 1912. 10.

33. *The Jackson Sun* (Jackson, TN). October 15, 1953. 19.

34. Jet. "Name Change of the Week." August 18, 1955. 26.

35. *The Pittsburgh Press* (Pittsburgh, PA). "'Nigger-Head'—A New Game." April 3, 1910.

36. *San Bernardino County Sun* (San Bernardino, CA). "Nigger Canyon Water Scheme." July 21, 1899. 7; *Los Angeles Evening Citizen News* (Hollywood, CA). "Palomar Lures Motorists with Beauty." May 7, 1924. 13.

37. *Times-Advocate* (Escondido, CA) January 9, 1967. 10; *Times-Advocate.* "Poets' Corner." August 27, 1949. 6.

38. *The Galveston Daily News* (Galveston, TX). "Two Miles Apart." March 16, 1911. 6; *News-Press* (Fort Myers, FL). "County Plans Nigger Head Action." December 9, 1959. 1.

39. Stephanie McCrummen. "Rick Perry family's hunting camp still known to many by old racially charged name." *Washington Post.* October 1, 2011.

40. *The Oshkosh Northwestern* (Oshkosh, WI). "A Green Colored Delegation." April 22, 1892. 4.

41. *Black Hills Weekly Pioneer* (Deadwood, SD). January 17, 1880. 2.

42. *The Daily Leader* (Lexington, KY). April 28, 1899. 4.

43. *The Weekly Times-Star* (Sedan, KS). August 9, 1901. 2.

44. *The Times* (Muster, IN). March 28, 1913. 6.

45. *Buffalo Courier* (Buffalo, NY). "The Conning Tower, Klan Song." July 27, 1924. 70.

46. Kenneth B. Clark and Mamie P. Clark. "Racial Identification and Preference in Negro Children." Unknown publication. 1947. 169–78.

47. Kenneth Clark quoted in Derrick Z. Jackson. "Kenneth Clark's unfulfilled dream." *The Boston Globe.* May 4, 2005. A19.

48. Clark and Clark. "Racial Identification and Preference in Negro children." 169–70.

49. Benjamin Fine. "White Woman Assists Negro Girl as 400 Jeer." *Des Moines Register* (Des Moines, IA). September 5, 1957. 1 and 4.

50. Hazel Bryan quoted in Benjamin

Fine. "Ugly Mob, Troops Bar Negro Pupils." *Detroit Free Press* (Detroit, MI). September 5, 1957. 1 and 6.

51. Fine. "White Woman Assists Negro Girl as 400 Jeer."

52. Carlton F. Wilson of the United Press International. *Pauls Valley Democrat* (Pauls Valley, OK). "Cheerleaders vow fight to the finish against integration." December 9, 1960. 1.

53. *The La Crosse Tribune* (La Crosse, WI). "2 Negro students Removed from Georgia U. After Riots, Violence." January 12, 1961. 1.

54. *San Francisco Examiner.* "Rebels Yell at Ole Miss." September 21, 1962. 14.

55. *Carlsbad Current-Argus* (Carlsbad, New Mexico). "Negro Jeered at Ole Miss Second Night." January 9, 1963. 2.

56. Leslie Houts Picca and Joe Feagin. *Two-Faced Racism: Whites in the Backstage and Frontstage.* New York: Routledge. 2007. 7.

57. Brad Kutrow. "Here's the @daily tarheel editorial..." Twitter. February 6, 2019 found at Martha Quillin and Jane Stancill. "UNC yearbook editor expected 'public outcry' over racist 1979 photos. This week, it finally came." *Newsobserver. com.* December 20, 2019. Retrieved from https://www.newsobserver.com/news/local/article226007650.html.

58. Sara L. Bernson and Robert J. Eggers. "Black People in South Dakota History." *South Dakota State Historical Society.* 1977. 242–44; Dick Day. "Federal Edict Changing Name of 'Nigger Hill' to "Negro Hill."" *Casper Star-Tribune* (Casper, WY). March 16, 1966. 12.

59. Tony Marro. "Merits of Renaming 'Niggerhead Pond' in Sharp Debate." *Rutland Daily Herald* (Rutland, VT). April 7, 1966. 19.

60. Frederick Stetson. "Deed Shows UVM Owns Portion of 'Niggerhead.'" *The Burlington Free Press* (Burlington, VT). March 18, 1871. 39.

61. Isabel Wilkerson. *Caste: The Origins of Our Discontents.* New York, NY: Penguin Random House LLC. 2020. 288.

62. Gordon W. Allport. *The Nature of Prejudice.* 25 Anniversary Edition. New York, NY: Basic Books. 1954, 1979.

63. Chris Berdik. "Invisible Bias." *Boston Globe* (Boston, MA). December 19, 2004. K1 and K5.

64. Michael Richards quoted in Leonard Pitts, Jr. "If not racism, then what?" *Standard-Speaker* (Hazleton, PA) November 2006. 20.

65. Paul Mooney quoted in Tim Clodfelter. "Richards incident forced Mooney to censor himself." *The Indiana Gazette* (Indiana, PA). February 19, 2007. 18.

Chapter 3

1. Jon Wiener. *Gimme Some Truth: The John Lennon FBI Files.* Berkeley, CA: University of California Press, 1999. 110.

2. *Detroit Free Press.* "Sinclair Convicted in Pot Case." July 26, 1969. A3; John Oppedahl. "Sinclair Given Sentence of 9½–10 years for Pot." *Detroit Free Press.* July 29, 1969. A3.

3. Wiener. *Gimme Some Truth.* 115.

4. Jeff Burger, ed. *Lennon on Lennon: Conversations with John Lennon.* Chicago, IL: Chicago Review Press, 2016. 352.

5. John Lennon quoted in *Detroit Free Press* (Detroit, MI). "Lennon to Join U–M Rally." December 9, 1971. 16-A; Peter Andrews. "Audio recording of John and Yoko's intent to come to Ann Arbor for the John Sinclair Freedom Rally." John and Leni Sinclair Papers, 1957–2003, Bentley Historical Library. Sound Cassettes series: Unit IV, no. 4, Box 28f. Retrieved from https://aadl.org/freeingjohnsinclair/recordings/audio_recording_of_john_and_yokos_intent

6. *Ibid.*

7. In the version of "John Sinclair" that appeared on *Some Time in New York City,* Lennon replaced "Judge Colombo" with "the judges" to avoid a defamation lawsuit.

8. Geoffrey Giuliano. *Lennon in America: 1971–1980, Based in Part on the Lost Lennon Dairies.* New York, NY: Cooper Square, Press, 2000. 38–39.

9. Weiner. *Gimme Some Truth.* 110.

10. Heather Ann Thompson. *Blood in the Water: The Attica Prison Uprising of 1971 and Its Legacy.* New York, NY: Vintage Books, 2017.

11. John Lennon television interview, May 11, 1972. *The Dick Cavett Show:* John and Yoko collection [video recording] DVD 2005.

12. Martin Luther King, Jr. "The Rising Tide of Racial Consciousness." Address

at the Golden Anniversary Conference of the National Urban League. September 6, 1960. New York, NY.

13. Shannon Sullivan. *Good White People: The Problem with Middle-Class White Anti-Racism*. New York, NY: State University of New York Press, 2016. 1–4, 119–20.

14. Malcolm X. "The Danger of White Liberals." December 4, 1963; Malcolm X. "The Danger of White Liberals." University of California, Berkeley. October 11, 1963. C-SPAN. Retrieved from https://www.c-span.org/video/?c4618921/user-clip-danger-white-liberals

15. Charles W. Mills in George Yancy. *What White Looks Like: African-American Philosophers on the Whiteness Question*. New York and London: Routledge, 2004. 49–50.

16. Derrick Bell. *Silent Covenants: Brown v. Board of Education and the Unfulfilled Hopes for Racial Reform*. Oxford and New York: Oxford University Press, 2004. 1–3; Derrick Bell. *Faces at the Bottom of the Well: The Permanence of Race*. New York, NY: Basic Books, 1989. ii–iv; Richard Delgado and Jean Stefancic. *Critical Race Theory: An Introduction*. New York and London: New York University Press, 2012. 20–24.

17. Television interview, May 11, 1972. *The Dick Cavett Show: John and Yoko* collection [video recording] DVD 2005.

18. Carlos E. Cortes. *The Making and Remaking of a Multiculturalist*. New York and London: Teacher's College Press, 2002. 18–19.

19. Bette Midler, Twitter Post. October 4, 2018, 4:50 p.m. (tweet deleted); Bette Midler. Twitter Post. October 4, 2018. 7:23 p.m. (tweet deleted).

20. Cydney Henderson. "Bette Midler apologizes for controversial 'women, are the n-word of the world' tweet." *USA Today*. October 4, 2018.

21. Television interview, May 11, 1972. *The Dick Cavett Show: John and Yoko* collection [video recording] DVD 2005.

22. Some of the documentaries referenced here are Michael Epstein. *John & Yoko: Above Us Only Sky*. Documentary, 2018; David Leaf. *The U.S. vs. John Lennon*. Documentary, 2006; Michiko Byers. *Inside John Lennon*. Documentary. 2003; Roger Appleton. *Looking for Lennon*. Documentary, 2018.

23. *Ottawa Citizen* (Ottawa, Ontario, Canada). "'Bed-in' in Bahamas was simply too hot." May 26, 1969. 40.

24. David Wigg. "John Lennon & Yoko Ono Interview: Apple Offices, London, May 8, 1969." *The Beatles Ultimate Experience*. Retrieved from http://www.beatlesinterviews.org/db1969.0508.beatles.html

25. Donald McGillivray of the *London Herald Bureau*, "Beatle wants tour to recoup fortune" printed in the *Edmonton Journal* (Edmonton, Alberta, Canada.) April 2, 1969. 37.

26. *Baltimore Sun* (Baltimore, MD). "Beatle Plans to Distribute Peace Acorns." April 2, 1969. 3; *Arizona Daily Star* (Tucson, AZ). "Beatle Lennon 'Plants' Acorns for Peace." April 2, 1969. B7.

27. John Lennon told a reporter that the inspiration for the Bed-In demonstrations came from documentarian Peter Watkins. He said, "[T]he thing that really struck it off was a letter we got from a guy called Peter Watkins who made a film called *The War Games*. It was a very long letter stating just what's happening—how the media is really controlled, how it's all run, and everything else that people really know deep down. He said, 'People in your position have a responsibility to use the media for world peace.' And we sat on the letter for about three weeks thinking, 'Well, we're doing our best. All you need is love, man.' That letter just sort of sparked it all off. It was like getting your induction papers for peace!" SOURCE: Geoffrey Giuliano. *The Beatles—A Celebration*. Book Sales, 1993. 144.

28. John Lennon and Yoko Ono were arrested by London police on October 18, 1968. They were taken from Lennon's London apartment in the Marylebone district and charged at Paddington Green Police Station with possessing cannabis. *Dayton Daily News* (Dayton, OH). "Lennons to Stage Bahamas Bed-In." May 25, 1969. 14-D; *Ottawa Citizen* (Ottawa, Ontario, Canada). "'Bed-in' in Bahamas was simply too hot." May 26, 1969. 40; *Philadelphia Inquirer* (Philadelphia, PA). "Beatle Is Held on Drug Charge." October 19, 1968. 12.

29. *Ottawa Citizen* (Ottawa, Ontario, Canada). "Beatle bedded down." May 28, 1969, 36; *Calgary Herald* (Calgary, Alberta,

Canada). "'Salesman' Lennon's Bed-In A Commercial for Peace." May 29, 1969. 9.

30. John Lennon gave co-authorship rights of "Give Peace a Chance" to Paul McCartney. He always regretted not rightfully granting songwriting credit to Yoko Ono, who co-wrote the song during the Montreal Bed-In. SOURCE: Ian MacDonald. *Revolution in the Head: The Beatles' Records and the Sixties* (3rd edition). Chicago, IL: Chicago Review Press, 2007. 358; Dave Chenoweth. "Half of Smothers Bros. cares about U.S." *The Gazette* (Montreal, Quebec, Canada.) June 2, 1969. 11.

31. Connolly. "The Beatle Backlash in Britain."

32. David Yates. "Beatle Crusades, Fans Wait in Rain." *Ottawa Journal* (Ottawa, Ontario, Canada). June 4, 1969. 3.

33. Kathy Frankovi. "When it comes to the n-word, most see it as offensive whoever says it." YouGov. August 23, 2018. Retrieved from https://today.yougov.com/topics/politics/articles-reports/2018/08/23/when-it-comes-n-word-most-see-it-offensive-whoever.

34. Dick Gregory. "Dick Gregory—How the 'N' Word Began & More on Smiles TV Talk Show." SmilesTV Stephanie a. Miles. November 12, 2013. YouTube. Retrieved from https://www.youtube.com/watch?v=9-iJAVdS8Uo&t=788s

35. Robert Hilburn. "A Letdown Album from John, Yoko." *Los Angeles Times* (Los Angeles, CA). June 23, 1972. 46.

36. Jeremy Roberts. *Bob Dylan: Voice of a Generation.* Minneapolis, MN: Lerner Publications Company, 2005. 7.

37. Television interview. April 28, 1975. *Tomorrow Show* with Tom Snyder. YouTube. TheMMProducties. March 5, 2012.

38. Henry Hanson of the *Miami Herald-Chicago Daily News Wire.* "Ban on Lennons' Women's Lib Song." *Miami Herald* (Miami, FL). May 10, 1972. 2-E.

39. Ray Connolly. *Being John Lennon: A Restless Life.* New York and London: Pegasus Books, 2018. 272–74, 320–21; Cynthia Lennon. *John.* London, UK: Hodder & Stoughton. 2005. 244–245; Albert Goldman. *The Lives of John Lennon.* Chicago, IL: Chicago Review Books, 1988. 441.

40. *The Arizona Republic* (Phoenix, AZ). "John Lennon Disco Spins Controversy." April 23, 1972. 10-A.

41. Connolly. *Being John Lennon.* 182–96, 212–74.

42. *The Arizona Republic* (Phoenix, AZ). "John Lennon Disco Spins Controversy." April 23, 1972. 10-A.

43. Television interview, May 11, 1972. *The Dick Cavett Show:* John and Yoko collection [video recording] DVD 2005; Jeff Burger, ed. *Lennon on Lennon: Conversations with John Lennon.* Chicago, IL: Chicago Review Press, 2016. 314.

44. Helen Reddy's "I Am Woman" debuted in May 1971, one year before Lennon's "Woman is the Nigger of the World." John Lennon quoted in Johnny Rogan. *Lennon: The Albums.* Calidore, 2010.

45. Allison Perlman. *Public Interests: Media Advocacy and Struggles over U.S. Television.* New Brunswick, NJ: Rutgers University Press, 2016. 75.

46. Ronald V. Dellums. "Rep. Dellums Objects to Quote In Record Ad." *JET* Magazine. June 15, 1972. 4.

47. Dick Cavett. *Brief Encounters: Conversations, Magic Moments, and Assorted Hijinks.* New York, NY: Henry Hold and Company, 2014. 82; Burger. *Lennon on Lennon.* 302.

48. John McWhorter. Email correspondence with the author. New York, NY. March 17, 2020; Richard Delgado and Jean Stefancic. *Critical Race Theory: An Introduction.* New York, NY: 2017; Richard Delgado and Jean Stefancic. *Critical Race Theory: The Cutting Edge.* Philadelphia, PA: Temple University Press, 2000.

49. Perlman. *Public Interests*; Burger. *Lennon on Lennon.* 314–15.

50. Dellums. 4.

51. Irv Kupcinet. "Nichols and May Reviving Old Act." *Miami Herald* (Miami, FL) May 13, 1972. 8-D; Cavett. *Brief Encounters,* 82.

52. "Ex-Beatle Tells How Black Stars Changed His Life." *JET.* October 26, 1972. 61–62; Irv Kupcinet of the *Chicago-Daily News* and *Sun-Time Service* reprinted in "Kup's Bowl of Vignettes." *York Dispatch* (York, PA). May 13, 1972, 6; Jann S. Wenner. *Lennon Remembers.* London and New York: Verso 2000, 21.

53. "Ex-Beatle Tells How Black Stars Changed His Life." *JET.* October 26, 1972, 62.

54. Julia Baird. *Imagine This: Growing Up With My Brother John* Lennon. Great

Britain: Hodder & Stoughton, 2007. 97–98; Connolly, *Being John Lennon*. 55–56, 65–66; Hunter Davies. *The Beatles*. New York, NY: W.W. Norton & Company. 1996 (1968). 69.

55. Quoted in *Being John Lennon* by Ray Connolly, 31–32; Mark Lewisohn. *Tune In: The Beatles: All These Years*. New York, NY: Three Rivers Press, 2013, 89–90.

56. *The Mike Douglas Show*. "John Lennon & Chuck Berry—The Mike Douglas Show, February 16, 1972." The BeatlesAtTheStudio231. March 19, 2017. Retrieved from https://www.youtube.com/watch?v=_UmnVdZkXSA

57. Television interview. April 28, 1975. *Tomorrow Show* with Tom Snyder. YouTube. TheMMProducties. March 5, 2012.

58. Elijah Wald. "Did the Beatles push black music aside?" CNN Opinion. August 25, 2014.

59. George Harrison quoted in Jon Garelick. "Tracing Lead Belly's unlikely path to stardom." *The Boston Globe*. February 22, 2015. N7.

60. *JET*. "What the Beatles Learned from Negroes." July 1, 1965. 60–62.

61. Lennon. *John*, 246–47.

62. Connolly, *Being John Lennon*. 302–04.

63. Heather Ann Thompson. *Blood in the Water: The Attica Prison Uprising of 1971 and Its Legacy*. New York, NY: Vintage Books, 2017.

64. Philip Norman. *John Lennon: The Life*. New York, NY: Ecco, Harper-Collins Publishers, 2008. 698–99.

65. Hunter Davies, ed. *The John Lennon Letters*. New York, Boston and London: Little, Brown, and Company, 2012. 245.

66. Lewisohn. *Tune In*. 83.

67. Lennon. *John*, 256–58.

68. Geoffrey Giuliano. *Lennon in America: 1971–1980, Based in Part on the Lost Lennon Dairies*. New York, NY: Cooper Square, Press, 2000. 39. Biographer Giuliano claims the album reached number 48 "on the charts," but gives no indication of the charts in question.

69. John Blaney. *John Lennon: Listen to This Book*. John Blaney, 2005. 103.

70. Connolly. *Being John Lennon*. 354; Norman. *John Lennon*, 2008. 698–700.

71. Giuliano. *Lennon in America*. 39.

72. Johnny Rogan. *Lennon: The Albums*. Calidore, 2010. 128.

73. Rogen. *Lennon*. 129

74. Robert Hilburn. "A Letdown Album from John, Yoko." *Los Angeles Times* (Los Angeles, CA). June 25, 1972, 46; Val Adams. "Top Executives Shifts at NBC-TV." *Daily News* (New York, NY). May 11, 1972. 120.

75. Robert Hilburn. "A Letdown Album From John, Yoko." *Los Angeles Times*. June 25, 1972 46; Al Rudis. "John and Yoko's Album Brings Back Memories of Pete Seeger." *Kingsport Times* (Kingsport, TN). July 12, 1972. 3D; Denny Delk. "Gallagher & Lyle': Another Good Album." *Austin American* (Austin, TX). May 20, 1972, 40; Lynn Van Matre. "Women Speak Out on Their Status." *Chicago Tribune* (Chicago, IL). June 28, 1972, 1–2.

76. *Ithaca Journal* (Ithaca, NY). "NOW Gives Special Citations." August 25, 1972. 8; *Hartford Courant* (Hartford, CT). "NOW Marks Women's Rights Day." August 26, 1972. 15; Laurie Johnston. "Women's Group to Observe Rights Day Here Today." *New York Times*. August 25, 1972. 40; *Times and Democrat* (Orangeburg, SC). "Women Observe Their Day." August 26, 1972. 6.

77. Robert Hillburn. *Corn Flakes with John Lennon: And Other Tales from a Rock 'n' Roll Life*. New York, NY: Rodale Inc., 2010. 119.

78. Benita Roth. *Separate Roads to Feminism: Black Chicana, and White Feminist Movements in America's Second Wave*. Cambridge, UK: Cambridge University Press, 2004. 3; Winifred Breines. *The Trouble Between Us: An Uneasy History of White and Black in the Feminist Movement*. New York: Oxford University Press, 2006. 3.

79. In 1964, Assistant Secretary of Labor Daniel Patrick Moynihan published a study of African American families hoping to inform the Johnson Administration that civil rights legislation alone would not close prevailing opportunity gaps between white and Black Americans. The report became the topic of heated debate a year later when critics found Moynihan's conclusions about the African American family troublesome, as conservatives saw data about loose family morality as providing ammo to the argument that racial separation is justified. Moynihan

was also criticized for shying away from structural racism by placing the onus of the problems in the Black community on fatherless households.

80. Roth. *Separate Roads to Feminism.* 6–7; Patricia Hill-Collins. *Black Feminist Thought: Knowledge, Consciousness, and the Politics of Empowerment.* New York: Routledge. 1990, 1999. vii, 11–12, 101–2.

81. Roth. *Separate roads to Feminism.* 105–06.

82. Kelsy Kretschmer. *Fighting for NOW.* University of Minnesota Press, 2019. 37–38.

83. Kate Millett. *The Loony-Bin Trip.* Champagne, IL: University of Illinois Press, 2000. 35; Jon Wiener. *Come Together: John Lennon in His Time.* Champagne, IL: University of Illinois Press, 1984. 118, 122.

84. *New York Times.* "Militant is Hanged by Trinidad After Long Fight for Clemency." May 17, 1975. 4.

85. Jacqui Ceballos. "Memories." Veteran Feminists of America. Date unknown. Retrieved from https://www. veteranfeministsofamerica.org/legacy/ JohnYoko.htm.

86. Carol Trapani. "Worldwide Feminists Meet: Problems Are Universal." *Poughkeepsie Journal* (Poughkeepsie, NY). June 14, 1973. 15; *The Oshkosh Northwest* (Oshkosh, WI). "Feminist solidarity crosses national lines." June 14, 1973. 12; Maria Karagianis. "Feminists of 27 nations vow 'to change society.'" *The Boston Globe* (Boston, MA). June 5, 1973. 28–30.

87. Ray Hilburn of the *Los Angeles Times* reprinted in the *Longview Daily News* (Longview, WA). "Beatle John Lennon comes out of hiding. October 24, 1980. C2.

Chapter 4

1. Federal Bureau of Investigation. "U.S. Dept. of Justice, Federal Bureau of Investigation. November 23, 2018. Federal Crime Data 2017." Retrieved from https://ucr.fbi.gov/crime-in-the.u.s/2017/ crime-in-the.u.s.-2017/additional-data-collections/federal-crime-data/federal-crime-data.pdf; Federal Bureau of Investigation; FBI Report reported in NPR. "FBI Reports Dip in Hate Crimes, But Rise in Violence." November 12, 2019.

Retrieved from https://www.npr.org/2019/ 11/12/778542614/fbi-reports-dip-in-hate-crimes-but-rise-in-violence; "About Hate Crimes Statistics, 2016 and Recent Developments." *Criminal Justice Information Services Division.* January 2017. Retrieved from https://ucr.fbi.gov/hate-crime/2016.

2. John McWhorter. "Stop Policing the N-Word." *TIME.* May 3, 2016. Retrieved from https://time.com/4316322/larry-wilmore-obama-n-word/.

3. The Situation Room with Wolf Blitzer. "CNN Anchor, analyst's heated spat over N-word's use." *CNN.* June 22, 2015. Retrieved from https://www.cnn. com/videos/us/2015/06/22/don-lemon-sunny-hostin-n-word-debate-tsr.cnn/ video/playlists/south-carolina-and-race/

4. Charles C. W. Cooke. "Obama's Use of the N-word was Judicious and Fair." *National Review.* June 22, 2015. Retrieved from https://www.nationalreview. com/corner/obamas-use-n-word-was-judicious-and-fair-charles-c-w-cooke/

5. Rory Carroll. "Donald Trump on tape saying 'every racist thing ever,' claims actor Tom Arnold." *The Guardian.* December 21, 2016. Retrieved from https://www. theguardian.com/us-news/2016/dec/20/ donald-trump-apprentice-outtakes-tape-tom-arnold; P.R. Lockhart. "The debate over Donald Trump's alleged n-word tape, explained." *Vox.* August 16, 2018. Retrieved from https://www.vox.com/ identities/2018/8/16/17693342/donald-trump-n-word-tape-racism-omarosa-manigault-controversy.

6. Alexandra Hutzler. "Most Donald Trump Voters don't think using the N-word is racist, or even offensive, new poll indicates." *Newsweek.* August 30, 2018. Retrieved from https://www. newsweek.com/donald-trump-voters-n-word-racist-1098127; David Badash. "Trump Voters Increasing Think It's OK to Use the N-Word." *New Civil Rights Movement.* July 30, 2019. Retrieved from https://www.thenewcivilrightsmovement. com/2019/07/trump-voters-increasingly-think-its-ok-to-use-the-n-word/

7. Jamie Ducharme. "Georgia Lawmaker says President Trump's Alleged N-Word Use Should be Held Separate From His Presidency." *TIME.* August 18, 2018. Retrieved from https://time.com/5371071/ michael-williams-trump-n-word/

8. Linton Weeks of the *Washington Post*. "Harvard professor is hoping to ease racial epithet's sting." *Chicago Tribune*. December 13, 2001.12.

9. Randall Kennedy. "Nigger: Strange Career of a Troublesome Word." WGBH-Forum. March 28, 2014. YouTube. Retrieved from https://www.youtube.com/watch?v=a0JA3QDzeU0.

10. Nicholas Sammond. *Birth of an Industry: Black face Minstrelsy and the Rise of American Animation*. Durham, NC: Duke University Press, 2015. 21–26.

11. Randall Kennedy. *Nigger: The Strange Career of a Troublesome Word*. New York, NY: Vintage Books, 2002. 4–5.

12. "Easing the N-word's sting with knowledge, history." *Lancaster Sunday News* (Lancaster, PA). January 6, 2002. P5.

13. Randall Kennedy. "Who can Say 'Nigger'? And Other Considerations." *The Journal of Blacks in Higher Education*. Winter 1999–2000. 90; Kennedy. *Nigger*. 145.

14. Kennedy. "Who can Say 'Nigger'?." 91–92.

15. Kennedy. *Nigger*. 145.

16. Randall Kennedy. "How the n-word became the 'atomic bomb of racial slurs.'" *PBS NewsHour*. YouTube. October 25, 2016. Retrieved from https://www.youtube.com/watch?v=t8g3V2gzY7Q; Kennedy. Who can Say 'Nigger'?. 92; Kennedy. *Nigger*. 146.

17. William Parris. "The N-Word and Power of Words in Language. Special Guest: Dr. Neal A. Lester, Ph.D." *Legitimate Matters*. YouTube. October 5, 2020. Retrieved from https://www.youtube.com/watch?v=wB91UCo8CF8.

18. Neal Lester. "'Sticks and stones may break my bones…': Airbrushing the Ugliest of Ugly in African American Children's Books." *Obsidian III*. 2001–2002. 13, 20, 27.

19. Neal A. Lester. "The N-Word: Lessons Taught and Lessons Learned." *Journal of Praxis in Multicultural education*. January 2014. 2; Neal A. Lester. "'Sticks and stones may break my bones…': Airbrushing the Ugliest of Ugly in African American Children's Books." *Obsidian III*. 2001–2002.

20. Lester. "'Sticks and stones may break my bones…'" 21.

21. Lester. "The N-Word." 5.

22. Neal Lester quoted in The University of Alabama. "The Power of Words." November 6, 2015. YouTube. Retrieved from https://www.youtube.com/watch?v=r0xG0626Faw.

23. Neal Lester quoted in Parris. "The N-Word and Power of Words in Language." October 5, 2020.

24. Neal Lester quoted in ASU ProjectHumanities. "N-word: A Perspective with Neal Lester." January 7, 2019. YouTube. Retrieved from https://www.youtube.com/watch?v=4z7Xn9WvtKg.

25. Jabari Asim. "After Words with Jabari Asim." C-SPAN. April 20, 2007. Retrieved from https://www.c-span.org/video/?197645-1/after-words-jabari-asim; Jabari Asim. *The N Word: Who Can Say It, Who Shouldn't, and Why*. Boston and New York: Houghton Mifflin Company, 2007.

26. Asim. "After Words with Jabari Asim."

27. Asim. *The N Word*. 190.

28. Randall Kennedy. "How the n-word became the 'atomic bomb of racial slurs.'" *PBS News Hour*. YouTube. October 25, 2016. Retrieved from https://www.youtube.com/watch?v=t8g3V2gzY7Q

29. Asim. *The N Word*. 228.

30. Jenice Armstrong. "No more n-word." *Philadelphia Daily News*. June 9, 2005. 29.

31. Michael Eric Dyson. "State of the Black Union 2005: Defining the Agenda, Part 2." C-SPAN. February 26, 2005. Retrieved from https://www.c-span.org/video/?185632-3/state-black-union-2005-defining-agenda-part-2.

32. Armstrong. "No more n-word." June 9, 2005.

33. Renee Graham. "In death, Tupac remains an idol." *Des Moines Register* (Des Monies, IA). September 9, 2001. 4E.

34. Michael Eric Dyson. *Holler If You Hear Me: Searching for Tupac Shakur*. New York, NY: Basic Civitas Books, 2002. 145.

35. Michael Eric Dyson. *Tears We Cannot Stop: A Sermon to White America*. New York, NY: St. Martin's Press, 2017. 166–67.

36. Dyson. *Tears We Cannot Stop*. 163.

37. Dyson. *Holler If You Hear Me*. 148–49.

38. Michael Eric Dyson quoted in Cornel West. "Never Forget: A Journey of Revelations." Hidden Beach. July 3, 2008.

39. Cornel West." "Never Forget: A

Journey of Revelations." Hidden Beach Recording. June 19, 2007.

40. Cornel West quoted in *Washington Post* "Cornel West discusses race, activism, music." August 9, 2007. D3.

41. West." "Never Forget." June 19, 2007.

42. Cornel West. "The Stream—The 'N' word." *Al Jazeera*. February 20, 2013. Retrieved from https://www.youtube.com/watch?v=GV1a8NhPZtE

43. Cornel West quoted in G. Jeffrey MacDonald. "Professor tries rap to reach new audience." *Star Tribune* (Minneapolis, MN). December 29, 2001. B7.

44. West. "The Stream." February 20, 2013.

45. John McWhorter. "There are Two N-Word." *Lexicon Valley Podcast.* January 9 2018.

46. Seth Mydans. "As English's dominance continues, linguists see few threats to its rule." *Boston Globe* (Boston, MA). April 29, 2007. 9.

47. John McWhorter. *Talking Back, Talking Black: Truths About America's Lingua Franca.* New York, NY: Bellevue Literary Press, 2017. 14.

48. Stokely Carmichael. *Stokely Speaks: From Black Power to Pan-Africanism.* Chicago, IL: Chicago Review Press. 1971. 4.

49. McWhorter. *Talking Back, Talking Black* 11–12.

50. McWhorter. *Talking Back, Talking Black.* 12.

51. McWhorter. *Talking Back, Talking Black.* 161.

52. McWhorter. *Talking Back, Talking Black.* 163.

53. John McWhorter. *Nine Nasty Words: English in the Gutter: Then, Now, and Forever.* New York: Avery. 2021. 202.

54. John McWhorter. Email Correspondence with the author. New York, NY. March 17, 2020.

55. John McWhorter. "The Idea That Whites Can't Refer to the N-Word." *The Atlantic.* August 27, 2019. Retrieved from https://www.theatlantic.com/ideas/archive/2019/08/whites-refer-to-the-n-word/596872/

56. John McWhorter. "If President Obama Can Say It, You Can Too." *TIME.* June 22, 2015. Retrieved from https://time.com/3930797/obama-maron-interview/

57. McWhorter. *Nine Nasty Words.* 208.

58. Elizabeth Stordeur Pryor. "The Etymology of Nigger: Resistance, Language, and the Politics of Freedom in the Antebellum North." *Journal of the Early Republic,* vol. 36, No. 2, Summer 2016. 212, 216.

59. Elizabeth Stordeur Pryor. *Colored Travelers: Mobility and the Fight for Citizenship before the Civil War.* Chapel Hill, NC: University of North Carolina Press, 2016. 40.

60. Kennedy. *Nigger.* 92–94.

61. Juliana Menasce Horowitz, Anna Brown, and Kiana Cox. "Race in America 2019." *Pew Research Center.* April 9, 2019. Retrieved from https://www.pewsocialtrends.org/2019/04/09/race-in-america-2019/

62. Elizabeth Stordeur Pryor. "The N-Word in the Classroom." TEDxEasthamptonWomen. January 28, 2020. Retrieved from https://www.youtube.com/watch?v=_LauLaVT_ZY

63. Stordeur Pryor. "The N-Word in the Classroom." January 28, 2020.

64. Imani Perry. *Prophets of the Hood: Politics and Poetics in Hip Hop.* Durham, NC: Duke University Press, 2004. 143.

65. Annette John-Hall. "N-word: Don't play with fire." *The Philadelphia Inquirer* (Philadelphia, PA). January 10, 2007. D1–4.

66. Perry. *Prophets of the Hood.* 142.

67. Imani Perry. *Breath: A Letter to My Sons.* Boston, MA: Beacon Press, 2019. 67–68.

68. Jessica McDonald. "Wise Words." *The Forum* (Salt Lake City, UT). September 19, 2006. 2.

69. Daniel T. Lichter, et al. "Toward a New Macro-Segregation? Decomposing Segregation within and between Metropolitan Cities and Suburbs." *American Sociological Review.* 2015.

70. Jennifer L. Eberhardt. *Biased: Uncovering the Hidden Prejudice That Shapes What We See, Think, and Do.* New York: Penguin Books. 2020; Mahzarin R. Banaji. *Blindspot: Hidden Biases of Good People.* New York: Bantam. 2016.

71. Tim Wise. *White Like Me: Reflections from a Privileged Son.* Soft Skull Press, 2011. 38.

72. Wise. *White Like Me.* 36; Allison Petty. "Confronting a Mess." *Herald and Review* (Decatur, IL). March 2, 2012. 3.

73. Michael Eric Dyson quoted in "Anti-racism activist Tim Wise to speak

May 20." *Glen Rock Gazette* (Glen Rock, NJ). May 6, 2005. 44.

74. Tim Wise. "Author: Use 3rd Grade Logic with the N Word." *CNN Tonight with Don Lemon*. July 1, 2013. Retrieved from https://www.youtube.com/watch?v=Ee3WQiqWhlw; Tim Wise. "CNN: Is the N-word ever OK?" *CNN Tonight with Don Lemon*. August 15, 2010. Retrieved from https://www.youtube.com/watch?v=RTJlfWPc09I

75. Tim Wise. "The Stream—The 'N' word." *Al Jazeera*. February 20, 2013. Retrieved from https://www.youtube.com/watch?v=GVla8NhPZtE

76. Joe Feagin. *Systemic Racism: A Theory of Oppression*. New York, NY: Routledge, 2006. 3–5; Joe R. Feagin. *Racist America: Roots, Current Realities, and Future Reparations*. New York, NY: Routledge 2014. 1–12.

77. Joe Feagin. *White Racist Frame: Centuries of Racial Framing and Counter-Framing*. New York, NY: Routledge, 2013. 141.

78. Joe Feagin. "The White Racial Frame: Historical and Contemporary." *Interpreting Joe R. Feagin*, 2013. Handout at Okogyeamon (Herbert A. Perkins) and Margery K. Otto. 2014 www.asdic-circle.org.

79. Feagin. "The White Racial Frame: Historical and Contemporary." 2013.

80. Joe Feagin. *White Racist Frame*. 126.

81. Joe Feagin. *White Racist Frame*. 94, 127–30.

Chapter 5

1. *New York Times News Service* quoted in *The Morning Call* (Allentown, PA). "200,000 Jam Catskills Hamlet for Woodstock rock festival." August 16, 1969. 2.

2. Jerry Shnay. "It's Keyed to Entertainment Culture is in the Offing on TV." *Chicago Tribune*. July 27, 1969. Sct. 5–5; Bryan Greene. "Parks and Recreation." *Poverty & Race Research Action Council*. April–June 2017. 5.

3. Hardeep Phull. *Story Behind the Protest Song: A Reference Guide to the 50 Songs that Changed the 20th Century*. Westport, CT: Greenwood Pres, 2008. 84–86.

4. Ice-T and Douglass Century. *Ice: A Memoir of Gangster Life and Redemption—from South Central to Hollywood*. New York, NY: One World Books, 2011. 131–32.

5. James Hetfield quoted in "Precious Metal." *SPIN*. October 1991. 45.

6. Michael Eric Dyson. *Long Time Coming: Reckoning with Race in America*. New York, NY: St. Martin's Press. 2020. 41–42.

7. Yoko Ono quoted in Ursula Macfarlane. *The Real Yoko Ono*. Documentary, 2001; Michael Epstein. *John & Yoko: Above Us Only Sky*. Documentary, 2018.

8. Geoffrey Giuliano. *Lennon in America: 1971–1980, Based in Part on the Lost Lennon Dairies*. New York, NY: Cooper Square, Press, 2000. 36.

9. Albert Goldman. *The Lives of John Lennon*. Chicago, IL: Chicago Review Books, 1988. 22.

10. David Bauder. "Lennon Remembered." *The Courier-News* (Bridgewater, NJ). December 7, 2005. E1-E3; Robert Hilburn. "A Letdown Album from John, Yoko." *Los Angeles Times* (Los Angeles, CA). June 25, 1972. 46.

11. Giuliano. *Lennon in America*. 33; Thom Akeman. "It's the John and Yoko Art Show." *Democrat and Chronicle* (Rochester, NY). October 9, 1971. 1C; Tom Zito. "Yoko Opens Art Show." *Pacific Daily News* (Agana Heights, Guam). October 16, 1971. 34; Suzy Knickerbocker. "Suzy Says: Unconquerable West Stole the Scene." *Hartford Courant* (Hartford, CT). October 17, 1971. 11E; Gertrude Lucey. "Losses at Yoko Ono Exhibit Cause Museum Head Concern." *The Post-Standard* (Syracuse, NY). October 19, 1971. 8 and 11.

12. Joan Hanauer. "Yoko Ono's 'instructions' help her to live." *Boston Globe* (Boston, MA). September 7, 1971. 39.

13. Ken Tucker and David Fricke. "Fearless Leader." *Rolling Stones*. October 10, 2012.

14. Mike Barber of *Postmedia News* found in *The Windsor Star* (Windsor, Ontario, Canada). "Dire Straits lyrics ruled offensive." January 14, 2011. C6.

15. Chris Selley. *National Post* (Toronto, Ontario, Canada). "Dire Straits and empty plates." January 14, 2011. A12.

16. Charmaine Kerridge. *National Post* (Toronto, Ontario, Canada). "Dire Straits Member Decries CBSC Ruling." January 15, 2011. A10.

17. *Red Deer Advocate* (Red Deer, Alberta, Canada). "Straits' fans decry ban on 'Money.'" January 15, 2011. A8.

18. Timothy Hampton. *Bob Dylan's Poetics: How the Songs Work.* New York, NY: Zone Books. 2019. 149; Richard F. Thomas. *Why Bob Dylan Matters.* New York, NY: HarperCollins Publishers, 2017. 303.

19. Ibram X. Kendi. *How To Be An Antiracist.* New York, NY: Random House, One World. 90; Ibram X. Kendi quoted in John Black. "Sure, black people can be racist too." *CNN.* September 22, 2019. Retrieved from https://www.cnn.com/2019/09/22/us/kendi-book-anti-racist-blake/index.html

20. Stephen Duncombe and Maxwell Tremblay. *White Riot: Punk Rock and the Politics of Race.* Verso Books. 2011. 18–23.

21. Patti Smith, quoted in Duncombe and Tremblay. *White Riot.* 18–23.

22. Duncombe and Tremblay. *White Riot.* 23.

23. Robert Hilburn. "Patti Smith's Double Victory." *Los Angeles Times* (Los Angeles, CA). March 25, 1978. 13.

24. Adam Bregman. "Song of Frankenchrist." *LA Weekly.* July 31, 1997. 41; S. Rick Czach. "'Dead Kennedys' can be fun." *The Tampa Times* (Tampa, FL). October 31, 1980. 51.

25. Jim Sullivan. "Punk rock band goads audience." *The Bangor Daily News* (Bangor, ME). April 20, 1981. 12.

26. Elvis Costello quoted in Prachi Gupta. "BBC gets heat for censoring Elvis Costello's 1979 hit 'Oliver's Army.'" *Salon.* March 19, 2013.

27. Elvis Costello quoted in Rob Patterson. "Are Elvis Costello's 'Armed Forces' Real?" *The Times and Democrat* (Orangeburg, SC). April 12, 1979. 10.

28. Elvis Costello quoted in Jack Lloyd. "Caustic comments from Elvis Costello erode image in U.S." *The Philadelphia Inquirer* April 6, 1979. 22.

29. *Longview Daily News* (Longview, WA). "British rock star copies Ali's technique." May 5, 1979. 13.

30. Ernie Santosouosso. "Randy Newman's 'Rednecks' a song of Lester Maddox." *The Boston Globe.* October 6, 1974. 78.

31. Randy Newman quoted in Art Harris. "Randy Newman." *Dayton Daily News* (Dayton, OH). October 27, 1974. 3.

32. Associated Press International featured in *The San Francisco Examiner.* "Ad decries bigotry in lyrics." September 23, 1989. A-17.

33. Vernon Reid quoted in *The Age* (Melbourne, Victoria, Australia). "Guns N' Roses: sneering all the way to the bank." February 4, 1990. 24; Tom Moon. "Neanderthal Axl Rose Erases Rock Progress." *Albuquerque Journal* (Albuquerque, NM). December 24, 1989. F2.

34. Arsenio Hall quoted in *The Age.* "Guns N' Roses." February 4, 1990. 24.

35. Axl Rose quoted in *The Age.* "Guns N' Roses." February 4, 1990. 24.

36. Roger Catlin. "The band that won't talk." *Daily Press* (Newport News, VA). June 21, 1991. 12.

37. Dan Leroy. "Coe Revisits Penitentiary." *Rolling Stone.* July 14, 2005.

38. Mark Kemp. *Dixie Lullaby: A Story of Music, Race, and New Beginnings.* Athens and London: The University of Georgia Press, 2004. 205.

39. Neil Strauss. "Songwriter's Racist Songs from the 1980's Haunt Him." *The New York Times.* September 4, 2000.

40. *Ibid.*

Chapter 6

1. *Decatur Daily Review* (Decatur, IL) "Racist Plot Against King Under Probe." February 26, 1965. 1; *Spokesman-Review* (Spokane, WA). "Dynamite Found; Suspect Hunted." February 26, 1965. 1.

2. Dennis Ogawa paraphrased in Alison Dundes Renteln. "A Psychohistorical Analysis of the Japanese American Internment." *Human Rights Quarterly.* The Johns Hopkins University Press. Nov. 1995. 632; John DeWitt quoted in Alison Dundes Renteln. "A Psychohistorical Analysis of the Japanese American Internment." *Human Rights Quarterly.* The Johns Hopkins University Press. Nov. 1995. 634.

3. Isabel Wilkerson. *Caste: The Origins of Our Discontents.* New York, NY: Penguin Random House LLC. 2020.

4. *Herald and Whig* (Somerset, PA). "Let the South Bear its Share of the Burdens." June 7, 1865. 2.

5. Tom O'Connor. "Portrait of a Lynch Town." *The Gazette and Daily* (York, PA). August 6, 1946. 2 and 27.

6. Randall Kennedy. *Nigger: The Strange Career of a Troublesome Word.* New York, NY: Vintage Books. 2002. 45–46.

7. Carolyn Bryant quoted in R.L. Nave. "Emmett Till murder; The full text testimony of Carolyn Bryant." July 12, 2018. *Mississippi Today.* Retrieved at https://mississippitoday.org/2018/07/12/emmett-till-murder-the-full-text-testimony-of-carolyn-bryant/

8. Hugh White quoted in Homer Bigart. "Mississippi Violently Opposes Integration." *Tampa Bay Times* (St. Petersburg, FL). September 24, 1955. 1.

9. Charles Conley "Connie" Lynch quoted in Tonya Jameson. "Any way you say n-word, it connotes inferiority." *The Charlotte Observer* (Charlotte, NC). January 27, 2002. 4D.

10. Tom Tiede. "Gibson Battles an Image." *The Daily Herald* (Provo, UT). July 1, 1970. 16.

11. J.B. Stoner quoted in Tim O'Brien. "FCC Rules Georgia Race Can Continue 'Nigger' Ad." *The Capital Times* (Madison, WI). August 4, 1972. 4.

12. *Parsons Weekly Globe* (Parsons, KS). "Mahara's Mammoth Minstrels." March 17, 1899. 1.

13. *The Evening Herald* (Parsons, KS). "Mahara Minstrels." October 27, 1902. 3.

14. *The Tennessean* (Nashville, TN). "Fisk Library to Get Handy's Documents." November 20, 1978. 11.

15. *Daily Press* (Newport News, VA). "Father of Blues, W.C. Handy, Buried." April 3, 1958. 6.

16. William T. Dargan. "Composer sets tone for generations." *The News and Observer* (Raleigh, NC). October 5, 1995. 10E.

17. Peter C. Muir. *Long Lost Blues: Popular Blues in America, 1850–1920.* Champaign, IL: University of Illinois Press. 2010. 28–36.

18. John Henrik Clarke quoted in Peggy Peterman. "Nigger: an ugly word out of the past ..." *Tampa Bay Times* (St. Petersburg, FL). July 29, 1979. E1.

19. Randall Kennedy. *Nigger: The Strange Career of a Troublesome Word.* New York, NY: Vintage Books, 2003. 3, 43–44.

20. Michael Eric Dyson. *Tears We Cannot Stop.* New York, NY: St. Martin's Press, 2017. 163.

21. Ijeoma Oluo. *So You Want To Talk About Race.* New York, NY: Seal Press, 2018. 140.

22. Todd Williams. *The N Word.* Documentary Film. Todd Larkins. June 26, 2004.

23. Elizabeth Stordeur Pryor. *Colored Travelers: Mobility and the Fight for Citizenship before the Civil War.* Chapel Hill, NC: University of North Carolina Press, 2016. 11; Elizabeth Stordeur Pryor. "The Etymology of Nigger: Resistance, Language, and the Politics of Freedom in the Antebellum North." *Journal of the Early Republic,* vol. 36, No. 2, Summer 2016. 206.

24. Pyror. "The Etymology of Nigger." 214, 243.

25. Lerone Bennett, Jr. "An Abolitionist Named Truth." *Dayton Daily News* (Dayton, OH). November 20, 1968. 42.

26. *Hartford Courant* (Hartford, CT). "A Man by Himself." February 21, 1895. 6.

27. David Henry and Joe Henry. *Furious Cool: Richard Pryor and the World That Made Him.* Chapel Hill, NC: Algonquin Books of Chapel Hill, 2014. 63–64.

28. Richard Pryor. "Richard Pryor 1964 Standup Comedy old but funny." YouTube. Black godztv. July 2, 2016. Retrieved from https://www.youtube.com/watch?v=JexB1MQaVhs

29. Henry Allen. "Pryor Exorcises the Devil in Him." *The Sacramento Bee* (Sacramento, CA). October 10, 1978. 2.

30. Richard Pryor. "Super Nigger [Explicit]." *The Anthology: 1968–1992.* Warner Records Inc. & Rhino Entertainment Company, 2002, 2015; Jabari Asim. *The N Word: Who Can Say It, Who Shouldn't, and Why.* Boston and New York: Houghton Mifflin Company, 2007. 207–08.

31. Richard Pryor. "President Pryor." YouTube. Buckum95. September 22, 2006. Retrieved from https://www.youtube.com/watch?v=EtlDVi_1JMg; David S. Silverman. *You Can't Air That: Four Cases of Controversy and Censorship in American Television Programming.* Syracuse, NY: Syracuse University Press, 2007. 70–71.

32. Robin DiAngelo. *White Fragility: Why It's So Hard for White People to Talk About Racism.* Boston, MA: Beacon Press, 2018. 103.

33. Coura Fall. "Is the N-Word Just A Word?" An Interview with Dr. Ibram X. Kendi." *The Blackprint.* April

12, 2019. Retrieved from https://www. theblackprintau.com/blog/2019/4/12/ interview-with-dr-ibram-x-kendi-on-the-n-word-incident

34. Richard Pryor. "The Motherland." Retrieved from Black Godztv. "Richard Pryor The N word." May 2, 2018. *YouTube.* Retrieved from https://www.youtube.com/ watch?v=ArxI3sbNrlI; Audrey Thomas McCluskey, editor. *Richard Pryor: The Life and Legacy of a "crazy" Black Man.* Bloomington, IN. Indiana University Press, 2008. 32; Liane Hansen. "With Biting Humor, Pryor Explored Race in America." *NPR Obituaries.* December 11, 2005. Retrieved from https://www.npr.org/templates/ story/story.php?storyId=5048040.

35. *Ebony.* "Richard Pryor: Talks About Richard Pryor (The Old, The New) Rejection That Led to Loneliness and Drugs, God, Prayer, 'Nigger,' And How He Was Burned." October 1980. 42.

36. Robert Wieder. "Bad Mooney Rising." *The San Francisco Examiner* (San Francisco, CA). February 21, 1993.

37. Wieder. "Bad Mooney Rising." February 21, 1993.

38. Paul Mooney quoted in Michel Marriott. "Can pop culture defuse sting of a racial epithet?" *The Atlanta Constitution* (Atlanta, GA). January 27, 1993. B1 and B5.

39. Paul Mooney quoted in Erin Texeira. "No more n-word." *The Times* (Munster, IN). December 1, 2006. C9.

40. Chris Rock quoted in David Gauder. "Chris Rock says to chill out." *Lansing State Journal* (Lansing, MI). September 5, 1998. 27.

41. Marty Gitlin. *Chris Rock: A Biography of a Comic Genius.* Berkeley Heights, NJ: Enslow Publishers, Inc. 2014. 16–17.

42. *The Courier-News* (Bridgewater, NJ). "And the winners are ..." September 15, 1997. 24.

43. Chris Rock quoted in Jonathan McDonald. "Between Rock and a Funny Place." *The Province* (Vancouver, British Columbia, Canada). January 16, 1998. C1.

44. Gitlin. *Chris Rock.* 17.

45. Chris Rock quoted in Al Hunter Jr. "N-ything Goes." *Philadelphia Daily News* (Philadelphia, PA). October 31, 1997. F16.

46. Donald Glover. "The N word." *Comedy Central Uncensored. Entertainment One Distribution. YouTube.* November 6, 2014. Retrieved from https://www. youtube.com/watch?v=k15g9iYsFRI

47. Tony Norman. "The hilariously dangerous world of Dave Chappelle." *Pittsburgh Post-Gazette* (Pittsburgh, PA). January 27, 2004. 7.

48. Dave Chappelle quoted in Bernard Weinraub. "Inspired by Cosby." *The Town Talk* (Alexandria, LA). August 24, 1993. C-7.

49. Dave Chappelle quoted in NBC. com. "Dave Chappelle Stand-Up Monologue." November 7, 2020. Retrieved from https://www.nbc.com/saturday-night-live/video/dave-chappelle-standup-monologue/4262843.

Chapter 7

1. Steve Dougherty. "Ali: Still the Greatest." *Atlanta Constitution* (Atlanta, GA). April 8, 1978. A1 and A4.

2. Muhammad Ali quoted in David J. Thomas. *The State of American Policing: Psychology, Behavior, Problems, and Solutions.* Santa Barbara, CA: Praeger. 2018. 15.

3. Muhammad Ali quoted in Shirley Povich of *The Washington Post.* "Muhammad Ali has predicted Super Bowl 'Will go distance.'" *The Times* (Shreveport, LA). January 17, 1971. 11.

4. Muhammad Ali quoted in William Hart. "Ali's a Knockout in Prison." *Detroit Free Press* (Detroit, MI). March 28, 1976. 1.

5. Muhammad Ali quoted in Dave Anderson of the *New York Times.* "Ali says Cuban would be no match." *Miami News* (Miami, FL. August 5, 1976. 16.

6. *The Atlanta Constitution* (Atlanta, GA). "Promoter Ali Steals the Show." September 12, 1978. D1 and D6.

7. Muhammad Ali quoted in *The Jackson Sun* (Jackson, TN). "Clay Heckles His Black Hecklers." January 30, 1970. 20.

8. Muhammad Ali quoted in *The Province* (Vancouver, British Columbia, Canada). "Polar Proposal Gets Yes." April 26, 1988. 42.

9. Dorothy Gilliam. "Crushing tolerance for racism at University of Kentucky." *The Washington Post.* April 11, 1988.

10. Touré. "How Muhammad Ali Invented Hip-Hop." *Noisey, Music by Vice.* Vice.com. June 6, 2016. Retrieved

from https://www.vice.com/en/article/nnkjvd/how-muhammad-ali-invented-hip-hop.

11. Randy Roberts and Johnny Smith. *Blood Brothers: The Fatal Friendship Between Muhammad Ali and Malcolm X.* New York, NY: Basic Books. 2016. 2.

12. Chuck D quoted in Jake Coyle. "New book claims Ali was the first rapper." *Indiana Gazette* (Indiana, PA). December 19, 2006. 20.

13. Darryl McDaniels quoted in Hess. *Hip Hop in America.* Xviii.

14. Imani Perry quoted in Mickey Hess. *Hip Hop in America: Regional Guide.* Santa Barbara, CA. Denver, CO. Oxford England: Greenwood Press. 2010. xviii.

15. Imani Perry. *Prophets of the Hood: Politics and Poetics in Hip Hop.* Durham, NC and London, England. Duke University Press, 2004. 58.

16. Perry. *Prophets of the Hood.* 59.

17. Roberts and Smith. *Blood Brothers.* 61.

18. Oprah quoted in *The Oprah Winfrey Show.* "Jay-Z on the N-word." September 2009, posted January 17, 2011. Retrieved from http://www.oprah.com/own-oprahshow/jay-z-on-the-n-word-video.

19. Jay-Z quoted in *O Magazine.* "Oprah Talks to Jay-Z." October 2009. Retrieved from https://www.oprah.com/omagazine/oprah-interviews-jay-z-october-2009-issue-of-o-magazine/8.

20. Ann Oldenburg. "Oprah: 'You cannot be my friend' and use n-word.'" *USA Today.* July 31, 2013. Retrieved from https://www.usatoday.com/story/life/people/2013/07/31/oprah-you-cannot-be-my-friend-and-use-n-word/2604587/.

21. Michael Eric Dyson. *Tears We Cannot Stop: A Sermon to White America.* New York, NY. St. Martin's Press, 2017. 164–67.

22. Michael Eric Dyson quoted in C-SPAN. "User Clip: Dyson on the 'n' word." November 12, 2017. Retrieved from https://www.c-span.org/video/?c4691208/user-clip-dyson-n-word

23. Neal Lester quoted in *The G-L Review.* "Dr. Neal Lester on Rap, Culture, and the N-Word." Found in Nathan Graber-Lipperman. "At the Intersection of Language and Culture: Rap and the N-Word." *Medium.* September 23, 2018.

Chapter 8

1. Ice-T. and Heidi Siegmund. *The Ice Opinion: Who Gives a Fuck?* United Kingdom: Pan, 1995.

2. Kathy Frankovic. "When it comes to the n-word, most see it as offensive whoever says it." YouGov. August 23, 2018. Retrieved from https://today.yougov.com/topics/politics/articles-reports/2018/08/23/when-it-comes-n-word-most-see-it-offensive-whoever.

3. Ray Winbush quoted in Rick de Yampert. "The N-word." *The Tennessean* (Nashville, TN). February 28, 1999. 1D-2D.

4. Delroy Lindo and Christian Miranda. "The Good Fight S02E06 Clip / 'So Say It.'" *The Good Fight.* YouTube. April 8, 2018. Retrieved from https://www.youtube.com/watch?v=S4pSp3Km6Mw

5. Jordan Zakarin. "Samuel L. Jackson Insists Reporter Say N-Word in 'Django Unchained' Interview (Video)." *Hollywood Reporter.* January 2, 2013. Retrieved from https://www.hollywoodreporter.com/news/samuel-l-jackson-insists-reporter-407425

6. George Yancy. *Across Black Spaces: Essays and Interviews from an American Philosopher.* New York, NY: Rowman & Littlefield. 2020. 41.

7. Dalton Higgins. *Hip Hop World: A Groundwork Guide by Dalton Higgins.* Berkeley, CA: Groundwood Books, 2009. 13.

8. Perry. *Profits of the Hood.* 143.

9. Gary Suarez. "When Latinx People Use the N-Word." *New York Times.* October 17, 2019.

10. Dylan Flynn. "White people should never rap the n-word: A linguist breaks it down." *The Conversation.* October 22, 2017 (Updated May 22, 2018). Retrieved from https://theconversation.com/white-people-should-never-rap-the-n-word-a-linguist-breaks-it-down-84673

11. Linda M. Harrington. "On Capitol Hill, a real rap session." *Chicago Tribune.* February 24, 1994. 1 and 18.

12. Snoop Dogg quoted in Sian Cain. "Jason Reynolds: 'Snoop Dogg once told white folks: 'I know you hate me. But your kids don't.' That's how I feel." *The Guardian.* November 20, 2020. Retrieved from https://www.theguardian.com/books/2020/nov/

20/jason-reynolds-snoop-dogg-once-told-white-folks-i-know-you-hate-me-but-your-kids-dont-thats-how-i-feel

13. Greg Botelho and Dana Ford. "Fraternity's house mom sings n-word." *CNN.* March 10, 2015. Retrieved from https://www.cnn.com/2015/03/10/us/oklahoma-fraternity-house-mom/index.html; Jake New. "Fraternity Caught on Video Singing Racist Song." *InsideHigherEd.* March 9, 2015. Retrieved from https://www.insidehighered.com/quicktakes/2015/03/09/fraternity-caught-video-singing-racist-song; *ABC News.* Oklahoma SAE Frat: Two Students Expelled Over Racist Chants." *YouTube.* March 11, 2015. Retrieved from https://www.youtube.com/watch?v=nU-ZbjB00k8.

14. Trinidad James quoted in Jay Balfour. "Trinidad James Reacts to Oklahoma University Fraternity's Racist Chant." *Hip Hop DX.* March 15, 2015. Retrieved from https://hiphopdx.com/news/id.32959/title.trinidad-james-reacts-to-oklahoma-sae-chapter-singing-racist-chant#;

15. Trinidad James quoted in Saeed Ahmed. "Rapper Trinidad James, commentator Ben Ferguson clash over use of N-word." *CNN Tonight.* March 17, 2015. Retrieved from https://www.cnn.com/2015/03/17/living/don-lemon-cnn-tonight-n-word-exchange-feat/index.html

16. Steven Elbow. "Negotiating the N-word." *The Capital Times* (Madison, WI). June 18, 2014. 18.

17. Ben Ferguson quoted in Saeed Ahmed. "Rapper Trinidad James, commentator Ben Ferguson clash over use of N-word." *CNN Tonight.* March 17, 2015. Retrieved from https://www.cnn.com/2015/03/17/living/don-lemon-cnn-tonight-n-word-exchange-feat/index.html

18. Frank Lombardi. "Council vote sends a message." *Daily News* (New York, NY). March 1, 2007. 4.

19. *Daily News* (New York, NY). "Council vs. the N-word." February 27, 2007. 13; Mary Vallis. "New York city council bans the N-word." *National Post* (Toronto, Ontario, Canada). March 2, 2007. A2.

20. *Daily News* (New York, NY). "Voices of the People." March 2, 2007. 28.

21. *Daily News* (New York, NY). "Ban the bans." August 2, 2007. 28.

22. Bruce Jablonsky quoted in *Daily News.* "Ha, ha, ha." August 3, 2007. 34.

23. Kilpatrick and Bond quoted in Corey Williams. "Burying racism's 'greatest child.'" *Victoria Advocate* (Victoria, TX). July 10, 2007. A6.

24. *The Daily News-Journal* (Murfreesboro, TN). "NAACP symbolic burial should put N-word to rest." July 16, 2007. 10.

25. Kurtis Blow quoted in Suzette Hackney. "NAACP puts unfriendly word to rest." *Greenville News* (Greenville, SC). July 10, 2007. 6.

26. *Alabama Journal* (Montgomery, AL). "NAACP Holds Funeral Rites for 'Jim Crow.'" April 4, 1955. 9.

27. John McWhorter quoted in Mary Vallis. "New York city council bans the N-word." *National Post* (Toronto, Ontario, Canada). March 2, 2007. A2.

28. John McWhorter quoted in Gene Demby. "How Would You Kill The N-Word?" *Code Switch.* Podcast. August 13, 2013.

29. Cary Darling. "Rap music going mainstream with successful 'Yo! MTV Raps.'" *The Pittsburgh Press.* February 9, 1990. C7.

30. Nichole Christian. "Rap Reaches New Ears." *Detroit Free Press.* September 27, 1989. B1 and B2.

31. Michael Endelman. "After Sept. 11, hip-hop raises dissenting voices." *The Boston Globe* (Boston, MAA). May 5, 2002. L10.

32. Russell Simmons and Nelson George. *Life and Def: Sex, Drugs, Money, and God.* New York, NY. Three Rivers Press. 2001. 70; Russell Simmons quoted in John McWhorter. "How Hip-Hop Holds Blacks Back: Violence, Misogyny, and Lawlessness are Nothing to Sing About." *City-Journal* (New York, NY), Summer 2003. Retrieved from https://www.city-journal.org/html/how-hip-hop-holds-blacks-back-12442.html

33. Schoolly D quoted in Jonathan Takiff. "The Rap Message." *Philadelphia Daily News* (Philadelphia, PA). November 2, 1988. 47; A.D. Amorosi. "Schoolly D." *Philadelphia Inquirer* (Philadelphia, PA). December 5, 2000. E1-E3.

34. Patrick Goldstein. "Geffen vs. Geto Boys: Double Standard?" *The Los Angeles Times.* August 26, 1990. 78.

35. Jimmy Magahern. "Geto Boys make no apologies." *Leader-Telegram* (Eau Claire, WI). January 6, 1991. 2G.

36. Peggy Fikac. "The Best New Musicians May be Found in the Independent Fringe." *The Kokomo Tribune* (Kokomo, IN). April 16, 1992. 19.

37. Jason Whitlock. "Changing to keep up with times, Geto Boys focus on bottom line." *The Charlotte Observer* (Charlotte, NC). November 29, 1991. 2E.

38. Paul Harris. *Black Rage Confronts the Law.* New York, NY: NYU Press, 1999. 186.

39. A.S. Rose. "Gangsta Rap. Nazi Rock." *San Francisco Examiner* (San Francisco, CA). January 10, 1993. D1 and D6.

40. Leonard Pitts Jr. "Gangsta on Trial." *Miami Herald* (Miami, FL). December 8, 1993. E1 and E3.

41. Calvin Butts quoted in Leonard Pitts Jr. "Gangsta on Trial." *Miami Herald* (Miami, FL). December 8, 1993. E3.

42. Paul George. "Rap on the knuckles." *The Guardian* (London, Greater London, England). January 18, 1995. 20.

43. Robbert Tilli. "Sweden: Sweden's Smorgasbord of Talent has something for every taste." *Billboard.* December 13, 1997. 58.

44. Zak Tell quoted in "Rage Fuels Clawfinger's European Success." *Billboard.* March 5, 1994.

45. Carrie Golus. *Tupac Shakur.* Lerner Publications. 2006.

46. Dan Quayle quoted in Chuck Philips. "Testing the Limits." *Los Angeles Times* (Los Angeles, CA). F1, F6-F7.

47. Gabe Meline. "Remembering the time Tupac Shakur Sued the Oakland Police for $10 Million." *KQED.* June 16, 2016.

48. Djvlad. Jermaine Hopkins. "I don't feel 2Pac turned into 'Bishop' after 'Juice.'" *YouTube.* June 4, 2019. Retrieved from https://www.youtube.com/watch?v=ROO1CEjTKnw.

49. Fernando Gonzalez. "Shakur's death foreshadowed in rhythms of his life." *Clarion-Ledger* (Jackson, MS). September 15, 1966. 12A.

50. *Atlanta Post.* "Remembering Tupac: His Musical Legacy and His Top Selling Albums." February 20, 2011.

51. Michael Eric Dyson. *Holler if You Hear Me.*

52. Kara Keeling. "'A Homegrown Revolutionary'?: Tupac Shakur and the Legacy of the Black Panther Party." *The Black Scholar.* 1999. 59.

53. Virginia C. Fowler. *Nikki Giovanni: A Literary Biography.* Santa Barbara, CA. Denver, CO. Oxford, England: Praeger. 2013. 37–38.

54. Nikki Giovanni. "Reflections of April 4, 1968."

55. Snoop Dogg quoted in Rock & Roll Hall of Fame. "Snoop Dogg Inducts Tupac Shakur into the Rock & Roll Hall of Fame 2017." *YouTube.* June 17, 2017. Retrieved from https://www.youtube.com/watch?v=VYFZFIZ5SBM.

56. Ice-T quoted in Rick de Yampert. "Once just a racist weapon, now a hip-hop icon, and that stirs worry among some blacks." February 28, 1999. 1D and 2D.

57. Henry Louis Gates quoted in Murray Forman and Mark Anthony Neal. *That's the Joint1: The Hip-Hop Studies Reader*; David Samuels. "The Rap on Rap: The 'Black Music' that isn't either.'" New York, NY: Routledge. 2004. 153.

58. Michael Endelman. "After Sept. 11, hip-hop raises dissenting voices." *The Boston Globe* (Boston, MAA). May 5, 2002. L10.

59. T.J. Crawford quoted in Andy Downing. "Hip-hop artists hope to build political power." *Chicago Tribune* (Chicago, IL). July 16, 2006. 8.

60. Halifu Osumare. "Attacks against rapper are smoke screen for larger issues." *The Sacramento Bee* (Sacramento, CA). May 22, 2011. E5; Jason Genegabus. "Common: A Conscious Rapper." *Honolulu Star-Bulletin* (Honolulu, HI). September 23, 2005. 1.

61. Roger Catlin. "More rappers putting accent on education, communication." *Messenger-Inquirer* (Owensboro, KY). September 1, 1989, D1 and D6.

62. *Arizona Daily Sun* (Flagstaff, AZ). September 6, 2018. A7.

Chapter 9

1. Peter Sblendorio. "Sorority slammed after members sing N-word in Kanye West song." *New York Daily News.* September 22, 2017. Retrieved from https://www.nydailynews.com/entertainment/music/sorority-investigated-girls-sing-n-word-kanye-song-article-1.3511331.

2. Piers Morgan. Twitter. June 22, 2015. 11:16 a.m.

3. Piers Morgan. "Don't get angry about a bunch of white girls singing n***as, blame Kanye and the rap industry for putting it in their songs in the first play." *Daily Mail.* September 21, 2017. Retrieved from https://www.dailymail.co.uk/news/article-4907740/PIERS-MORGAN-mad-Kanye-not-girls-singing-n-as.html

4. Derald Wing Sue. "Race Talk: The Psychology of Racial Dialogues." *American Psychologist.* November 2013. 663–672; Kotler, J.A. Haider, T.Z. & Levine, M.H. (2019). *Identity Matters: Parents' and educators' perceptions of children's social identity development.* New York: Sesame Workshop. 14–21.

5. Kotler, J.A. Haider, T.Z. & Levine, M.H. (2019). *Identity Matters: Parents' and educators' perceptions of children's social identity development.* New York: Sesame Workshop. 14–21.

6. Jeremy Helligar. "Kendrick Lamar's Onstage Outrage: Why Rap Should Retire the N-Word for Good." *Variety.* May 22, 2018. Retrieved from https://variety.com/2018/music/opinion/kendrick-lamar-rappers-should-stop-using-n-word-1202818977/

7. Barry Jenkins. "Chapter V." *Dear White People.* Netflix. April 28, 2017.

8. Monnica T. Williams. "Cultural Adaptations of Prolonged Exposure therapy for Treatment and Prevention of Post-traumatic Stress Disorder in African Americans." *Behavioral Sciences.* 2014. 4; J.A. Himle, R.E. Baser, R.J. Taylor, R.D. Campbell, and J.S. Jackson. "Anxiety disorders among African Americans, Blacks of Caribbean Descent, and Non-Hispanic Whites in the United States." *Journal of Anxiety Disorder.* 2009.

9. Jonathan W. Kanter, Monnica T. Williams, Adam M. Kuczynski, Tatherine E. Manbeck, Marlena Debreaux, and Daniel C. Rosen. "A Preliminary Report on the Relationship Between Microaggressions Against Black People and Racism Among White College Students." *Race and Social Problems.* August 30, 2017. Retrieved from https://link.springer.com/article/10.1007/s12552-017-9214-0

10. Scott O. Lilienfeld paraphrased in Todd Mealy. *Race Conscious Pedagogy: Disrupting Racism at Majority White Schools.* Jefferson, NC: McFarland Publishing, 2020. 265.

11. John McWhorter. *Authentically Black: Essays for the Black Silent Majority.* New York, NY: Gotham Books, 2003. 2.

12. Broderick Hunter. Twitter. @BroderickHunter. April 26, 2020. 3:38 p.m.

13. Broderick Hunter. Twitter. @BroderickHunter. April 26, 2020. 3:59 p.m.

14. Bradley Campbell and Jason Manning. *The Rise of Victimhood Culture: Microaggressions, Safe Spaces, and the New Culture Wars.* New York, NY: Palgrave and MacMillan, 2018. 13–14.

15. Daniel Rutledge. "Trevor Noah says all hip-hop songs should have 'no N-word' version." *Newshub.* October 27, 2019. Retrieved from https://www.newshub.co.nz/home/entertainment/2019/10/trevor-noah-says-all-hip-hop-songs-should-have-no-n-word-versions.html

16. Noname (@noname). "when I go to work …" Twitter. November 30, 2019; Noname quoted in Wren Graves. "Noname may quit music, says she won't perform for mostly white audiences." *Consequence of Sound.* November 30, 2019. Retrieved from https://consequenceofsound.net/2019/11/noname-may-quit-music-wont-perform-for-mostly-white-audiences/

17. Eric Diep. "2 Georgia High School Students Expelled After Using the N-word in Racist TikTok." *Complex.* April 18, 2020. Retrieved from https://amp-www-complex-com.cdn.ampproject.org/c/s/amp.www.complex.com/life/2020/04/high-school-students-expelled-using-the-n-word-racist-tik-tok; Mariel Padilla. "2 Georgia High Schoolers Posted Racist Video, Officials Say." *The New York Times.* April 18, 2020. Retrieved from https://www.nytimes.com/2020/04/18/us/racist-tik-tok-video-carrollton.html.

18. Joe Feagin. *The White Racial Frame: Centuries of Racial Framing and Counter-Framing.* New York, NY: Routledge, 2009. 22.

19. Maria Cramer. "Announcer Caught on Open Mic Using Racial Slur at Basketball Game." *The New York Times.* March 13, 2021.

20. Dyson. *Tears We Cannot Stop.* 167–68.

21. Michael Eric Dyson. "A Conversation with Michael Eric Dyson." *Real Time with Bill Maher.* June 10, 2017.

22. Charles Barkley. *Who's Afraid of a Large Black Man?* New York, NY: Penguin

Press, 2005. 236. Note: This story was refuted in 2010 by Woods' kindergarten teacher Maureen Decker.

23. John McWhorter. "The Idea That Whites Can't Refer to the N-Word." *The Atlantic*. August 27, 2019.

Chapter 10

1. Elizabeth Pryor. "Why it's so hard to talk about the N-word." *Ted*. YouTube. April 16, 2020. https://youtu.be/CVPl8jRa AqM

2. Chris Rickert. "Teacher who said n-word says she was correcting student's use of another slur." *Wisconsin State Journal*. April 14, 2019. Retrieved from https://apnews.com/3c412aacb8684cea9b116e6ab18c6f20

3. Madeleine Carlisle. "Black Security Guard Fired for Repeating the N-Word When Telling a Student Not to Call Him It to Get His Job Back." *TIME*. October 22, 2019. Retrieved from https://time.com/5706848/black-security-guard-wisconsin-n-word/; Molly Beck. "Black school guard fired for telling student not to call him the N-word by using it himself." *USA Today*, October 20, 2019.

4. Eric Perry. "Richmond teacher fired after calling student the "N-word." *NBC12*. October 17, 2019. Retrieved from https://www.nbc12.com/2019/10/17/rps-teacher-fired-after-calling-student-n-word/

5. Dom Calicchio. "Tennessee students stage walkout in support of teacher placed on leave over N-word assignment." *Fox-News*. November 24, 2019. Retrieved from https://www.foxnews.com/us/tennessee-students-stage-walkout-over-n-word-assignment-after-teacher-placed-on-leave; Matthew Torres. "MNPS teacher placed on leave for homework about the n-word." *News Channel 5*. November 22, 2019. Retrieved from https://www.newschannel5.com/news/mnps-teacher-placed-on-leave-for-homework-about-the-n-word; CNN Wire. "Students walk out to support Nashville teacher who assigned homework about the N-word." *Fox 40*. November 23, 2019. Retrieved from https://fox40.com/news/students-walk-out-to-support-nashville-teacher-who-assigned-homework-about-the-n-word/.

6. Radio Iowa Contributor. "Denison teacher placed on leave over use of 'n' word in class." *Radio Iowa*. November 18, 2019. Retrieved from https://www.radioiowa.com/2019/11/18/denison-teacher-placed-on-leave-after-use-of-n-word-in-class/; *WHOtv.com*. "Iowa High School Students Protest Teacher Accused of Using Racial Slur." November 19, 2019. Retrieved from https://whotv.com/news/iowa-high-school-students-protest-teacher-accused-of-using-racial-slur/; Tyler J. Davis. "Iowa teacher who used racial slur in class will return to work as district closes investigation." *Des Moines Register*. November 21, 2019. Retrieved from https://www.desmoinesregister.com/story/news/2019/11/21/denison-iowa-teacher-who-used-racial-slur-class-return-steven-holt/4266242002/

7. Peyton Yager. "Mustang teacher recorded reading aloud racial slur several times; student takes issue." *Oklahoma's News 4*. November 22, 2019. Retrieved from https://kfor.com/news/mustang-teacher-recorded-reading-aloud-racial-slur-several-times-student-takes-issue/

8. Janelle Griffith. "Maine student called N-word by assistant principal, mom says." *NBC News*. October 111, 2019. https://www.nbcnews.com/news/nbcblk/maine-student-called-n-word-assistant-principal-mom-says-n1065096; Sarah Jackson. "Pennsylvania teacher placed on leave for racist rant to parent after fender bender." *NBC News*. October 11, 2019. https://www.nbcnews.com/news/us-news/pennsylvania-teacher-placed-leave-racist-rant-parent-after-fender-bender-n1065121

9. Colleen Flaherty. "Too Taboo for Class?" *Inside Higher Ed*. February 1, 2019. Retrieved from https://www.insidehighered.com/news/2019/02/01/professor-suspended-using-n-word-class-discussion-language-james-baldwin-essay

10. *Ibid*.

11. Tom Steward. "Augsburg Faces Backlash After Professor's Suspension Over 'N-Word' Controversy." *American Experiment*. February 4, 2019. Retrieved from https://www.americanexperiment.org/2019/02/augsburg-faces-backlash-after-professors-suspension-over-n-word-controversy/

12. Sammie Schenk quoted in Tom Steward, "Augsburg Faces Backlash After

Professor's Suspension Over 'N-Word' Controversy." February 4, 2019.

13. Hans-Joerg Tiede, et al. "Letter to Dr. Paul Pribbenow, Augsburg University." *American Association of University Professors*. January 22, 2019. 1. Retrieved from https://www.aaup.org/sites/default/files/Augsburg%20University%201-22-19.pdf

14. Tiede. "Letter." 1.

15. Randall Kennedy. "How a Dispute Over the N-Word Became a Dispiriting Farce." *The Chronicle of Higher Education*. February 22, 2019.

16. Colleen Flaherty. "Too Taboo for Class?" *Inside Higher Ed*. February 1, 2019. Retrieved from https://www.insidehighered.com/news/2019/02/01/professor-suspended-using-n-word-class-discussion-language-james-baldwin-essay

17. Laurie Sheck. "White professor: My university investigated me for quoting James Baldwin's use of 'N-word'." Twitter. August 21, 2019. Retrieved at https://twitter.com/lauriesheck/status/1164211967529238528: My University investigated me for quoting James Baldwin's use of 'N-word.'" *USA Today*. August 21, 2019.

18. Sheck, "White professor." August 21, 2019; Colleen Flaherty. "N-Word at the New School." *Inside Higher Ed*. August 7, 2019. Retrieved from https://www.insidehighered.com/news/2019/08/07/another-professor-under-fire-using-n-word-class-while-discussing-james-baldwin

19. Brittany Bernstein. "USC Professor Who Used Chinese Word That Sounds Like English Slur 'Not Dismissed Nor Suspended,' Admin Says." *National Review*. September 10, 2020. Retrieved from https://www.nationalreview.com/news/usc-professor-who-used-chinese-word-that-sounds-like-english-slur-not-dismissed-nor-suspended-admin-says/; Brittany Bernstein. "USC professor placed on leave after Black students complained his pronunciation of a Chinese word affected their mental health." *National Review*. September 3, 2020. Retrieved from https://www.nationalreview.com/news/usc-professor-placed-on-leave-after-black-students-complained-his-pronunciation-of-a-chinese-word-affected-their-mental-health/; Robby Soave. "USC Suspended a

communications professor for saying a Chinese word that sounds like a racial slur." *Reason*. September 3, 2020. Retrieved from https://reason.com/2020/09/03/usc-greg-patton-chinese-word-offended-students/

20. Jason McGahan. "How a Mild-Mannered USC Professor Accidentally Ignited Academia's Latest Culture War." *Los Angeles Magazine*. October 21, 2020. Retrieved from https://www.lamag.com/citythinkblog/usc-professor-slur/.

21. Trevor Noah. "Did that USC Professor Actually Say the N-Word?" *The Daily Show*. YouTube. September 11, 2020. Retrieved from https://www.youtube.com/watch?v=cijQ-gddGCE.

22. *Pittsburgh Action News 4*. "Duquesne University has fired professor who used racial slur in class video." October 7, 2020. Retrieved from https://www.wtae.com/article/duquesne-university-professor-who-used-n-word-in-class-video-on-paid-leave-pending-investigation/33997792

23. Nicole Acevedo and Ali Gostanian. "Duquesne University professor who used racial slur in class is put on leave." *NBC News*. September 12, 2020. Retrieved from https://www.nbcnews.com/news/us-news/duquesne-university-professor-who-used-racial-slur-class-put-leave-n1239957?cid=sm_npd_nn_fb_ma&fbclid=IwAR1_Jdl5-ctvRoIn7HJdrc_6myp6y4C8YYhy43Cqu9p8kTewonspajDlruc

24. Bill Schackner. "Duquesne faculty panel says professor should not have been fired for racial slur." *Pittsburgh Post Gazette*. January 26, 2021. Retrieved from https://www.post-gazette.com/news/education/2021/01/26/Duquesne-University-race-racism-slur-gary-Shank-AAUP-fired-academic-freedom-class/stories/202101260122

25. Bill Schackner. "Duquesne University professor who used racial slur can be reinstated but faces sanctions, including suspension." *Pittsburgh Post-Gazette*. February 5, 2021.

26. Andrew Koppelman. "Is this Law Professor Really a Homicidal Threat?" *Chronicle of Higher Education*. January 19, 2021. Retrieved from https://www.chronicle.com/article/is-this-law-professor-really-a-homicidal-threat; Greg

Piper. "Law school claims exam question that offended students is not protected by academic freedom." *The College Fix*. February 16, 2021. https://www.thecollegefix.com/law-school-claims-exam-question-that-offended-students-is-not-protected-by-academic-freedom/

27. Glenn Loury quoted in Bloggingheds.tv. "Critical race theory's rising hegemony Glenn Loury & John McWhorter." *The Glenn Show*. YouTube. February 2, 2021. https://www.youtube.com/watch?v=BNfzT-S6LHE

28. Erik Wemple. "Opinion: Slate clarifies guidelines on use of racial slurs following suspension of podcaster Mike Pesca." *Washington Post*. February 26, 2021.

29. Arienne Thompson. "Tom Hanks' son defends using the N-word." *USA Today*. June 2, 2015. Retrieved from https://www.usatoday.com/story/life/people/2015/06/02/tom-hanks-son-defends-his-use-of-the-n-word/28369727/

30. Van Lathan. "034—Tom Hanks' Used PT Cruiser w/Chet Hanks." *The Red Pill Podcast*. Soundcloud. October 10, 2018. Retrieved from https://soundcloud.com/redpillpodcast/034-tom-hanks-used-pt-cruiser-w-chet-hanks; Bryan Hood. "Chet Haze explains why he used the N-word." *Page Six*. October 16, 2018. Retrieved from https://pagesix.com/2018/10/16/chet-haze-explains-why-he-used-the-n-word/

31. Joe Feagin. *Two-Faced Racism: Whites in the Backstage and Frontstage*. New York, NY: Routledge. 2007. 91.

32. Michael Eric Dyson quoted on *Real Time with Bill Maher*, "A Conversation with Michael Eric Dyson." June 10, 2017.

33. Jose Bastidas. "Tim Allen's 2013 Interview About Using the N-Word Resurfaces to Social Media Backlash." *Pop Culture*. March 23, 2019. Retrieved from https://popculture.com/celebrity/2019/03/22/tim-allen-2013-interview-using-n-word-resurfaces-social-media-backlash/; Brian Logan. "Tim Allen demands to use the n-word." *The Guardian*. July 30, 2013. Retrieved from https://www.theguardian.com/stage/2013/jul/30/tim-allen-n-word-row.

34. *The View*. "Tim Allen on Political Correctness in Comedy Today." November 25, 2019. YouTube. Retrieved from https://www.youtube.com/watch?v=XhBhyd2LfO0.

Conclusion

1. Aaron A. Fox. *Real Country: Music and Language in Working-Class Culture*. Durham and London: Duke University Press. 2004.

2. Ishena Robinson. "NAACP and BeBe Winans to Educate Country Singer Morgan Wallen on Why the N-Word is Bad." *The Root*. February 5, 2021; David Oliver. "Morgan Wallen used a racist slur but his popularity is skyrocketing. How did we get here?" *USA Today*. February 10, 2021; TMZ "Morgan Wallen Hurls N-word After Rowdy Night." February 2, 2021. Retrieved from https://www.tmz.com/2021/02/02/morgan-wallen-n-word-nashville-neighbors/; CMT. "After learning of Morgan Wallen's..." Twitter. February 3, 2021. 11:39 a.m.; Paul Resnikoff. "Cumulus Media—The First Company to Ban Morgan Wallen Reinstates the Artist on Multiple Radio Stations." *Digital Musical News*. March 17, 2021. Retrieved from https://www.digitalmusicnews.com/2021/03/17/cumulus-media-morgan-wallen/

3. Mickey Guyton. "When I read comments ..." Twitter. February 3, 2021. 8:55 a.m. https://twitter.com/MickeyGuyton/status/1356964476793180161

4. Mickey Guyton. "This is not the first time ..." Twitter. February 2, 2021. 10:12 p.m. https://twitter.com/MickeyGuyton/status/1356802598200700928

5. Kelsea Ballerini. "The news out of Nashville ..." Twitter. February 2, 2021. 11:53. https://twitter.com/KelseaBallerini/status/1356828160780820480

6. Maren Morris. "It actually IS ..." Twitter. February 3, 2021. 12:14 a.m. https://twitter.com/MarenMorris/status/1356833333502599170

7. Valerie Ponzio. "One Time I met ..." Twitter. February 27, 2021. 5:31 p.m. https://twitter.com/valerieponzio/status/1365791716616384516

8. Sara Taylor. "Following N-word controversy, Morgan Wallen breaks 65-year Billboard chart record, surpasses Garth Brooks, the Eagles, and more." *The Blaze*. March 9, 2021. Retrieved from https://www.theblaze.com/

news/morgan-wallen-n-word-billboard-chart-record

9. Morgan Wallen. "Update from me." *YouTube.* February 10, 2021. Retrieved from https://www.youtube.com/watch?v=GB3OII1pZI8.

10. Dayton Duncan and Ken Burns. *Country Music: An Illustrated History.* New York: Alfred A. Knopf. 2019. 3.

11. Bryn Elise Sanberg and Lesley Goldberg. "Netflix Fires PR Chief After Use of N-Word in Meeting." *Hollywood Reporter.* June 22, 2018. Retrieved from https://www.hollywoodreporter.com/live-feed/jonathan-friedland-exits-netflix-1122675; Shalini Ramachandran and Joe Flint. "At Netflix, Radical Transparency and Blunt Firings Unsettle the Ranks." *Wall Street Journal.* October 25, 2018. Retrieved from https://www.wsj.com/articles/at-netflix-radical-transparency-and-blunt-firings-unsettle-the-ranks-1540497174?mod=hp_lead_pos4

12. Adrian Sol. "Papa John's Pizzas Disgusted with Anti-White NFL, Pulls Ads." *Daily Stormer.* November 2, 2017. Retrieved from https://dstormer6em3i4km.onion.link/papa-johns-pizzas-disgusted-with-anti-white-nfl-pulls-ads/

13. Noah Kirsh. "Papa John's Founder Used N-Word on Conference Call." *Forbes.* July 11, 2018. Retrieved from https://www.forbes.com/sites/noahkirsch/2018/07/11/papa-johns-founder-john-schnatter-allegedly-used-n-word-on-conference-call/#357cbcaa4cfc; Chauncey Alcorn. "Papa John's is still haunted by its founder using the n-word." *CNN Business.* November 5, 2019. Retrieved from https://www.cnn.com/2019/11/05/business/papa-johns-schnatter/index.html

14. Steve Ritchie. "Papa John's Founder on using N-word: It wasn't a slur." *CNN.* Video. July 15, 2018. Retrieved from https://www.youtube.com/watch?v=Ox7Nslbxyu8.

15. James Baldwin. *Notes of a Native Son.* Boston, MA: 1984. 175.

Epilogue

1. Intel Software. "Billions of Gamers Thousands of Needs Millions of Opportunities / GDC 2021 Showcase / Intel Software." *YouTube.* March 18, 2021. Retrieved at https://youtu.be/97Qhj299zRM; Michael Kan. "Intel 'Bleep' Software Filters Out Toxic Slurs in Voice as You Game." *PC Magazine.* www.pcmag.com. March 18, 0221.

2. *Ibid.*

3. Luke Plunkett. "Inntel, A 'White Nationalism' Slider Ain't It." *Kotaku.* April 7, 2021.

4. Patricia Hernandez. "Playing Red Dead Online as a Black character Means Enduring Racist Garbage." *The Verge.* January 15, 2019. Retrieved at https://www.theverge.com/2019/1/15/18183843/red-dead-online-black-character-racism.

5. Christina Ingersoll. "Free to Play? Hate, Harassment and Positive Social Experiences in Online Games 2020." *The Anti-Defamation League.* 2020. Retrieved at https://www.adl.org/media/15349/download.

6. Roger Chandler. "Billions of Gamers Thousands of Needs Millions of Opportunities / GDC 2021 Showcase / Intel Software." *Intel Software. YouTube.* March 18, 2021. Retrieved at https://youtu.be/97Qhj299zRM

7. Jeremy White. "It's time for Alexa, Google Assistant and Siri to Swear." *Wired UK.* July 17, 2021

Bibliography

Books

Abbott, Lynn, and Doug Seroff. "They Cert'ly Sound Good to Me": Sheet Music, Southern Vaudeville, and the Commercial Ascendancy of the Blues" in David Evans (ed.) *Ramblin' On My Mind*. Urbana and Chicago: University of Illinois Press. 2008.

Allport, Gordon W. *The Nature of Prejudice*. 25th Anniversary Edition. New York: Basic Books. 1954, 1979.

Ammen, Saron. *May Irwin: Singing, Shouting, and the Shadow of Minstrelsy*. Champaign, IL: University of Illinois Press, 2017.

Asim, Jabari. *The N Word: Who Can Say It, Who Shouldn't, and Why*. Boston and New York: Houghton Mifflin Company, 2007.

Badger, Reid. *A Life in Ragtime: A Biography of James Reese Europe*. New York and Oxford: Oxford University Press, 1995.

Baird, Julia. *Imagine This: Growing Up with My Brother John Lennon*. Great Britain: Hodder & Stoughton, 2007.

Baldwin, James. *Notes of a Native Son*. Boston, MA: 1984.

Banaji, Mahzarin R. *Blindspot: Hidden Biases of Good People*. New York: Bantam, 2016

Barkley, Charles. *Who's Afraid of a Large Black Man?* New York: Penguin Press, 2005.

Bell, Derrick. *Faces at the Bottom of the Well: The Permanence of Race*. New York: Basic Books, 1989.

Bell, Derrick. *Silent Covenants: Brown v. Board of Education and the Unfulfilled Hopes for Racial Reform*. Oxford: Oxford University Press, 2004.

Blaney, John. *John Lennon: Listen to This Book*. John Blaney, 2005.

Blight, David. *Frederick Douglass: Prophet of Freedom*. New York: Simon & Schuster, 2018.

Boyd, Todd. *Am I Black Enough for You? Popular Culture From the 'Hood and Beyond*. Bloomington, IN. Indiana University Press, 1997.

Boyd, Todd. *Young, Black, Rich, and Famous: The Rise of the NBA, the Hip Hop Invasion, and the Transformation of American Culture*. Lincoln, NE: University of Nebraska Press, 2003.

Breines, Winifred. *The Trouble Between Us: An Uneasy History of White and Black in the Feminist Movement*. New York: Oxford University Press, 2006.

Burger, Jeff, ed. *Lennon on Lennon: Conversations with John Lennon*. Chicago, IL: Chicago Review Press

Campbell, Bradley, and Jason Manning. *The Rise of Victimhood Culture: Microaggressions, Safe Spaces, and the New Culture Wars*. New York: Palgrave and MacMillan, 2018.

Carmichael, Stokely. *Stokely Speaks: From Black Power to Pan-Africanism*. Chicago, IL: Chicago Review Press, 1971.

Cavett, Dick. *Brief Encounters: Conversations, Magic Moments, and Assorted Hijinks*. New York: Henry Hold and Company, 2014.

Clinton, George. *Brothas Be, Yo Like George Ain't That Funkin' Kinda Hard on You?* New York: Atria Books, 2017.

Cochran, Johnnie, and David Fisher. *A Lawyer's Life*. Macmillan, 2003.

Connolly, Ray. *Being John Lennon: A Restless Life*. New York: Pegasus Books, 2018.

243

Cortes, Carlos E. *The Making and Remaking of a Multiculturalist*. New York: Teacher's College Press, 2002.

Davies, Hunter. *The Beatles*. New York: W.W. Norton, 1996 (1968).

Davies, Hunter, ed. *The John Lennon Letters*. New York: Little, Brown, and Company, 2012.

Davis, Thomas J., and Brenda M. Brock. *Documents of the Harlem Renaissance*. Santa Barbara, CA: ABC-CLIO. 2021.

Delgado, Richard, and Jean Stefancic. *Critical Race Theory: An Introduction*. New York: 2012, 2017.

Delgado, Richard, and Jean Stefancic. *Critical Race Theory: The Cutting Edge*. Philadelphia, PA: Temple University Press, 2000.

Dent, Gina. *Black Popular Culture: A Project by Michele Wallace*. Seattle, WA: Bay Press, 1992.

DiAngelo, Robin. *White Fragility: Why It's So Hard for White People to Talk About Racism*. Boston, MA: Beacon Press, 2018.

Duncombe, Stephen, and Maxwell Tremblay. *White Riot: Punk Rock and the Politics of Race*. Verso Books, 2011.

Dyson, Michael Eric. *Holler If You Hear Me: Searching for Tupac Shakur*. New York: Basic Civitas Books, 2002.

Dyson, Michael Eric. *Long Time Coming: Reckoning with Race in America*. New York: St. Martin's Press, 2020.

Dyson, Michael Eric. *Tears We Cannot Stop*. New York: St. Martin's Press, 2017.

Eberhardt, Jennifer L. *Biased: Uncovering the Hidden Prejudice That Shapes What We See, Think, and Do*. New York: Penguin Books, 2020.

Feagin, Joe. *Systemic Racism: A Theory of Oppression*. New York: Routledge, 2006.

Feagin, Joe. *Two-Faced Racism: Whites in the Backstage and Frontstage*. New York: Routledge, 2007.

Feagin, Joe. *The White Racial Frame: Centuries of Racial Framing and Counter-Framing*. New York: Routledge, 2009.

Feagin, Joe R. *Racist America: Roots, Current Realities, and Future Reparations*. New York: Routledge, 2014.

Fowler, Virginia C. *Nikki Giovanni: A Literary Biography*. Santa Barbara, CA. Denver, CO. Oxford, England: Praeger, 2013.

Gitlin, Marty. *Chris Rock: A Biography of a Comic Genius*. Berkeley Heights, NJ: Enslow, 2014.

Giuliano, Geoffrey. *Lennon in America: 1971–1980, Based in Part on the Lost Lennon Dairies*. New York: Cooper Square Press, 2000.

Goldman, Albert. *The Lives of John Lennon*. Chicago, IL: Chicago Review Books, 1988.

Goodwin, Brady Jr. *Navigating the 'N' Word: How Keeping "Niggas" Alive Is Killing Black Folk*. Self-Published, Urbanremixproject.com, 2016.

Hampton, Timothy. *Bob Dylan's Poetics: How the Songs Work*. New York: Zone Books, 2019

Harris, Paul. *Black Rage Confronts the Law*. New York: New York University Press, 1999.

Hart, Mrs. Alfred. "Adam's Picaninny." *The Sketch: A Journal of Art and Actuality, Volume 10*. London, England: Ingram Brothers Publisher, 1895.

Henry, David, and Joe Henry. *Furious Cool: Richard Pryor and the World That Made Him*. Chapel Hill, NC: Algonquin Books, 2014.

Hess, Mickey. *Hip Hop in America: Regional Guide*. Santa Barbara: Greenwood Press, 2010.

Higgins, Dalton. *Hip Hop World: A Groundwork Guide by Dalton Higgins*. Berkeley, CA: Groundwood Books, 2009.

Hill-Collins, Patricia. *Black Feminist Thought: Knowledge, Consciousness, and the Politics of Empowerment*. New York: Routledge, 1990, 1999.

Hillburn, Robert. *Corn Flakes with John Lennon: And Other Tales from a Rock 'n' Roll Life*. New York: Rodale, 2010.

Horne, Gerald. *Jazz and Justice: Racism and the Political Economy of the Music*. New York: Monthly Review Press, 2019.

Ice-T, and Douglass Century. *Ice: A Memoir of Gangster Life and Redemption—from South Central to Hollywood*. New York: One World Books, 2011.

Ice-T, and Heidi Siegmund. *The Ice Opinion: Who Gives a Fuck?* United Kingdom: Pan, 1995.

Kelley, Robin D.G. *Race Rebels: Culture, Politics and the Black Working Class*. New York: Simon & Schuster, Free Press, 1994.

Kemp, Mark. *Dixie Lullaby: A Story of Music, Race, and New Beginnings*. Athens: University of Georgia Press, 2004.

Kendi, Ibram X. *How To Be an Antiracist.* New York: Random House, One World.

Kennedy, Randall. *Nigger: The Strange Career of a Troublesome Word.* New York: Vintage Books, 2003.

Kretschmer, Kelsy. *Fighting for NOW.* University of Minnesota Press, 2019.

Lennon, Cynthia. *John.* London, UK: Hodder & Stoughton, 2005.

Lewisohn, Mark. *Tune In: The Beatles: All These Years.* New York: Three Rivers Press, 2013.

Lhamon, W.T. Jr. *T.D. Rice: Jim Crow, American Selected Songs and Plays.* Cambridge, MA and London: The Belknap Press of Harvard University Press, 2009.

MacDonald, Ian. *Revolution in the Head: The Beatles' Records and the Sixties* (3rd edition). Chicago, IL: Chicago Review Press, 2007.

McCluskey, Audrey Thomas, ed. *Richard Pryor: The Life and Legacy of a "Crazy" Black Man.* Bloomington, IN. Indiana University Press, 2008.

McWhorter, John. *All About the Beats: Why Hip-Hop Can't Save Black America.* New York: Gotham Books, 2008.

McWhorter, John. *Authentically Black: Essays for the Black Silent Majority.* New York: Gotham Books, 2003.

McWhorter, John. *Nine Nasty Words: English in the Gutter: Then, Now, and Forever.* New York: Avery, 2021.

McWhorter, John. *Talking Back, Talking Black: Truths About America's Lingua Franca.* New York: Bellevue Literary Press, 2017.

Meacham, John, and Tim McGraw. *Songs of America: Patriotism, Protest, and the Music That Made a Nation.* New York: Random House, 2019.

Mealy, Todd. *Biography of an Antislavery City.* Frederick, MD: PublishAmerica, 2008.

Mealy, Todd. *Race Conscious Pedagogy: Disrupting Racism at Majority White Schools.* Jefferson, NC: McFarland, 2020.

Millett, Kate. *The Loony-Bin Trip.* Champagne, IL: University of Illinois Press, 2000.

Muir, Peter C. *Long Lost Blues: Popular Blues in America, 1850–1920.* Champaign, IL: University of Illinois Press, 2010.

Norman, Philip. *John Lennon: The Life.* New York: HarperCollins, 2008.

Obama, Barack. *Dreams from My Father: A Story of Race and Inheritance.* New York: Crown Publishers, 1995.

O'Connell, Joanne. *The Life and Songs of Stephen Foster.* Lanham: Rowman & Littlefield, 2016.

Oluo, Ijeoma. *So You Want To Talk About Race.* New York: Seal Press, 2018.

Perry, Imani. *Breath: A Letter to My Sons.* Boston, MA: Beacon Press, 2019.

Perry, Imani. *Prophets of the Hood: Politics and Poetics in Hip Hop.* Durham, NC: Duke University Press, 2004.

Phull, Hardeep. *Story Behind the Protest Song: A Reference Guide to the 50 Songs that Changed the 20th Century.* Westport, CT: Greenwood Press, 2008.

Picca, Leslie Houts, and Joe Feagin. *Two-Faced Racism: Whites in the Backstage and Frontstage.* New York: Routledge, 2007.

Pryor, Elizabeth Stordeur. *Colored Travelers: Mobility and the Fight for Citizenship before the Civil War.* Chapel Hill, NC: University of North Carolina Press, 2016.

Pryor, Richard Jr., and Ron Brawer. *In A Pryor Life.* Bear Manor Media, 2019.

Roberts, Jeremy. *Bob Dylan: Voice of a Generation.* Minneapolis, MN: Lerner Publications Company, 2005.

Roberts, Randy, and Johnny Smith. *Blood Brothers: The Fatal Friendship Between Muhammad Ali and Malcolm X.* New York: Basic Books, 2016.

Ross, Lawrence. *Blackballed: The Black and White Politics of Race on America's Campuses.* New York: St. Martin's Press, 2015.

Roth, Benita. *Separate Roads to Feminism: Black Chicana, and White Feminist Movements in America's Second Wave.* Cambridge, UK: Cambridge University Press, 2004.

Sammond, Nicholas. *Birth of an Industry: Black Face Minstrelsy and the Rise of American Animation.* Durham, NC: Duke University Press, 2015

Sedler, Michael D. *What to Do When Words Get Ugly.* Grand Rapids, MI: Revel, 2001.

Shapiro, Robert L., with Larkin Warren. *Search For Justice.* New York: Warner Books, 1996.

Silverman, David S. *You Can't Air That: Four Cases of Controversy and Censorship in American Television Programming.*

Syracuse: Syracuse University Press, 2007.

Simmons, Russell, and Nelson George. *Life and Def: Sex, Drugs, Money, and God.* New York. Three Rivers Press, 2001.

Sullivan, Shannon. *Good White People: The Problem with Middle-Class White Anti-Racism.* New York: State University of New York Press, 2016.

Thomas, David J. *The State of American Policing: Psychology, Behavior, Problems, and Solutions.* Santa Barbara, CA: Praeger, 2018.

Thomas, Richard F. *Why Bob Dylan Matters.* New York: HarperCollins Publishers, 2017.

Thompson, Heather Ann. *Blood in the Water: The Attica Prison Uprising of 1971 and Its Legacy.* New York: Vintage Books, 2017.

Watkins, S. Craig. *Hip Hop Matters: Politics, Pop Culture, and the Struggle for the Soul of a Movement.* Boston, MA: Beacon Press, 2005.

Wenner, Jann S. *Lennon Remembers.* London: Verso, 2000.

Wiener, Jon. *Come Together: John Lennon in His Time.* Urbana and Chicago, IL: University of Illinois Press, 1984.

Wilkerson, Isabel. *Caste: The Origins of Our Discontents.* New York: Penguin Random House, 2020.

Wise, Tim. *White Like Me: Reflections from a Privileged Son.* New York: Soft Skull Press, 2011.

Yancy, George. *Across Black Spaces: Essays and Interviews from an American Philosopher.* New York: Rowman & Littlefield, 2020.

Yancy, George. *What White Looks Like: African-American Philosophers on the Whiteness Question.* New York: Routledge, 2004.

Yancy, George, ed. *White on White/Black on Black.* New York: Rowman & Littlefield, 2005.

Young, Vershawn Ashanti. *Your Average Nigga Performing Race Literacy and Masculinity.* Detroit, MI: Wayne State University Press, 2007.

Film/Documentaries

Marlon Riggs. *Ethnic Notions: African American Stereotypes and Prejudice.* California Newsreel, 1987.

Interviews

McWhorter, John. Email correspondence with the author. New York. March 17, 2020.

Journals

Eisenstadt, Leora F. "The N-Word at Work: Contextualizing Language in the Workplace." *Berkeley Journal of Employment and Labor Law.* Vol. 33, No. 2 (2012).

Himle, J.A., R.E. Baser, R.J. Taylor, R.D. Campbell, and J.S. Jackson. "Anxiety Disorders Among African Americans, Blacks of Caribbean Descent, and Non-Hispanic Whites in the United States." *Journal of Anxiety Disorder.* 2009.

Kanter, Jonathan W., Monnica T. Williams, Adam M. Kuczynski, Tatherine E. Manbeck, Marlena Debreaux, and Daniel C. Rosen. "A Preliminary Report on the Relationship Between Microaggressions Against Black People and Racism Among White College Students." *Race and Social Problems.* August 30, 2017.

Kennedy, Randall. "Who can Say 'Nigger'? And Other Considerations." *The Journal of Blacks in Higher Education.* Winter 1999–2000.

Lester, Neal A. "The N-Word: Lessons Taught and Lessons Learned." *Journal of Praxis in Multicultural Education.* January 2014.

Lester, Neal A. "'Sticks and Stones May Break My Bones...': Airbrushing the Ugliest of Ugly in African American Children's Books." *Obsidian III.* 2001–2002.

Lichter, Daniel T., et al. "Toward a New Macro-Segregation? Decomposing Segregation Within and Between Metropolitan Cities and Suburbs." *American Sociological Review.* 2015.

Nowlin, Michael. "James Weldon Johnson's 'Black Manhattan' and the Kingdom of American Culture." *African American Review.* Johns Hopkins University Press. Fall 2005.

Parks, Gregory S., and Shayne E. Jones. "'Nigger': A Critical Race Realist Analysis of the N-Word Within Hate Crimes Law." *The Journal of Criminal Law and Criminology (1973–)*, Vol. 98, No. 4 (Summer 2008). 1306.

Pryor, Elizabeth Stordeur. "The Etymology of Nigger: Resistance, Language, and the Politics of Freedom in the Antebellum North." *Journal of the Early Republic*, Vol. 36, No. 2, Summer 2016.

Renteln, Alison Dundes. "A Psychohistorical Analysis of the Japanese American Internment." *Human Rights Quarterly*. The Johns Hopkins University Press. November 1995.

Williams, Monnica T. "Cultural Adaptations of Prolonged Exposure therapy for Treatment and Prevention of Posttraumatic Stress Disorder in African Americans." *Behavioral Sciences*. 2014.

Media Resources

Alcorn, Chauncey. "Papa John's is Still Haunted by Its Founder Using the N-Word." *CNN Business*. November 5, 2019.

Badash, David. "Trump Voters Increasingly Think It's OK to Use the N-Word." *New Civil Rights Movement*. July 30, 2019.

Bastidas, Jose. "Tim Allen's 2013 Interview About Using the N-Word Resurfaces to Social Media Backlash." *Pop Culture*. March 23, 2019.

Carlisle, Madeleine. "Black Security Guard Fired for Repeating the N-Word When Telling a Student Not to Call Him It to Get His Job Back." *TIME*. October 22, 2019.

Carroll, Rory. "Donald Trump On Tape Saying 'Every Racist Thing Ever,' Claims Actor Tom Arnold." *The Guardian*. December 21, 2016.

Diep, Eric. "2 Georgia High School Students Expelled After Using the N-word in Racist TikTok." *Complex*. April 18, 2020.

Ducharme, Jamie. "Georgia Lawmaker says President Trump's Alleged N-Word Use Should be Held Separate From His Presidency." *TIME*. August 18, 2018.

Ebony. "Richard Pryor: Talks About Richard Pryor (The Old, The New) Rejection That Led to Loneliness and Drugs, God, Prayer, 'Nigger,' And How He Was Burned." October 1980.

Flaherty, Colleen. "N-Word at the New School." *Inside Higher Ed*. August 7, 2019.

Flaherty, Colleen. "Too Taboo for Class?" *Inside Higher Ed*. February 1, 2019.

Flynn, Dylan. "White People Should Never Rap The N-Word: A Linguist Breaks It Down." *The Conversation*. October 22, 2017.

Helligar, Jeremy. "Kendrick Lamar's Onstage Outrage: Why Rap Should Retire the N-Word for Good." *Variety*. May 22, 2018.

Hutzler, Alexandra. "Most Donald Trump Voters Don't Think Using the N-Word is Racist, Or Even Offensive, New Poll Indicates." *Newsweek*. August 30, 2018.

JET. "Ex-Beatle Tells How Black Stars Changed His Life." October 26, 1972.

JET. "What the Beatles Learned from Negroes." July 1, 1965.

Kennedy, Randall. "How a Dispute Over the N-Word Became a Dispiriting Farce." *The Chronicle of Higher Education*. February 22, 2019.

Kirsh, Noah. "Papa John's Founder Used N-Word on Conference Call." *Forbes*. July 11, 2018.

Lockhart, P.R. "The Debate Over Donald Trump's Alleged N-Word Tape, Explained." *Vox*. August 16, 2018.

McWhorter, John. "The Idea That Whites Can't Refer to the N-Word." *The Atlantic*. August 27, 2019.

McWhorter, John. "If President Obama Can Say It, You Can Too." *TIME*. June 22, 2015.

McWhorter, John. "Stop Policing the N-Word." *TIME*. May 3, 2016.

Ramachandran, Shalini, and Joe Flint. "At Netflix, Radical Transparency and Blunt Firings Unsettle the Ranks." *Wall Street Journal*. October 25, 2018.

Ritchie, Steve. "Papa John's Founder on Using N-Word: It Wasn't A Slur." *CNN*. Video. July 15, 2018.

Rutledge, Daniel. "Trevor Noah Says All Hip-Hop Songs Should Have 'No N-Word' Version." *Newshub*. October 27, 2019.

Sanberg, Bryn Elise, and Lesley Goldberg. "Netflix Fires PR Chief After Use of N-Word in Meeting." *Hollywood Reporter*. June 22, 2018.

Sheck, Laurie. "White professor." August 21, 2019.

Sol, Adrian. "Papa John's Pizzas Disgusted with Anti-White NFL, Pulls Ads." *Daily Stormer*. November 2, 2017.

Steward, Tom. "Augsburg Faces Backlash After Professor's Suspension Over 'N-Word' Controversy." *American Experiment*. February 4, 2019.

Tucker, Ken, and David Fricke. "Fearless Leader." *Rolling Stones*. October 10, 2012.

Wigg, David. "John Lennon & Yoko Ono Interview: Apple Offices, London, May 8, 1969." *The Beatles Ultimate Experience*.

Multimedia

Appleton, Roger. *Looking for Lennon*. Documentary, 2018.

Bruce, Lenny. "Are There Any Niggers Here Tonight?" December 13, 1962. Retrieved at Robert D. Farber University Archives & Special Collections. Brandeis University. Goldfarb Library.

Byers, Michiko. *Inside John Lennon*. Documentary, 2003.

Carlin, George. "George Carlin—They are only Words!" dcg13lj. Video. April 8, 2011.

The Dick Cavett Show. Television interview, May 11, 1972. John and Yoko Collection [videorecording] DVD 2005.

Epstein, Michael. *John & Yoko: Above Us Only Sky*. Documentary, 2018.

"The Good Fight S02E06 Clip / 'So Say It.'" *The Good Fight*. YouTube. April 8, 2018.

Gregory, Dick. "Dick Gregory—How the 'N' Word Began & More on SMiles TV Talk Show." SmilesTV Stephanie a. Miles. November 12, 2013.

Jenkins, Barry. "Chapter V." *Dear White People*. Netflix. April 28, 2017.

Leaf, David. *The U.S. vs. John Lennon*. Documentary, 2006.

Lindo, Delroy and Christian Miranda. "The Good Fight S02E06 Clip / 'So Say It.'" *The Good Fight*. YouTube. April 8, 2018. Retrieved from https://www.youtube.com/watch?v=S4pSp3Km6Mw.

Macfarlane, Ursula. *The Real Yoko Ono*. Documentary, 2001.

Mike Douglas Show. "John Lennon & Chuck Berry—The Mike Douglas Show, February 16, 1972." The BeatlesAtTheStudio231. March 19, 2017.

Real Time with Bill Maher. "A Conversation with Michael Eric Dyson." HBO. June 10, 2017.

Tomorrow Show with Tom Snyder. Television interview. April 28, 1975. YouTube. TheMMProducties. March 5, 2012.

West, Cornel. "Never Forget: A Journey of Revelations." Hidden Beach. July 3, 2008.

Zakarin, Jordan. "Samuel L. Jackson Insists Reporter Say N-Word in 'Django Unchained' Interview (Video)." *Hollywood Reporter*. January 2, 2013.

Newspapers

Anti-Slavery Bugle (Lisbon, OH)
Arizona Daily Star (Tucson, AZ)
Arizona Republic (Phoenix, AZ)
Atlanta Constitution (Atlanta, GA)
Austin American (Austin, TX)
Baltimore Sun (Baltimore, MD)
Black Hills Weekly Pioneer (Deadwood, SD)
Boston Globe (Boston, MA)
Buffalo Courier (Buffalo)
Calgary Herald (Calgary, Alberta, Canada)
Chicago Daily News Wire (Chicago, IL)
Chicago Tribune (Chicago, IL)
Courier (Waterloo, IA)
Daily Leader (Lexington, KY)
Daily Mail (London, England)
Dayton Daily News (Dayton, OH)
Decatur Daily Review (Decatur, IL)
Des Moines Register (Des Moines, IA)
Detroit Free Press (Detroit, MI)
The Forum (Salt Lake City, UT)
Frederick Douglass Paper (Rochester)
Gazette (Montreal, Quebec, Canada)
Glen Rock Gazette (Glen Rock, NJ)
Harrisburg Telegraph (Harrisburg, PA)
Hartford Courant (Hartford, CT)
Herald and Review (Decatur, IL)
Ithaca Journal (Ithaca)
Kingsport Times (Kingsport, TN)
Lancaster Sunday News (Lancaster, PA)
Liberator (Boston, MA)
London Herald Bureau (Edmonton, Alberta, Canada)
Longview Daily News (Longview, WA)
Los Angeles Times (Los Angeles, CA)
Miami Herald (Miami, FL)
National Post (Toronto, Ontario, Canada)
New York Daily News (New York)
New York Times (New York)
Oshkosh Northwest (Oshkosh, WI)
Ottawa Citizen (Ottawa, Ontario, Canada)
Philadelphia Daily News (Philadelphia, PA)
Pittsburgh Post Gazette (Pittsburgh, PA)
Post-Standard (Syracuse)
Poughkeepsie Journal (Poughkeepsie)

Red Deer Advocate (Red Deer, Alberta, Canada)

St. Johnsbury Caledonian (St. Johnsbury, VT)

Spokesman-Review (Spokane, WA)

Sydney Morning Herald (Sydney, New South Wales, Australia)

Tampa Bay Times (St. Petersburg, FL)

Times and Democrat (Orangeburg, SC)

Times (Muster, IN)

USA Today

Washington Post (District of Columbia)

Weekly Times-Star (Sedan, KS)

Windsor Star (Windsor, Ontario, Canada)

Wisconsin State Journal (Madison, WI)

York Dispatch (York, PA)

Studies/Surveys

Asian American Bar Association of New York. "A Rising Tide of Hate and Violence against Asian Americans in New York During COVID-19: Impact, Causes, Solutions." Paul, Weiss, Rifkind, Wharton & Garrison LLP.

Clark, Kenneth B. and Mamie P. Clark. "Racial Identification and Preference in Negro Children." 1950.

Horowitz, Juliana Menasce, Anna Brown, and Kiana Cox. "Race in America 2019." *Pew Research Center.* April 9, 2019.

Podcasts

Charlamagne Tha God. "Can White People Use the N-Word in Hip Hop Context?" *The Breakfast Club.* November 14, 2017.

McWhorter, John. "There are Two N-Words." *Lexicon Valley Podcast.* January 9, 2018.

Index

251

Index